Flickr™
Mashups

Flickr™
Mashups

David Wilkinson

Wiley Publishing, Inc.

Flickr™ Mashups

Published by
Wiley Publishing, Inc.
10475 Crosspoint Boulevard
Indianapolis, IN 46256
www.wiley.com

Library of Congress Cataloging-in-Publication Data

Wilkinson, David.
  Flickr mashups / David Wilkinson.
     p. cm.
  Includes index.
  ISBN-13: 978-0-470-09774-8 (paper/website)
  ISBN-10: 0-470-09774-4 (paper/website)
  1. Flickr (Electronic resource) 2. Photography—Digital techniques. 3. Image processing—Digital techniques. I. Title.
  TR267.5.F55W55 2007
  775—dc22
                                2006036645

To Sue

About the Author

David Wilkinson is a highly skilled freelance technical consultant and programmer with more than 20 years' experience in the IT industry, delivering business-critical systems to many blue-chip companies, including BP, Jaguar, Land Rover, Tesco, and Lloyds TSB. He also acts as operations manager at Utata, a community web site supporting photographers all over the world, and is responsible for the operation of the Utata site and its integration with Flickr. A keen amateur photographer, he discovered Flickr in its very early days and been a staunch advocate of it ever since.

Credits

Exccecutive Editor
Chris Webb

Development Editor
Brian MacDonald

Technical Editor
Sam Judson

Production Editor
Michael Koch

Copy Editor
S. B. Kleinman

Editorial Manager
Mary Beth Wakefield

Production Manager
Tim Tate

Vice President and Executive Group Publisher
Richard Swadley

Vice President and Executive Publisher
Joseph B. Wikert

Project Coordinator
Kristie Rees

Graphics and Production Specialists
Jonelle Burns, Barbara Moore, Alicia B. South

Quality Control Technician
John Greenough

Proofreading and Indexing
Techbooks

Anniversary Logo Design
Richard Pacifico

Acknowledgments

Although it's my name that gets printed on the front cover, a book like this is never the work of a single individual. Not only were many different people involved in the production of this book, there were many others who helped pave the path that led here.

The first credit has to go to Chris Webb at Wiley. He is the man who persuaded me to embark on such an insane venture as writing a book in the first place. To him, I have just one thing to say—Chris, thank you for convincing me; I have thoroughly enjoyed the experience. Next, we have my development editor, Brian MacDonald, who very patiently guided me through the process of taking a series of random thoughts and turning them into a (hopefully) coherent printed book, and Sam Judson, author of the Flickr.Net API library, who did a grand job as technical reviewer. Thank you all. There are many other people behind the scenes at Wiley/Wrox who played a valuable role in getting this book out into the world, but I would especially like to mention Carol Kessel, who helped my wife get to grips with the American taxation system. Thank you, Carol — you were much more help than the man at the IRS.

I'd like to thank my long-time friend and colleague Nick Holloway, who got lumbered with the task of checking over my code to make sure I didn't do anything really dumb. If you find any remaining errors, it's almost certainly because I ignored his advice. A number of other people provided vast amounts of moral support during the writing of this book. In particular, Catherine Jamieson was never without an encouraging word, and Paul May's regular Skype calls were a great boost. Thank you both. And Richard Williams — I promised I would mention you in the acknowledgments, so here is your moment of fame.

Of course, life isn't one great long book-writing session — there's other work that has to be done too. I'd like to thank the other people I was supposed to be doing work for, for being both patient and forgiving during the writing of this book — especially Chris Pring and Mark Menzies, both of whom had to wait their turn in the queue.

Just about all of the photos you see featured in this book are mine and you can find them in my Flickr photostream. The Utata badges featured in Chapter 10, however, incorporate photos from a number of the Utata group admins. Catherine Jamieson, Carolynn Primeau, Bryan Partington, Brenda Anderson, Greg Fallis, Brittney Bush, Carrie Musgrave, Karl Randay, and Shari DeAngelo — thank you all for very kindly allowing me to use your photographs here.

No book about Flickr would be complete without a word of acknowledgment for some of the people who helped create it in the first place: Stewart Butterfield, Caterina Fake, George Oates, and Eric Costello, with Heather Champ helping to keep the unruly masses in some kind of order — they all deserve a mention. It is they, and the rest of the Flickr staff, whom I must thank for creating one of the best online communities I have come across in a very long time. There is, of course, another name to mention here. In this book, I must reserve a special mention for Cal Henderson, the man behind the Flickr API. Without his contribution to Flickr, there would be no reason for this book to exist.

Many third-party pieces of software are used in the projects in this book — PHP, MySQL, Greasemonkey, and many others. I would also like to thank the very many people involved in the cre-

Acknowledgments

ation of these various tools for making them available to us — without them, building mashups such as those featured in this book would be nigh impossible. I'd especially like to thank Dan Coulter, whose phpFlickr library is used extensively throughout this book.

Flickr isn't just about the photos — it's also about the community, the people who take part. Without them, Flickr would be a very different place. Through Flickr I've met a wide variety of people, scattered all over the globe — from curiouskiwi on the other side of the world in New Zealand to chapmonkey, who lives just a dozen or so miles away. Thanks to Flickr, I've exchanged food parcels with coffeefloat in Jakarta and chotda in Guam, I've swapped Moo Minicards with missyasmina in Milan, and as part of Swaptata I've received prints of fabulous photos from people all around the world. I've made some very good friends on Flickr — there's Kathya Ethington in Wiesbaden (who shares my great love of food), there's Cindi Miller Herleman in Colorado, and, well, there's just too many more to name individually. Thank you all for making Flickr such a great place to be. Speaking of community, the finest community of all is to be found in the Utata group — in all my years of using the Internet, I've yet to find a better group of people to hang out with. Above all else, it is the Utatans who inspired me to build the systems that run the Utata web site, and the Utata web site is, I think, the greatest Flickr mashup of all.

And finally, because one always saves the best until last, I thank my wife, Sue, for all her help and encouragement throughout the writing of this book. Without her support, none of this would be possible. Thank you.

Contents

Contents

Contents

Contents

Contents

Introduction

When Flickr was launched in early 2004, few would have expected that a little more than a year later it would not only have become one of the top photo-sharing sites on the Internet, but also have caught the eye of the Internet giant Yahoo!, which acquired Flickr and its parent company Ludicorp in March 2005.

Many things could be said to have contributed to Flickr's enormous success: the intuitive user interface, the friendly tone of the text scattered about the site, the emphasis on the social aspects of building a web-based community, perhaps even just its being in the right place at the right time. One thing is clear — the decision to open up Flickr to the outside world was a smart one. Allowing developers to create applications that can fully interact with Flickr, storing and retrieving photos, together with all the other details stored alongside them, has spawned a whole secondary industry in Flickr-based applications. It seems that you can find practically everything out there — from tools to help you upload your photos to applications to turn your photostream into a bound and printed book. Everyone, from hobbyists to businesses, is getting in on the act.

The emergence of mashups as a means of building systems presents a whole new world of possibilities. No longer do you have to wait for a company to implement the features you know you need — you can just do it yourself. If Flickr doesn't provide a way to automatically build sets of your most interesting photos, you don't need to sit waiting in despair — you can go ahead and create the necessary functionality. Perhaps you want to geotag your photos, but Flickr's maps don't cover your local area very well? That's not a problem — use the Flickr API to enable you to overlay your photos onto Google maps instead. If you don't like Google Maps, take your own aerial photographs and use those! No matter how niche your requirements are, the fact that companies like Flickr are opening up their systems to outside developers means that you can supplement the services they provide to get just what you need, regardless of how bizarre or offbeat that need is.

Flickr is a great starting point for building mashups — a picture is worth a thousand words, and pictures are something Flickr has in abundance. You only have to visit Flickr fleetingly to realize that it is packed full of great photographs — pictures of pretty much everywhere in the world. From Antarctic survey stations to Brazilian rain forests, from New York skyscrapers to African desert scenes — with such an abundance of spectacular imagery, it is little wonder that people want to build new ways to explore and interact with this vast photographic database. Whatever it is you want to display, chances are you will find it on Flickr.

Whom This Book Is For

If you are interested in building software that interfaces with Flickr in some way, then this book is for you. You'll need to be comfortable with a few things first, though. In this book, I won't teach you how to program from scratch — you should at least be familiar with basic programming techniques. If you know what a `for` loop is, though, you're well on the way.

As you work through this book, you'll come across a wide range of different tools and technologies — everything from AJAX to MySQL, from Greasemonkey to ImageMagick. You're not expected to be an expert in each of them — in fact, you're not expected to know very much about them at all. As you go through, you will find enough about each new piece of software or technology to enable you to easily follow the examples and understand what is going on. Where possible, additional references are provided so that readers who want to pursue in more detail some of the topics covered can easily do so at their leisure.

You'll be using PHP for most of the examples shown, so a passing familiarity with PHP or similar scripting languages would be very helpful. If you're not already familiar with PHP, all is not lost — PHP is a pretty straightforward language and very easy to learn. If you've used other programming languages, such as JavaScript, Perl, C++, or Java, the code in this book should present you with very little difficulty. The documentation on the PHP web site at `www.php.net/` contains everything you need to bring you up to speed.

Pretty much all the examples presented here are web-based, and so a working knowledge of basic HTML and some familiarity with JavaScript is assumed. All the basics of setting up a web server and PHP are covered in Chapter 3, so even if you've never looked under the covers of a web server before, this book should tell you everything you need to get you started.

One chapter, Chapter 10, uses Perl. Even if you don't know Perl, the code used is fairly straightforward and most developers should be able to follow the example and get it up and running without any problems. Again, you're gently walked though the process of getting Perl installed and running on your computer, so there's really no excuse not to give it a try. If you really, really loathe it, however, the chapter is completely optional — skipping it won't spoil your enjoyment of the rest of the book in any way whatsoever.

What This Book Covers

In this book, you will be walked through a variety of ways to build software that interacts in some way with Flickr. You'll see how to use feeds to retrieve information, how to use Greasemonkey to change the Flickr web site to suit your own needs, and how to use the Flickr API to build whole systems that use Flickr as a source of information.

As this book is being written, Flickr is in what the developers call, in typical tongue-in-cheek fashion, "gamma" status. Gamma is the next letter in the Greek alphabet after beta — so the implication is that they consider the site to be out of beta, but still not ready for final release. In fact, a site like Flickr can never be considered "final" — some things can always be improved and new features added. It is inevitable that as time goes on, some parts of this book will grow dated — in particular those bits that say things like "Flickr doesn't do this yet." Although some of the details may change, and newer and cooler ways of building things will emerge, the basic principles covered in this book will remain valid. The techniques you will see used here will stand you in good stead all the way through to Flickr omega.

It's not only Flickr that changes over time — in this book you will use a wide variety of software packages, and those too can be expected to grow and evolve. If you want to catch up on the latest changes made to either Flickr or the software packages used here, in particular with regard to how they may affect anything you read in this book, you should check out my web site at `www.dopiaza.org/`. You will find information there about changes that have an impact on anything you read here. You'll also find some other Flickr remixes and mashups to play with. If you dig deeper, the site features also a whole bunch of things that you are probably not the slightest bit interested in — including some great recipes — but don't worry, you're not obliged to read those. The chicken with chili and nuts is pretty good, though, even if I say so myself.

How This Book Is Structured

This book is very much about learning by doing. It includes many hands-on examples to help you understand how things work, and each chapter includes one or more exercises to help you put all your newly-learned skills to the test. Don't worry if you get stuck, though — Appendix A contains full answers to all of the exercises.

The book is divided into three parts. Part I, "Building a New Internet" is aimed at bringing you up to speed with the world of mashups, and getting you ready to start building them. Chapter 1 talks about remixes and mashups, and the differences between them. It describes the world of Web 2.0 and introduces many of the technologies you will be using during the course of this book. Chapter 2 then takes you on a short guided tour of Flickr — even if you're already familiar with the Flickr web site, this chapter helps identify some of the interesting bits from the mashup author's perspective. Chapter 3 makes sure that you are fully equipped to start developing your mashups. It walks you through the process of setting up a development web server, and it shows you how to configure PHP and install Perl — by the end of this chapter, you will have all the software you need in place, ready to start mashing. Part I concludes with Chapter 4, "The Flickr API." This chapter explains the main programmatic interface you will be using to build the projects in this book.

Parts II and III are all about building software. In these sections you are guided, step-by-step, through a series of software projects. Some of the projects are complete stand-alone applications, while others build upon earlier projects to add new features. Each project introduces you to a new aspect of building mashups with Flickr, guiding you through the process of creating your own working application. Part II focuses on remixes — taking content from Flickr and presenting it on your own web site, or even changing the look of the Flickr web site itself by using Firefox and Greasemonkey. Part III concentrates on mashing. In this section you will take content from both Flickr and a variety of other sources to build a range of projects, from finding photographs to illustrate news feeds through to displaying your photos on Google Maps. The final chapter of the book looks at some more advanced mashup techniques and shows you how to use a local database to improve the performance and scalability of your software.

By the end of the book you will have built a variety of remixes and mashups, each building upon the core services provided by Flickr, and you will be well prepared to embark on new mashup projects of your own.

What You Need to Use This Book

All the software used in this book — web servers, PHP, Perl, ImageMagick, MySQL — is cross-platform. Whatever your choice of computing environment, it is more than likely that you will be able to build the projects described here. It is, however, impractical to give full instructions on how to set up every kind of computer out there. The chapters that discuss installation and setup of software packages such as Apache, PHP, Perl, and MySQL are written principally from the point of view of a user running Windows XP Professional. Users of other variants of Windows will probably find their experiences largely similar, but possibly subtly different.

Linux users will find, on the whole, that all the software they need is already included within their Linux distribution, and should consult their distribution's documentation for instructions on how to make sure that the necessary packages are installed.

All the software packages needed for the exercises in this book are also available for Mac OSX and, wherever possible, additional notes are given to help you locate the necessary software and installation and configuration information.

Conventions

To help you get the most from the text and keep track of what's happening, we've used a number of conventions throughout the book.

> **Boxes like this one hold important, not-to-be forgotten information that is directly relevant to the surrounding text.**

Tips, hints, tricks, and asides to the current discussion are offset and placed in italics like this.

As for styles in the text:

❑ We *italicize* new terms and important words when we introduce them.

❑ We show keyboard strokes like this: Ctrl+A.

❑ We show filenames, URLs, and code within the text like so: `persistence.properties`.

❑ We present code in two different ways:

```
In code examples we highlight new and important code with a gray background.
```

```
The gray highlighting is not used for code that's less important in the present
context, or that has been shown before.
```

Source Code

As you work through the examples in this book, you may choose either to type in all the code manually or use the source-code files that accompany the book. All the source code used in this book is available for download at `www.wrox.com`. Once at the site, simply locate the book's title (either by using the Search box or by using one of the title lists) and click the "Download Code" link on the book's detail page to obtain all the source code for the book.

Because many books have similar titles, you may find it easiest to search by ISBN; this book's ISBN is 978-0-470-09774-8.

Once you download the code, just decompress it with your favorite compression tool. Alternately, you can go to the main Wrox code download page at `www.wrox.com/dynamic/books/download.aspx` to see the code available for this book and all other Wrox books.

Errata

We make every effort to ensure that there are no errors in the text or in the code. However, no one is perfect, and mistakes do occur. If you find an error in one of our books, such as a spelling mistake or faulty piece of code, we would be very grateful for your feedback. By sending in errata you may save another reader hours of frustration and at the same time you will be helping us provide even higher-quality information.

To find the errata page for this book, go to www.wrox.com and locate the title using the Search box or one of the title lists. Then, on the book details page, click the "Book Errata" link. On this page you can view all errata that have been submitted for this book and posted by Wrox editors. A complete book list, including links to each's book's errata, is also available at www.wrox.com/misc-pages/booklist.shtml.

If you don't spot "your" error on the Book Errata page, go to www.wrox.com/contact/techsupport .shtml and complete the form there to send us the error you have found. We'll check the information and, if appropriate, post a message to the book's errata page and fix the problem in subsequent editions of the book.

p2p.wrox.com

For author and peer discussion, join the P2P forums at p2p.wrox.com. The forums are a Web-based system enabling you to post messages relating to Wrox books and related technologies and to interact with other readers and technology users. The forums offer a subscription feature to e-mail you when new posts on topics of interest to you are made to the forums. Wrox authors, editors, other industry experts, and your fellow readers are present on these forums.

At http://p2p.wrox.com you will find a number of different forums that will help you not only as you read this book, but also as you develop your own applications. To join the forums, just follow these steps:

1.   Go to p2p.wrox.com and click the Register link.
2.   Read the terms of use and click Agree.
3.   Complete the required information to join as well as any optional information you wish to provide and click Submit.
4.   You will receive an e-mail with information describing how to verify your account and complete the joining process.

   You can read messages in the forums without joining P2P, but in order to post your own messages you must join.

Once you join, you can post new messages and respond to messages other users post. You can read messages at any time on the Web. If you would like to have new messages from a particular forum e-mailed to you, click the Subscribe to this Forum icon by the forum name in the forum listing.

For more information about how to use the Wrox P2P, be sure to read the P2P FAQs for answers to questions about how the forum software works as well as to many common questions specific to P2P and Wrox books. To read the FAQs, click the FAQ link on any P2P page.

Flickr™
Mashups

Part I

Building a New Internet

Rewriting the Web

Over the past few years, the Web has seen dramatic growth — both in the actual number of users and in the sheer volume of information available to them. As more and more people start making use of the Web, more web sites appear. The volume of available information is overwhelming — and more importantly, the number of ways in which people wish to use the information available to them is increasing rapidly.

Service providers have come to realize that they simply cannot keep up with demand — they cannot hope to satisfy all of the people all of the time. The audience out there is so large and diverse that it is no longer possible to build all the systems their customers desire. Realizing this, some service providers have addressed the problem in a rather innovative way — instead of closely guarding their corporate data and systems, they have taken the bold step of opening them up to the world. Now, if the service you desire isn't available, the tools are there to take an existing service and enhance it yourself. The distinction between service provider and service consumer is blurring. Consumers are taking control of what they see and sometimes even becoming providers themselves. Companies like Google, Yahoo!, Amazon.com, and Flickr are among the first to embrace this new, open Internet, but where they tread, others will surely follow. This first chapter takes a brief wander through some of the different technologies that have made this shift possible.

Web 2.0: Power to the People

Web 2.0 is the new, open Internet — the latest, and indeed greatest, incarnation of the World Wide Web. But what does Web 2.0 actually mean? The version number suggests a new iteration of technology, a new software release, but Web 2.0 isn't actually a technological advancement. There is no new technology involved — all those Web 2.0 systems that you hear people talking could have been built several years ago. So what has changed?

The change has been a social one. At the core of Web 2.0 is the idea of collaboration, the common thread across Web 2.0 systems being the online sharing of information and the networking of human beings as well as computers. In the world of Web 2.0, web sites are no longer stand-alone entities. Instead of simply displaying their wares to passing visitors, they become data centers — feeding information to other applications on the web. The information is not only shared, it is enriched. Users of shared data are encouraged to add to it, to annotate it. They identify points of interest on Google Maps, add tags to photos on Flickr, and write book reviews on Amazon.com. Users help identify connections between pieces of data — they place their photos on maps of the world, they tag related links in del.icio.us and they create lists of related items on Amazon.com. Each connection made is stored away — an extra data point is created.

By encouraging both the sharing and the enhancement of data, the overall value of those data is increased. The idea that the whole is greater than the sum of its parts is central to Web 2.0, and at the very heart of it is the key element, the user community itself — the very people who enrich the data and give them value.

Remixes and Mashups

The words *remix* and *mashup* are regularly bandied about, but the two are often confused and used interchangeably. Both refer to the presentation of third-party content in a form that is different from the original, but each refers to a slightly different approach.

A *remix* is a piece of content taken from somewhere and presented in a different form. There's typically no significant modification to the content itself — only to the mode of presentation. A very simple example of creating a remix might be applying a user-defined style sheet to change the background color of a web site you are viewing, and perhaps hiding the banner advertisements at the same time. A more complex example might be building a custom web site to display photographs stored on Flickr in your own online gallery. In each case, the content is being derived from a single source, but a custom mode of presentation used.

A *mashup*, on the other hand, involves content from a variety of sources mashed together to produce a brand new dataset — one that is richer than any of the original sources on their own. For example, taking your photographs from Flickr and displaying them as an overlay onto Google Maps would be creating a mashup of Flickr content (the photos and the location information held against them) and Google's mapping data.

Remixes and mashups aren't necessarily distinct — all mashups, for example, could well be considered to be remixes, but remixes may or may not also be mashups, depending on the number of data sources they use. In practice, the distinction between the two terms is minor. In this book, when I'm discussing the projects, I'll use the term that seems most appropriate based on the number of data sources. In more general passages, it quickly becomes tedious to keep having to use the phrase "remix or mashup," so for ease of reading I'll interchangeably use one or the other of the terms. If ever the distinction is important, it will be made explicitly clear.

What Makes a Mashable System?

So, is any source of content out on the Internet mashable? Well, in theory, yes — if you can see it, you can mash it. There are, however, a number of things to consider.

Are You Allowed to Mash the Content?

If the content is owned by somebody else — and this is true in many cases — then you most likely need permission from the copyright owner before you can reuse the content. The content owner may explicitly make content available, although usually there will be restrictions on how you can use it.

On Flickr, and some other systems, the matter is slightly more complicated. The content made available by Flickr isn't typically owned by Flickr itself — it's actually the property of Flickr's users. The photos you see on Flickr are owned by millions of people across the globe. Obviously, use of your own photos is not a problem — you are free to use those where you choose — but you should be careful about how you use photos that do not belong to you. Flickr allows its members to assign different copyright licenses to photos from the Creative Commons set of licenses, and so explicitly allow their use in other applications. These licenses are discussed in more detail in Chapter 2.

When deciding what content to include in your mashup, always check that you will be using the content in ways that are permitted by the copyright owner.

How Easy Is It to Get the Content?

It's often said that if you can see the content on the web, you can write software to retrieve it — after all, that's all your web browser is doing. Strictly speaking, that's absolutely correct. The real question, however, isn't whether or not you can get the content, but rather how *easy* it is to get the content. Suppose, for example, that the piece of text you need to include in your mashup is buried in the middle of somebody else's web page. You need to retrieve and parse the HTML on the page and try to locate the piece you're interested in. If the content of the page is regularly updated, this may in itself be a fairly tricky task. Add to that the prospect of having to deal with cookies, web server authentication, and a whole bunch of other things that happen quietly behind the scenes when you are browsing the Web, and the seemingly straightforward task of getting your piece of text can quickly become a nightmare.

On the other hand, if the content is explicitly made available to you by the content provider, perhaps via a defined programmatic interface or web service, then retrieving it can be extremely straightforward.

When planning your remix or mashup, you should always consider just how you will obtain the content you will be using. In particular, you should check that it is made available in ways that will help rather than hinder you.

Mashup Architectures

From an architectural viewpoint, the most fundamental decision you have to make when starting to design your remix or mashup is where the remixing occurs. Does it occur on the server, or does it occur on the client? Quite possibly, it's a combination of the two. So how do you decide where to do the remixing? As you work through this book, you'll see many examples of both server-side and client-side mashups in action, but let's first take a look at the pros and cons of each.

For the sake of simplicity, we'll assume here that all of the remixes and mashups we discuss are web-based systems. Of course that doesn't have to be the case — you could just as easily write a native Microsoft Windows application that mashes different kinds of data together. The basic mashing principles are, however, basically the same, no matter how you choose to build and deploy your mashup.

Mashing on the Client

Building your mashup so that it executes on the user's client machine is often an attractive option. For a start, it means that you don't need any special software running on your own web server. You may not even need a web server of your own at all. The downside, however, is clear — you are completely dependent on the end user to be using a computer capable of running your mashup. You can see a typical client-side configuration in Figure 1-1.

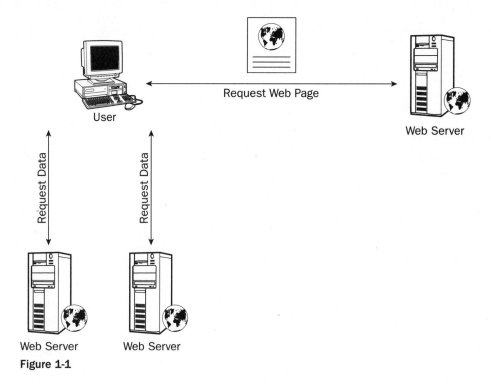

Request Web Page

User

Web Server

Request Data

Request Data

Web Server

Web Server

Figure 1-1

In a client-side mashup, the user first retrieves the web page containing the mashup. Typically, other code within this page then executes within the client browser and retrieves further data from other web servers on the Internet, and then integrates it into the original page, finally displaying the resulting page to the user.

For client-side mashups to work, you need to either have the end user install all the required software, or rely on it already being there. In most cases you can reasonably expect a user to have certain software available — a relatively up-to-date web browser, JavaScript, maybe even the Flash plug-in. You should remember, however, that the more demands you place on the client, the smaller the potential audience for your mashup becomes. Many users won't install extra software just so they can see your mashup — no matter how good it is. Ideally, all they should need to do is point their web browsers in the right direction.

Mashing on the Server

For maximum control and flexibility, mashing on the server is usually by far the best option. You will often have much more control as to the software available to you, installing anything that you need. The server takes control, retrieving content from the various different sources, assembling it all, and then sending the finished result back to the client. You can see all this in action in Figure 1-2.

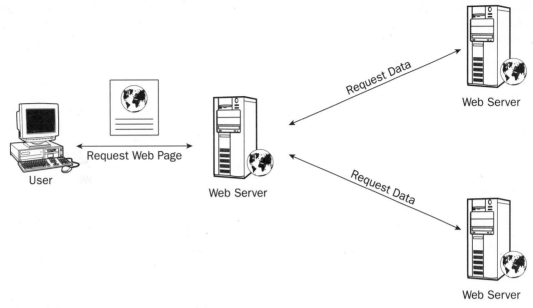

Figure 1-2

The creation of server-side mashups can be a little more complicated — you need to set up and configure all the elements you need on a server first. Despite this, the advantage of server-side mashups is clear — your users don't need any special software. All they need to view your creation is a web browser.

Understanding Mashup Tools and Technologies

Many different tools and technologies are useful in the masher's toolkit. In this next section, we take a brief look at a few of these and see how they might be of use. In a book of this size, it clearly isn't possible to provide full tutorials on each of the subjects mentioned here — each one could easily warrant a whole book in its own right, so here we can do little more than give them a passing mention. Some of these topics are also discussed in more detail in later sections of the book where they are put to use, while Appendix D contains many useful references if you want more detailed information.

HTML, XHTML, and CSS

You almost certainly already have at least a passing familiarity with this family of technologies, starting with HTML, or *Hypertext Markup Language*, which provides the foundation for the entire Web. HTML is a simple, text-based markup language used to structure documents published on the World Wide Web. The HTML standards are defined by the World Wide Web Consortium (W3C) and can all be found on the W3C web site at http://www.w3.org/.

XHTML, or *Extensible Hypertext Markup Language*, is a variant of HTML represented as XML (discussed later) and is the successor to HTML, which it is now starting to replace. For maximum flexibility, most new documents should be created with XHTML rather than HTML.

CSS, or *cascading style sheets*, is a mechanism for attaching style information to HTML and XHTML documents. Style information includes such things as font, color, and page layout information. The first incarnation of HTML provided very little ability to specify much in the way of style information, and decisions about how to render the document were left entirely to the browser. Before long, support for additional HTML elements and attributes was added, so that content creators can make documents that specify various elements of style.

```
<html>
  <head>
    <title>My Document</title>
  </head>
  <body bgcolor="#FF33FF">
    <h1><font face="Arial" size="2" color="#0000FF">Welcome to My
         Web Site</font></h1>
    <p>
      <font face="Arial" size="4" color="#00FF00">Hello, world!</font>
    </p>
  </body>
</html>
```

As you can imagine, maintenance of web sites made up of documents styled in this way was a nightmare—every time you wanted to change a font size, for example, you would have go through each document, changing the size attribute everywhere it occurred. This approach also increased the complexity of the document structure enormously, resulting in a great deal of document bloat. Fortunately, CSS came along to save the day.

CSS provides complete separation of document content and document presentation. With CSS, it is possible to take the same HTML document and present it in different ways and via different media. For example, you might use one set of CSS to render an HTML document for the Web, and a different set to format your document in a way that allows it to be printed easily.

Used properly, CSS can reduce document bloat enormously. For example, with CSS, the HTML above becomes:

```
<html>
  <head>
    <title>My Document</title>
    <link href="styles.css" rel="stylesheet" type="text/css" />
  </head>
  <body>
    <h1>Welcome to My Web Site</h1>
    <p>Hello, world!</p>
  </body>
</html>
```

Here is the associated CSS file:

```
body {
    color: #00FF00;
```

```
        background-color: #FF33FF;
        font-family: Arial;
        font-size: 14pt;
    }

    h1 {
        color: #0000FF;
        font-family: Times New Roman;
        font-size: 24pt;
    }
```

When you consider that many pages across a web site will share the same CSS, and that the CSS files will normally only be loaded by the browser on first access (subsequent page accesses will use the CSS then stored in the browser's cache), it's easy to see that the reduced page bloat can result in dramatically improved page load times — especially on large and complex pages.

The separation of style from content provided by CSS makes creating and maintaining web sites dramatically easier. Changes to the look and feel of the entire site can be made simply by the modification of a single CSS file.

XML and XPath

XML, or *Extensible Markup Language*, is a simple, extensible text format, primarily used for transferring and exchanging data structures. Being text-based, it is easily human-readable and is widely used in interfacing with web-based systems. Along with HTML, it is derived from SGML (Standard Generalized Markup Language) and follows a similar tag-based model. XML specifications are managed by the World Wide Web Consortium and may be found on its web site.

Each XML application is free to define its own data structures, which may then be formally described within a DTD (document type definition) or XML schema. A discussion of these documents is beyond the scope of this book, but again, details can be found on the W3C web site.

Creation of XML documents is very simple — here's a sample document describing part of a book publisher's catalog:

```
<?xml version="1.0"?>
<books>
  <book>
    <title>Flickr Mashups</title>
    <author>David Wilkinson</author>
    <isbn>0470097744</isbn>
  </book>
  <book>
    <title>Google Maps Mashups</title>
    <author>Virender Ajmani</author>
    <isbn>0470097752</isbn>
  </book>
  <book>
    <title>del.icio.us Mashups</title>
    <author>Brett O'Connor</author>
    <isbn>0470097760</isbn>
  </book>
```

```
   <book>
     <title>Amazon.com Mashups</title>
     <author>Francis Shanahan</author>
     <isbn>0470097779</isbn>
   </book>
   <book>
     <title>Yahoo! Maps Mashups</title>
     <author>Charles Freedman</author>
     <isbn>0470097787</isbn>
   </book>
 </books>
```

Every XML document must start with a header that declares it as XML:

```
<?xml version="1.0"?>
```

The header is then followed by a single root element — in this case `<books>`. Within the root element sits the rest of the document. In the example here, the `<books>` element contains a list of individual `<book>` elements. Each `<book>` element contains, in turn, `<title>`, `<author>`, and `<isbn>` elements.

XPath, or *XML Path Language*, enables you to address different parts of an XML document. It is a very powerful tool often used in processing and manipulating XML. XPath treats an XML document as a tree of nodes, with each element and each attribute represented by a node in that tree. An *XPath query* returns a set of nodes from the tree. A typical XPath query consists of an expression representing the path to one or more nodes. So, for example, in the sample XML document here, the XPath query

```
/books
```

will return the root `<books>` node, while the query

```
/books/book
```

returns the set of `<book>` nodes contained within `<books>`, and

```
/books/book/title
```

returns the set of `<title>` nodes.

To return the third book in the list, you would use the following XPath query:

```
/books/book[3]
```

And the last book could be found with

```
/books/book[last()]
```

If you don't want to specify the whole path to an element, you can use the following notation:

```
//title
```

— which in this example will return all the `<title>` nodes within the document — regardless of location.

In this book we only scratch the surface of XPath's capabilities, but if you want to learn how to build more complex XPath expressions, you can read more about the language and its capabilities on the W3C web site.

JavaScript and DOM

JavaScript is another scripting language, widely known for its use in web-based applications. The name JavaScript is something of a misnomer, as it bears only a superficial resemblance to the Java programming language. It first appeared in Netscape's web browser in 1995, and was incorporated into the international standard ECMA-262 as ECMAScript. Most modern browsers incorporate an ECMAScript-compatible scripting language — the one found in Microsoft's Internet Explorer is known as Jscript. JavaScript is actually a registered trademark of Sun Microsystems, but is widely used as a generic reference to the scripting language used within web browsers.

Within the scripting language, web browsers typically implement the W3C standard DOM, or *document object model*. The DOM specifies how HTML and XML documents are represented as a tree structure within the browser. The DOM specification also specifies the programmatic interface by which the various elements within the document tree can be manipulated.

JavaScript used to manipulate the DOM within a browser is often referred to as *dynamic HTML*. Here's a simple example of how you might use dynamic HTML to provide interaction on a web page.

```html
<html>
  <head>
    <title>Arithmetic</title>
    <script type="text/javascript">
      function showAnswer()
      {
        var answerNode = document.getElementById('answer');
        answerNode.innerHTML = "<h2>Answer</h2><p>" + (2 + 2) + "</p>";
      }
    </script>
  </head>
  <body>
    <h1>Question</h1>
    <form onsubmit="showAnswer(); return false;">
      <p>
      What is the answer to the sum <code>2 + 2</code>?
      </p>
      <input type="submit" value="Show Answer" />
    </form>

    <div id="answer">
        The answer will appear here
    </div>
  </body>
</html>
```

In this example, the question is placed inside a form, with a button to submit the form and show the answer. A placeholder <div> element is added at the end of the document and is where the answer to the question will appear.

In the `<head>` section of the page, a JavaScript function is defined, `showAnswer()`. This function uses the DOM method `getElementById()` to find the HTML element with an `id` of `answer` — that's the placeholder `<div>` at the bottom of the page. Once the element is found, the method replaces the HTML contained within the element with new HTML containing the answer to the sum.

Finally, the form defines an `onsubmit` event handler that calls the `showAnswer()` function. This event handler is invoked immediately before the form is submitted to the server (when the button is pressed). Because the JavaScript function does all that is needed here, `return false` is added to the event handler to prevent the submission to the server from actually happening.

AJAX

AJAX, or *Asynchronous Javascript and XML*, is simply a new name for a set of tools that have actually been around for a long time. AJAX has become almost synonymous with Web 2.0, but the techniques that form the basis for AJAX have actually been around since the late 1990s.

Traditional web applications are *page-based*. Every time a new piece of information is requested, or data are updated, a request is sent to the server and a new page is retrieved. This results in many web applications being somewhat laborious to use.

AJAX is intended to overcome this inherent clunkiness of web applications by enabling developers to display or manipulate data within a web page, but without performing a page refresh. This is achieved by means of a JavaScript object called `XmlHttpRequest`. This object allows an HTTP request to be sent to a web server, and the response processed. All this happens behind the scenes of the current page. The requests are carried out *asynchronously* — in other words, the user can continue interacting with the current page while the asynchronous request is being carried out in the background. The result is that web applications can be made to appear much more responsive to a user's actions.

AJAX applications are often much more network-friendly. As usually only part of a page is refreshed in response to a user action, the amount of data transferred across the network is often significantly less than is found in traditional page-based applications.

One of the problems with building AJAX applications has always been supporting the wide variety of web browsers in everyday use. Each web browser has its own individual set of quirks to cope with, and creating an application that works reliably and consistently for the majority of users can be quite a challenge. To this end, a number of toolkits have appeared that take some of the pain out of building AJAX applications. One of the most popular toolkits is Sam Stephensons's Prototype JavaScript framework, available from `http://prototype.conio.net/`, which you will be putting to good use in Chapter 6.

JSON

JSON, or *JavaScript Object Notation*, is a lightweight data-exchange format based on JavaScript syntax. It is designed to be easy for humans to read and write, and also for machines to parse.

It is based around two types of data:

❑   **Objects:** a JavaScript object is a set of name/value pairs. The order of the items in the object is not significant.

❑   **Lists:** a JavaScript list or array is an ordered set of values.

Objects are defined in JSON like this:

```
{
    "title" : "Flickr Mashups",
    "author" : "David Wilkinson",
    "isbn" : "0470097744"
}
```

Each object is surrounded by braces and within those is a comma-separated list of elements. Each element in the object has a name and a value, separated by a colon.

Lists are comma-separated and enclosed by square brackets:

```
["red", "green", "blue"]

[1, 2, 3, 4, 5]

["cat", 312, true]
```

The values represented in JSON may be strings (enclosed in double-quotes as shown above), numbers, Boolean values (`true` and `false`), or the keyword `null`. Whitespace that isn't part of a string is not significant.

Objects and arrays can be combined to form more complex data structures. For example, the data used in the sample XML document shown earlier in this chapter could be represented in a JSON structure as a list of objects — like this:

```
[
    {
        "title" : "Flickr Mashups",
        "author" : "David Wilkinson",
        "isbn" : "0470097744"
    },
    {
        "title" : "Google Maps Mashups",
        "author" : "Virender Ajmani",
        "isbn" : "0470097752"
    },
    {
        "title" : "del.icio.us Mashups",
        "author" : "Brett O'Connor",
        "isbn" : "0470097760"
    },
    {
        "title" : "Amazon.com Mashups",
        "author" : "Francis Shanahan",
        "isbn" : "0470097779"
    },
    {
        "title" : "Yahoo! Maps Mashups",
        "author" : "Charles Freedman",
        "isbn" : "0470097787"
    }
]
```

You can find out more about JSON at `http://www.json.org`.

Web Servers and HTTP

The key piece of software behind any web-based system is the one that is often taken the most for granted — that is, the web server itself. There are many different web servers available, but the two most commonly encountered are the *Apache Web Server* from the Apache Software Foundation (`http://www.apache.org`) and Microsoft's *Internet Information Services* (`http://www.microsoft.com/iis/`), commonly known as IIS.

The web server's role is to listen for incoming requests and then return an appropriate response. Incoming requests commonly come from web browsers, but a significant number may arrive from other software applications — sites that provide an external interface for developers to use, such as Flickr, usually use a web server to handle incoming requests.

The protocol used by web servers is HTTP, or *Hypertext Transfer Protocol*. HTTP is a simple message-based protocol used to transfer information across the web. HTTP supports a number of different types of message, but the two you are most likely to come across are GET and POST.

Most of the time, when you are using your web browser to access web pages, your browser is sending a series of GET requests to one or more web servers. Every page you access is retrieved via an HTTP GET request, as is every image and graphic, every external style sheet, and every external JavaScript file used by the page — assembling all the different pieces of content required to build up a single page can easily result in a couple of dozen GET requests being sent.

A typical GET request to retrieve the contents of the URL `http://www.flickr.com/photos/` looks something like this:

```
GET /photos/ HTTP/1.1
Host: www.flickr.com
User-Agent: Mozilla/5.0 (Windows; U; Windows NT 5.1; en-US; rv:1.8.0.6)
    Gecko/20060728 Firefox/1.5.0.6
Accept: text/xml,application/xml,application/xhtml+xml,text/html;q=0.9,text/plain;
    q=0.8,image/png,*/*;q=0.5
Accept-Language: en-us,en;q=0.5
Accept-Encoding: gzip,deflate
Accept-Charset: ISO-8859-1,utf-8;q=0.7,*;q=0.7
Keep-Alive: 300
Proxy-Connection: keep-alive
Cookie: cookie_epass=b451d297bd19680bea0012147c34c68b; CP=null*;
    cookie_accid=492257; cookie_session=492257%b451d297bd19680bea0012147c34c68b;
    use_master_until=1157985652
```

The first line of an HTTP request consists of the method (in this case, GET), then the name of the resource being requested (`/photos/`), and finally the version of the HTTP protocol being used (`HTTP/1.1`). There then follow a series of headers, which provide additional information that the web server can use to decide how best to handle the request. At the end of the headers is a blank line. Most of these headers you can safely ignore unless you are particularly interested in delving into the inner workings of HTTP. A couple, however, are worth explaining.

The `Host` header is used to specify the name of the host machine on which the client is trying to access a resource. At first glance, that seems a somewhat redundant piece of information — after all, surely the host machine knows what it is called? It is specified in the header of the message because a single web server might be responsible for hosting many different sites. Each web site is a *virtual host* configured within the web server. Probably the majority of the web sites on the Internet are, in fact, virtual hosts, each one sharing a web server with many other web sites.

The other header of interest here is the `Cookie` header. Many web sites use cookies to store information within the client browser. This is typically how web sites remember who you are — every time you visit, your browser presents your cookie to the web server, and the web server can use that to identify you. Cookies are sent in the HTTP headers. In this case, the cookie is sent from the client to the server. When the cookie value is initially set, or whenever it changes, a `Set-Cookie` header is sent from the server back to the client in the response.

Let's take a look at a typical HTTP response. The response shown below is to the request above:

```
HTTP/1.1 200 OK
Date: Sun, 10 Sep 2006 15:14:23 GMT
Server: Apache/2.0.52
Cache-Control: private
Connection: close
Content-Type: text/html; charset=utf-8

<!DOCTYPE HTML PUBLIC "-//W3C//DTD HTML 4.01 Transitional//EN">
<html>
<head>
   <title>Flickr: Photos from everyone in Flickr</title>


   ...
```

The first line consists of a string identifying the protocol version being used, a three-digit status code, and finally a human-readable message describing the meaning of the status code. Here the status is `200`, which means that everything is fine and the requested resource is contained in the body of the response. Status codes of the form 2*xx* indicate success. 3*xx* means that further action is required from the client — perhaps the resource has moved and a new request should be sent to retrieve it from the new location. Status codes of the form 4*xx* indicate an error on the part of the client — the most commonly seen is 404, which means that the requested resource was not found on the server. Finally, 5*xx* codes indicate an error on the part of the server.

After the HTTP status, there follow a number of headers. The most important one shown here is the `Content-Type` header — this contains the MIME type of the requested resource. Here it is `text/html`, so the web browser knows to render this as a web page. After the HTTP headers is a blank line, followed by the requested resource itself — here, an HTML page.

The other web server method you are likely to come across is POST. Whereas GET requests a resource from the web server, POST is used to send data to a resource on the web server. The most common use of POST is for filling in a form on a web page: the data included in the form are sent in the body of the POST request.

Web Browsers

The web browser is, in many ways, the companion to the web server. It is the software that handles the client side of an HTTP transaction. Web browsers have become such a fundamental part of our everyday lives that you might wonder why they even warrant a mention here — for many people, the web browser is one of the primary tools on a computer.

Taking the browser for granted is one of the most common mistakes people make when building web applications. All too often, people fall into the trap of forgetting that the browser they use isn't the only one in existence. Because they are built around a common set of standards, you would expect all web browsers to work with all web sites. Well, by and large, they do — but once you start building more interesting applications, using a wider variety of technologies, you notice that there are, in practice, inconsistencies. Sometimes, there are things that the standards don't actually specify, or that may be open to interpretation, or perhaps a browser only partially implements a particular standard. Some differences may even be caused by bugs in the browser itself.

People use a wide variety of browsers: Internet Explorer, Firefox, Netscape, Safari, and Opera are some of the more common browsers in use — but that list is far from complete. To complicate matters, each browser typically exists in many different versions — each with its own different idiosyncrasies, and each still in use by someone somewhere on the Internet.

To compound the problem, most browsers are capable of running on a variety of platforms — Microsoft Windows, Linux, OS X — and for each platform are usually a number of different variants: Windows XP, Windows 2000, Windows Me, and Vista, for example. Each browser may behave slightly differently on each of those platforms.

If you think that sounds like a daunting set of variations — you're right; it is. What's more, there is no real answer. The total combination of browser/platform combinations is too large for all but the largest development teams to consider testing against. The important thing to remember is that just because your mashup works fine for you, you must not assume that everyone else will see it in exactly the same way.

At the very least, you should always check your mashup under a couple of different browsers. On Windows, try with Internet Explorer and Firefox. On a Mac, try both Firefox and Safari. If you can, try it out with both Mac and Windows. Simply doing this will catch the vast majority of problems. All too often, people are disappointed when they go to check out the latest cool mashup they've heard about, only to find that it doesn't work with their chosen browser. Don't let this happen to you!

PHP and Perl

PHP and Perl are two of the most commonly used scripting languages in use on the Internet today, and most of the examples in this book make use of one of them.

PHP is a recursive acronym for *PHP: Hypertext Preprocessor*. It is a general-purpose scripting language, although it is most commonly encountered in the generation of web pages — a task to which it is ideally suited. Rather than writing lots of code to output HTML tags, you can embed PHP directly into standard HTML pages:

```
<html>
  <head>
    <title>Arithmetic</title>
```

```
      </head>
      <body>
        <h1>Question</h1>
        <p>
          What is the answer to the sum <code>2 + 2</code>?
        </p>
        <h2>Answer</h2>
        <?php
          echo 2 + 2 ;
        ?>
      </body>
    </html>
```

I'll be making a lot of use of PHP in the chapters that follow, and some experience of PHP is assumed throughout most of this book. If you need to brush up on your PHP skills, the main PHP web site at http://www.php.net/ is always a good place to start. There you will find the PHP documentation and tutorials.

Like PHP, Perl is a scripting language, and it has a very long history. Created by Larry Wall in the mid 1980s, it has become one of the most widely used tools around. System administrators refer to it as the "duct tape of the Internet": its versatility and almost ubiquitous availability allow it to be easily applied in most situations.

Perl is available for a large variety of computing platforms, and is supported by a comprehensive library of add-on modules available from CPAN — the *Comprehensive Perl Archive Network* — which can be found at http://cpan.perl.org/.

Regular Expressions

A *regular expression* is a string that defines a *pattern* that is used to match one or more strings, and is typically used to search for specific patterns within a larger string. The easiest way to understand what this means is by seeing an example or two — let's look at a few examples of typical regular expressions.

Many types of regular expressions exist — in this book, I use only *Perl-style* regular expressions.

Here's a very simple regular expression:

```
/Flickr/
```

The regular expression, often shortened to *regexp*, is delimited by forward slashes. Within the slashes is the pattern to be matched. Here the pattern is very simple — it's the word Flickr. This pattern will match any string that contains the text Flickr. The following are all strings that match the pattern.

```
Flickr Mashups
The Flickr web site
I like Flickr
```

Most regular expressions aren't that straightforward, however. Many special characters can be used within a regexp pattern to perform more complex matches. For example, the caret character (^) is used to match the start of a string, and the dollar sign ($) matches the end of a string. Look at this regexp:

```
/^Flickr/
```

The ^ character at the start of the pattern means that only strings that begin with the word `Flickr` will be matched. In the three sample strings, only one matches:

```
Flickr Mashups
```

Similarly, this regexp

```
/Flickr$/
```

only matches the string that ends with `Flickr`:

```
I like Flickr
```

The period (`.`) will match any character, so the following pattern will match any string that has an `F` and an `r` separated by four characters:

```
/F....r/
```

That means it will match all three of the Flickr strings, and will also match these two:

```
Farmer Giles has a herd of cows
Fly around the world
```

The asterisk (`*`) is a modifier that means "zero or more occurrences" of the preceding character. So, the regexp

```
/che*se/
```

will match

```
cheese
cheeeeeeeese
chse
```

Similarly, the plus (`+`) and question mark (`?`) characters are modifiers that mean *one or more occurrences* and *exactly zero or one occurrences*, respectively.

You can use square brackets to enclose a set of alternatives, so the regexp

```
/br[eo]ad/
```

will match both `bread` and `broad`.

You can use `\d` to match a numeric digit (0–9) and `\w` to represent a "word" character (a letter or digit, or the underscore character), so the regexp

```
/\d\d\d\d-\d\d-\d\d/
```

can be used to match dates in the format *yyyy-mm-dd*.

Regular expressions are a very powerful tool, and there's much more to them than can be covered in a brief introduction such as this. You'll be using them in various places in this book, often within PHP. The PHP web site has a handy description of regular expression pattern syntax at `http://www.php.net/manual/en/reference.pcre.pattern.syntax.php`.

REST

REST, or *Representational State Transfer*, is a term that is often misused. Strictly speaking, REST describes an architectural approach to building software systems. The term REST was first used by Roy Fielding, one of the principal authors of the HTTP specification, in his PhD dissertation: "Representational State Transfer is intended to evoke an image of how a well-designed Web application behaves: a network of web pages (a virtual state-machine), where the user progresses through an application by selecting links (state transitions), resulting in the next page (representing the next state of the application) being transferred to the user and rendered for their use."

A web application built on REST principles would model each object stored in the system as a unique URL. So, a bookstore might use URLs of the following form:

```
http://www.somebookstore.com/books/0470097744
```

Here, 0470097744 is the ISBN of the book in question. When the URL is accessed, a document representing the book is returned — on the web, this is most likely an HTML page. Of course, there isn't really a different HTML page for every single book in the store — the pages are all dynamically generated based on the information passed in the URL.

The HTML page for the book might include a link to a list of reviews of the book:

```
http://www.somebookstore.com/books/0470097744/reviews
```

Each review would also have its own URL:

```
http://www.somebookstore.com/books/0470097744/reviews/1
```

Each time the user follows a link to new URL, the new URL contains all of the context required to service the request — there is no state required to be stored on the server; it is stored entirely in the URL. This is a key feature of a REST system.

In the Web 2.0 world, the term REST is also often used to refer to any simple HTTP interface that exchanges information (usually XML) without the aid of an additional messaging layer such as SOAP (see the following section). The Flickr API has such a REST interface, which is covered in detail in Chapter 4.

REST interfaces such as the one offered by Flickr are URL-based, and represent a very concise way of sending a request to the remote system. A typical REST request URL might look something like this:

```
http://www.flickr.com/services/rest/?method=flickr.photos.search
    &user_id=50317659@N00&per_page=6&api_key=1f2811827f3284b3aa12f7bbb7792b8d
```

This URL performs a search for a user's recent photos on Flickr. Don't worry about the details of what all those parameters mean right now — we'll look at this request in more detail in Chapter 4. You can see, however, that the whole of the request is found in the URL. One of the big advantages of using REST is that you can try things out simply by typing the URL into your web browser — there are no complicated messaging protocols to conform to. As far as application interfaces go, REST is as close to instant gratification as you are likely to get as a software developer.

> *If you do try typing this example URL into your browser, it won't actually work. Before you can use Flickr's services, you will need to get an API key from it. We'll explain all about what API keys are, how you get one, and how you use them in the next few chapters.*

SOAP

SOAP is an XML-based messaging format, widely used as the means of communication with web services. The SOAP standard is maintained by W3C. Originally, SOAP was an acronym for *Simple Object Access Protocol*, but that particular definition has been dropped in recent years.

SOAP requests and responses are both XML documents, and as such can be very verbose. For example, when converted to a SOAP message, the simple Flickr REST request shown previously becomes something like this:

```
<?xml version="1.0" encoding="utf-8" ?>
<s:Envelope
 xmlns:s="http://www.w3.org/2003/05/soap-envelope"
 xmlns:xsi="http://www.w3.org/1999/XMLSchema-instance"
 xmlns:xsd="http://www.w3.org/1999/XMLSchema"
>
    <s:Body>
        <x:FlickrRequest xmlns:x="urn:flickr">
            <method>flickr.photos.search</method>
            <api_key>1f2811827f3284b3aa12f7bbb7792b8d</api_key>
            <user_id>50317659@N00</user_id>
            <per_page>6</per_page>
        </x:FlickrRequest>
    </s:Body>
</s:Envelope>
```

Many web services that provide SOAP interfaces use WSDL, or *Web Services Description Language*, as a means of formally describing the services available and defining how to both construct the request-message documents and understand the response documents.

Because of the widespread use of SOAP, many SOAP toolkits are available, and many development environments provide direct support for SOAP. Such toolkits, however, typically rely on the existence of a WSDL description of the web service, and if this is not available, they are of limited use.

XML-RPC

XML-RPC is another commonly used XML-based messaging format and is a mechanism for providing *remote procedure calls* using XML. A remote procedure call is simply a means of executing a service on another computer. XML-RPC was the precursor to SOAP and, as with SOAP, the message format is somewhat verbose. A typical XML-RPC message might look something like this:

```xml
<?xml version="1.0" encoding="utf-8" ?>
<methodCall>
    <methodName>flickr.photos.search</methodName>
    <params>
        <param>
            <value>
                <struct>
                    <member>
                        <name>api_key</name>
                        <value>
                            <string>1f2811827f3284b3aa12f7bbb7792b8d</string>
                        </value>
                    </member>
                    <member>
                        <name>user_id</name>
                        <value>
                            <string>50317659@N00</string>
                        </value>
                    </member>
                    <member>
                        <name>per_page</name>
                        <value>
                            <int>6</int>
                        </value>
                    </member>
                </struct>
            </value>
        </param>
    </params>
</methodCall>
```

XML-RPC isn't in quite such widespread use as SOAP, and less toolkit support is available for it within the developer community.

Databases

Most systems of any complexity make use of a database somewhere behind the scenes. For very small amounts of data, and small numbers of users, you can get by with storing any data you need to keep track of in files on disk, or perhaps in cookies, but before long you'll find yourself needing a proper *database management system*. A database management system provides an efficient means of storing, searching, and maintaining large quantities of information.

One of the most popular database systems in use in web systems today is MySQL. MySQL is a freely available open-source database from MySQL AB and is available from http://www.mysql.com. MySQL is a relational database, and as might be expected from the name, uses *Structured Query Language* (SQL) to manage and query the data.

SQL and MySQL database administration are a large and complex topic — and one impossible to cover in any depth in a book like this. Chapter 14 contains instructions for setting up a MySQL database, together with a brief introduction to basic SQL commands, and many more resources on the Internet explore these subjects in much more detail. The main MySQL web site has full documentation and includes a brief tutorial on using MySQL.

Curl

Earlier on in this chapter, you saw how easy it was to send a REST-style query to a web server — you can simply type it into the address bar of your web browser. But what if you don't want to use your web browser? Perhaps you want to see exactly what is being returned, or perhaps you want to save the results to a file. What about more complicated messages such as SOAP or XML-RPC? How can you try out sending those kinds of message? The answer is a little application called *curl*.

Curl is a command-line tool for sending and retrieving files using URL syntax. It supports a wide range of protocols including, most importantly, HTTP. Curl is free and available for a very wide variety of platforms. You can download it from `http://curl.haxx.se/`.

When you come to run curl, you have a huge number of command-line options to choose from. These are all documented on the curl web site, but here are a few common ones. To retrieve the contents of a URL such as `http://www.flickr.com/`, simply type the following:

```
curl http://www.flickr.com/
```

To retrieve the page, but save it to a file:

```
curl -o file.html http://www.flickr.com/
```

And to POST the contents of a file to a URL:

```
curl -d @request.xml http://www.flickr.com/services/soap/
```

Curl is a very powerful and versatile tool; it is well worth spending a little time to read through the manual.

Summary

This chapter introduced you to the world of mashups. You saw the difference between client- and server-side mashups and were introduced to many of the technologies that make mashups possible. Now, let's move on and take a closer look at Flickr, the system that will be the focus of our mashups for the rest of this book.

Flickr: A Short Tour

If you're reading this book, you probably already have a Flickr account and are familiar with at least some aspects of Flickr. It is, however, a large and continually growing web site and there may well be areas you are not yet familiar with. In this chapter, you will be taken on a brief guided tour of Flickr. I won't show you all the wide variety of different features available — the aim of this chapter isn't to be a comprehensive Flickr user guide. Instead, I'll take a look at things from the mashup developer's point of view. I'll show you how the main features at Flickr are set up, with a few rest stops along the way to highlight specific areas of interest.

Creating an Account

The first step in the Flickr experience is creating an account. You probably already have a Flickr account, but if you don't, this is a very good time to go ahead and sign up. You can create a new account from the Flickr home page at `http://www.flickr.com/` by following the sign-up instructions there. Each new Flickr account is tied to a Yahoo! account — as part of the Flickr sign-up process, you will be asked to create a new Yahoo! account, or sign in to an existing one.

When you create your Flickr account, you will also get to choose your *screen name*. This is the name that people see when they look at your photos on Flickr, and can be your real name or an alias — it's entirely up to you. Your screen name is unique at any point in time, but you are free to change it as you wish. The variability of the screen name means that it isn't particularly reliable as a means of identification, so behind the scenes Flickr allocates you another unique identifier, known as the NSID, or *Network Services ID*. A typical NSID looks like this:

```
50317659@N00
```

Your NSID is fixed and can never be changed. Most Flickr users go through their whole time on Flickr without ever really being aware of NSIDs. To you, as a mashup developer, however, the NSID is especially important — throughout this book, you'll be making extensive use of NSIDs to uniquely identify users.

Account Types

Two types of Flickr accounts are available — free and *pro*. When you first create a Flickr account, you will have a free account by default, although you can upgrade to a pro account at any time by going to the `http://www.flickr.com/account/` page. There are some subtle but significant differences between free and pro accounts — some of which you may need to bear in mind when building your mashups.

The principal limitation on free accounts is in the number of photos they are allowed to have visible in their photostream on Flickr at any one time. For pro users, the number of photos is unlimited, but free accounts may only have the 200 most recently uploaded photographs available. Once a free-account holder reaches the 200-photo limit, as new photos are uploaded, the older ones disappear from view. Free accounts are also restricted in the amount of upload bandwidth they are allowed to use. Flickr regulates how much you upload by measuring the total number of bytes uploaded rather than the number of bytes stored on Flickr — meaning that even if you delete your photos off Flickr, the bandwidth used does not change. Free-account holders are allowed a total of 20 MB of bandwidth per calendar month, whereas pro-account holders are allowed up to 2 GB per month. You can see how much bandwidth you have left at any time by going to the Flickr Upload page at `http://www.flickr.com/photos/upload/`.

Another restriction on free-account holders is in the number of photo sets they are allowed to create — free-account holders may only create three sets, whereas pro-account holders have no limit on the number of sets allowed.

Some other Flickr features are also restricted to pro-account holders only, and more differences may well be added over time. For example, the ability to replace a photo in your photostream is only available to pro users.

Setting a URL

One of the most important decisions you can make with your Flickr account is in choosing its URL. By default, the URL to your photos contains your NSID, and looks something like this:

```
http://www.flickr.com/photos/50317659@N00/
```

As URLs go, that's not particularly memorable, so Flickr enables you to set an alternative, friendlier URL, which might look more like this:

```
http://www.flickr.com/photos/dopiaza/
```

You can set your URL very easily by going to the Your Account page and clicking the Set up your URL link, or by going straight to `http://www.flickr.com/profile_url.gne`.

When you set your URL, you must choose carefully. Once set, it can never be changed. Setting your URL is a once-only decision.

Uploading Photographs

Once you have a Flickr account, the next step is to upload some photos. The simplest way is to use the Flickr Upload page at `http://www.flickr.com/photos/upload/`, shown in Figure 2-1.

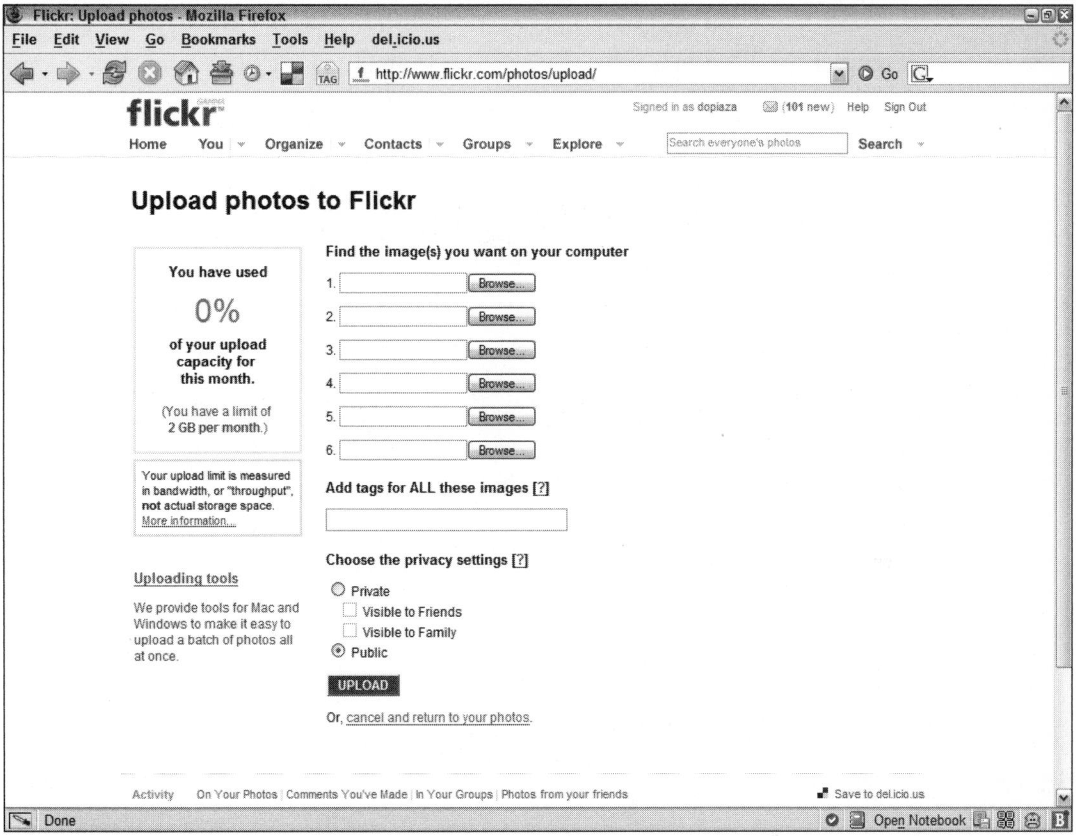

Figure 2-1

The Upload page also enables you to see just how much of your available bandwidth you have used in the current month. The Upload page is very handy for quickly uploading an image, but as you can see, it only allows you to upload six photos at a time. A number of additional uploading tools for a variety of platforms are available from the tools page (http://www.flickr.com/tools/)—many people use one of these. Later on in this book, you will see how you can build your own uploader, but to start with, you should easily find something here that meets your immediate needs.

One of the most common applications used for uploading is the Flickr Uploadr, which is available for Windows and Mac OS X. This is a stand-alone application that enables you to drag and drop photos onto it and then upload them as a batch. You can see Uploadr in action in Figure 2-2.

Pro accounts are limited to a maximum individual photo size of 10 MB, and free accounts are limited to a total of 5 MB per file. Uploadr will warn you if you attempt to upload a file larger than the permitted size and ask you to resize it. You can also set Uploadr to resize all images uploaded to Flickr if you like—you do this via the options dialog, which you can find by clicking the light switch button at the far right of the row of Uploadr buttons. The options dialog is shown in Figure 2-3.

Figure 2-2

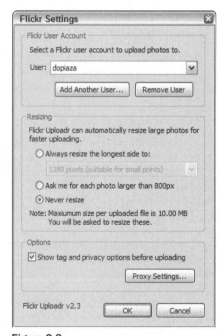

Figure 2-3

From here, you can not only tell Uploadr to resize your images, but also configure it to allow access to multiple accounts — a very useful feature if you share your computer with other users or manage multiple accounts on Flickr.

Photo Formats and Sizes

Flickr enables you to upload photos in a variety of common formats:

❑   JPEG

❑   GIF (non-animated)

❑   PNG

❑   TIFF

Whenever a file is uploaded, the original is stored away and is not modified by Flickr at all, expect in the case of TIFF files, in which the original is first converted to JPG. Flickr then generates a series of smaller files — ranging from small thumbnails to larger sizes suitable for display on a web page. Regardless of the format of your original photo, all Flickr-generated images will be in JPEG format. You can see these resized images if you go to any of your photo pages and press the All Sizes button above the photo. Note that if you have a free account the original-size photo is not available — it is still stored at Flickr and will become available if you upgrade your account to pro.

Photo IDs and URLs

When you upload a photo to Flickr, it is allocated a unique identifier known as the *photo ID*. This ID is fixed for the life of the photo — even if you replace the photo, the ID remains the same. In accordance with the REST principles I talked about in Chapter 1, each photo has its own unique URL. I'll discuss photo URLs in more detail in Chapter 4, but if you take a look at one of your photo pages, you can see that it looks something like this:

```
http://www.flickr.com/photos/dopiaza/231699414/
```

The ID for the photo is the number on the end of the URL — in this case, 231699414. At the time of this writing, the photo ID is simply an incremental count of the number of photos stored on Flickr — when this photo was posted, there were over 231 million photos already posted to Flickr. Of course, there will be fewer photos actually stored on Flickr — some of those millions of photos will have since been deleted, and many of the remainder will be private and therefore unavailable to you. Flickr reserves the right to change how photo IDs get allocated in the future, but until they do so, the photo ID you are allocated is a good indication of just how vast the Flickr databases are.

Organizing Your Photographs

Flickr offers a number of different ways to organize your photographs. In this section, I'll introduce the different methods available to you.

The Photostream

The default view of your photos is your *photostream*. The photostream shows all the photos you have uploaded to Flickr — sorted by upload date, with the most recently uploaded photos at the start of the stream and the oldest photos at the end. Every time you upload a new photo, it appears at the head of your photostream. You can see a typical photostream view in Figure 2-4.

The only way to change the order of photos within your photostream is to manually edit the upload date. If you look the main photo page for one of your photographs, under the Additional Information section on the right-hand side, you will see a line giving the date the photo was taken, together with an edit link. Clicking the edit link takes you to the Edit Date screen, where you have two tabs to select between, Date Taken and Date Posted, as shown in Figure 2-5.

Figure 2-4

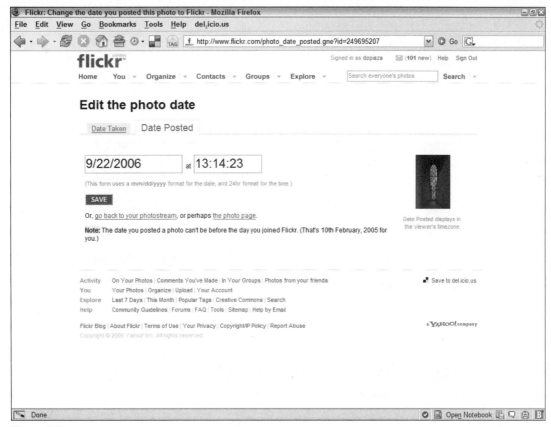

Figure 2-5

By selecting the Date Posted tab, you can modify the time and date that Flickr has stored as the upload date for the photo. Once you save a new time and date here, Flickr will reorder your photostream to reflect the new timestamps. You can easily see this in action—go to any older photo in your stream and modify the date taken to be the current date and time. If you then go back to the photostream view, you will see that the photo has moved to the head of the photostream—as far as Flickr is concerned, it is now the most recently uploaded photo in your photostream and as such takes prime position at the top of the page.

Sets

The photostream view is ideal for quickly seeing what is new in a series of photographs, but isn't well suited to grouping related photos for display. To do this, Flickr provides another feature called *sets*. A set, sometimes called a *photoset*, is a collection of photographs from your photostream—you can use sets to group photographs with a common theme, a collection from an event, or any selection of pictures you choose. Once you have created some sets, you will see them appear down the right-hand side of the first page of your photostream, and also on your sets page, which will look something like Figure 2-6.

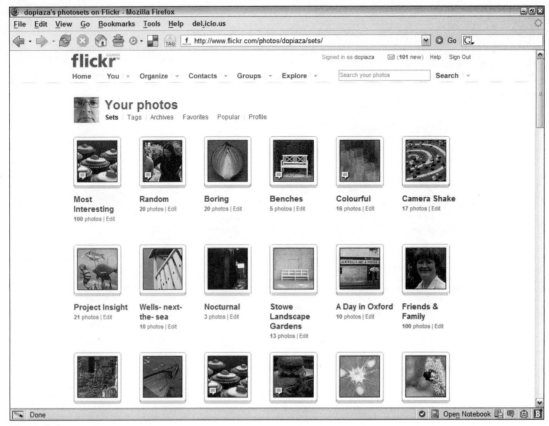

Figure 2-6

You can easily add a photo to a new or existing set by clicking the Add to Set button above the photo on the main photo page. When you click the Add to Set button, you are presented with a list of available sets, or the option to create a new set. Any sets that already contain the photo are shown in this list as gray with an [X] symbol next to them—clicking this [X] will remove them from that set. A photo can be in any number of sets at once, and removing a photo from a set, or deleting an entire set, does not delete any of the photos—they remain in your photostream until they themselves are explicitly deleted.

You might notice that each photoset, just like each photo, has its own ID, and the URL for a photoset looks something like this:

```
http://www.flickr.com/photos/dopiaza/sets/72057594090101718/
```

Here, the set ID is 72057594090101718. Unlike photo IDs, set IDs don't simply increase by one each time you create a new set—if you create two sets in quick succession, you will see that their IDs are significantly different.

Organizr

The Flickr Organizr is a very useful tool to help organize your photos. You can find it at `http://www`
`.flickr.com/photos/organize`, or simply by clicking the Organize link at the top of any Flickr page.

It is worth taking a closer look at Organizr — it is an AJAX application created with the Flickr API, and
as such an excellent example of the kind of application that can be built this way. I'll look at the Flickr
API in detail in Chapter 4 and then make extensive use of it throughout the rest of this book. For the
moment, however, let's take a closer look at Organizr and the capabilities it offers.

The Organizr application consists of a series of tabs along the top of the window, each one enabling the
user to switch among the different major tasks that Organizr performs. Across the bottom of the Organizr
window is a strip of photographs, together with a number of controls to enable searching and selection of
photos from the user's photostream. The central area of Organizr is the main working area. When you
first open Organizr, it is in batch organize mode, and you can select photos from the bottom strip and
drag them into the central area in order to perform batch operations on them. You can see this view in
Figure 2-7.

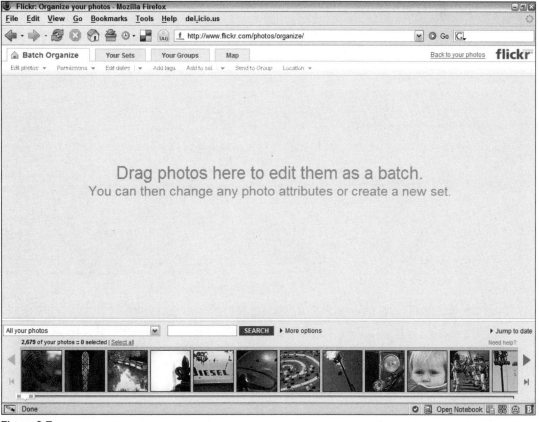

Figure 2-7

When selecting photos to drag into the main area, you can use the usual key combinations to make multiple selections — Shift-click to select a range and Control-click to select noncontiguous items. Once you have selected your photos, the menu underneath the tabs enables you to make a variety of changes to the photos, such as by modifying dates, tags, titles, and descriptions.

The next tabs enable you to easily manage your sets — you can create new sets and delete existing ones, add and remove photos from your sets, and change the order in which your sets appear, along with the photos inside them. Many of Flickr's set-management features, such as the ability to reorder sets and change the primary photo of the set, are available only from within Organizr.

The third Organizr tab provides a screen form that lets you easily post photographs to one or more group pools, and the fourth tab, Map, enables you to add location information to your photos. As with sets, the Map tab provides functionality that is not found elsewhere on Flickr. When you click it, Flickr's Geotagging interface will load and show you a map of the world — rather like that shown in Figure 2-8.

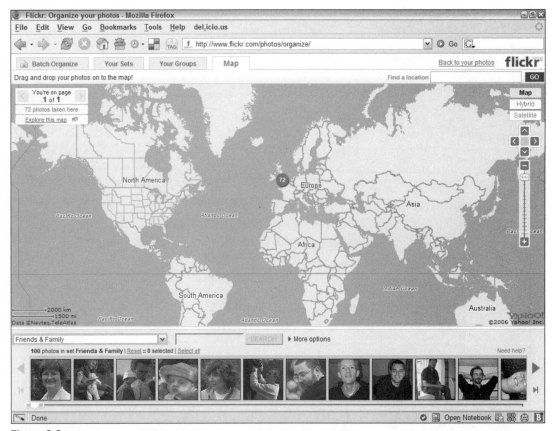

Figure 2-8

You can zoom in closer on the map using the slider on the right-hand side of the page, and you can click anywhere on the map and drag to reposition it. To add your photos to the map, just drag them from the bar at the bottom and drop them onto the map at the appropriate location. I'll talk about geotagging and location information in much more detail in Chapter 13.

Tags

Tags are a key part of the organizational structure of photos on Flickr. For each photo on Flickr, you can add one or more tags. These tags may be descriptive of the objects in the photograph (*me, cat, flower, sunset*), they may describe the event or time the photo was taken (*vacation, Christmas, summer, 2006*), the location (*Paris, London, Canada*) or perhaps something much more abstract (*fun, happy, sad*). In short, you can add any kind of tag you like to your photograph—there is no formal tag vocabulary.

Tagging is one of the easiest means of finding photos—just search for the word *cat*, for example, and you will find many thousands of photos with that tag. The lack of a fixed tagging structure makes the process of adding tags to a photo very simple and straightforward—just click the Add a tag link on one of your photo pages and type in any words and phrases you want to use as tags. You can see this in Figure 2-9.

Figure 2-9

You can add more than one tag at once—just separate the tags by spaces. If you want to tag with a phrase rather than a single word, just enclose the phrase in double quotes. A typical set of tags added might look something like this:

```
party fun "Sue's birthday" 2006
```

This would result in four different tags being added: *party, fun, Sue's birthday, and 2006.* Flickr always stores the exact tag you entered, and when the tag is displayed you see it exactly as you typed it. Internally, however, Flickr also stores a second representation of the tag, which is the version it uses when conducting tag searches. It constructs this internal form of the tag by removing all the characters that aren't letters or numbers from the tag entered and converting the rest to lowercase. So, for example, the tags *Sue's birthday, sues birthday, sues_birthday,* and *suesbirthday* are all treated by Flickr as being identical—a search on any one of those tags would result in a match.

Some common words are automatically removed from the tag list when you try to add them. When people are new to the idea of tagging, they often type a descriptive phrase in the tag box. By removing certain common words such as *the, of,* and *and,* Flickr includes only the key words in the phrase as tags. Try this: go to one of your photos and add this phrase as a tag: *the cat is sitting on the mat.* Make sure, though, that you do *not* enclose the phrase in quotes. Once the tags are added, you will see that only the words *cat, is, sitting* and *mat* are actually added as tags. The words *the* and *on* are not added.

You can, if you wish, allow other users to add tags to your photographs. The ability to add tags is configurable—you can set it by modifying your default photo privacy settings at http://www.flickr.com/account/prefs/photoprivacy/.

A free-form user-driven and collaborative tagging system such as that used by Flickr is often referred to as a *folksonomy*—in contrast to a *taxonomy*, which is a more formal, well-defined system of categorization.

Of course, having no formal method for allocating tags has its disadvantages too—the tag space is easily polluted by irrelevant or confusing tags. Some people will add a variety of popular tags to all of their photos, regardless of their relevance, in an effort to garner more views. This method isn't usually that successful, but it does cause irrelevant matches to be returned during tag searches. Another potential pitfall here is that different people's ideas of what is an appropriate tag can vary enormously. If someone has a dog named Chester, for example, somebody searching for photos of the English town might be surprised to see a large collection of photos of a family pet. Similarly, somebody else searching on the tags *paris* and *hilton* might not be expecting to find a collection of architectural photographs of French hotels. Yet another common source of confusion is the fact that Flickr members are scattered across the globe and the membership has a wide variety of native languages. Many people tag photographs in their native tongue and a search for photos tagged *cat*, for example, would fail to find any from French members who tagged them *chat*. There can also be much confusion where the same word means different things in different languages—the word *ape* is Italian for *bee*, so a search for primates might well also turn up Italian winged insects. There is no easy solution to the problem of tags meaning different things to different people—there is no arbiter to say what usage is correct and what usage isn't. Just don't be surprised to find occasional unexpected results when you perform a search.

NIPSA

Some Flickr accounts are marked as *NIPSA*, or *Not in Public Site Areas*. As the name suggests, NIPSA accounts are, at least to some extent, hidden from public view. Photos from accounts marked as NIPSA won't appear if you perform a tag search across everyone's photos. If you go to the URL of a NIPSA'd account, you can still see the photos—they're not actually hidden from view, they're simply excluded from search results. There are a number of different reasons that an account may be marked as NIPSA.

Every new account is marked as NIPSA when it is first created. Each account is manually reviewed by staff to verify that the initial contents of the account are acceptable for public viewing. Note that this review does not take place until the account has had a certain number of publicly visible photos uploaded to it— the number of public photos currently required to trigger a staff review is five. This is a manual process and it can be a few days before the review actually takes place.

Accounts will also be marked as NIPSA if they contain content that is contrary to the Flickr terms of use. The most common type of content that causes accounts to be marked as NIPSA is non-photographic imagery. This includes computer-generated graphics, illustrations, and screenshots.

As a mashups developer, you should be aware that content from NIPSA accounts will not show up in any *public* searches you make to retrieve content from Flickr. You should specifically note the word *public* there—in this context, it means a search executed across everyone's photos. If you perform a search against a specific account, you will find all matching content—even if that account is marked as NIPSA.

The Social Network: Contacts, Friends and Family

Flickr isn't just a place to store photographs—one of its much-advertised features is the ability to *share* your photos. By default, your photos are visible to other users—both Flickr members and non-members. Equally, you are free to browse other users' photostreams. If you find a Flickr user whose photographs you particularly like and would like to be able to easily find again, you can mark that user as a *contact*. To add someone as a contact, you simply place your cursor over the user's buddy icon and click the drop-down menu that appears. Here you will see a variety of options relating to that user—including the option to add him or her as a contact. If you select that option, you will be asked to confirm your action, and also given the option to mark the user as a friend or family member. You can see this screen in Figure 2-10.

Once you've added someone as a contact, that person's most recent photos appear on your Photos from Your Contacts page, which you can get to by clicking the Contacts menu at the top of each page. This means that by adding somebody as a contact, you can easily keep track of when he or she uploads new photos.

Figure 2-10

People who are new to Flickr can sometimes find the contact system a little strange, and are reluctant to add people as contacts. Creating contacts is really just a form of bookmarking—there is no implied social connection. Adding someone as a contact does not automatically make you a contact of that person—he or she has to explicitly add you in order to reciprocate the relationship. Every time somebody adds you as a contact, you are sent a FlickrMail message informing you of the fact—this gives you the opportunity to look at the person's profile and photostream to decide whether or not you want to add that person.

When marking people as contacts, you can optionally designate them as friends, family, or both. By doing so, you can restrict who gets to see your photos. You can mark each of your photos as public or private—just click the link under each photo in the photostream view, or the privacy link in the Additional Information section on the Photo page.

On the Privacy page, you can set not only who can view the photo, but who can add comments and who can add notes and tags. You can see this page in Figure 2-11.

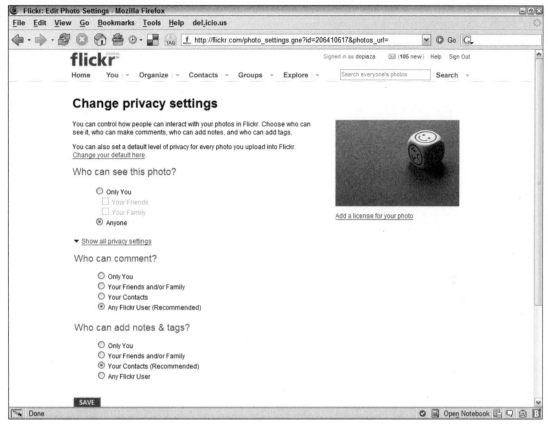

Figure 2-11

Note that if your photos are marked as private, they are not generally visible. If you have selected the option Visible to Friends or Visible to Family, they will be visible to contacts you have marked as being friends or family as appropriate. If you have marked a photo as private but selected neither Visible to Friends nor Visible to Family, then the photo will only be visible to you. Later on, when you build your mashups, the privacy of your photos will become important. If you want to be able to access your private photos through your mashup, you will need to authenticate yourself with Flickr before you are allowed to see them. Authentication is covered in detail in Chapter 7.

Groups

Groups are the places on Flickr where like-minded users gather, discuss things, and share pictures. There are many thousands of groups on Flickr covering every subject imaginable, from groups that collect pictures of cats and sunsets through to a whole range of groups dedicated to traffic cones. Groups vary wildly in popularity. The most popular, such as FlickrCentral, have tens of thousands of members, other more specialist groups a mere handful.

Groups can be public, invitation-only, or private. Public groups are, as the name suggests, open to all, whereas private groups are not generally visible and are accessible only by invitation. Invitation-only groups are somewhere between the two. They are publicly visible, but new members can join only if they are invited.

```
Groups are identified in the same way as users are—each group has its own unique
NSID. Take FlickrCentral as an example: it has an NSID of 34427469792@N01, and a
URL of http://www.flickr.com/groups/34427469792@N01/.
```

Groups can have their own "friendly" URLs, just as people can. FlickrCentral's friendly URL is `http://www.flickr.com/groups/central/`.

Just as member URLs cannot change once they are set, nor can group URLs. Despite the fact that member URLs and group URLs have different prefixes (`http://www.flickr.com/photos/` and `http://www.flickr.com/groups/`) they share a common namespace. Using FlickrCentral as an example, since that group has already chosen the URL `http://www.flickr.com/groups/central/`, no user can then set `http://www.flickr.com/photos/central/` as his or her personal URL. As far as Flickr is concerned, the name `central` has been taken.

Each group has a discussion area, where members can post messages and engage in conversation. Only group members can post in discussions, although group administrators can decide whether or not the discussions are visible to non-members.

Alongside the discussion area is a group *pool*. The pool is a place where group members can add photos that are then visible to all group members—regardless of the privacy settings on the photos themselves. Each group usually has its own rules about the type of photos that are acceptable in its pool, and group pools are often actively policed by group administrators, with photos that do not conform to the pool rules being removed. Group pools are potentially of interest to the mashups developer as they are a great source of themed photographs. As group pool submissions are usually monitored by group administrators to ensure that they fit into the group's theme, they can often provide a more useful source of photographs than the random results that a simple tag search can generate.

Interestingness

A key concept within Flickr is that of *interestingness*. If you look at the Explore section of Flickr at `http://www.flickr.com/explore/`, you can see a selection of the *most interesting* photos uploaded to Flickr. But what makes an interesting photo? Who decides whether a photograph is interesting or not? This is a much-asked question on the Flickr Forums, and the usual joke answer supplied is that the Flickr Magic Donkey chooses the photographs every day. The real answer is actually that no individual decides—it's all done algorithmically. Flickr invented the concept of interestingness to identify which photos should be shown in the Explore section of the site, and created an algorithm that assigns an interestingness value to every photograph on Flickr. The algorithm itself is a closely guarded secret and is regularly modified to prevent people from reverse-engineering it.

The whole point of interestingness isn't to make qualitative judgments on the photos shown on Flickr, but rather to allow the selection of photos that are in some way interesting. Remember, *interesting* does not necessarily mean *good*—a very bad photograph may be interesting if it depicts an unusual event.

Exactly what counts as interesting in Flickr's eyes is of course a secret, but it's possible to make some educated guesses as how it works. First of all, and perhaps most importantly, it is almost certain that the interestingness score is not dependent in any way on the image itself. Human beings are very good at recognizing visual patterns quickly. When looking at a photograph, you can tell in an instant the difference between a landscape scene and a close-up of a bee. For a piece of software, it's really not that simple. Considering the volume of photographs being uploaded at Flickr — currently running at over a million new photos a day — the thought of performing any sort of image analysis would be daunting.

So what does interestingness consist of? Well, anything a little out of the ordinary is likely to be considered more inherently interesting than something that is commonplace. A photo tagged with *diplodocus* is, on average, likely to be more interesting than a photograph tagged with *cat* — not because the photograph is necessarily any better than the one of the cat, but simply because it's more unusual. There are currently 242 matches returned for a search on *diplodocus* and 982,886 for a search on *cat*. But unusual tags aren't, on their own, enough. Photos with more comments and that more users have added as a favorite might also be more interesting. More importantly, just *who* comments and adds an image as a favorite might well be a factor — a comment from a stranger who isn't a contact undoubtedly means more than a comment from a close family member. Equally, deviations from normal patterns help identify interesting photos. If a member typically receives a dozen or so views for every photo and suddenly has one photo that receives over a hundred views, than there is clearly something more interesting than the rest about it. All these factors and more undoubtedly have a bearing on the interestingness algorithm used by Flickr.

To you as a mashup developer, interestingness can be a very useful thing. Depending on how you want to use them, any public search for photos sorted by interestingness will likely yield better results than a search sorted by, for example, date. If you were building a slideshow of cat photographs, for example, the photos that score high in interestingness would likely provide a better display than those chosen randomly — they will simply be more *interesting*.

Copyright

An important note is that when you upload your photos to Flickr, copyright remains with the original photographer. Flickr makes no claim to any photos uploaded, although it does enable you to set a variety of copyright licenses.

The rules surrounding copyright are very complex and vary from country to country. You should never assume that you have the right to use a photograph simply because it appears on Flickr. If you are ever in any doubt as to whether you can use a photograph in a particular context, you should consult a legal professional, although often the easiest and safest choice is to simply not to use the photo.

All Rights Reserved

The most common type of license in use on Flickr is the All Rights Reserved license, the one applied to your photos by default. This license simply means that the copyright owner has not relinquished any statutory rights over the photo.

Creative Commons

Creative Commons licenses are a series of copyright licenses devised to encourage the sharing of creative works such as photographs. By applying a Creative Commons license to your photos, you can give away some of the rights you have on your photos in a controlled and well-defined way. You can read more about Creative Commons and the different types of license available at its web site: `http://creativecommons.org/`.

A number of different types of Creative Commons licenses are designed to cover a variety of situations, each featuring a different combination of the main license types — *Attribution, NonCommercial, NoDerivs,* and *ShareAlike*. Here is a very brief summary of the main license types. For full details you must consult the license documents themselves, which are available on the Creative Commons web site at `http://creativecommons.org/licenses/`.

❑　**Attribution:** All the Creative Commons licenses require attribution. This means that when you use a work licensed under Creative Commons, you must give credit to the person owning the work you are using, in the manner specified by the author of the work.

❑　**NonCommercial:** You may not use any work licensed under this type of license for commercial purposes. The license defines such use as one "primarily intended for or directed toward commercial advantage or private monetary compensation."

❑　**NoDerivs:** You may not modify the licensed work in any way, so photos used under this license may not be manipulated, but they can be used as part of a collection of material.

❑　**ShareAlike:** If you create a derivative work using materials licensed under this type of license, you may only distribute the resulting work under a license identical to the one used.

Linking Back to Flickr

Flickr actively encourages people to use it as a place to store photographs that are then used on other web sites such as blogs. It does, however, put some restrictions on how these photos may be displayed. In particular, every time you display a photograph from Flickr, you must provide a link back to the relevant photo page.

The Flickr Terms of Use state that "The Flickr service makes it possible to post images hosted on Flickr to outside websites. This use is accepted (and even encouraged!). However, pages on other websites which display images hosted on flickr.com must provide a link back to Flickr from each photo to its photo page on Flickr."

You'll be making plenty of use of Flickr-hosted photos while building your mashups, both throughout the course of this book and no doubt later on when you start devising mashups of your own. Always make sure you link back to the Flickr photo page whenever you display a photo.

Summary

In this chapter, you have been taken on a whirlwind tour of some of the main features of Flickr. I haven't covered everything there is to see — for that, there is no real substitute for sitting down and actively using the site yourself for a while. What you have seen here are some of the important features that will be relevant as you progress through this book. You've been introduced to a number of aspects of Flickr, including:

- ❑ Using the photostream
- ❑ How the tagging system works
- ❑ Flickr's privacy system
- ❑ Interestingness
- ❑ Copyright licenses

If you're already a seasoned user of Flickr, you can move straight on to the next chapter, where you'll see how to get everything set up so that you're ready to mash. If you're relatively new to Flickr, here are a couple of exercises to help you explore the Flickr user interface a little.

Exercises

1. If you haven't already done so, go to `http://www.flickr.com/` and create an account. Log into your account, go to the Upload page, and upload a couple of photos.

2. Go to the photo page for one of your photos and try adding some tags to it. Add a variety, including tags consisting of multiple words and tags containing non-alphabetic characters.

3. Try searching for photos on Flickr. See if you can find any photos featuring the word *cat* — you should find there are quite a lot of cat photos on Flickr. Now try searching for photos that have both the words *cat* and *banana* — with a little luck, you should easily find some of these too. Pick some other odd word combinations — see if you can find a pair of everyday words that result in no matches.

4. If you know other people with Flickr accounts, try searching for them and find their profile pages. Add them as contacts. If you don't know any other Flickr users, try searching for me — my username is `dopiaza`.

5. FlickrCentral is one of the most popular groups on Flickr. Search for the FlickrCentral group and join it.

Getting Ready to Mash

Before you can commence work on your mashups, there are a few things you need to do. In this chapter you'll put together a development environment and put the various pieces of software in place so that you can get started.

Getting an API Key

The most important thing you need to build most of the mashups described in this book is a Flickr API key. This is an identifier generated by Flickr that enables you to write applications that can communicate with Flickr's servers. You'll learn all about the Flickr API, what it is, and what you can do with it in the next chapter, but as part of getting everything set up and ready, you will first need to obtain your API key.

Getting a key is very straightforward. Make sure you are signed in to Flickr and go to the API keys page at `http://www.flickr.com/services/api/keys/`. Click on the link to apply for an API key. You will be presented with a form similar to that shown in Figure 3-1.

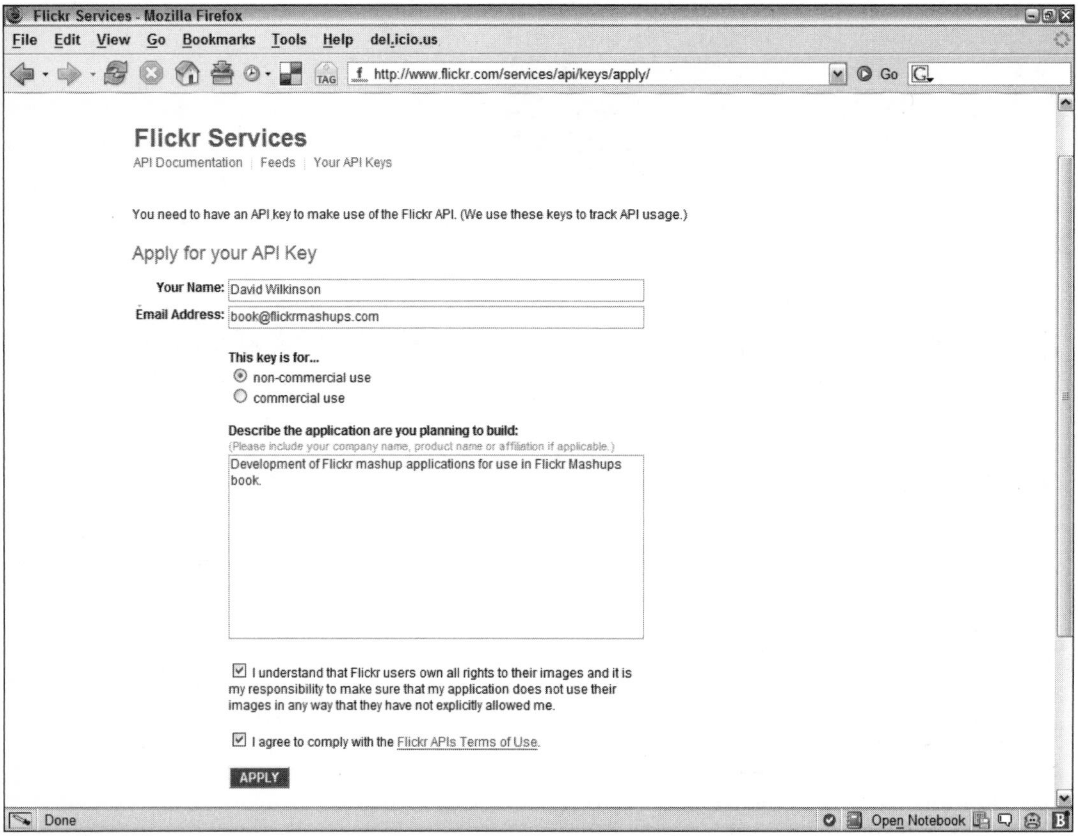

Figure 3-1

When you fill in the form, be sure to specify that your key is for noncommercial use — while you're simply working through the examples in this book, a noncommercial key will be sufficient. If you decide you want to build a mashup to use commercially, you must apply for a commercial API key. All commercial requests are manually reviewed by staff, and so there will be a delay before any commercial key is issued.

Once you submit the form, you will be presented with your API key — you'll see a screen like that shown in Figure 3-2.

It's worth taking note of the API key — but don't just simply follow the advice on the screen and write it down, it's far too easy to make mistakes when copying long hexadecimal strings by hand. Copy and paste the key into a text file locally so that you have it available for reference. Don't worry if you lose it, though; you can always retrieve any API key you create. Just go to the API keys page (http://www .flickr.com/services/api/keys/) and you will see all of your keys listed.

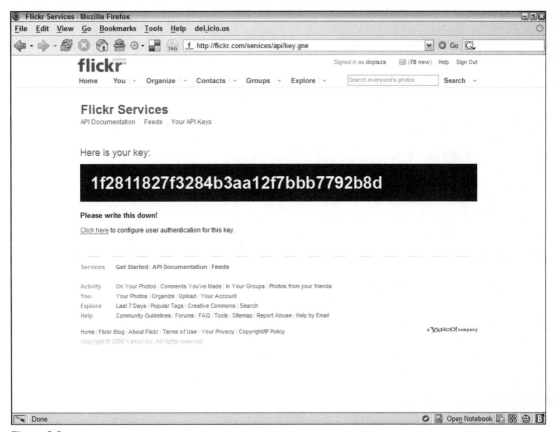

Figure 3-2

Setting Up a Development Environment

Now you've got your API key, the other thing you need is somewhere to develop your mashups. In this book you'll be building a variety of mashups, the majority of which will be web-based, so you will need a web development environment. You'll be using PHP as the server-side scripting language and for one of the projects you will need Perl. You may, of course, already have a suitable development environment set up, in which case you can probably skip much of this chapter—make sure you check through all the sections first to be sure you have everything you need.

The mechanics of setting up a development environment will vary a great deal depending on the operating system you are running. There are far too many variations for me to be able to cover them all in detail here, so in this chapter I'll focus on one of the most common development platforms—Microsoft Windows. If you are running a Unix-based platform such as Linux or Mac OS X, don't despair: there will be some pointers later in this chapter to help you get your machine set up.

Before I launch into details about setting up your computer, it's worth pointing out that if you don't want to go to the trouble of setting up a local development environment, you don't need to. If you have web space with an ISP, you may well be able to use that—all you need to do is make sure that it allows you to run PHP scripts. If it doesn't, you might like to shop around. Hosting packages are cheap and widely available these days and most providers will include facilities such as PHP and MySQL databases as part of their standard offering. You will have to copy files to your server in order to test them, but it is a very quick and low-hassle way of getting started.

Setting Up Your Web Server

I'll look at two different web server configurations here—Microsoft's Internet Information Services HTTP server and the Apache HTTP server. Note that you will need to have administrator privileges to perform many of the tasks outlined here.

Microsoft IIS

Modern versions of Microsoft Windows, such as Windows XP Professional, come complete with a web server as part of Microsoft's *Internet Information Services*, or *IIS*. The instructions here apply to a default installation of Windows XP Professional, although installation under other versions of Windows will be similar. If you find that IIS isn't already installed on your computer, you may need to install it manually by inserting your Windows installation CD and choosing to install optional Windows components. If you are running Windows XP Home Edition, you'll find that IIS is not included—in that case, you should instead look at the next section, which describes how to install the Apache web server.

Finding Your Document Root

Once IIS is installed, you will find an Internet Information Services icon in the Windows Control Panel under Administrative Tools. If you double-click this, you will see the IIS Management Console, as shown in Figure 3-3.

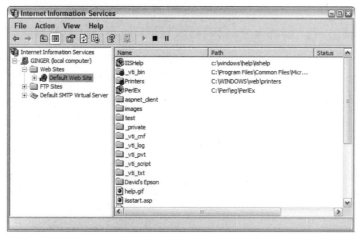

Figure 3-3

If you select Default Web Site, you will be able to use the controls at the top of the screen to stop and start the web server. Right-click the Default Web Site entry in the left-hand pane and select Properties. You will see a dialog box that enables you to configure your web server. You don't need to change anything in here yet, but select the Home Directory tab, as shown in Figure 3-4, and make a note of the path specified. This is the root of your web site, where all the web pages live. It is usually called the *document root*.

Figure 3-4

By default, the document root for IIS is `c:\inetpub\wwwroot`.

Installing PHP

The next step is to install PHP. You can find full installation instructions for PHP on the PHP web site, but we will quickly walk through the process here. First of all, you need to download the latest version of PHP from `http://www.php.net/downloads.php`. A number of different versions and formats are available — you should download the latest version of the Windows binary zip package, and make sure you download PHP 5, rather than PHP 4. Once it is downloaded, unzip the file into `c:\php`.

Next, you need to add the `c:\php` directory to your system path. To do this, open up the System icon in the Control Panel, select the Advanced tab, and click the Environment Variables button. You will see a dialog box like that shown in Figure 3-5.

In the System variables section, scroll down until you find the entry for Path. Select it and click the Edit button. You will see another dialog box appear, as shown in Figure 3-6.

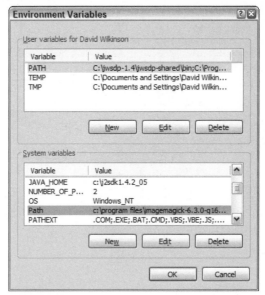

Figure 3-5

Figure 3-6

Place the cursor at the end of the text in the Variable value text box (make sure you scroll all the way to the right here) and append this to the end of the line:

```
;c:\php
```

(Make sure you include the semi-colon.) Click OK in all the dialog boxes to close them. You will now need to restart your computer for these changes to take effect — services such as IIS read their environments at system start-up, so simply logging out and back in again is not sufficient.

You now need to set up the PHP configuration file. In your c:\php directory is a file called php.ini-dist. Copy this to a new file called php.ini in your Windows directory, which is usually c:\windows. The PHP installation instructions on the PHP web site suggest that you should be able to create the php.ini file in the c:\php directory, but this often seems to be problematic — putting it in the Windows directory is less tidy, but more reliable. Open up this php.ini file in a text editor. Find the line that looks like this:

```
doc_root =
```

Edit it so that it reflects the document root value you noted from your IIS settings earlier. If you are using the default values, it should then look like this:

```
doc_root = c:\inetpub\wwwroot
```

Next, find the line that sets up `extension_dir`, which will probably look like this:

```
extension_dir = "./"
```

Change it so that it points to the directory containing PHP extensions. By default, this should be an `ext` directory within your PHP installation, in which case the line should look like this:

```
extension_dir = "./ext/"
```

Configuring IIS

Now you need to tell IIS about PHP. Open up the IIS Management Console again, right-click Default Web Site and choose Properties. Select the ISAPI Filters tab, as shown in Figure 3-7.

Figure 3-7

Click the Add button and add a new filter, as shown in Figure 3-8.

Figure 3-8

The filter name should be set to PHP, and the executable is the php5isapi.dll in your PHP directory.

Next, go to the Home Directory tab — the one you saw in Figure 3-4. Make sure Execute Permissions is set to Scripts Only. Now click the Configuration button and you will see a dialog like that in Figure 3-9.

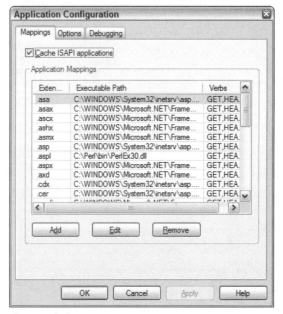

Figure 3-9

Make sure the Mappings tab is selected, click the Add button, and add a new mapping. The executable should be the php5isapi.dll in your PHP directory and the extension should be set to .php. Set the other options as shown in Figure 3-10. Click OK until you are back at the main properties dialog box.

Finally, you need to set index.php as a default document. Select the Documents tab, as shown in Figure 3-11.

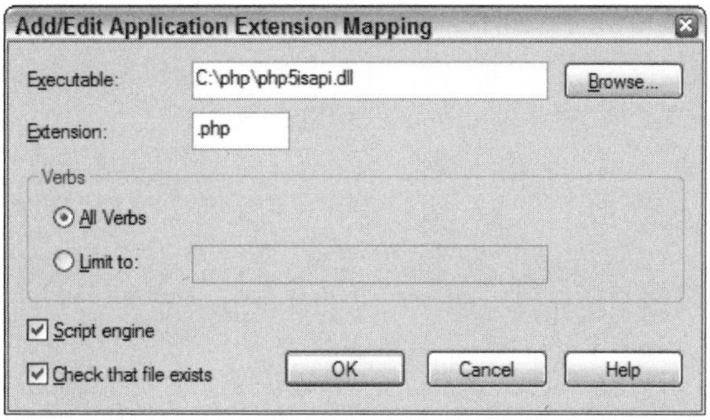

Figure 3-10

Figure 3-11

Click the Add button and add index.php as a default document. Once you have added it, select index.php in the list of documents and use the arrow buttons to move it to the top of the list.

Now you have to restart IIS. Open up a command window and type:

```
net stop w3svc
```

followed by

```
net start w3svc
```

Testing Your Setup

PHP is now installed on IIS — all that remains is to test it. Create a new file called `info.php` in your document root directory, with the following contents:

```php
<?php

phpinfo();

?>
```

You now need to open this file in your browser. If you enter the URL `http://localhost/info.php` into your web browser, you should see a screen full of information about your PHP installation, as shown in Figure 3-12.

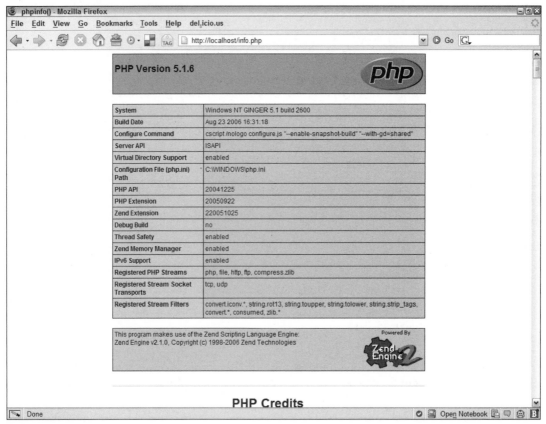

Figure 3-12

If, instead of the PHP info screen, you see a "file not found" error, check that you have placed your `info.php` in the correct place — it must be in the document root that you specified in your IIS configuration. By default, this is `c:\inetpub\wwwroot` — check that this value is correct.

If you find that your web server is trying to serve up a document, but doesn't seem to be executing it as PHP, go back through the Configuring IIS section and check that all of the settings are correct and as described in this section. You can also try rebooting your computer to ensure that all services are restarted.

Apache

The most popular web server in use on the Internet today is the Apache HTTP server, which sits behind over 60 percent of web sites. It's the web server you are most likely to be running under when you put your mashups live on the Internet and so you may well want to use it for development too. Apache is free to download and use—you can find both source code and ready-to-install binary versions on the Apache web site at `http://httpd.apache.org/`. You should download the Win32 Binary (MSI Installer) version of the web server.

You need to ensure compatibility between the versions of Apache and PHP you are running. At the time of writing, use of Apache 2.2.x requires PHP 5.2 or later, but PHP 5.2 has not yet been formally released— PHP 5.1.6 is the latest stable version. In this case, you need to use the latest 2.0.x version of Apache and PHP 5.1.x. By the time you read this, the PHP 5.2 code is likely to have been released, and you should use Apache 2.2.x and PHP 5.2.x.

Installing Apache

When you run the installer, you will be presented with an installation wizard. After accepting the terms of the license agreement, you will be prompted for information about your server, as shown in Figure 3-13.

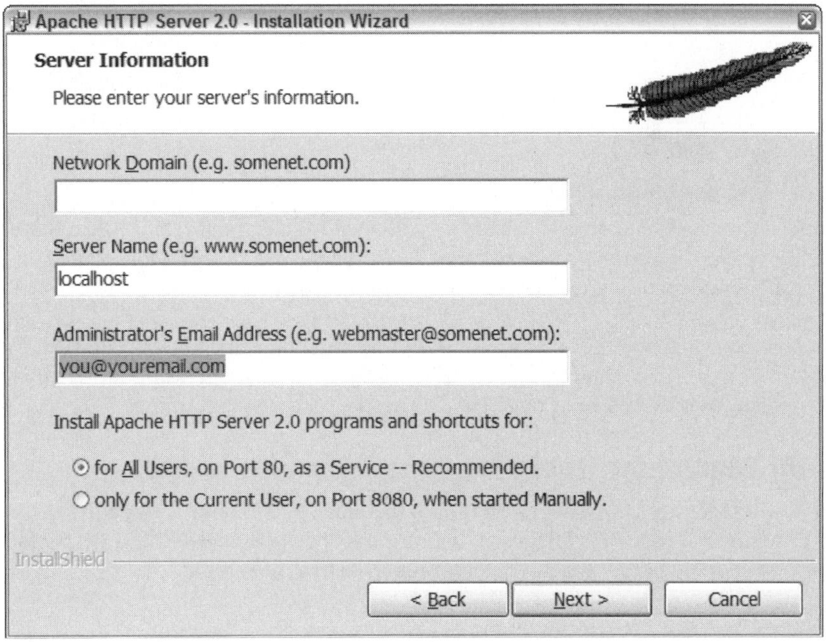

Figure 3-13

You can most likely accept the default values for the Network Domain and Server Name text boxes, but if you are in doubt, you should leave Network Domain blank and enter `localhost` as the server name. Put your e-mail address into the Administrator's Email Address text box.

If this is the only web server you are running on your computer, you can choose to install it as a service on port 80. If you are already running a web server, such as IIS, you should choose to run Apache on port 8080 instead. Click Next and complete the installation.

Now you need to start up the Apache server. If you installed Apache as a service on port 80, look in the system tray and there will be a new icon for the Apache Monitor program. Right-click it and choose Open Apache Monitor. From here you can start and stop the installed Apache server. You can see Apache Monitor in Figure 3-14.

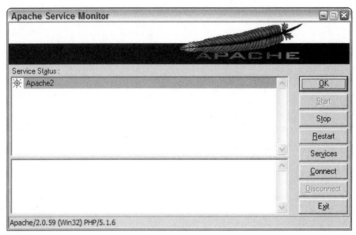

Figure 3-14

If you installed Apache to run on port 8080, you will need to start it manually. Select Start⇨All Programs⇨ Apache HTTP Server⇨Control Apache Server⇨Start Apache in Console. (The procedure you use might be slightly different, depending on the version of Apache you are using.)

Once Apache is running, open a web browser window and enter the appropriate URL for your server. It will be either `http://localhost/` or `http://localhost:808`, depending on whether you installed on port 80 or 8080. You should see a page confirming that Apache is running.

Finding Your Document Root

Next, you need to identify your document root — the place where your web pages are stored. Select Start⇨All Programs⇨Apache HTTP Server⇨Configure Apache Server⇨Edit the Apache `httpd.conf` Configuration File to open the Apache configuration file in a text editor.

Search through this document until you find a line similar to the following:

```
DocumentRoot "C:/Program Files/Apache Software Foundation/Apache2.2/htdocs"
```

This configuration directive identifies your document root. If you like, you can change it to a different path elsewhere on your disk, but you will then need to restart the web server before the changes take effect. Make a note of the path to your document root.

Installing PHP

The next step is to install PHP. The instructions for downloading and installing PHP to run under Apache are almost identical to those given for IIS earlier in this chapter — so follow the instructions in the "Installing PHP" section for IIS, with the following differences:

❑   When creating the php.ini file, create it in the c:\php directory rather than c:\windows.

❑   When setting the doc_root parameter, be sure to use the document root you have set in the Apache configuration file above and not the default value used by IIS.

Configuring Apache

Next, you need to configure Apache to use PHP. Select Start⇨All Programs⇨Apache HTTP Server⇨ Configure Apache Server⇨Edit the Apache httpd.conf Configuration File.

At the end of the file, add the following lines.

For Apache 2.0.x, add

```
LoadModule php5_module "c:/php/php5apache2.dll"
AddType application/x-httpd-php .php
PHPIniDir "C:/php"
```

and for Apache 2.2.x, add

```
LoadModule php5_module "c:/php/php5apache2_2.dll"
AddType application/x-httpd-php .php
PHPIniDir "C:/php"
```

Save the file and restart Apache. You can do this by using the Apache Monitor if you are running it as a service. If you started Apache manually in a console window, simply click in the console window to select it and press Ctrl+C to stop the server. You can then start it up again as usual via the Start menu.

Testing Your Setup

PHP is now installed in Apache — all that remains is to test it. Create a new file called info.php in your document root directory, with the following contents:

```
<?php

phpinfo();

?>
```

You now need to open this file in your browser. Enter the URL to the file into your web browser. This will be either http://localhost/info.php or http://localhost:8080/info.php, depending on which port you set Apache to run on. You should see a screen full of information about your PHP installation, similar to that shown earlier in Figure 3-12.

If, instead of that, you get a "cannot find server" error, you need to check that Apache is running. If it is running as a service, you can go to the Windows Control Panel and click Administrative Tools and then Services. Find Apache in the list of services and start it if necessary. If it is running on port 8080, be sure you started it from the Start menu and that no error messages were displayed.

If you get a "document not found" error, check that you saved the `info.php` file in the directory specified as `DocumentRoot` in your Apache configuration file.

If the document is being found, but not processed as PHP, you should check the Configuring Apache section earlier in this chapter — in particular, make sure that all the paths specified are correct and that they correspond to your PHP installation.

Setting Up Other Systems

If you are running a Linux-based system, you probably already have everything you need here — all the major Linux distributions include Apache and PHP as standard. You should check in your manual or on the distribution's web site for information on installing the Apache and PHP packages. When installation is complete, there is usually no further configuration needed, but you should check your local documentation or configuration files to find out the directory for your document root — this is the place you need to put your web pages.

For Mac OSX users, a number of prepackaged installations of PHP are available on the web that enable you to easily set up Apache and PHP. See the PHP Mac OS X section at `http://www.php.net/manual/en/install.macosx.php` for some useful links.

Setting Up Directories

Now that you've got PHP up and running within your chosen web server, you need to set up a basic directory structure to keep your files in. Create two new directories in your document root, `lib` and `css`. Throughout the course of this book, you'll be installing a number of third-party libraries and you'll also be creating some reusable components of your own — you'll store all these in the `lib` directory. In the `css` directory, you'll store a selection of cascading style sheets that will be used in the various projects.

Finally, as you'll be building a number of web pages for the various projects, you should define a few basic CSS styles you can use across the site. In the CSS directory, create a new file called `main.css`, with the following contents:

```css
body {
    font-family: Geneva, Arial, Helvetica, sans-serif;
    font-size: 14px;
    color: #000000;
    background-color: #FFFFFF;
    margin: 2em;
}
a {
    color: #000099;
    text-decoration: none;
}
a:hover {
    text-decoration: underline;
}
```

Here, you set the default font for everything residing in the body of the document, together with some page colors and margins, and then define the colors and hover effects for hyperlinks.

Setting Up Perl

For the purposes of most of this book, setting up Perl is optional—it's only used in Chapter 10. If you want to see that mashup in action, you will need to set up Perl, together with a few libraries.

Installing Perl Under Microsoft Windows

The easiest way to get Perl running under Windows is to use ActiveState's ActivePerl, which is available as a free download from http://www.activestate.com/. Installation of Perl itself is very straightforward—allowing the Windows installer to run its course, accepting the default configuration options, should work fine for most people. One thing you must make sure of is that when you are prompted, the option to add Perl to your PATH is selected, as shown in Figure 3-15.

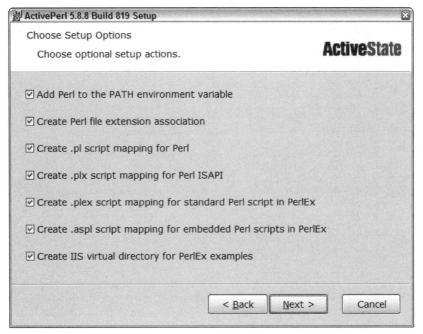

Figure 3-15

After the installer has finished, open a command prompt and type perl -v. You should see output something like this:

```
C:\>perl -v

This is perl, v5.8.8 built for MSWin32-x86-multi-thread
(with 33 registered patches, see perl -V for more detail)
```

```
Copyright 1987-2006, Larry Wall

Binary build 819 [267479] provided by ActiveState http://www.ActiveState.com
Built Aug 29 2006 12:42:41

Perl may be copied only under the terms of either the Artistic License or the
GNU General Public License, which may be found in the Perl 5 source kit.

Complete documentation for Perl, including FAQ lists, should be found on
this system using "man perl" or "perldoc perl". If you have access to the
Internet, point your browser at http://www.perl.org/, the Perl Home Page.
```

Next you need to install a couple of Perl packages to enable you to talk to Flickr easily. From the command prompt, type ppm to launch the Perl Package Manager. In earlier versions of ActiveState Perl the Package Manager was a command-line tool, but in more recent versions it has had a full GUI. You should see a window pop up like that shown in Figure 3-16.

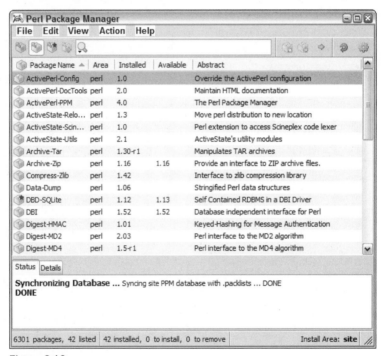

Figure 3-16

Now you need to select the packages to install. Select View⇨All Packages, and then type Flickr into the search box on the toolbar. Several matches will appear; select the one called Flickr-API, right-click it and select Install.

Next, clear the search box and type XPath into it. Again, several matches will appear. Right-click the one called XML-Parser-Lite-Tree-XPath, and select Install.

Now clear the search box again and select View⇨Packages to Install/Remove. You should see the two packages you just selected, as shown in Figure 3-17.

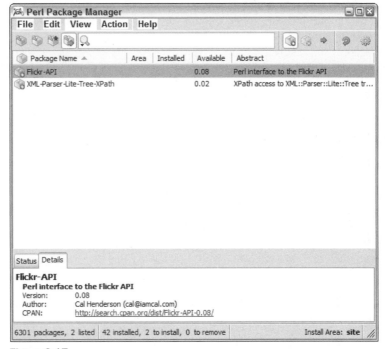

Figure 3-17

Select File⇨Run Marked Actions. You will be asked if you wish to install these two packages together with additional prerequisite packages — you should say OK to this. The requested packages will now be downloaded and installed.

Installing Perl on Unix Systems

Almost all Unix-based systems will already have Perl installed — if not, consult your system documentation about how to install it. You will, however, have to install the modules needed to allow easy access to Flickr. You will need super-user access to do this.

When logged in as root, from the command line, type the following:

```
perl -MCPAN -eshell
```

On some systems, in order to get super-user access rights, you may need to log in as a normal user and use the following command instead:

```
sudo perl -MCPAN -eshell
```

This will cause the CPAN shell to start running. CPAN is the Comprehensive Perl Archive Network and contains a wide selection of Perl modules. If this is the first time CPAN has been run, you will be asked if you want to configure it. The default values are almost always right, so you can say no to manual configuration when asked. If you do choose to answer yes, you will be asked lots of questions about the configuration of your machine — again, the default values are usually correct, so you can just press return to accept the default.

Next, you need to install four modules, so enter the four commands shown below. After each one is entered, the module will be downloaded, compiled, and installed. Wait for each one to complete before moving on to the next. If you are asked any questions during this process, just press return to accept the default value.

```
install SOAP::Lite
install XML::Parser::Lite::Tree
install XML::Parser::Lite::Tree::XPath
install Flickr::API
```

Once these modules are installed, you have all you need in place to use Flickr with Perl.

Summary

In this chapter you have seen how to put together a basic development environment for your mashups. You've seen how to set up IIS and Apache web servers, install and configure PHP, install and configure Perl, and obtain a Flickr API key.

In the next chapter you'll take a closer look at the Flickr API itself and see how to use it to retrieve information about your photos stored on Flickr. If you're relatively new to PHP development, there are a couple of very simple PHP warm-up exercises below, just to help you get into the swing of writing a little PHP code and to test out your new PHP installation to make sure it's all working as you would expect — you may well find the documentation on http://www.php.net/ helpful here. If you're already comfortable with PHP development, feel free to skip these and move straight on to the Flickr API.

Exercises

1. Create a web page that creates an array of a thousand random numbers, each between 1 and 1,000. Use a `for` loop to populate the array. After you have created the array, loop through the array again, this time using a `foreach` loop, calculate the average of the numbers, and display the result.

2. Create a web page containing a form with three text boxes in which numbers can be entered. When the form is submitted, display the sum of the three numbers. Hint: you will find the form field values in the `$_REQUEST` array.

The Flickr API

The key to building any successful mashup is getting hold of the data in the first place. All of the interesting bits and pieces you see on Flickr — photo titles and descriptions, comments, group discussions — are held in databases on the internal network of Yahoo! Before you can build your mashup, you first need to get those data.

This chapter explains how Flickr makes some of its data available to the world. It shows what data are available and how to access them.

What Is an API?

API stands for *application programming interface*. It is a formal definition of how to interact with a system. In a programming library, it often refers to the description of the functions and methods that the software developer can call to make use of that library. In a web service, it refers to the messages and responses sent between the requesting client application and the server. It defines not only the content of those messages, but also the mechanism by which they are passed between the client application and the server.

Talking to Flickr

Flickr is a web-based system, and so all requests to the Flickr servers are sent using HTTP — basically, they are no different from any other request you make from your web browser. The URL that requests are sent to is known as the *API endpoint*.

All Flickr requests consist of a number of parameters, each sent as a pair of data items — the name of the parameter and the value it takes. Although the number of parameters sent will depend on which API method you are trying to invoke, all API calls must contain at least two parameters: `api_key` and `method`.

The `api_key` parameter is your API key — a string of hexadecimal digits — and will look something like `1f2811827f3284b3aa12f7bbb7792b8d`. Every single API call you make to Flickr *must* contain this key — Flickr uses your key to track who is using the API and how. It also means that Flickr can trace all API activity back to the user account to which the key was assigned. If you do not send a valid API key with your call, it will be rejected.

The Flickr API is divided into a series of *methods*, where each method represents a specific operation that can be performed, such as "search for a photo," or "set a photo's title." I'll show you what methods are available later on in this chapter. Whenever you make an API call, you need to specify which of the available methods you wish to invoke. You do this by setting the `method` parameter. All API calls must include this parameter.

Character Encoding

With the exception of uploading images, which is covered in Chapter 8, all Flickr API requests and responses are text-based. Flickr has users spread all over the world, and so has to cope with character sets other than standard ASCII — users will often want to write their photo titles and descriptions in their native language, whether that be English, German, Japanese, or any other. To cope with this, all Flickr requests are required to use UTF-8 character encoding. UTF-8 is a *Unicode Transformation Format* that uses eight-bit sequences to represent characters.

The aim of Unicode is to allow all text to be represented in an unambiguous and consistent way. In the words of the Unicode Consortium (`http://www.unicode.org/`), "Unicode provides a unique number for every character, no matter what the platform, no matter what the program, no matter what the language."

A Unicode Transformation Format is a means of representing those Unicode characters as a stream of bytes. UTF-8 is a commonly used transformation format, because it leaves the standard ASCII character set unchanged. This means that for most purposes, the standard text files that you use in everyday life are already valid UTF-8-encoded documents.

Request Format

Flickr accepts API calls in three different formats: REST, SOAP, and XML-RPC. Although the functionality provided in each case is exactly the same, the API endpoint address and the format of the requests and responses themselves are significantly different in each case.

REST

REST (Representational State Transfer) is the simplest means of communicating with Flickr, and is by far the most commonly used. It is the method I've used in all the examples in this book.

API Endpoint

The address used for all REST requests is `http://api.flickr.com/services/rest/`.

You can easily see REST in action. All you need to do is to enter a valid REST URL into your web browser. Remember, though, that to use the Flickr API you need a valid API key. If you've already signed up for one, now is the time to dig it out. If you haven't signed up for one yet, don't worry; look back at Chapter 3, which walks you through the process — it's very simple and only takes a couple of minutes.

> In case you forgot or lost your API key, you can easily find it again—just log into Flickr and go to http://www.flickr.com/services/api/keys/. This page lists all the API keys registered to your account.

Try It Out   Using REST

In this exercise you'll see what a REST request looks like.

1. Fire up your web browser and enter the following URL (where it says YOUR-API-KEY, substitute your own API key). Note that the URL is long and is split over two lines here for readability—make sure you enter it all on a single line in your web browser.

```
http://api.flickr.com/services/rest/?method=flickr.photos.search
    &user_id=50317659@N00&per_page=6&api_key=YOUR-API-KEY
```

2. Your browser should display something like this.

```
<rsp stat="ok">
    <photos page="1" pages="392" perpage="6" total="2350">
        <photo id="157113860" owner="50317659@N00" secret="70060bada9" server="68"
            title="No Parking" ispublic="1" isfriend="0" isfamily="0"/>
        <photo id="157113453" owner="50317659@N00" secret="99166dec9f" server="52"
            title="66" ispublic="1" isfriend="0" isfamily="0"/>
        <photo id="154833256" owner="50317659@N00" secret="a94893da5e" server="60"
            title="Decay" ispublic="1" isfriend="0" isfamily="0"/>
        <photo id="153615581" owner="50317659@N00" secret="e8e0bdb260" server="59"
            title="My Workspace" ispublic="1" isfriend="0" isfamily="0"/>
        <photo id="150681007" owner="50317659@N00" secret="84cc7afd68" server="52"
            title="Cool" ispublic="1" isfriend="0" isfamily="0"/>
        <photo id="148967487" owner="50317659@N00" secret="66ecb49990" server="44"
            title="Utata Goes To The Movies" ispublic="1" isfriend="0"
            isfamily="0"/>
    </photos>
</rsp>
```

How It Works

If you look at the URL you entered in more detail, you can see that it has a base part:

```
http://api.flickr.com/services/rest/
```

This is the API endpoint, the address to which all REST requests are sent.

Tagged onto the end is the *query string:*

```
method=flickr.photos.search&user_id=50317659@N00&per_page=6&api_key=YOUR-API-KEY
```

A question mark (?) is used to separate the base URL from the query string. The query string contains all the parameters that make up the API call as name/value pairs. Each name/value pair is separated from the next by an ampersand (&).

The parameters in the query string are *URL-encoded*. This means that any special characters in the parameter values (such as the question mark or ampersand) are converted to the form %nn, where nn is the two-digit hexadecimal representation of the UTF-8 code for the character. This means that you would use %3F to represent a question mark and %26 for an ampersand. If you needed to use the percent sign itself as a value in a parameter, you would encode it as %25.

Examining the query string shows that you have the following parameters:

❑ api_key: Your API key

❑ method: flickr.photos.search

❑ user_id: 50317659@N00

❑ per_page: 6

The first two parameters are api_key and method, mentioned above. As you can see, the method being invoked here is flickr.photos.search. As the name suggests, this method enables you to search for photos on Flickr and is probably one of the methods you'll be making most use of.

The next parameters are the ones you require to define exactly what it is you want flickr.photos.search to search for.

The first is user_id. This parameter is set to the Flickr user ID (often called the NSID) of the person whose photos you wish to find. Unlike screen names, NSIDs are fixed when you sign up for a Flickr account and never change. The user ID shown in the example, 50317659@N00, is my NSID.

The last parameter you sent is per_page. At the time of this writing, I have over two thousand photos available on Flickr — clearly it would be impractical to retrieve information about all of them in a single request, so Flickr returns search results in pages. Here, the per_page parameter is saying that six results should be sent in each response. The default value for per_page is 100, and the maximum value that can be specified is 500.

You may notice that the parameters above do not specify *which* six photographs you want returned — by default Flickr will return the most recently uploaded.

The *response* is an XML document, and the tag and attribute names are, on the whole, reasonably descriptive. You can usually read through the response received and easily understand most of what it means without having to refer to the API specification.

The first thing you will notice is that the whole response is enclosed in an rsp tag:

```
<rsp stat="ok">
```

The rsp tag has a single attribute, stat, which can take the values ok or fail to indicate the success of the call. Within the rsp tag, the format of the response depends on the actual method being called. The flickr.photos.search method returns a set of photos, so in this case, the next tag you see is a photos tag. The photos tag has its own set of attributes that summarize the search results:

```
<photos page="1" pages="392" perpage="6" total="2350">
```

Here you can see that a total of 2,350 photos match the search criteria specified. As the request asked for them to be sent six per page, the response contained page one out of a total of 392 pages.

> **The parameter name you sent in the request for the number of photos to be returned per page was called** per_page. **The attribute returned in the** photos **tag in the response is** perpage. **Note the lack of an underscore!**
>
> **The Flickr API contains a number of naming inconsistencies like this. If things don't behave the way you expect, carefully check the API specification for the method you are using to make sure you are using the correct names for everything.**

Within the photos tag is a list of photo tags, one for each photo being returned — in this case, six. Each photo tag has its own set of attributes that describe the photo:

```
<photo id="157113860" owner="50317659@N00" secret="70060bada9" server="68"
title="No Parking" ispublic="1" isfriend="0" isfamily="0"/>
```

Every photo stored on Flickr has its own unique ID — this is shown here in the id attribute. The owner attribute is the NSID of the owner of the photograph — as NSID was the search criterion used in the API call, all the photos returned have the same NSID — the one that was requested.

The next attributes, secret and server, are both used in constructing the URL for the photo, which is described later in this chapter. The title attribute contains, as you might expect, the title of the photo.

The last three attributes returned — ispublic, isfriend, and isfamily — describe the permissions set on the photo. A 1 indicates that the permission is enabled, and a 0 indicates that it is not. Here, the photo is set to be public rather than private, and there is no requirement that a user be marked as a friend or as family in order to view the photo.

Note that the photos returned as a result of the flickr.photo.search method will depend on their individual permissions. Normally, only photos marked as public will be returned. In order to see photos marked as private, you will need to make an authenticated API call. Authentication is covered in detail in Chapter 7.

REST Error Response

If your REST request fails for any reason, you will receive a REST error response. It will look something like this:

```
<rsp stat="fail">
    <err code="100" msg="Invalid API Key (Key not found)"/>
</rsp>
```

The actual error code and message will vary, depending on the reason for failure. You can find a list of the possible error codes for each method's page in the API documentation on the Flickr web site.

SOAP

Flickr also provides a SOAP (Simple Object Access Protocol) interface to the API. If you intend to use the SOAP interface for any reason, you should note that Flickr does not provide WSDL (Web Service Definition Language) for its SOAP service. Many applications and SOAP toolkits rely on WSDL to allow the SOAP service to be used. This lack of available WSDL means that much of the convenience of SOAP is lost, and so many developers simply opt to use the REST interface instead.

API Endpoint

The address used for all SOAP requests is `http://api.flickr.com/services/soap/`.

Try It Out   Using SOAP

Although the SOAP protocol is not as straightforward as the REST protocol, it is still fairly easy to see SOAP in action. To do this, you will need to have installed curl (see Chapter 1 for a description of curl). Curl is free and available for a wide variety of platforms. You can download the latest version from `http://curl.haxx.se/`.

1.   With REST you can simply send all the API parameters on the command line, but with SOAP you need to POST a well-formed SOAP request to the API endpoint URL. In a text editor, create a file with the following contents and save it as `SOAPRequest.xml` — don't forget to replace YOUR-API-KEY with your own API key.

```
<?xml version="1.0" encoding="utf-8" ?>
<s:Envelope
 xmlns:s="http://www.w3.org/2003/05/soap-envelope"
 xmlns:xsi="http://www.w3.org/1999/XMLSchema-instance"
 xmlns:xsd="http://www.w3.org/1999/XMLSchema"
>
    <s:Body>
        <x:FlickrRequest xmlns:x="urn:flickr">
            <method>flickr.photos.search</method>
            <api_key>YOUR-API-KEY</api_key>
            <user_id>50317659@N00</user_id>
            <per_page>6</per_page>
        </x:FlickrRequest>
    </s:Body>
</s:Envelope>
```

2.   Now you are ready to send this SOAP request to Flickr using curl. From the command line, type the following command:

```
curl -d @SOAPRequest.xml http://api.flickr.com/services/soap/
```

You should then see a response that looks something like this:

```
<?xml version="1.0" encoding="utf-8" ?>
<s:Envelope
    xmlns:s="http://www.w3.org/2003/05/soap-envelope"
    xmlns:xsi="http://www.w3.org/1999/XMLSchema-instance"
    xmlns:xsd="http://www.w3.org/1999/XMLSchema"
>
    <s:Body>
```

```
        <x:FlickrResponse xmlns:x="urn:flickr">
&lt;photos page=&quot;1&quot; pages=&quot;392&quot; perpage=&quot;6&quot;
total=&quot;2350&quot;&gt;
    &lt;photo id=&quot;157113860&quot; owner=&quot;50317659@N00&quot;
secret=&quot;70060bada9&quot; server=&quot;68&quot; title=&quot;No Parking&quot;
ispublic=&quot;1&quot; isfriend=&quot;0&quot; isfamily=&quot;0&quot;/&gt;
    &lt;photo id=&quot;157113453&quot; owner=&quot;50317659@N00&quot;
secret=&quot;99166dec9f&quot; server=&quot;52&quot; title=&quot;66&quot;
ispublic=&quot;1&quot; isfriend=&quot;0&quot; isfamily=&quot;0&quot;/&gt;
    &lt;photo id=&quot;154833256&quot; owner=&quot;50317659@N00&quot;
secret=&quot;a94893da5e&quot; server=&quot;60&quot; title=&quot;Decay&quot;
ispublic=&quot;1&quot; isfriend=&quot;0&quot; isfamily=&quot;0&quot;/&gt;
    &lt;photo id=&quot;153615581&quot; owner=&quot;50317659@N00&quot;
secret=&quot;e8e0bdb260&quot; server=&quot;59&quot; title=&quot;My Workspace&quot;
ispublic=&quot;1&quot; isfriend=&quot;0&quot; isfamily=&quot;0&quot;/&gt;
    &lt;photo id=&quot;150681007&quot; owner=&quot;50317659@N00&quot;
secret=&quot;84cc7afd68&quot; server=&quot;52&quot; title=&quot;Cool&quot;
ispublic=&quot;1&quot; isfriend=&quot;0&quot; isfamily=&quot;0&quot;/&gt;
    &lt;photo id=&quot;148967487&quot; owner=&quot;50317659@N00&quot;
secret=&quot;66ecb49990&quot; server=&quot;44&quot; title=&quot;Utata Goes To The
Movies&quot; ispublic=&quot;1&quot; isfriend=&quot;0&quot;
isfamily=&quot;0&quot;/&gt;
&lt;/photos&gt;
        </x:FlickrResponse>
    </s:Body>
</s:Envelope>
```

How It Works

The request is a standard SOAP request. The payload for the request is contained within the FlickrRequest tag. As you can see from the XML document, the payload is simply a list of tags, each one of which corresponds to the parameters that need to be sent in the API call.

```
<x:FlickrRequest xmlns:x="urn:flickr">
    <method>flickr.photos.search</method>
    <api_key>YOUR-API-KEY</api_key>
    <user_id>50317659@N00</user_id>
    <per_page>6</per_page>
</x:FlickrRequest>
```

Each name/value pair is represented by a single XML tag — the parameter name is used as the tag name and the value of the tag is the parameter value itself.

When you run the following curl command, the -d option tells curl to perform an HTTP POST request:

```
curl -d @SOAPRequest.xml http://api.flickr.com/services/soap/
```

The @ sign at the start of @SOAPRequest.xml indicates that rather than be specified on the command line, the data should be read from the named file — SOAPRequest.xml in this case. So curl reads in the data from the file and sends them as the body of an HTTP POST request to the specified URL, which here is the SOAP API endpoint.

The response is a standard SOAP response message. Just like the SOAP request, the payload is held within a `FlickrResponse` tag. If you look closely at that response, you can see that it is in fact an XML document. The angle brackets (`<`, `>`) and double quotes (`"`) have been converted to the entities `&lt;`, `&gt;` and `&quot;` to allow them to be embedded in the XML response document, but apart from that it is exactly the same as the body of the response you saw sent back from the REST request before.

If you take the first line of the response body —

```
&lt;photos page=&quot;1&quot; pages=&quot;392&quot; perpage=&quot;6&quot;
total=&quot;2350&quot;&gt;
```

— and replace the entities with their corresponding characters, you get this, just as you saw in the REST response:

```
<photos page="1" pages="392" perpage="6" total="2350">
```

SOAP Error Response

If your SOAP request fails for any reason, you will receive a standard SOAP error response. This will look something like the following:

```
<?xml version="1.0" encoding="utf-8" ?>
<s:Envelope xmlns:s="http://www.w3.org/2003/05/soap-envelope">
    <s:Body>
        <s:Fault>
            <faultcode>flickr.error.100</faultcode>
            <faultstring>Invalid API Key (Key not found)</faultstring>
            <faultactor>http://www.flickr.com/services/soap/</faultactor>
            <details>Please see http://www.flickr.com/services/api/ for more
details</details>
        </s:Fault>
    </s:Body>
</s:Envelope>
```

The actual error code and message will vary, depending on the reason for failure.

XML-RPC

The third way of accessing the Flickr API is through its XML-RPC interface. Like SOAP, this interface uses HTTP POST to send XML messages to the API endpoint.

API Endpoint

The address used for all XML-RPC requests is http://api.flickr.com/services/xmlrpc/.

Try It Out   Using XML-RPC

You can use curl to send an XML-RPC-formatted message to the XML-RPC API endpoint in exactly the same way that you sent the SOAP request earlier. The process is exactly the same; only the message format and API endpoint are different.

1. In a text editor, create a file with the following contents and save it as XMLRPCRequest.xml —
again, don't forget to replace YOUR-API-KEY with your own API key.

```
<?xml version="1.0" encoding="utf-8" ?>
<methodCall>
    <methodName>flickr.photos.search</methodName>
    <params>
        <param>
            <value>
                <struct>
                    <member>
                        <name>api_key</name>
                        <value>
                            <string>YOUR-API-KEY</string>
                        </value>
                    </member>
                    <member>
                        <name>user_id</name>
                        <value>
                            <string>50317659@N00</string>
                        </value>
                    </member>
                    <member>
                        <name>per_page</name>
                        <value>
                            <int>6</int>
                        </value>
                    </member>
                </struct>
            </value>
        </param>
    </params>
</methodCall>
```

2. Now you are ready to send this XML-RPC request to Flickr using curl. From the command line,
type the following command:

```
curl -d @XMLRPCRequest.xml http://api.flickr.com/services/xmlrpc/
```

You should then see a response that looks something like this:

```
<?xml version="1.0" encoding="utf-8" ?>
<methodResponse>
    <params>
        <param>
            <value>
                <string>
&lt;photos page=&quot;1&quot; pages=&quot;392&quot; perpage=&quot;6&quot;
total=&quot;2350&quot;&gt;
    &lt;photo id=&quot;157113860&quot; owner=&quot;50317659@N00&quot;
secret=&quot;70060bada9&quot; server=&quot;68&quot; title=&quot;No Parking&quot;
ispublic=&quot;1&quot; isfriend=&quot;0&quot; isfamily=&quot;0&quot;/&gt;
    &lt;photo id=&quot;157113453&quot; owner=&quot;50317659@N00&quot;
secret=&quot;99166dec9f&quot; server=&quot;52&quot; title=&quot;66&quot;
ispublic=&quot;1&quot; isfriend=&quot;0&quot; isfamily=&quot;0&quot;/&gt;
```

```
&lt;photo id=&quot;154833256&quot; owner=&quot;50317659@N00&quot;
secret=&quot;a94893da5e&quot; server=&quot;60&quot; title=&quot;Decay&quot;
ispublic=&quot;1&quot; isfriend=&quot;0&quot; isfamily=&quot;0&quot;/&gt;
    &lt;photo id=&quot;153615581&quot; owner=&quot;50317659@N00&quot;
secret=&quot;e8e0bdb260&quot; server=&quot;59&quot; title=&quot;My Workspace&quot;
ispublic=&quot;1&quot; isfriend=&quot;0&quot; isfamily=&quot;0&quot;/&gt;
    &lt;photo id=&quot;150681007&quot; owner=&quot;50317659@N00&quot;
secret=&quot;84cc7afd68&quot; server=&quot;52&quot; title=&quot;Cool&quot;
ispublic=&quot;1&quot; isfriend=&quot;0&quot; isfamily=&quot;0&quot;/&gt;
    &lt;photo id=&quot;148967487&quot; owner=&quot;50317659@N00&quot;
secret=&quot;66ecb49990&quot; server=&quot;44&quot; title=&quot;Utata Goes To The
Movies&quot; ispublic=&quot;1&quot; isfriend=&quot;0&quot;
isfamily=&quot;0&quot;/&gt;
&lt;/photos&gt;
                    </string>
                </value>
            </param>
        </params>
</methodResponse>
```

How It Works

The request is a standard XML-RPC request — you can find the full definition for XML-RPC at http://www.xmlrpc.com/, but the XML format is relatively easy to read without it. The first thing you might notice when you examine the request is the methodName tag:

```
<methodName>flickr.photos.search</methodName>
```

In both REST and SOAP, method was treated just like any other parameter and sent along as part of the parameter list. The XML-RPC request format, on the other hand, has a special field for the method name: <methodName>.

The XML for the other parameters for the request looks a little complicated at first. As far as XML-RPC is concerned, however, only one parameter is sent. This is a struct, which contains a list of member tags. Each member tag corresponds to one of the parameters in the Flickr API call. As the method has already been specified earlier in the body of the request, it doesn't appear in this list.

```
<member>
    <name>user_id</name>
    <value>
        <string>50317659@N00</string>
    </value>
</member>
```

This is no different really from the REST or SOAP examples you saw earlier — it's just a more verbose way of representing the data you need to send. One significant difference of XML-RPC is that the parameter values are typed — the example above shows that user_id is of data type string.

The response is a standard XML-RPC response message. Just as with the SOAP request, a single parameter is returned, which is an encoded string representing the XML document containing the response.

XML-RPC Error Response

If your XML-RPC request fails for any reason, you will receive a standard XML-RPC error response. This will look something like the following:

```
<?xml version="1.0" encoding="utf-8" ?>
<methodResponse>
    <fault>
        <value>
            <struct>
                <member>
                    <name>faultCode</name>
                    <value><int>100</int></value>
                </member>
                <member>
                    <name>faultString</name>
                    <value><string>Invalid API Key (Key not found)</string></value>
                </member>
            </struct>
        </value>
    </fault>
</methodResponse>
```

The actual error code and message will vary, depending on the reason for failure.

Flickr Methods and Objects

The Flickr API is broken down into sections, with each section corresponding to a specific area of functionality. Many of these areas relate to a specific kind of object that is manipulated — photos, groups, or blogs, for example, while other areas of functionality are based around more abstract concepts, such as interestingness.

Over 80 methods are currently contained in the Flickr API, but in practice, most of the work in any Flickr application is done with a very small number of the API methods. In this section we will look at a couple of examples of common API methods and the responses they return. If you want to look at the API in detail, Appendix B contains a comprehensive list of Flickr API methods, and Appendix C covers all the major data structures returned. You should also bear in mind that Flickr is still growing, and the API continues to evolve as new features are added — you should check the official Flickr API web pages (http://www.flickr.com/services/api/) for the latest details.

Methods and Responses

An API method name consists of a series of identifiers separated by dots. All methods have flickr as the first element. The second element identifies the section of the API that this method belongs to. Next is an optional subsection. Finally, the last element is the method name itself. This is shown in Figure 4-1.

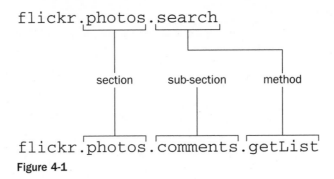
Figure 4-1

Many API method calls return a common set of data structures. Each time a list of photos is returned, for example, the basic XML structure in the response is the same — regardless of whether the photos in question are your own, a contact's, a list of favorites, or the results of a tag search.

Any given data structure within the API often appears in two formats. First, it exists in a *summary format* containing just the key pieces of information for that item. You will see the summary format when you request a list of things — each item in the response represents a summary of one particular item in the response. The second format is the *detailed format*, and contains comprehensive details for the item represented.

You've already seen how a photo is represented in summary form when you were trying out the REST call earlier. Now take a look at the detailed view of a photo.

Try It Out   **Retrieving Photo Details**

In this exercise, you will retrieve a photo's details using the `flickr.photos.getInfo` API method.

1.   Enter the following URL into your browser:

```
http://api.flickr.com/services/rest/?api_key=YOUR-API-KEY
    &method=flickr.photos.getInfo&photo_id=148878052
```

   Again, the URL has been split over two lines for ease of reading. You must also remember to substitute your own API key in the appropriate place.

2.   When the result has loaded into your browser, you should see something like the following:

```
<?xml version="1.0" encoding="utf-8" ?>
<rsp stat="ok">
<photo id="148878052" secret="108e958747" server="55" dateuploaded="1147980255"
    isfavorite="0" license="0" rotation="0" originalformat="jpg">
  <owner nsid="50317659@N00" username="dopiaza" realname="David Wilkinson"
      location="Northamptonshire, United Kingdom" />
  <title>Wells Beach Hut</title>
  <description>[DSC_1578]</description>
  <visibility ispublic="1" isfriend="0" isfamily="0" />
  <dates posted="1147980255" taken="2006-05-12 14:47:51" takengranularity="0"
```

```
        lastupdate="1147980278" />
    <editability cancomment="0" canaddmeta="0" />
    <comments>0</comments>
    <notes />
    <tags>
      <tag id="296457-148878052-8904" author="50317659@N00" raw="wells">wells</tag>
      <tag id="296457-148878052-178492" author="50317659@N00"
          raw="wells-next-the-sea">wellsnextthesea</tag>
      <tag id="296457-148878052-6876" author="50317659@N00"
          raw="norfolk">norfolk</tag>
      <tag id="296457-148878052-279" author="50317659@N00"
          raw="england">england</tag>
      <tag id="296457-148878052-110" author="50317659@N00" raw="uk">uk</tag>
      <tag id="296457-148878052-704" author="50317659@N00" raw="beach">beach</tag>
      <tag id="296457-148878052-12640" author="50317659@N00" raw="hut">hut</tag>
    </tags>
    <urls>
      <url type="photopage">http://www.flickr.com/photos/dopiaza/148878052/</url>
    </urls>
  </photo>
</rsp>
```

How It Works

The URL you entered points to the REST API endpoint. The query string of the URL (the part after the question mark) contains a number of parameters:

- ❑ api_key: Your API key
- ❑ method: flickr.photos.getInfo
- ❑ photo_id: 148878052

This invokes the flickr.photos.getInfo API method, passing in the parameter photo_id containing the value 148878052. This causes Flickr to return a response describing the photo with an ID of 148878052. As you can see, the response contains all of the details you saw when you used flickr.photos.search, together with many other items not found in the summary form. The <photo> object is described in detail in Appendix C, but many of the tags and attributes you see here are fairly self-explanatory.

In the detailed <photo> object, you can see that the <description> tag gives you the description attached to the photo, whereas in the summary form only the title was provided. You can also see the number of comments that have been made on the photo, which is given by the <comment> tag.

The <tags> section of the response lists all the tags applied to the photo, in both the raw form (as typed by the user) and the clean form used for searching, together with the NSID of the user who created the tag. The <urls> section provides the URL to the photo page.

This full response also provides a little more information about the owner of the photo in the <owner> tag. All the information you see is sourced from the owner's profile.

73

You've now seen how to retrieve information about a photo using the `flickr.photos.getInfo` method — all you need to know is the photo's ID. You can also find out more about Flickr users, if you know their unique identifiers, by using the API method `flickr.people.getInfo`.

Try It Out   **Retrieving a User's Details**

In this exercise, you will retrieve a user's details using the `flickr.people.getInfo` API method.

1.   Enter the following URL into your browser:

```
http://api.flickr.com/services/rest/?api_key=YOUR-API-KEY
   &method=flickr.people.getInfo&user_id=50317659@N00
```

Don't forget to substitute your own API key in the appropriate place.

2.   After the result has loaded into your browser, you should see something like the following:

```
<?xml version="1.0" encoding="utf-8" ?>
<rsp stat="ok">
<person id="50317659@N00" nsid="50317659@N00" isadmin="0" ispro="1"
      iconserver="56">
  <username>dopiaza</username>
  <realname>David Wilkinson</realname>
  <mbox_sha1sum>bb000a20aca3da32bcacb609b7f7c23557f286cd</mbox_sha1sum>
  <location>Northamptonshire, United Kingdom</location>
  <photosurl>http://www.flickr.com/photos/dopiaza/</photosurl>
  <profileurl>http://www.flickr.com/people/dopiaza/</profileurl>
  <mobileurl>http://www.flickr.com/mob/photostream.gne?id=296457</mobileurl>
  <photos>
    <firstdatetaken>1976-01-01 00:00:00</firstdatetaken>
    <firstdate>1108051836</firstdate>
    <count>2423</count>
  </photos>
</person>
</rsp>
```

How It Works

Just as with the `flickr.photos.getInfo` call you made in the previous example, the URL you entered points to the REST API endpoint. This time, the query string contains the following parameters:

❏   `api_key`: Your API key

❏   `method`: `flickr.people.getInfo`

❏   `user_id`: `50317659@N00`

The method invoked this time is `flickr.people.getInfo`, which takes a single parameter, the NSID of the user for whom you want to retrieve information. You passed in `50317659@N00`, which is my NSID.

Once again, the `<person>` object returned is described in detail in Appendix C, although you can probably figure out what many of the fields mean. The `<username>`, `<realname>`, and `<location>` tags all contain information derived from the user's profile.

You'll see that the `<photos>` tag contains some interesting pieces of information about the user's photostream — the earliest date taken, the earliest upload date, and the number of public photos in the stream.

Building URLs

In your mashups, you will often want to link to particular locations on Flickr — a user's photostream or profile, or perhaps a specific photo page. You may just want to access a photo on Flickr in order to display it within your mashup. For all of these things, you need to be able to get the URL of the page or image you are after. In this section, you will see how to construct URLs for all of these items.

The Photostream URL

The photostream URL for a user is the base element for many URLs used by Flickr. Each user may have two photostream URLs. A user's photostream can always be accessed by a URL of the form `http://www`
`.flickr.com/photos/NSID/`, where `NSID` is replaced with the NSID of the required user. My NSID is 50317659@N00, and so my photostream can be found at `http://www.flickr.com/photos/`
`50317659@N00/`. Try entering that URL into your browser and you should see my most recently uploaded photos.

NSIDs are both ugly and unmemorable, so users have the option of choosing a friendlier URL — these take exactly the same form as above except that the NSID is replaced by an identifier chosen by the user. For my URL, I chose the identifier `dopiaza`, as that is also my Flickr screen name, so my friendly photostream URL is `http://www.flickr.com/photos/dopiaza/`.

Enter that URL in your browser and you will see that it goes to exactly the same page as the NSID version above.

The photostream URL for a user is also returned by the `flickr.people.getInfo` and `flickr.urls`
`.getUserPhotos` methods. If the user has set a friendly URL, then that will be returned; otherwise the NSID version will be returned.

The Profile URL

A user's profile URL is returned by the `flickr.people.getInfo` and `flickr.urls.getUserProfile` methods. It can also be built in exactly the same way as a user's photostream URL, but with `photos` instead of `people`. So, just as above, my profile can be found at either `http://www.flickr.com/`
`people/50317659@N00/` or `http://www.flickr.com/people/dopiaza/`.

Enter each of those URLs into your browser. Once again, you will see that they both point to the same page — my Flickr profile.

The Photo Page URL

Every photo on Flickr is featured on its own *photo page*. You can build a photo page URL for a photo in a number of ways. The simplest is through the `flickr.photos.getInfo` API call. As you saw in the earlier example, this method call returns the photo page URL directly in the `urls` section of the response.

You won't always want to make an extra API call to get the photo page URL, though; sometimes you may already have enough information to work it out. You need to know both the ID of the photo and the owner of the photo, and you may remember from earlier that `flickr.photos.search` does indeed return both the photo ID and the owner's NSID.

Take Wellington as an example — you can see him in Figure 4-2.

Figure 4-2

I have a photo of him in my photostream — photo ID 160244291. To see the photo page for his photo, you simply take the URL of my photostream:

```
http://www.flickr.com/photos/50317659@N00/
```

and append the ID of the photo:

```
http://www.flickr.com/photos/50317659@N00/160244291/
```

If you go to that URL, you will see Wellington's photo page in all its glory.

If you happen to know the photo owner's friendly URL, it works with that too — so Wellington also resides at `http://www.flickr.com/photos/dopiaza/160244291/`.

Once again, the two URLs point to exactly the same page.

The Image URL

More often, you will just want to get the direct URL of the image file itself. Once again, the information returned by `flickr.photos.search` contains everything you need. Here's what the `<photo>` tag contains when Wellington appears in the search results:

```
<photo id="160244291" owner="50317659@N00" secret="bd2ff55b61" server="70"
title="Wellington" ispublic="1" isfriend="0" isfamily="0"/>
```

To get the URL of the image file itself, you need to know the photo ID, the server, and the secret, and combine them like this:

```
http://static.flickr.com/SERVER/PHOTOID_SECRET.jpg
```

where SERVER is the `server` attribute, PHOTOID is the `id` attribute and SECRET is the `secret` attribute. So the URL of Wellington's image is:

```
http://static.flickr.com/70/160244291_bd2ff55b61.jpg
```

Enter that URL into your browser and you will see the image file displayed.

Images are available in several sizes, which are obtained by appending a suffix to the end of the secret in the image URL. The following sizes are available.

Name	Suffix	Size
Square	_s	75 × 75
Thumbnail	_t	100 on longest side
Small	_m	240 on longest side
Medium	None	500 on longest side
Large	_b	1024 on longest size (Only exists for large original images)
Original	_o	Original image dimensions (only available to pro users)

To see a large version of Wellington, you would go to `http://static.flickr.com/70/160244291_bd2ff55b61_b.jpg`,

```
and you would find his thumbnail image at http://static.flickr.com/70/
160244291_bd2ff55b61_t.jpg.
```

Note that except for TIFF files, the file type of the original image will be the same as the file type originally uploaded. All other sizes are always .jpg. For TIFF files, the original is also stored as a JPEG.

Photoset URLs

You can find a user's photosets page by simply appending `sets` to the end of his or her photostream URL, so you can see my sets at either `http://www.flickr.com/photos/50317659@N00/sets/` or `http://www.flickr.com/photos/dopiaza/sets/`.

To get to an individual photoset, you append the photoset ID to the end. I have a set entitled "Cats," containing photos of, surprisingly enough, cats. This set has a photoset ID of 160910, so you can view it at `http://www.flickr.com/photos/50317659@N00/sets/160910/` or `http://www.flickr.com/photos/dopiaza/sets/160910/`.

The Buddy Icon URL

The buddy icon is the small 48 × 48–pixel graphic shown alongside each user's name on Flickr. If you look at the response you got from the call to `flickr.people.getInfo`, you will see the following:

```
<person id="50317659@N00" nsid="50317659@N00" isadmin="0" ispro="1"
    iconserver="56">
```

The `iconserver` attribute, together with the user's NSID, is used to construct the URL of the buddy icon, like this:

```
http://static.flickr.com/ICON-SERVER/buddyicons/NSID.jpg
```

So, based on the information above, my buddy icon has the following URL:

```
http://static.flickr.com/56/buddyicons/50317659@N00.jpg
```

If you enter that into your browser, you will see my current buddy icon. If you change your buddy icon, the icon server, and hence the URL, will stay the same. If, however, you delete your buddy icon and then create a new one, the icon server is likely to change.

If the `iconserver` attribute is set to 0, it means that the user has not set a buddy icon and so the default gray blockhead icon should be shown. This icon's URL is `http://www.flickr.com/images/buddyicon.jpg`.

The Group Icon URL

The group icon URL is created in exactly the same way as a buddy icon URL — except that you use the NSID of the group rather than that of a user. A list of groups for a user retrieved using `flickr.people` `.getPublicGroups` would contain items like this:

```
<group nsid="81474450@N00" id="81474450@N00" name="Utata" admin="1" privacy="3"
photos="44958" iconserver="6"/>
```

Using the group's NSID and icon server, you can see that the group icon would be found at `http://` `static.flickr.com/6/buddyicons/81474450@N00.jpg`.

Using the API Explorer

The API Explorer is an invaluable tool for learning more about the API — it provides a user interface that enables you to call any Flickr API method, setting any parameters needed. You can get to the API Explorer by looking at any of the API Method reference pages on Flickr — you will see a link at the bottom of each method page.

The URL for the API Explorer is `http://www.flickr.com/services/api/explore/?method=` `METHOD-NAME`, where `METHOD-NAME` is the name of the Flickr method you are interested in.

Try It Out   API Explorer

In this exercise, you'll get some practice using the API Explorer.

1. Go to the Flickr API reference page for the method `flickr.people.getInfo`. You can find it at `http://www.flickr.com/services/api/flickr.people.getInfo.htm`.

    This page contains a brief description of the function, describes its arguments, and shows a sample response. Below this, you should see a link to the API Explorer for this method. Click the link and you will be taken to the API Explorer page at

    `http://www.flickr.com/services/api/explore/?method=flickr.people.getInfo`.

    You can see an example of this page in Figure 4-3.

2. On the API Explorer page you will see the method name, and below it a list of arguments. The `flickr.people.getInfo` method only has one argument — the user ID of the person you want to get information about.

    You will also see, on the right-hand side of the Explorer page, a list of useful values. It shows your own NSID, photo IDs for some of your recently uploaded photos, photoset IDs for some of your recent photosets, group IDs for some of your groups, and finally a list of some of your contacts' NSIDs. These values are displayed so that you always have some test data at hand if you want to try out methods in the API to see how they work.

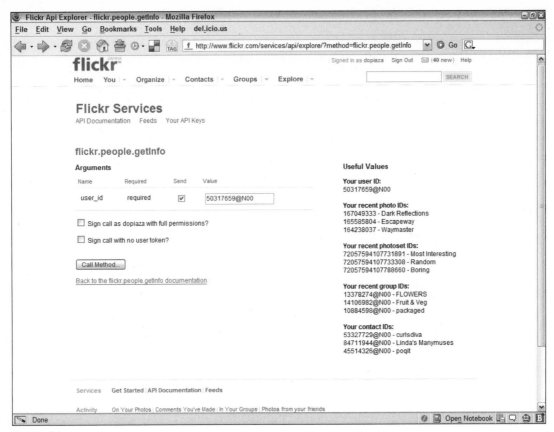

Figure 4-3

3. Select the value of your NSID in the right-hand column under the heading "Your User Id" — it will look something like 12345678@N00. Copy this text to the clipboard and then paste it into the text box in the arguments list for the argument `user_id`. Clear the Sign call as <your user name> with full permissions? and Sign call with no user token? check boxes below the arguments list. These will become important when you start making authenticated API calls, which is covered in Chapter 7. For now, you can safely ignore them. Finally, when you've done all that, click the Call Method button. If you scroll down the resulting page, you should see something that looks like Figure 4-4.

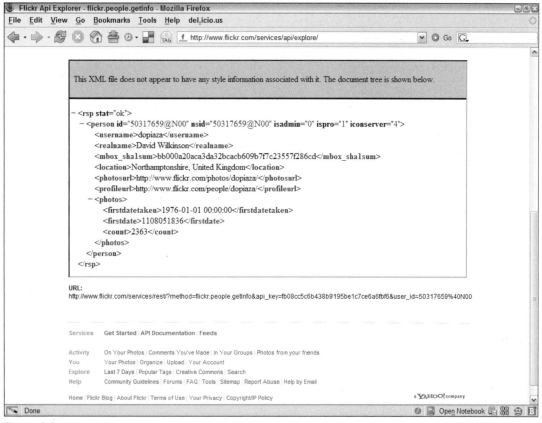

Figure 4-4

The XML file you see is the response from the Flickr API for the method you have just called — the `flickr.people.getInfo` method for your user ID.

How It Works

The API Explorer knows, from the method parameter in the URL, which method you are invoking and what arguments it requires (it can find out this information itself by using the `flickr.reflection` `.getMethodInfo` method call).

When you fill in the arguments and submit the form, the API Explorer simply builds the REST URL for this method invocation. In fact, if you look below the XML document displayed on the response page you can see the REST URL that was used — it will look something like this:

```
http://api.flickr.com/services/rest/?method=flickr.people.getInfo&
    api_key=1f2811827f3284b3aa12f7bbb7792b8d&user_id=50317659%40N00
```

The XML document you see displayed is simply the output from that REST URL. You can easily verify that by selecting the URL and copying and pasting it into another browser window. You should see the same XML response returned.

Using an API Kit

Constructing Flickr API requests by hand and manually decoding the responses can quickly become cumbersome. To make the process of creating Flickr applications easier, a number of API kits have been created. These API kits provide a wrapper around the Flickr API and take care of all of the hard work of building requests and unraveling responses.

API kits are not officially part of the Flickr API, and are neither provided nor endorsed by Flickr. Despite this lack of official endorsement, API kits are very popular and have sprung up for most major development languages, including PHP, Perl, Java, Actionscript, .NET, Python, and many more. They are usually written by independent authors and often licensed under an open-source license such as the GNU General Public License (GPL).

In most cases there is little point in reinventing the wheel, and the majority of Flickr applications make use of one or more of these API kits. The PHP projects in this book, for example, use Dan Coulter's excellent phpFlickr library, which is available under the GPL and can be found at `http://www.phpflickr.com/` or downloaded directly from SourceForge at `http://sourceforge.net/projects/phpflickr`.

Be a Good Flickr Citizen

The API is open to use by all—after all, any Flickr user can get an API key just by filling in the form on the web site. It's important, however, that you behave sensibly in your use of the API and that you don't abuse that privilege. In practice, there are only a few things that you need to watch out for.

Commercial Use

Most API keys are issued for non-commercial use, and so should not be used in a commercial application or on a commercial web site. So what constitutes commercial use? Clearly, if you are using your Flickr API key on a web site that sells or promotes the sale of goods or services, that would be described as commercial. On the other hand, if you keep a blog about life with your pet cat, and also happen to have a few Google ads running alongside it, that probably doesn't constitute commercial. Between these two extremes are a vast number of possibilities. Often common sense will tell you if your use of the API is really commercial or not. If you are in any doubt, however, you should ask. You can find a Help via Email link at the bottom of every page on the Flickr web site. If you use that and describe your situation, you should then be able to get a definitive answer from the Flickr team.

If you know that your use of the API is going to be commercial, you should indicate this on the form you fill in to request your API key. Your application will then be reviewed by a member of the Flickr staff— so do make sure you give them enough information to allow them to make a decision.

Minimizing API calls

One of the main things you can and should do to be a good Flickr citizen is to ensure that you don't generate an unnecessary or unreasonable amount of traffic to their servers. Bandwidth and processing power don't come for free, and every API application or mashup created adds a little to the total computing resources needed to run Flickr. Now, that's not to say that you should try to avoid sending any traffic at all — after all, the whole point of giving you an API key was to give you access to Flickr's data — but you should be careful not to be too greedy, and never ask for more than you actually need. You will also benefit from being efficient in the way you use the API — the less time your code has to spend waiting for Flickr, the faster and more responsive your application will become.

Here are some tips for minimizing the number of API calls you make. They may seem obvious, but people fall into these same traps time and time again.

❑ **Don't call methods more than once.** If you display the title of a photograph twice on a page, make sure you request it from Flickr only once — try to store it away, in a global variable perhaps, for when you need it the second time.

❑ **Get as much information with each method call as you can.** Many API methods return much more information in a single call than might be obvious just from the name or from a cursory read of the API specification. The `flickr.photos.search` method that you saw earlier returns the NSID of the owner for each photo it returns. If, however, you specify `owner_name` in the `extras` parameter, it will return the owner's screen name as well. It is worth reading carefully the specification of the methods you intend to use in order to ensure that you get the most out of each method call that you can.

❑ **Don't request data you don't need.** Be careful of what you ask for — it's easy to request data that you end up never using. For example, if you want to display your five most recent photos, be sure to specify that you want only five returned. The default behavior for many of the API methods is to return details for 100 photos if no actual value is specified — that's an awful lot of data to transfer and process if you don't need to.

❑ **Cache data wherever you can.** A good technique for reducing the number of API calls you have to make in any application is to cache data wherever you can. You can store cached data in many places in a web application — in cookies, in the user's session, or in a local database. You can even simply write the data to disk. By judicious use of caching, you can avoid having to go back to Flickr for information each time the user loads a new page.

Flickr Resources

There are a number of resources that as a Flickr developer you should not only be aware of, but consulting regularly.

Flickr Services Page

The Flickr Services Page at `http://www.flickr.com/services/` should be your first port of call for information. From here you can find all the API documentation, manage your API keys, and find links to many third-party applications that show off just what you can do with the Flickr API.

Flickr Developer Support Group

You can find the Flickr Developer Support Group at http://groups.yahoo.com/group/yws-flickr/. If you can't find the answer to your Flickr API questions by reading through the documentation, you can post them here — the group is read by many experienced Flickr developers as well as members of the Flickr staff. There is also a searchable archive of past posts, so you can see if your question has been asked before.

If you want to post to the group, or have posts mailed to you, you will need to have a Yahoo! account.

Flickr API Group

There is an unofficial Flickr group dedicated to discussions of the API, which you can find at http://www.flickr.com/groups/api/. In it you will find not only discussions of various aspects of the API, but also details of new API applications that various members have created.

Summary

In this chapter you have been presented with an overview of the Flickr API. You have learned how to send messages to Flickr via REST, SOAP, and XML-RPC, construct URLs to access a variety of Flickr pages and images, understand some of the common data structures returned by Flickr, and use the API Explorer to invoke Flickr methods.

Now that's more than enough background information. You are now ready to start building your first Flickr mashup. In the next chapter you will discover how to use feeds to get information from Flickr, and then how to process and display the content of those feeds in your web page.

Exercises

1. Construct a REST URL to use the flickr.photos.getRecent method to retrieve summary information for the 10 most recent public photos uploaded to Flickr. Enter the URL in your browser to verify that it returns the information correctly.

2. Use the API Explorer to find the most interesting photos on Flickr that have the tag cat. Hint: you will need to use the flickr.photos.search API method.

3. Take the results returned from the previous exercise and use the API Explorer for the flickr.photos.getInfo method to return details about the most interesting photo.

Part II
Remixing Flickr

Flickr Feeds

Flickr makes a number of *feeds* available to the world at large, and in a variety of formats. In this chapter you will find out just what a feed is, what kinds of feed are available, and also how you can make use of them. You will see how you can make a Flickr badge to include in your web pages to show off your (or anyone else's) photos on your web site using a publicly accessible feed from Flickr.

What Is a Feed?

A *feed* is a means of keeping track of a set of information that changes over time. The kinds of content usually associated with feeds are things like news stories and blog postings, but any kind of data that can be categorized as a list of individual items can be represented by a feed. A feed is just an electronic document containing such a list. Each item in the list represents a particular piece of content, usually in summary form. A web site that regularly changes information or adds new content will often publish a feed so that users can easily track changes and additions to the site. Feeds are not static data; each access to a feed will usually return an up-to-date set of items — a snapshot of the items available at that moment in time. Feeds are typically retrieved across the web, with each feed having its own unique URL. The process of making content available via a feed is known as *syndication*.

A number of web services and software applications, or *aggregators*, will let you view a set of feeds. Typically they will enable you to categorize and view a number of different feeds, so that you can easily see when new information is published from a wide variety of sources. Examples of aggregators are Bloglines (`http://www.bloglines.com`) and FeedDemon (`http://www.newsgator.com/`).

Try It Out   **Getting a Feed**

Getting hold of a feed is as simple as requesting a URL.

1.   Enter the following URL into your browser:

```
http://api.flickr.com/services/feeds/photos_public.gne
```

2.   You should then see the feed displayed in your browser window, something like this:

```
<?xml version="1.0" encoding="utf-8" standalone="yes"?>
<feed xmlns="http://www.w3.org/2005/Atom"
  xmlns:dc="http://purl.org/dc/elements/1.1/">

  <title>Everyone's Photos</title>
  <link rel="self" href="http://www.flickr.com/services/feeds/photos_public.gne" />
  <link rel="alternate" type="text/html" href="http://www.flickr.com/photos/"/>
  <id>tag:flickr.com,2005:/photos/public</id>
  <icon>http://www.flickr.com/images/buddyicon.jpg</icon>
  <subtitle>A feed of Everyone's Photos</subtitle>

  <updated>2006-07-08T13:57:15Z</updated>
  <generator uri="http://www.flickr.com/">Flickr</generator>

  <entry>
    <title>Blue Corner</title>
    <link rel="alternate" type="text/html"
href="http://www.flickr.com/photos/dopiaza/179701217/"/>

    <id>tag:flickr.com,2005:/photo/179701217</id>
    <published>2006-07-02T12:13:37Z</published>
    <updated>2006-07-02T12:13:37Z</updated>
    <dc:date.Taken>2006-07-02T12:42:04-08:00</dc:date.Taken>
    <content type="html">&lt;p&gt;&lt;a
href=&quot;http://www.flickr.com/people/dopiaza/&quot;&gt;dopiaza&lt;/a&gt; posted
a photo:&lt;/p&gt;

&lt;p&gt;&lt;a href=&quot;http://www.flickr.com/photos/dopiaza/179701217/&quot;
title=&quot;Blue Corner&quot;&gt;&lt;img
src=&quot;http://static.flickr.com/52/179701217_1f521ae2c9_m.jpg&quot;
width=&quot;240&quot; height=&quot;160&quot; alt=&quot;Blue Corner&quot;
style=&quot;border: 1px solid #ddd;&quot; /&gt;&lt;/a&gt;&lt;/p&gt;

&lt;p&gt;[DSC_2408]&lt;/p&gt;</content>
    <author>
      <name>dopiaza</name>
      <uri>http://www.flickr.com/people/dopiaza/</uri>
    </author>
    <category term="blue" scheme="http://www.flickr.com/photos/tags/" />
    <category term="corner" scheme="http://www.flickr.com/photos/tags/" />
    <category term="painting" scheme="http://www.flickr.com/photos/tags/" />
    <category term="picture" scheme="http://www.flickr.com/photos/tags/" />
    <category term="frame" scheme="http://www.flickr.com/photos/tags/" />
  </entry>
</feed>
```

How It Works

The URL you entered, http://www.flickr.com/services/feeds/photos_public.gne, is the URL for Flickr's Everyone's Photos feed and represents a snapshot of some of the most recently uploaded public photos. The feed that you see is an XML document in the Atom format — Atom is the format used for all Flickr feeds unless a different one is specified. If you look at the XML, it has an outer <feed> element followed by some elements containing general information about the feed. The <feed> element contains a series of <entry> elements. There's only one <entry> element shown here for reasons of space — you should see a number of <entry> elements in the feed opened in your browser. Each <entry> represents an individual item in the feed — in this case, a new photo uploaded to Flickr.

Available Flickr Feeds

Flickr generates feeds for a wide selection of its content. In fact, many of the pages you see on Flickr have associated feeds available for them — you can quickly tell whether a feed exists for a page by looking for the Feed link at the bottom of the page. Here are some of the most commonly used Flickr feeds:

❑   Recent public photos:

    http://api.flickr.com/services/feeds/photos_public.gne

❑   Any user's public photos:

    http://api.flickr.com/services/feeds/photos_public.gne?id=USER-NSID

❑   Recent comments on a user's public photos:

    http://api.flickr.com/services/feeds/activity.gne?id=USER-NSID

❑   Activity on photos a user has commented on:

    http://api.flickr.com/services/feeds/photos_comments.gne?user_id=USER-NSID

❑   Group discussions (only for public groups in which the discussions are visible to non-members):

    http://api.flickr.com/services/feeds/groups_discuss.gne?id=GROUP-NSID

❑   Group photo pool (only for public groups in which the pool is visible to non-members):

    http://api.flickr.com/services/feeds/groups_pool.gne?id=GROUP-NSID

Feed Formats

Feeds are usually published in a well-defined format — RSS and Atom being the most commonly used. Flickr offers its feeds in all the usual formats, but also in a variety of others that you may be surprised to come across. This section looks at the various formats supported by Flickr.

All feed formats are accessed via the same URL, but are differentiated by means of a `format` parameter in the query string of the feed URL — so, for example, the feed for recent public photos in the Atom format would be as follows:

```
http://www.flickr.com/services/feeds/photos_public.gne?format=atom
```

The following table lists the valid values for the `format` parameter:

Parameter	Description
`rss_200` or `rss2`	RSS 2.0
`atom_1` or `atom`	Atom
`rss_091`	RSS 0.91
`rss_092` or `rss`	RSS 0.92
`rss_100` or `rdf`	RSS 1.0
`rss_200_enc`	RSS 2.0 (with enclosures)
`php`	PHP code
`php_serial`	Serialized PHP Object
`csv`	Comma Separated Value
`json`	JavaScript Object Notation
`sql`	Structured Query Language
`yaml`	YAML Ain't Markup Language
`cdf`	Channel Definition Format

Most of the feed formats contain broadly the same information, although you should note that the actual contents do vary from feed to feed — if you are planning on using a feed, you should make sure that it contains the information you need. Each feed starts with a set of elements describing the feed itself, including fields such as title, description, URL, and publication date, followed by a list of all of the items found in the feed. The number of items returned varies from feed to feed, but it is typically between 10 and 20.

The list of available feed formats is updated from time to time, so check the main Flickr feed web page at `http://www.flickr.com/services/feeds/` for any updates to this list.

Let's now take a look at each of the currently available feed formats. To illustrate just what they look like, sample output is shown for each of the feed formats — this sample is the output from the public photos feed for the author of this book:

```
http://www.flickr.com/services/feeds/photos_public.gne?id=50317659@N00
```

Note that although each feed returns a number of feed items, only one feed item is shown in each example in order to keep the size of the sample code blocks down.

If you're impatient and just want to get on with writing some code, you don't need to look through all of the different formats right now — you can jump ahead to the "Creating a Flickr Badge" section of this chapter. When you need to know what a specific feed format looks like, you can always come back and leaf through this section later.

RSS

RSS, otherwise known as *Really Simple Syndication* or *Rich Site Summary,* is discussed further in Chapter 10. It is one of the most commonly used feed formats on the Internet.

Flickr supports a number of different versions of RSS; the example shown here is RSS 2.0.

```
<?xml version="1.0" encoding="utf-8"?>
<rss version="2.0"
        xmlns:media="http://search.yahoo.com/mrss"
xmlns:dc="http://purl.org/dc/elements/1.1/"
>
  <channel>
    <title>dopiaza's Photos</title>
    <link>http://www.flickr.com/photos/dopiaza/</link>
    <description>A feed of dopiaza's Photos</description>
    <pubDate>Sun, 2 Jul 2006 11:04:04 -0800</pubDate>
    <lastBuildDate>Sun, 2 Jul 2006 11:04:04 -0800</lastBuildDate>

    <generator>http://www.flickr.com/</generator>
    <image>
      <url>http://static.flickr.com/56/buddyicons/50317659@N00.jpg?1151240153</url>
      <title>dopiaza's Photos</title>
      <link>http://www.flickr.com/photos/dopiaza/</link>
    </image>

    <item>
      <title>Blue Corner</title>
      <link>http://www.flickr.com/photos/dopiaza/179701217/</link>

      <description>&lt;p&gt;&lt;a
href=&quot;http://www.flickr.com/people/dopiaza/&quot;&gt;dopiaza&lt;/a&gt; posted
a photo:&lt;/p&gt;

&lt;p&gt;&lt;a href=&quot;http://www.flickr.com/photos/dopiaza/179701217/&quot;
title=&quot;Blue Corner&quot;&gt;&lt;img
src=&quot;http://static.flickr.com/52/179701217_1f521ae2c9_m.jpg&quot;
width=&quot;240&quot; height=&quot;160&quot; alt=&quot;Blue Corner&quot;
style=&quot;border: 1px solid #ddd;&quot; /&gt;&lt;/a&gt;&lt;/p&gt;

&lt;p&gt;[DSC_2408]&lt;/p&gt;</description>
      <pubDate>Sun, 2 Jul 2006 05:13:37 -0800</pubDate>
      <dc:date.Taken>2006-07-02T12:42:04-08:00</dc:date.Taken>
      <author>nobody@flickr.com (dopiaza)</author>
      <guid isPermaLink="false">tag:flickr.com,2004:/photo/179701217</guid>
      <media:content url="http://static.flickr.com/52/179701217_1f521ae2c9_m.jpg"
        type="image/jpeg"
        height="160"
```

```
            width="240"/>
        <media:title>Blue Corner</media:title>
        <media:text type="html">&lt;p&gt;&lt;a
href=&quot;http://www.flickr.com/people/dopiaza/&quot;&gt;dopiaza&lt;/a&gt; posted
a photo:&lt;/p&gt;

&lt;p&gt;&lt;a href=&quot;http://www.flickr.com/photos/dopiaza/179701217/&quot;
title=&quot;Blue Corner&quot;&gt;&lt;img
src=&quot;http://static.flickr.com/52/179701217_1f521ae2c9_m.jpg&quot;
width=&quot;240&quot; height=&quot;160&quot; alt=&quot;Blue Corner&quot;
style=&quot;border: 1px solid #ddd;&quot; /&gt;&lt;/a&gt;&lt;/p&gt;

&lt;p&gt;[DSC_2408]&lt;/p&gt;</media:text>
        <media:thumbnail url="http://static.flickr.com/52/179701217_1f521ae2c9_s.jpg"
height="75" width="75" />
        <media:credit role="photographer">dopiaza</media:credit>
        <media:category scheme="urn:flickr:tags">blue corner painting picture
frame</media:category>

    </item>
  </channel>
</rss>
```

The RSS feed is an XML document—the feed (known as a *channel* here) is contained within a `<channel>` element and each item is held within an `<item>` element. The contents of most of the elements within the document are reasonably self-explanatory, although a few of them are worth noting.

The `<media:text>` element contains a text description of the item. It contains HTML and has had the angle bracket and double-quote characters converted to their equivalent entities: `&lt;`, `&gt;`, and `&quot;`. Note that this description is not simply the description of the photo as found on Flickr, but a piece of HTML that when decoded takes the following form:

```
<p><a href="http://www.flickr.com/people/dopiaza/">dopiaza</a> posted a photo:</p>

<p><a href="http://www.flickr.com/photos/dopiaza/179701217/" title="Blue
Corner"><img src="http://static.flickr.com/52/179701217_1f521ae2c9_m.jpg"
width="240" height="160" alt="Blue Corner" style="border: 1px solid #ddd;"
/></a></p>

<p>Flickr photo description goes here</p>
```

The `<guid>` element contains a unique identifier for this photo. The identifier generated here uses the *tag URI* scheme, which defines an algorithm to enable the creation of unique identifiers. If you are interested in the details of this scheme, you can find them at `http://taguri.org/`.

Finally, the `<media:category>` element contains a space-separated list of the Flickr tags for the photo.

Atom

Atom is another very popular XML-based format for publishing feeds on the Internet—it is the only format other than the various flavors of RSS in widespread use on the Internet for the syndication of content. Remember, this is the same data you saw in the RSS feed in the previous section; it's just presented here in a different format.

```
<?xml version="1.0" encoding="utf-8" standalone="yes"?>
<feed xmlns="http://www.w3.org/2005/Atom"
      xmlns:dc="http://purl.org/dc/elements/1.1/">

  <title>dopiaza's Photos</title>
  <link rel="self"
href="http://www.flickr.com/services/feeds/photos_public.gne?id=50317659@N00&amp;fo
rmat=atom" />
  <link rel="alternate" type="text/html"
href="http://www.flickr.com/photos/dopiaza/"/>
  <id>tag:flickr.com,2005:/photos/public/296457</id>
  <icon>http://static.flickr.com/56/buddyicons/50317659@N00.jpg?1151240153</icon>
  <subtitle>A feed of dopiaza's Photos</subtitle>

  <updated>2006-07-02T18:04:04Z</updated>
  <generator uri="http://www.flickr.com/">Flickr</generator>

  <entry>
    <title>Blue Corner</title>
    <link rel="alternate" type="text/html"
href="http://www.flickr.com/photos/dopiaza/179701217/"/>

    <id>tag:flickr.com,2005:/photo/179701217</id>
    <published>2006-07-02T12:13:37Z</published>
    <updated>2006-07-02T12:13:37Z</updated>
    <dc:date.Taken>2006-07-02T12:42:04-08:00</dc:date.Taken>
    <content type="html">&lt;p&gt;&lt;a
href=&quot;http://www.flickr.com/people/dopiaza/&quot;&gt;dopiaza&lt;/a&gt; posted
a photo:&lt;/p&gt;

&lt;p&gt;&lt;a href=&quot;http://www.flickr.com/photos/dopiaza/179701217/&quot;
title=&quot;Blue Corner&quot;&gt;&lt;img
src=&quot;http://static.flickr.com/52/179701217_1f521ae2c9_m.jpg&quot;
width=&quot;240&quot; height=&quot;160&quot; alt=&quot;Blue Corner&quot;
style=&quot;border: 1px solid #ddd;&quot; /&gt;&lt;/a&gt;&lt;/p&gt;

&lt;p&gt;[DSC_2408]&lt;/p&gt;</content>
    <author>
      <name>dopiaza</name>
      <uri>http://www.flickr.com/people/dopiaza/</uri>
    </author>
    <category term="blue" scheme="http://www.flickr.com/photos/tags/" />
    <category term="corner" scheme="http://www.flickr.com/photos/tags/" />
    <category term="painting" scheme="http://www.flickr.com/photos/tags/" />
    <category term="picture" scheme="http://www.flickr.com/photos/tags/" />
    <category term="frame" scheme="http://www.flickr.com/photos/tags/" />
  </entry>
</feed>
```

Although the structure is somewhat different, the basic data contained within an Atom feed are very similar to those in the RSS feed — after all, both feeds are trying to do exactly the same job. There are a few differences — for example, the Flickr photo tags are held in multiple <category> elements rather than a space-separated list — but once again, the XML structure is largely self-explanatory.

PHP

The PHP feed returns a block of PHP code that, when executed, initializes an array called a $feed.

```php
<?php
  $feed = array(
    'title' => "dopiaza's Photos",
    'url'   => "http://www.flickr.com/photos/dopiaza/",
    'description' => "A feed of dopiaza's Photos",
    'pub_date' => "1151863444",
    'image' =>
"http://static.flickr.com/56/buddyicons/50317659@N00.jpg?1151240153",
    'items' => array(
      array(
        'title' => "Blue Corner",
        'url'   => "http://www.flickr.com/photos/dopiaza/179701217/",
        'description'=> "<p><a
href=\"http://www.flickr.com/people/dopiaza/\">dopiaza</a> posted a
photo:</p>\n\n<p><a href=\"http://www.flickr.com/photos/dopiaza/179701217/\"
title=\"Blue Corner\"><img
src=\"http://static.flickr.com/52/179701217_1f521ae2c9_m.jpg\" width=\"240\"
height=\"160\" alt=\"Blue Corner\" style=\"border: 1px solid #ddd;\"
/></a></p>\n\n<p>[DSC_2408]</p>",
        'date' => "1151842417",
        'guid' => "/photo/179701217",
        'author_name' => "dopiaza",
        'author_url'=> "http://www.flickr.com/people/dopiaza/",
      ),
    ),
  );
?>
```

This may look a little bizarre at first, but it is very useful if you want to fetch a feed from within a PHP application. The PHP feed means that you don't need to worry about parsing a complex XML structure like RSS or Atom; you can simply use the PHP feed itself, which creates a PHP object directly for you.

The $feed array is an associative array that contains a series of fields containing information about the feed. The individual items in the feed are held in the $feed['items'] array.

Once again, most of the fields stored in the array are self-explanatory. The date fields are stored as Unix timestamps rather than in a more readable form, but you can use the PHP date function to format them.

The guid field in this feed uses a shorter form of the unique identifier than the previous feeds described — it is simply a string of the form /photo/photo_id. Note that this is *not* the path to the image or photo page on the Flickr web site.

You will see an example of how to use the PHP feed later in this chapter.

Serialized PHP

The serialized PHP feed is similar to the PHP feed, except that it generates a serialized PHP object rather than executable code. You can use the PHP unserialize function to convert this into a PHP object, which you can then use in the same way as the $feed object described in the PHP section above.

```
a:7:{s:5:"title";s:16:"dopiaza's
Photos";s:3:"url";s:37:"http://www.flickr.com/photos/dopiaza/";s:11:"description";s
:26:"A feed of dopiaza's
Photos";s:8:"pub_date";s:10:"1151863444";s:5:"image";s:66:"http://static.flickr.com
/56/buddyicons/50317659@N00.jpg?1151240153";s:4:"guid";s:21:"/photos/public/296457"
;s:5:"items";a:10:{i:0;a:16:{s:5:"title";s:11:"Blue
Corner";s:3:"url";s:47:"http://www.flickr.com/photos/dopiaza/179701217/";s:11:"desc
ription";s:339:"<p><a href="http://www.flickr.com/people/dopiaza/">dopiaza</a>
posted a photo:</p>

<p><a href="http://www.flickr.com/photos/dopiaza/179701217/" title="Blue
Corner"><img src="http://static.flickr.com/52/179701217_1f521ae2c9_m.jpg"
width="240" height="160" alt="Blue Corner" style="border: 1px solid #ddd;"
/></a></p>

<p>[DSC_2408]</p>";s:9:"photo_xml";s:0:"";s:4:"date";s:10:"1151842417";s:10:"date_t
aken";s:25:"2006-07-02T12:42:04-
08:00";s:4:"guid";s:16:"/photo/179701217";s:11:"author_name";s:7:"dopiaza";s:10:"au
thor_url";s:37:"http://www.flickr.com/people/dopiaza/";s:9:"photo_url";s:54:"http:/
/static.flickr.com/52/179701217_1f521ae2c9_m.jpg";s:9:"thumb_url";s:54:"http://stat
ic.flickr.com/52/179701217_1f521ae2c9_s.jpg";s:6:"height";s:3:"160";s:5:"width";s:3
:"240";s:4:"tags";s:34:"blue corner painting picture
frame";s:10:"photo_mime";s:10:"image/jpeg";s:9:"tags_list";a:5:{i:0;s:4:"blue";i:1;
s:6:"corner";i:2;s:8:"painting";i:3;s:7:"picture";i:4;s:5:"frame";}}}}
```

JSON

The JSON (JavaScript Object Notation) feed works in a similar way to the PHP feed, but generates a piece of JavaScript code.

```
jsonFlickrFeed({
  "title": "dopiaza's Photos",
  "link": "http://www.flickr.com/photos/dopiaza/",
  "description": "A feed of dopiaza's Photos",
  "modified": "2006-07-02T18:04:04Z",
  "generator": "http://www.flickr.com/",
  "items": [
  {
    "title": "Blue Corner",
    "link": "http://www.flickr.com/photos/dopiaza/179701217/",
    "date_taken": "2006-07-02T12:42:04-08:00",
    "description": "&lt;p&gt;&lt;a
href=&quot;http://www.flickr.com/people/dopiaza/&quot;&gt;dopiaza&lt;/a&gt; posted
a photo:&lt;/p&gt; &lt;p&gt;&lt;a
href=&quot;http://www.flickr.com/photos/dopiaza/179701217/&quot; title=&quot;Blue
Corner&quot;&gt;&lt;img
src=&quot;http://static.flickr.com/52/179701217_1f521ae2c9_m.jpg&quot;
width=&quot;240&quot; height=&quot;160&quot; alt=&quot;Blue Corner&quot;
style=&quot;border: 1px solid #ddd;&quot; /&gt;&lt;/a&gt;&lt;/p&gt;
&lt;p&gt;[DSC_2408]&lt;/p&gt;",
    "published": "2006-07-02T12:13:37Z",
    "author": "nobody@flickr.com (dopiaza)",
    "tags": "blue corner painting picture frame"
  }]
})
```

This generated JavaScript calls a `jsonFlickrFeed` function that takes a single argument—a JavaScript object that is generated in the feed as JSON. To use this feed, you need to define in your web page a `jsonFlickrFeed` function that will then be automatically invoked when the feed JavaScript is executed.

Once again, the contents of the feed are very similar to those of the previous feeds. It is worth noting that the URLs of the photostream and photo pages are called `link` here, whereas in the PHP feed they are called `url`. You will see an example of how to use the JSON feed later in this chapter.

CSV

The CSV (Comma-Separated Values) feed generates a list of items in CSV format. In the following sample, the different fields are shown on separate lines, with a blank line separating the feed information from the item information. This is done purely to make the example readable—the actual feed has all the fields on a single line, with no blank lines separating the items.

```
"dopiaza's Photos",
"http://www.flickr.com/photos/dopiaza/",
"A feed of dopiaza's Photos",
"1151863444",
"http://static.flickr.com/56/buddyicons/50317659@N00.jpg?1151240153"

"Blue Corner",
"http://www.flickr.com/photos/dopiaza/179701217/",
"<p><a href=\"http://www.flickr.com/people/dopiaza/\">dopiaza</a> posted a
photo:</p>\n\n<p><a href=\"http://www.flickr.com/photos/dopiaza/179701217/\"
title=\"Blue Corner\"><img
src=\"http://static.flickr.com/52/179701217_1f521ae2c9_m.jpg\" width=\"240\"
height=\"160\" alt=\"Blue Corner\" style=\"border: 1px solid #ddd;\"
/></a></p>\n\n<p>[DSC_2408]</p>",
"1151842417",
"/photo/179701217",
"dopiaza",
"http://www.flickr.com/people/dopiaza/"
```

The first line in the CSV feed contains details about the feed itself. The fields are feed title, feed URL, feed description, feed publication date, and feed icon. The rest of the lines in the CSV feed correspond to the items in the feed. Each feed item has the field's title, photo page URL, description, posted date, GUID, author name, and author URL. The CSV feed is particularly useful if you need to import data into spreadsheets or applications with limited text-processing capabilities.

YAML

YAML, which is a recursive acronym for YAML Ain't Markup Language, is a text-based data feed.

```
guid        : /photos/public/296457
title       : dopiaza's Photos
url         : http://www.flickr.com/photos/dopiaza/
image       : http://static.flickr.com/56/buddyicons/50317659@N00.jpg?1151240153
description : A feed of dopiaza's Photos
pubdate     : 1151863444
items       :
    - guid        : /photo/179701217
```

```
    title       : Blue Corner
    url         : http://www.flickr.com/photos/dopiaza/179701217/
    date        : 1151842417
    description : |
        <p><a href="http://www.flickr.com/people/dopiaza/">dopiaza</a> posted a
photo:</p>

        <p><a href="http://www.flickr.com/photos/dopiaza/179701217/" title="Blue
Corner"><img src="http://static.flickr.com/52/179701217_1f521ae2c9_m.jpg"
width="240" height="160" alt="Blue Corner" style="border: 1px solid #ddd;"
/></a></p>

        <p>[DSC_2408]</p>
    authorname  : dopiaza
    authorurl   : http://www.flickr.com/people/dopiaza/
    tags        :
        - blue
        - corner
        - painting
        - picture
        - frame
```

YAML was designed to be easily human-readable, and uses whitespace and indentation to identify the structure of the data being described. Items in a list in YAML are denoted by a leading hyphen, so you can see in the example above that there is a single item in the items list. The item object starts with the guid item, and contains everything else that appears with that level of indentation. The final object in the item object is tags, which is itself a list—as can be seen by the further level of indentation and the leading hyphens on its members.

If you are interested in using YAML, you can read more about it at http://www.yaml.org/.

SQL

One of the more unusual feeds that Flickr provides is the SQL feed. It generates a set of SQL statements that enable you to directly store the feed data in a database.

```
CREATE TABLE IF NOT EXISTS feeds (
  guid varchar(255) NOT NULL default '',
  title varchar(255) NOT NULL default '',
  url varchar(255) NOT NULL default '',
  image_url varchar(255) NOT NULL default '',
  description text NOT NULL,
  pud_timestamp int(10) unsigned NOT NULL default '0',
  PRIMARY KEY (guid)
);

DELETE FROM feeds WHERE guid='/photos/public/296457';
INSERT INTO feeds VALUES (
  '/photos/public/296457',
  'dopiaza\'s Photos',
  'http://www.flickr.com/photos/dopiaza/',
  'http://static.flickr.com/56/buddyicons/50317659@N00.jpg?1151240153',
  'A feed of dopiaza\'s Photos',
```

```
    '1151863444'
);

CREATE TABLE IF NOT EXISTS feed_items (
  item_guid varchar(255) NOT NULL default '',
  feed_guid varchar(255) NOT NULL default '',
  title varchar(255) NOT NULL default '',
  url varchar(255) NOT NULL default '',
  pub_timestamp mediumint(8) unsigned NOT NULL default '0',
  description text NOT NULL,
  author_name varchar(255) NOT NULL default '',
  author_url varchar(255) NOT NULL default '',
  tags varchar(255) NOT NULL default '',
  PRIMARY KEY (item_guid)
);

DELETE FROM feed_items WHERE item_guid='/photo/179701217';
INSERT INTO feed_items VALUES (
  '/photo/179701217',
  '/photos/public/296457',
  'Blue Corner',
  'http://www.flickr.com/photos/dopiaza/179701217/',
  '1151842417',
  '<p><a href="http://www.flickr.com/people/dopiaza/">dopiaza</a> posted a
photo:</p>

<p><a href="http://www.flickr.com/photos/dopiaza/179701217/" title="Blue
Corner"><img src="http://static.flickr.com/52/179701217_1f521ae2c9_m.jpg"
width="240" height="160" alt="Blue Corner" style="border: 1px solid #ddd;"
/></a></p>

<p>[DSC_2408]</p>',
  'dopiaza',
  'http://www.flickr.com/people/dopiaza/',
  '\"blue\",\"corner\",\"painting\",\"picture\",\"frame\"'
);
```

The SQL generated as part of the feed uses two database tables, feeds and feed_items. Each table is created in the database if it does not already exist. The SQL then checks to see if the feed and feed item data are already present in the database, deleting them if there is already an entry present, and then inserts the new data items.

CDF

CDF, or Channel Definition Format, is another XML format for the syndication of data feeds. It was devised by Microsoft for use with its Active Channel technologies.

```
<?xml version="1.0" encoding="utf-8"?>
<CHANNEL
  HREF="http://www.flickr.com/photos/dopiaza/"
  LASTMOD="2006-07-02T18:04:04"
  PRECACHE="YES"
  LEVEL="0"
```

```
>
  <TITLE>dopiaza's Photos</TITLE>
  <ABSTRACT>A feed of dopiaza's Photos</ABSTRACT>
  <SCHEDULE><INTERVALTIME HOUR="1"/></SCHEDULE>
  <LOGO HREF="http://static.flickr.com/56/buddyicons/50317659@N00.jpg?1151240153"
STYLE="ICON"/>
  <ITEM
     HREF="http://www.flickr.com/photos/dopiaza/179701217/"
     LASTMOD="2006-07-02T12:13:37">
    <TITLE>Blue Corner</TITLE>
    <ABSTRACT>&lt;p&gt;&lt;a
href=&quot;http://www.flickr.com/people/dopiaza/&quot;&gt;dopiaza&lt;/a&gt; posted
a photo:&lt;/p&gt;

&lt;p&gt;&lt;a href=&quot;http://www.flickr.com/photos/dopiaza/179701217/&quot;
title=&quot;Blue Corner&quot;&gt;&lt;img
src=&quot;http://static.flickr.com/52/179701217_1f521ae2c9_m.jpg&quot;
width=&quot;240&quot; height=&quot;160&quot; alt=&quot;Blue Corner&quot;
style=&quot;border: 1px solid #ddd;&quot; /&gt;&lt;/a&gt;&lt;/p&gt;

&lt;p&gt;[DSC_2408]&lt;/p&gt;</ABSTRACT>
    <LOGO HREF="http://static.flickr.com/52/179701217_1f521ae2c9_s.jpg"
STYLE="IMAGE"/>
  </ITEM>
</CHANNEL>
```

Creating a Flickr Badge

Many people like to show off their affiliation with a particular web site by placing a *badge* on their own web pages. Badges are basically small advertisements used to promote a web site or community, and it is quite common to see them included in personal web sites or blogs. As a photography web site, Flickr lends itself to the production of visually interesting badges. There is an official Flickr badge available at http://www.flickr.com/badge_new.gne, and a very nice badge it is, too—but of course it's always far more interesting to make your own from scratch, and feeds offer a very simple means of doing this. Next you'll look at two fundamentally different ways of achieving exactly the same end result. You'll create a Flickr badge using two very different architectures—the first will be a server-side version using PHP to embed a badge on a web page, and the second will be a client-side version implemented in JavaScript.

Designing the Badge

The badge, as seen by the browser, will be a block of HTML. It would be useful if the badge could be easily restyled to match the look and feel of the web page it sits on, so this project will keep the HTML very simple and generic and use CSS for the presentation of the badge. So the first thing to do is consider how to structure the HTML. The HTML should represent the structure of the badge, but not impose any restrictions on the presentation—that is left entirely to the CSS.

If you consider the structure of a typical badge, it is a block-level element—a chunk of content that can be slotted into any arbitrary position on a page. Within that block, it typically contains a title followed by a list of images. Note that so far I have simply described how the badge is structured — I haven't said anything yet about what it should look like. So, translating that description into equivalent HTML, you get something like this:

```
<div class="badge">
  <p class="badge-title">
    <a href="/link/to/user/photostream">Badge Title</a>
  </p>
  <ul class="badge-items">
    <li class="badge-item">
      <a href="/link/to/photo/page">
        <img src="/path/to/image" />
      </a>
    </li>
    <li class="badge-item">
      ...
    </li>
  </ul>
</div>
```

The whole badge is contained within a `<div>` element to help isolate this block of HTML from its surroundings. The first item in the badge is the title — this is simply a piece of text describing the badge, so it has been placed with a `<p>` element. The badge then contains a list of images, so this is represented in the HTML as an unordered list. The `<ul>` element, in turn, contains an `<li>` element for each image displayed.

All the HTML elements have been annotated with an appropriately named `class` attribute — this means that it will be easy to refer to them in the CSS when you style the badge later.

A Server-Side Badge Using PHP

Now it's time to implement the badge. The first version will be created in PHP, with all the work building the HTML being performed on the server. You will use the PHP Flickr feed described earlier to get information about your latest photos.

When the user's browser requests the web page from the web server, the server must first construct the badge's HTML. To do this, the web server sends a request to Flickr to retrieve the PHP feed for the badge. It then builds the HTML for the badge and returns it to the browser. The flow of information is shown in Figure 5-1.

If you remember from the earlier section on feed types, the PHP feed is returned as a block of PHP code that initializes a `$feed` variable:

```
<?php
  $feed = array(
    ...
  );
?>
```

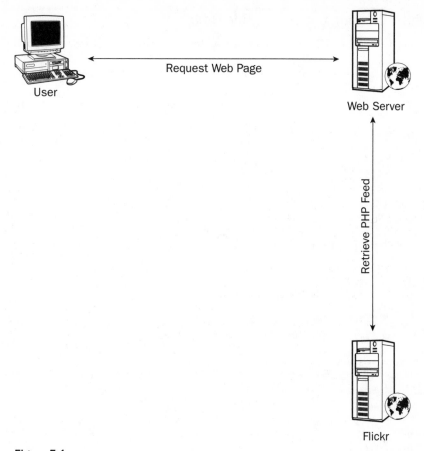

Figure 5-1

To execute a block of PHP code from a remote URL, you use the PHP `include` directive. So, for example, you could retrieve the PHP feed and output its raw contents with the following code:

```php
<?php

include("http://flickr.com/services/feeds/photos_public.gne?id=50317659@N00&format=php");

print_r($feed);

?>
```

You don't need to declare or assign the `$feed` variable yourself — that's all done for you in the included code. After the `include` statement, `$feed` is available to you for use.

Try It Out   **Creating the Server-Side Badge**

Now it's time to take the PHP feed and format the contents into your HTML badge, defined previously.

1.   Create a `badge` directory on your web server and within that create a `badge.php` file with the
     following contents:

```php
<?php

include("http://api.flickr.com/services/feeds/photos_public.gne?id=50317659@N00&
format=php");

$s = "";

$s .= '<div class="badge">';
$s .= '<p class="badge-title"><a href="' . $feed['url'] . '">' . $feed['title'] .
'</a></p>';
$s .= '<ul class="badge-items">';

$items = $feed['items'];

for ($i = 0; $i < count($items); $i++)
{
  if (preg_match('/(http:\/\/static.flickr.com\/\d+\/\d+_[0-9a-z]+)_m\.jpg/',
    $items[$i]['description'], $result))
  {
    $image = $result[1] . '_s.jpg';
    $s .= '<li class="badge-item"><a href="' . $items[$i]['url'] . '"><img src="' .
$image . '" /></a></li>';
  }
}

$s .= '</ul></div>';

echo($s);

?>
```

2.   The feed URL in the code above uses my NSID (`50317659@N00`) and so will retrieve my photos.
     Feel free to replace it with your own NSID so that you can see your own photos displayed in the
     badge.

     *If you can't remember what your own NSID is, the easiest way to find it is to go to the Flickr API
     Explorer page for any API method — for example:*

     `http://www.flickr.com/services/api/explore/?method=flickr.test.echo`

     You will find your NSID listed in the Useful Values column on the right-hand side of the page.

How It Works

If you look at the PHP code, you will see that it builds up a string of HTML in the `$s` variable and at the
end calls `echo($s)` to output the HTML. The structure of the HTML is exactly as outlined earlier, so let's
now take a look to see how the different parts of the badge details are extracted from the feed.

The first part of the badge is the title, which is linked back to the user's photostream. Generating this part is easy — both the feed title and the link are fields in the `$feed` array:

```
$s .= '<p class="badge-title"><a href="' . $feed['url'] . '">' . $feed['title'] .
'</a></p>';
```

Fishing out the actual images is a little trickier. The image URL isn't directly included in the feed. It is, however, embedded within the text in the description field:

```
'description'=> "<p><a href=\"http://www.flickr.com/people/dopiaza/\">dopiaza</a>
posted a photo:</p>\n\n<p><a
href=\"http://www.flickr.com/photos/dopiaza/179701217/\" title=\"Blue Corner\">
<img src=\"http://static.flickr.com/52/179701217_1f521ae2c9_m.jpg\" width=\"240\"
height=\"160\" alt=\"Blue Corner\" style=\"border: 1px solid #ddd;\"
/></a></p>\n\n<p>[DSC_2408]</p>",
```

The badge code loops through each element in the `items` array, using a regular expression to match the image URL.

```
if (preg_match('/(http:\/\/static.flickr.com\/\d+\/\d+_[0-9a-z]+)_m\.jpg/',
   $items[$i]['description'], $result))
{
   $image = $result[1] . '_s.jpg';
   $s .= '<li class="badge-item"><a href="' . $items[$i]['url'] . '"><img src="' .
$image . '" /></a></li>';
}
```

The regular expression looks for a string that matches the URL of an image. The pattern starts with the string `http://static.flickr.com/`. The next component, `\d+`, will match a sequence of one or more digits — this is the server ID for the photo. The final component of the URL is matched by the pattern `\d+_[0-9a-z]+)_m\.jpg`, which is a sequence of one or more digits followed by an underscore and then a sequence of one or more alphanumeric characters, ending with the string `_m.jpg`.

The image embedded in the description field is the small size, which measures 240 pixels on the longest side. That's large for a badge, so when the image URL is retrieved by the regular expression, only the first part of the URL is extracted — the part indicated by the parentheses in the regular expression. The `_m.jpg` is left off the end and replaced with `_s.jpg` — that's the square size, which is still a little large at 75 pixels, but at least they will fit together quite neatly into a grid.

One thing you may have noticed is that the sample HTML structure shown earlier was neatly laid out, whilst the HTML generated by the PHP badge code is all on a single line — it contains no whitespace between the tags. This does make the resulting source harder to read, but it makes styling the HTML much easier — if you have whitespace between your image elements, browsers will sometimes insist on rendering it, making it nigh impossible to get your images to butt up against each other. The simplest solution is to make sure you don't put any whitespace there in the first place.

The `badge.php` page you have just created isn't a compete HTML page — it only generates the badge `<div>` and its contents, so the next step is to create the containing web page and include the badge code within it.

Try It Out   **Displaying the Server-Side Badge**

In this exercise you'll create an HTML page for displaying your server-side badge.

1.   Create a new file called `php-badge.php` in your badge directory, with the following contents.

```
<!DOCTYPE html PUBLIC "-//W3C//DTD XHTML 1.0 Transitional//EN"
  "http://www.w3.org/TR/xhtml1/DTD/xhtml1-transitional.dtd">
<html xmlns="http://www.w3.org/1999/xhtml">
<head>
  <title>Flickr Mashups: Flickr PHP Badge</title>
  <link href="../css/main.css" rel="stylesheet" type="text/css" />
</head>
<body>

<?php include('badge.php') ?>

</body>
</html>
```

2.   Load this file into your web browser, and you should see something like Figure 5-2.

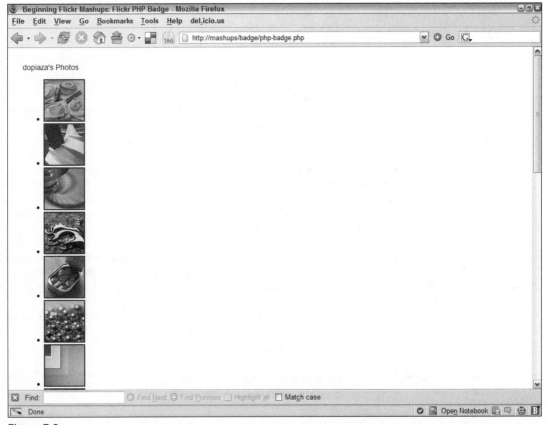

Figure 5-2

3.   Well, that's a badge of sorts, but it looks pretty ugly! Perhaps it's time to start work on the style sheet. Create a new style sheet called `badge.css` in the site's `css` directory — you can leave it empty for now, you're going to start adding style rules to it in a moment. Then modify your `php-badge.php` file to reference this new style sheet:

```
<!DOCTYPE html PUBLIC "-//W3C//DTD XHTML 1.0 Transitional//EN"
  "http://www.w3.org/TR/xhtml1/DTD/xhtml1-transitional.dtd">
<html xmlns="http://www.w3.org/1999/xhtml">
<head>
  <title>Flickr Mashups: Flickr PHP Badge</title>
  <link href="../css/main.css" rel="stylesheet" type="text/css" />
  <link href="../css/badge.css" rel="stylesheet" type="text/css" />
</head>
<body>

<?php include('badge.php') ?>

</body>
</html>
```

4.   The first thing to address is the image size — 75 pixels is just too big, something a little smaller would be much better. And that blue border around the images just has to go, so add the following to `badge.css`:

```
.badge-item img{
  border: 1px solid #333333;
  width: 48px;
  height: 48px;
}
```

5.   The next step is to remove the bullet next to each image, and to stop the images being displayed on separate lines. Add the following rule to `badge.css`:

```
.badge-item {
  display: inline;
  list-style-type: none;
}
```

By now you should have a page that looks something like Figure 5-3.

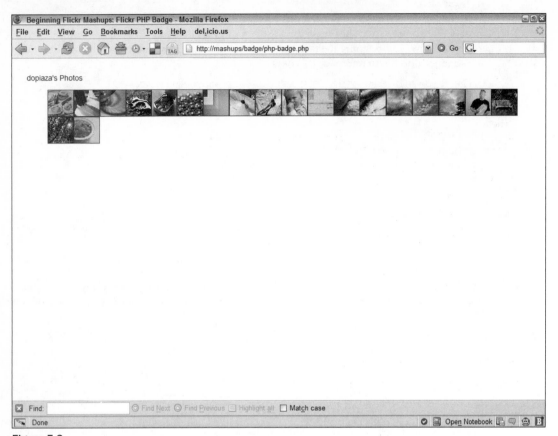

Figure 5-3

6. Now the images are in a horizontal line — it's time for a rule that arranges them into a grid. The feed for a user's photos returns 20 images, so a 2 × 10 grid would probably be suitable for a badge to run down the edge of a page. Add the following code to `badge.css`:

```
.badge-items {
  width: 100px;
  margin: 0;
  padding: 0;
}
```

7. View the `php-badge.css` page, and you should see that the badge is starting to take shape, as shown in Figure 5-4.

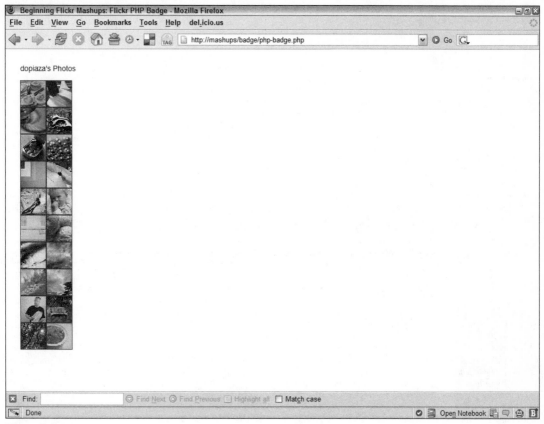

Figure 5-4

8. Now you need to tidy up the badge title a little — tweak the font size and ensure it is centered above the badge. Here's a copy of the finished `badge.css` in its entirety, with the newly added CSS rules highlighted.

```
.badge {
  width: 100px;
}
.badge-title {
  font-size: 12px;
  font-weight: 600;
  text-align: center;
}
.badge p {
  margin: 0;
  padding: 0;
}
```

```
.badge-items {
  width: 100px;
  margin: 0;
  padding: 0;
}
.badge-item {
  display: inline;
  list-style-type: none;
}
.badge-item img{
  border: 1px solid #333333;
  width: 48px;
  height: 48px;
}
```

9.   Update your `badge.css` and reload `php-badge.php` in your browser. You will see the finished badge in all its glory — it should appear as in Figure 5-5.

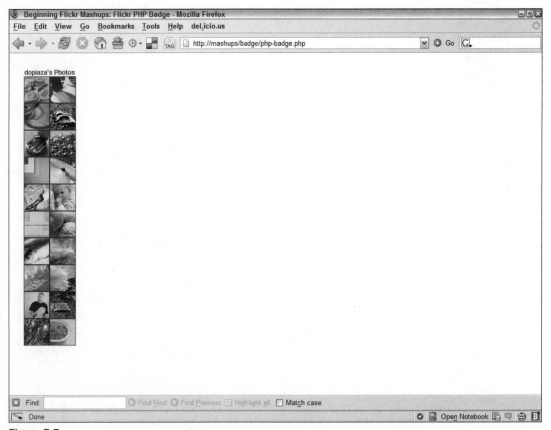

Figure 5-5

How It Works

You added a number of separate CSS rules to your `badge.css` file in this exercise, each of which refined the appearance of the badge a bit more. I'll go over what those rules did here.

```
.badge-item img{
   border: 1px solid #333333;
   width: 48px;
   height: 48px;
}
```

This CSS rule says that for all `<img>` elements contained within an element that has a class of `badge-item`, the image width and height should be reduced to 48 pixels, and the border set as a dark gray one-pixel line.

The next rule removes the bullets, and displays the images on one line:

```
.badge-item {
   display: inline;
   list-style-type: none;
}
```

This rule sets the `list-style-type` to `none` — which effectively means that no bullet is displayed alongside the list item. It also sets the display mode to `inline`, which means there is no forced line break after each element.

The next thing you did was add a rule to display the images in a 2 × 10 grid. After resizing, each image is now 48 pixels wide and has a one-pixel border on each of its sides. That means that each image occupies a total of 1 + 48 + 1, or 50, pixels on each side. So a 2 × 10 grid of images will be 100 pixels wide. The images sit within a `<ul>` element that has a class of `badge-items`, so the width of this element can be forced to be 100 pixels with this rule:

```
.badge-items {
   width: 100px;
   margin: 0;
   padding: 0;
}
```

The `margin` and `padding` tags are there to override the browser default settings for lists and force these values to zero.

The final rule adjusts the font size and ensures that it is centered above the badge:

```
.badge {
   width: 100px;
}
.badge-title {
   font-size: 12px;
   font-weight: 600;
   text-align: center;
}
.badge p {
   margin: 0;
   padding: 0;
}
```

A Client-Side Badge Using JavaScript

Now that you've built a Flickr badge, let's look at an alternative approach. The previous example used PHP on the server to construct the HTML for the badge — in this example, you'll build an identical badge, but using JavaScript to generate the HTML in the browser. You might want to create your badge on the client rather than the server for a number of reasons. Most importantly, you may want to host the badge somewhere that doesn't support PHP, or you may simply wish to reduce the amount of work your server has to do. Of course, for such a badge to work, the user's browser must provide support for JavaScript. All major browsers do support JavaScript, but the user can elect to disable it — your badge would remain hidden from anybody who does this.

With a client-side badge, the user's browser requests a copy of the web page from the web server. The browser then executes the JavaScript contained within the page and sends a second request, this time to Flickr, to retrieve the Flickr feed. The JavaScript running within the browser then processes the feed and generates the appropriate HTML. The flow of information is shown in Figure 5-6.

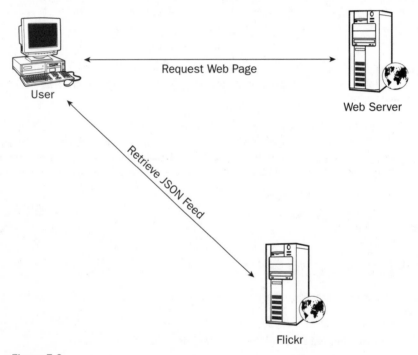

Figure 5-6

If a user looks at your web page multiple times, the JavaScript to create the badge is likely to be held in the browser's cache and so will not need to be retrieved from the server each time, resulting in lower bandwidth use between the user's machine and your server. This advantage, however, is balanced by the fact that the user's machine must then itself retrieve a copy of the feed from Flickr.

The goal here is to build identical HTML to that generated by the PHP badge, but to do it in JavaScript. If you look at the list of feed formats outlined earlier, you will see that there is a JSON feed. JSON (JavaScript Object Notation) is ideally suited to JavaScript applications. In fact, rather like the PHP feed, it generates a block of JavaScript code to be executed within the browser:

```
jsonFlickrFeed({
    ...
})
```

Try It Out   Creating the Client-Side Badge

Whereas the PHP feed initialized a `$feed` variable, the JSON feed calls a JavaScript function called `jsonFlickrFeed()`, which takes a single argument — a JavaScript object representing the feed. To process the feed, you need to define a JavaScript function, `jsonFlickrFeed()`, in your document.

1.   Create a new file called `badge.js` within your `badge` directory:

```
function jsonFlickrFeed(feed)
{
  var imgPattern = /(http:\/\/static.flickr.com\/\d+\/\d+_[0-9a-z]+)_m\.jpg/;
  var s = "";

  s += '<div class="badge">';
  s += '<p class="badge-title"><a href="' + feed['link'] + '">' + feed['title']
      + '</a></p>';
  s += '<ul class="badge-items">';

  var items = feed['items'];
  for (var i = 0; i < items.length; i++)
  {
    var result = imgPattern.exec(items[i]['description']);

    if (result != null)
    {
      var image = result[1] + '_s.jpg';
      s += '<li class="badge-item"><a href="' + items[i]['link'] + '"><img src="'
          + image + '" /></a></li>';
    }
  }

  s += '</ul></div>';

  document.writeln(s);
}
```

How It Works

Apart from the obvious syntactical differences, the code here is almost identical to that in the PHP version from earlier. The HTML is built up in a variable called `s`, and then `document.writeln(s)` is called at the end to output the HTML into the document.

The most significant difference is in the naming of some of the fields. In the PHP feed, you accessed the link to the photostream and photo pages though a field in the associative array called `url`. The equivalent field in the JavaScript object is `link`. A number of inconsistencies like this are scattered throughout the feeds — whenever you are using a feed, always look at its output yourself to be sure you are accessing it correctly.

Now that you've created the badge, you need to create a page with which to display it.

Displaying the Client-Side Badge

In this exercise, you'll create an HTML page to display your client-side badge.

1.   Create an HTML page, `javascript-badge.html`, in the `badge` directory.

```
<!DOCTYPE html PUBLIC "-//W3C//DTD XHTML 1.0 Transitional//EN"
  "http://www.w3.org/TR/xhtml1/DTD/xhtml1-transitional.dtd">
<html xmlns="http://www.w3.org/1999/xhtml">
<head>
  <title>Flickr Mashups: Javascript Badge</title>
  <link href="../css/main.css" rel="stylesheet" type="text/css" />
  <link href="../css/badge.css" rel="stylesheet" type="text/css" />
</head>
<body>

<script src="badge.js" type="text/javascript"></script>
<script
src="http://api.flickr.com/services/feeds/photos_public.gne?id=50317659@N00&format=
json" type="text/javascript"></script>

</body>
</html>
```

How It Works

The HTML simply includes two JavaScript files. `badge.js` is included first to ensure that the JavaScript function `jsonFlickrFeed` is defined. Then the Flickr feed itself is included — remember, the format of the JSON Flickr feed is a line of ready-to-execute JavaScript that calls the `jsonFlickrFeed` function.

When you view the `javascript-badge.html` file in your browser, you should see the badge displayed — in fact it should be identical to the badge displayed by the PHP version of the script in Figure 5-5.

Summary

In this chapter, you have learned about the different feeds available at Flickr, and also the different feed formats available. You have seen how to request the content of a feed via your web browser, fetch a PHP feed into a PHP script, fetch a JSON feed into a JavaScript script, and format the content of a feed into an HTML badge.

In the next chapter you will see how to use the Flickr API to do things that can't be achieved with the standard feeds available from Flickr. Before moving on to that, however, try customizing your Flickr badge further with the following exercises.

Exercises

1. The Flickr badge built in this chapter lays out the images in a 2 × 10 grid, which is fine for positioning down the edge of a page. In other contexts, a wider grid might be more appropriate. Change the CSS for the badge to display images in a 5 × 4 grid.

2. There are Flickr feeds available for group pools as well as individuals' photostreams. Modify the Flickr badge code to display pictures from the Utata group pool. You can find the Utata group at `http://www.flickr.com/groups/utata/` and its NSID is 81474450@N00.

6

Remixing Flickr
Using the API

In the previous chapter you used various Flickr feeds to generate a customized view of some of the photos on Flickr. Feeds are somewhat limited, though — you can get only certain sets of photos and you have limited metadata about the photos. If you want to build something a little more sophisticated, you need to use the Flickr API.

In this chapter, you will use the Flickr API to build a gallery web site displaying a selection of your recent photos. You will also see how to use the API to find images in your photostream and to display them as dynamically generated sets.

The Basics: A Simple Photo Gallery

Along with many other Flickr remixes, the photo gallery application has a fairly straightforward architecture. All page requests by the end user are sent to the web server. The web server retrieves information from Flickr to help build the requested page, and then returns the finished page to the user. The photos themselves reside on Flickr's servers and are retrieved directly from there by the client browser. The information flow is shown in Figure 6-1.

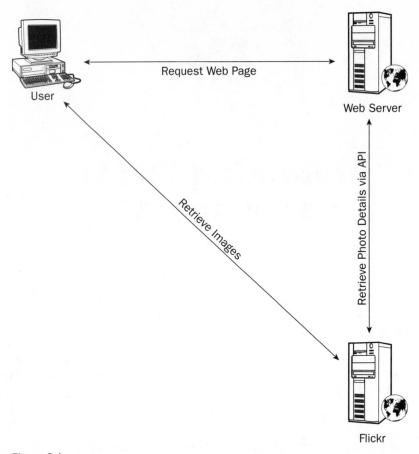

Figure 6-1

Setting Things Up

In Chapter 4 you were introduced to the idea of using an API kit. Most applications built around Flickr use one or another of the popular API kits to take care of the rather tedious business of constructing request messages and parsing responses — you could, of course, always do everything from first princi- ples, but there is little point in reinventing the wheel. In this and later chapters, you will be using the phpFlickr library created by Dan Coulter. PhpFlickr is distributed under the GNU General Public License (GPL) and can be downloaded from SourceForge at `http://sourceforge.net/projects/phpflickr`, whereas the main phpFlickr web site is at `http://www.phpflickr.com/`.

Installation is very straightforward — simply download the latest version and unpack it into your site `lib` directory. The created directory will probably contain the version number (for example, `phpFlickr-1.6.1`) — if it does, rename it to just `phpFlickr`.

As this book was being prepared, version 2 of phpFlickr was released. This version works in a slightly different way from the 1.x releases and does not provide backwards compatibility. To work with the examples in this book, you should download a 1.*x* version of phpFlickr — the latest version at the time of writing is 1.6.1, and the 1.*x* versions are all available for download from SourceForge alongside the version 2 release.

Try It Out   **Using phpFlickr**

Using phpFlickr to talk to Flickr is very simple, as you'll see in this exercise.

1.   Create a new directory for this project called `gallery`, and within that create a new file called `6-1.php` with the following contents — be sure to replace the text `YOUR-API-KEY` with your actual Flickr API key.

```php
<?php

include (dirname(__FILE__) . '/../lib/phpFlickr/phpFlickr.php');

$nsid = '50317659@N00';
$flickr = new phpFlickr('YOUR-API-KEY', NULL, false);

$args = array(
  'user_id' => $nsid,
  'sort' => 'date-posted-desc',
  'page' => 1,
  'per_page' => 5
);

$p = $flickr->photos_search($args);

if ($flickr->getErrorCode())
{
  echo ("Error fetching photos: " . $flickr->getErrorMsg());
}

echo "<pre>\n";
print_r($p);
echo "</pre>\n";
?>
```

2.   When you've done that, point your browser at the `6-1.php` file and you should see something like the following:

```
Array
(
    [_name] => photos
    [_attributes] => Array
        (
            [page] => 1
            [pages] => 478
            [perpage] => 5
            [total] => 2389
        )

    [_value] =>
    [page] => 1
```

```
[pages] => 478
[perpage] => 5
[total] => 2389
[photo] => Array
    (
        [0] => Array
            (
                [_name] => photo
                [_attributes] => Array
                    (
                        [id] => 191649377
                        [owner] => 50317659@N00
                        [secret] => 0d3e1a54ed
                        [server] => 61
                        [title] => Door
                        [ispublic] => 1
                        [isfriend] => 0
                        [isfamily] => 0
                    )

                [_value] =>
                [id] => 191649377
                [owner] => 50317659@N00
                [secret] => 0d3e1a54ed
                [server] => 61
                [title] => Door
                [ispublic] => 1
                [isfriend] => 0
                [isfamily] => 0
            )


...

)
```

3. The PHP object displayed contains a list of the most recent photos in my photostream. If you want to try this out on your own photostream, simply enter your own NSID in the PHP file:

```
$nsid = '50317659@N00';   // <-- put your NSID here
```

How It Works

The first line of the PHP script is an `include` statement that sets up the phpFlickr library. Next, an instance of a `phpFlickr` object is created:

```
$flickr = new phpFlickr('YOUR-API-KEY', NULL, false);
```

The first parameter is your Flickr API key. The second parameter is only used when you need to make authenticated calls. You will learn more about this in Chapter 7; for now, you can just leave that as `NULL`. The third parameter is a Boolean that tells phpFlickr whether to abort if it receives an error response from the Flickr API. This parameter is set to `false` here, as the script explicitly checks for an error code. If you prefer, you can set it to `true`, in which case, if the Flickr API returns an error response at any time, phpFlickr will print out an error message and the script will terminate immediately.

Next, the script needs to make a call to the Flickr API method `flickr.photos.search`. Most phpFlickr methods take a list of parameters, but the number of parameters taken by the `flickr.photos.search` method is so large that an associative array is used instead. Whereas an ordinary array uses numeric indices, an associative array enables you to use a string as the index.

```
$args = array(
  'user_id' => $nsid,
  'sort' => 'date-posted-desc',
  'page' => 1,
  'per_page' => 5
);
```

The `$args` array now holds the values for all the different parameters you need to pass into the `flickr.photos.search` method. In the array initialization shown here, the value on the left-hand side of each arrow symbol (=>) is the array *key*—the value used as the index in the array. The value on the right-hand side is the value stored against that key. So in our `$args` array, the `per_page` parameter, for example, is stored at `$args['per_page']` and takes the value 5.

The parameters set up here request the five most recent photos from the user with the specified NSID, sorted in descending order of the date they were posted to Flickr.

Next, the phpFlickr method `photos_search` is called.

```
$p = $flickr->photos_search($args);
```

Every method in the Flickr API has a corresponding method in the phpFlickr library. The phpFlickr method names follow the same naming convention as the Flickr API method names—for each API method, the corresponding phpFlickr method is similar, but with no `flickr.` prefix and underscores in place of any remaining dots.

The code then checks for an error response and finally prints out the object returned by the `photos_search()` method.

```
echo "<pre>\n";
print_r($p);
echo "</pre>\n";
```

The output is wrapped in a `<pre>` element to preserve formatting.

If you look at the output from the `print_r` method, you will see that the returned object is an array that maps directly onto the XML response from the `flickr.photos.search` method. Using the API Explorer with the same parameters gives the following XML:

```
<?xml version="1.0" encoding="utf-8" ?>
<rsp stat="ok">
  <photos page="1" pages="478" perpage="5" total="2389">
    photo id="191649377" owner="50317659@N00" secret="0d3e1a54ed" server="61"
title="Door" ispublic="1" isfriend="0" isfamily="0" />
    <photo id="189531316" owner="50317659@N00" secret="b123455c1b" server="61"
title="I Win" ispublic="1" isfriend="0" isfamily="0" />
    <photo id="189362479" owner="50317659@N00" secret="3f4ba7e6f7" server="78"
```

```
        title="Handwriting Meme" ispublic="1" isfriend="0" isfamily="0" />
            <photo id="188749900" owner="50317659@N00" secret="fc4f38b67d" server="73"
        title="Cheese and Onion Crackers" ispublic="1" isfriend="0" isfamily="0" />
            <photo id="194257908" owner="50317659@N00" secret="544ab536df" server="60"
        title="Chicken and Fennel Risotto" ispublic="1" isfriend="0" isfamily="0" />
        </photos>
    </rsp>
```

PhpFlickr simply takes the body of the `<rsp>` element in the Flickr response and copies the XML structure directly into the PHP data structure. For each element in the XML document, _name, _value, and _attributes array elements are created. _name contains the name of the node, _attributes is another associative array containing the element's attributes, and for text nodes, _value contains the value of the element — for non-text nodes, _value is left blank. So for the top-level `<photos>` element in the response you just saw, the following PHP data are created:

```
Array
(
    [_name] => photos
    [_attributes] => Array
        (
            [page] => 1
            [pages] => 478
            [perpage] => 5
            [total] => 2389
        )

    [_value] =>
)
```

So, to access the `total` attribute in the array, you would write the following code:

```
// $p is the name of the array returned by phpFlickr
$total = $p['_attributes']['total'];
```

As a convenience, phpFlickr copies these attributes up to the array for the element itself, so the PHP array then looks like this:

```
Array
(
    [_name] => photos
    [_attributes] => Array
        (
            [page] => 1
            [pages] => 478
            [perpage] => 5
            [total] => 2389
        )

    [_value] =>
    [page] => 1
    [pages] => 478
    [perpage] => 5
    [total] => 2389
)
```

This then means that your code to access the total attribute is simplified to this:

```
$total = $p['total'];
```

Finally, a new array is created for each of the child elements and the process repeated. This example features a list of photo elements, so a new array is created for the photo element list, each member of which is itself an array, containing details of that particular photo element:

```
Array
(
    [_name] => photos
    [_attributes] => Array
        (
            [page] => 1
            [pages] => 478
            [perpage] => 5
            [total] => 2389
        )

    [_value] =>
    [page] => 1
    [pages] => 478
    [perpage] => 5
    [total] => 2389
    [photo] => Array
        (
            [0] => Array
                (
                    [_name] => photo
                    [_attributes] => Array
                        (
                            [id] => 191649377
                            [owner] => 50317659@N00
                            [secret] => 0d3e1a54ed
                            [server] => 61
                            [title] => Door
                            [ispublic] => 1
                            [isfriend] => 0
                            [isfamily] => 0
                        )

                    [_value] =>
                    [id] => 191649377
                    [owner] => 50317659@N00
                    [secret] => 0d3e1a54ed
                    [server] => 61
                    [title] => Door
                    [ispublic] => 1
                    [isfriend] => 0
                    [isfamily] => 0
                )

        ...

)
```

If you are ever unsure about the structure being returned from a phpFlickr method, using `print_r` is a quick and easy way to inspect it to understand how to access the different elements.

Displaying the Photos

As you've just seen, it's very easy to embed a little PHP code into a web page to retrieve photo details from Flickr using phpFlickr. Next you'll see how to make use of the data structures returned and turn them into HTML to display your photos. Throughout this and later chapters, you'll be working a lot with the code you're writing here, so it's also time to start imposing a little structure and organization.

Try It Out Creating Your Photo Gallery

It's time to start building your photo gallery. By the time you've finished, a number of web pages will be involved in displaying the different parts of the gallery, so rather than duplicate code in each of those pages, a good place to start with a project like this is to build up a library of code that can be reused.

1. The first step is to build a PHP class to handle most of the work. Create a new file called `FlickrGallery.php` and put it in the site's `lib` directory:

```php
<?php

class FlickrGallery
{
  var $flickr;
  var $nsid = '50317659@N00';

  function FlickrGallery()
  {
    global $flickrApiKey;
    global $flickrApiSecret;

    $this->flickr = new phpFlickr($flickrApiKey, $flickrApiSecret, false);
  }

  function findRecentPhotos($n = 20)
  {
    $args = array(
    'user_id' => $this->nsid,
    'sort' => 'date-posted-desc',
    'page' => 1,
    'per_page' => $n
    );

    $p = $this->flickr->photos_search($args);
    if ($this->flickr->getErrorCode())
    {
      echo ("Error fetching photos: " . $this->flickr->getErrorMsg());
    }

    return $p['photo'];
  }
}

?>
```

2.   Create a file called `apikey.php` in the site's `lib` directory, replacing the text YOUR-API-KEY with your actual Flickr API key:

```php
<?php

$flickrApiKey = 'YOUR-API-KEY';
$flickrApiSecret = NULL;

?>
```

You might notice that we've given this file a name that is all lowercase, whereas the previous file, `FlickrGallery.php`, was mixed-case. We're using the convention that files that contain PHP classes are named after the class they contain—and the usual convention is that class names are mixed-case with an initial capital letter. You are, of course, free to use any naming convention you like, but sticking to a common and consistent system like this makes it much easier to follow the structure of the code.

3.   Next, create a new file, `gallery.php`, in the site's `lib` directory:

```php
<?php

require_once(dirname(__FILE__) . '/apikey.php');
require_once(dirname(__FILE__) . '/phpFlickr/phpFlickr.php');
require_once(dirname(__FILE__) . '/FlickrGallery.php');

header("Content-Type: text/html; charset=utf-8");

?>
```

4.   Now for the HTML page. Create a new file called `index.php` in your `gallery` directory:

```php
<?php include (dirname(__FILE__) . '/../lib/gallery.php') ?>
<!DOCTYPE html PUBLIC "-//W3C//DTD XHTML 1.0 Transitional//EN"
  "http://www.w3.org/TR/xhtml1/DTD/xhtml1-transitional.dtd">
<html xmlns="http://www.w3.org/1999/xhtml">
<head>
  <title>Flickr Gallery</title>
  <link href="../css/main.css" rel="stylesheet" type="text/css" />
</head>
<body>
<?php
  $gallery = new FlickrGallery();
?>
  <ul class="photo-set">
  <?php
    $recentPhotos = $gallery->findRecentPhotos();
    foreach ($recentPhotos as $photo)
    {
      $title = htmlentities($photo['title']);
      $img = 'http://static.flickr.com/' . $photo['server'] . '/' . $photo['id']
        . '_' . $photo['secret'] . '_s.jpg'
?>
    <li><img src="<?php echo $img ?>" alt="<?php echo $title ?>" title="<?php echo
$title ?>" /></li>
  <?php
```

```
        }
    ?>
        </ul>
    </body>
    </html>
```

5. If you look at the `index.php` page in your browser, you'll see something that looks like Figure 6-2.

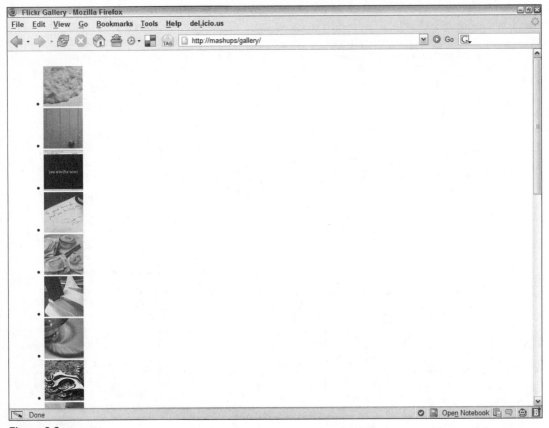

Figure 6-2

How It Works

As I mentioned earlier, the first thing you did was build a PHP class. The `FlickrGallery` class takes the code that you used in the earlier example and wraps it up into a PHP class. The class provides a constructor and a single method — `findRecentPhotos()` — that calls phpFlickr's `photos_search` method to retrieve a list of photos. The `$n` parameter specifies how many photos are to be returned and its default value is `20`. The return value is the `photo` array.

Every time you access Flickr, you need to use your API key. To eliminate the need to have this sit around in many different files, you can create a single file defining your key that can be included in any files that need to refer to it. That's why you created the file `apikey.php`. This file defines two global variables containing your Flickr API key and your API secret. Don't worry about the API secret; that will be explained in Chapter 7 — for now it is just a placeholder.

The file `gallery.php` that you created just gathers together the `require` statements for different files needed into one place, so that when you come to create the HTML file they can all be included easily. It also ensures that the content-type header returned with the page has the character encoding set to UTF-8. Remember that all messages sent back from Flickr are encoded as UTF-8 and that if you want any special characters to display correctly, you must tell the browser which character encoding is being used.

Finally, the PHP to generate the HTML is very straightforward — it instantiates a new `FlickrGallery` object and calls `findRecentPhotos()`. It then loops through each photo returned, creating a list as it goes.

Each list item generated contains an image — in this case the square version. The `alt` and `title` attributes are set so that in most browsers, you will see the photo title appear as a tooltip if you place the mouse cursor over the image.

```
<li><img src="<?php echo $img ?>" alt="<?php echo $title ?>" title="<?php echo
$title ?>" /></li>
```

Now it's time for some CSS.

Styling the Results

Although the gallery you have works now, it doesn't necessarily look very good. The next thing for you to do is add to your site a CSS file that contains some style directives to improve the appearance of your gallery.

Try It Out   **Styling the Photo Gallery**

In this exercise, you're going to add the CSS directives that style the gallery properly.

1. Create a new file, `gallery.css`, in the site `css` directory:

```css
.photo-set {
  list-style-type: none;
  width: 655px;
  margin: 2em 0 0 60px;
  padding: 0;
}
.photo-set li {
  float: left;
  width: 131px;
  text-align: center;
  margin-bottom: 1em;
}
.photo-set img {
  margin: 20px 20px 5px 20px;
  padding: 5px;
  border: 3px solid #EEEEEE;
}
```

2. Then update the gallery `index.php` file to reference this style sheet:

```
<?php include (dirname(__FILE__) . '/../lib/gallery.php') ?>
<!DOCTYPE html PUBLIC "-//W3C//DTD XHTML 1.0 Transitional//EN"
   "http://www.w3.org/TR/xhtml1/DTD/xhtml1-transitional.dtd">
<html xmlns="http://www.w3.org/1999/xhtml">
<head>
  <title>Flickr Gallery</title>
  <link href="../css/main.css" rel="stylesheet" type="text/css" />
  <link href="../css/gallery.css" rel="stylesheet" type="text/css" />
</head>
<body>

  ...

</body>
</html>
```

3. With the style sheet added, you now have something that looks like Figure 6-3.

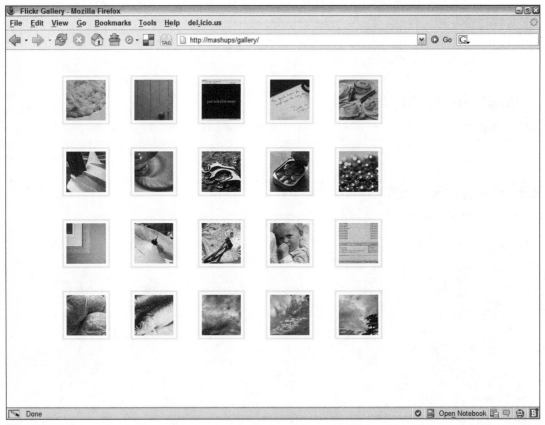

Figure 6-3

How It Works

The style sheet sets margins, padding and borders for the main elements in the gallery, as you saw done in the Flickr badge in Chapter 5.

Each square image retrieved from Flickr is 75 × 75 pixels. The style sheet defines a left and right margin of 20 pixels, a border of three pixels and padding of five pixels. That means that the on-screen width of each image is 20 + 3 + 5 + 75 + 5 + 3 + 20, or 131 pixels. By setting the photo set width to 655 pixels, you can display them in a five-wide grid.

The Photo Page

Now it's time to start using another bit of the Flickr API, the method `flickr.photos.getInfo`, which will enable you to find out a little more about a photo.

Try It Out   Creating the Photo Page

It's all very well displaying a set of thumbnails, but you need to be able to see the full-size image too. Next you will add a page to display a larger version of the photo, together with some other information obtained from Flickr.

1.   Add a new method to the `FlickrGallery.php` file:

```php
<?php

class FlickrGallery
{

    ...

    function getPhotoInfo($id)
    {
      $p = $this->flickr->photos_getInfo($id);
      if ($this->flickr->getErrorCode())
      {
        echo ("Error getting photo info: " . $this->flickr->getErrorMsg());
      }

      return $p;
    }

}

?>
```

2. Create a page called `photo.php` in your `gallery` directory:

```php
<?php include (dirname(__FILE__) . '/../lib/gallery.php') ?>
<!DOCTYPE html PUBLIC "-//W3C//DTD XHTML 1.0 Transitional//EN"
  "http://www.w3.org/TR/xhtml1/DTD/xhtml1-transitional.dtd">
<html xmlns="http://www.w3.org/1999/xhtml">
<head>
  <title>Flickr Gallery</title>
  <link href="../css/main.css" rel="stylesheet" type="text/css" />
  <link href="../css/gallery.css" rel="stylesheet" type="text/css" />
</head>
<body>
<?php
  $gallery = new FlickrGallery();
  $id = $_REQUEST['id'];
  if (!empty($id))
  {
    $info = $gallery->getPhotoInfo($id);
    $title = $info['title'];
    $img = 'http://static.flickr.com/' . $info['server'] . '/' . $info['id']
      . '_' . $info['secret'] . '.jpg';
    $photoPage = 'http://www.flickr.com/photos/' . $info['owner']['nsid'] . '/'
      . $id . '/';
  }
?>

  <div class="photo-display">
    <p class="photo-title"><?php echo $title ?></p>
    <p class="photo-image"><a href="<?php echo $photoPage ?>"><img src="<?php echo
$img ?>" alt="<?php echo $title ?>" title="<?php echo $title ?>" /></a></p>
  </div>
</body>
</html>
```

3. Make some additions to the `gallery.css` style sheet to lay out the photo page:

```css
.photo-display {
    width: 530px;
    margin: 2em 0 0 60px;
    padding: 0;
    text-align: center;
}
.photo-display .photo-title {
    font-size: large;
    font-weight: bold;
    text-align: center;
}
.photo-display .photo-image img {
    margin: 0;
    padding: 5px;
    border: 3px solid #EEEEEE;
}
```

4. Modify the gallery `index.php` so that the thumbnail images link to the photo page:

```php
<?php include (dirname(__FILE__) . '/../lib/gallery.php') ?>
<!DOCTYPE html PUBLIC "-//W3C//DTD XHTML 1.0 Transitional//EN"
"http://www.w3.org/TR/xhtml1/DTD/xhtml1-transitional.dtd">
<html xmlns="http://www.w3.org/1999/xhtml">
<head>
<meta http-equiv="Content-Type" content="text/html; charset=iso-8859-1" />
<title>Flickr Gallery</title>
<link href="../css/main.css" rel="stylesheet" type="text/css" />
<link href="../css/gallery.css" rel="stylesheet" type="text/css" />
</head>
<body>
<?php
  $gallery = new FlickrGallery();
?>
  <ul class="photo-set">
  <?php
    $recentPhotos = $gallery->findRecentPhotos();
    foreach ($recentPhotos as $photo)
    {
      $title = $photo['title'];
      $img = 'http://static.flickr.com/' . $photo['server'] . '/' . $photo['id']
        . '_' . $photo['secret'] . '_s.jpg'
?>
    <li><a href="photo.php?id=<?php echo $photo['id'] ?>"><img src="<?php echo $img
?>" alt="<?php echo $title ?>" title="<?php echo $title ?>" /></a></li>
  <?php
    }
?>
  </ul>
</body>
</html>
```

5. Open this `index.php` page in your browser and click one of the thumbnails — you should see the photo page looking something like Figure 6-4.

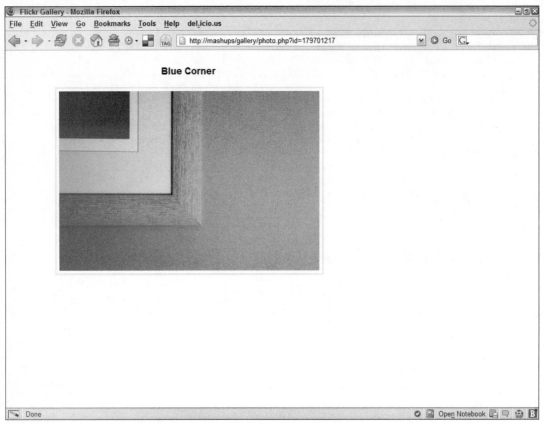

Figure 6-4

How It Works

The new method you added to `FlickrGallery.php`, called `getPhotoInfo()`, calls the phpFlickr method `photos_getInfo()`, which in turn calls the Flickr `flickr.photos.getInfo` method for the specified photo. `photos_getInfo()` takes a single parameter here, the ID of the photo being requested. The parameters for phpFlickr methods are usually clear if you look at the Flickr API documentation, but if you are in doubt, or need to check, just look at the `phpFlickr.php` file itself and search for the method name — you will then see the list of parameters required.

Each thumbnail shown on the index page is now a link to a new `photo.php` page. This page starts off by getting the `id` parameter from the HTTP request — this is the photo ID of the photo to be displayed. The photo info is then retrieved and the photo displayed. The photo itself is enclosed in an `<a>` tag so that it is a hyperlink back to the Flickr page for that photo — remember, Flickr's terms of use require you to include a link back to the Flickr photo page when you display an image like this.

A few new classes are defined in `gallery.css` to make the `photo.php` look presentable. The photo display area is sized to 530 pixels wide, and the contents centered. The font for the photo title is defined and a gray border drawn around the photo.

Using AJAX

It would be nice to display more information on the photo page, such as the photo description or tags, but the photo page as it stands now is relatively uncluttered without too much extraneous information to detract from the image. You could simply link to another page containing the photo description, but that's a rather clunky approach. A better way to include more information would be to add a More info link at the bottom of the photo and have the description appear below the photo when the link is clicked.

AJAX, or Asynchronous JavaScript and XML, enables you to request another document from the web server behind the scenes (asynchronously) — in other words, without reloading the page. You can then modify the contents of the page being displayed using standard dynamic HTML techniques. It is a very popular technique for displaying information in situations like this, and one that Flickr uses extensively on its own web site. The main problem with this approach is coping with the huge number of differences among the wide variety of browsers in use. All modern browsers support AJAX in one form or another, but the way in which they do this varies from browser to browser.

Rather than spend time here dealing with the never-ending complexities of cross-browser compatibility, we will turn to the Internet. With the current popularity of AJAX, a number of AJAX toolkits have appeared to simplify the creation of AJAX applications — using an established library can drastically reduce your application development time and help avoid many sleepless nights.

The prototype.js library

A very popular toolkit is the Prototype library by Sam Stephenson. It's completely free to use and can be downloaded from `http://prototype.conio.net/`. It is a JavaScript framework that is intended to make the development of dynamic web applications easier and is described as "quickly becoming the codebase of choice for web application developers everywhere."

Download the `prototype.js` file and create a `js` directory for it within your site `lib` directory — the package you download will contain a number of files, but you only need `prototype.js` for this example. The `prototype.js` file is around 40K in size, so it may increase the load time for your application a little. This is a one-time cost, however, as web browsers will typically only load the file the first time and will use a cached copy for subsequent accesses to the page.

Documentation for the prototype library can be found at `http://wiki.script.aculo.us/scriptaculous/show/Prototype`

Try It Out   **Using the prototype.js Library**

The first step to building the AJAX enhancement to the gallery is to generate the new information to be displayed. A common method for doing this, and one that will be adopted here, is to generate an HTML fragment that can simply be dropped into place at the appropriate point in the document.

  1.   Create a new file, `info.php`, in the `gallery` directory:

```php
<?php

include (dirname(__FILE__) . '/../lib/gallery.php');

function decodeHTML($text)
{
```

```php
    $s = str_replace("&lt;", "<", $text);
    $s = str_replace("&gt;", ">", $s);
    $s = str_replace("&quot;", "\"", $s);
    $s = str_replace("&amp;", "&", $s);

    return $s;
}

$gallery = new FlickrGallery();
$id = $_REQUEST['id'];
if (!empty($id))
{
    $info = $gallery->getPhotoInfo($id);
    $description = nl2br(decodeHTML($info['description']));
    $tags = $info['tags']['tag'];

?>
<div class="photo-info">
    <div class="photo-description"><?php echo $description ?></div>
    <ul class="photo-tags">
<?php
    if (!empty($tags))
    {
        foreach ($tags as $tag)
        {
?>
        <li><?php echo $tag['raw'] ?></li>
<?php
        }
    }
?>
    </ul>
</div>
<?php
}
?>
```

2. This page isn't designed to be viewed directly, but to test it out, you can try out this PHP script via your web browser — just enter the URL for the page and append the ID of the photo you wish to view. The actual URL will depend on how you have set up your web server, but should look something like this:

```
http://localhost/gallery/info.php?id=185608819
```

where 185608819 is the ID of the photo being viewed. If you view the source of the resulting page, you will see the following:

```
<div class="photo-info">
    <div class="photo-description">For <a
href="http://www.flickr.com/groups/projectinsight/">projectinsight</a><br />
<br />
Theme: liquid<br />
```

```
<br />
[DSC_2451]</div>
  <ul class="photo-tags">
    <li>black</li>
    <li>liquid</li>
    <li>water</li>
    <li>slate</li>
    <li>projectinsight</li>
  </ul>
</div>
```

The HTML here isn't a complete page — just the fragment of HTML that is to be displayed within the context of the existing photo page.

3. The next step is to create a JavaScript function to request the HTML fragment from `info.php`. Create a new file called `gallery.js` in your site `lib/js` directory:

```
function displayInfo(id)
{
  var s = 'id=' + id;

  new Ajax.Request('info.php',
  {
    parameters: s,
    method: "post",
    onSuccess:function(response)
    {
      var node = $('photo-info-' + id);
      node.innerHTML = response.responseText;
    },
    onFailure:function(response)
    {
      alert('Error: ' + response.status + ' ' + response.statusText);
    }
  });
}
```

4. The `photo.php` page needs updating to include the More info link. Modify `photo.php` as follows:

```
<?php include (dirname(__FILE__) . '/../lib/gallery.php') ?>
<!DOCTYPE html PUBLIC "-//W3C//DTD XHTML 1.0 Transitional//EN"
"http://www.w3.org/TR/xhtml1/DTD/xhtml1-transitional.dtd">
<html xmlns="http://www.w3.org/1999/xhtml">
<head>
  <title>Flickr Gallery</title>
  <link href="../css/main.css" rel="stylesheet" type="text/css" />
  <link href="../css/gallery.css" rel="stylesheet" type="text/css" />
  <script type="text/javascript" src="../lib/js/prototype.js"></script>
  <script type="text/javascript" src="../lib/js/gallery.js"></script>
</head>
<body>
<?php
```

```php
   $gallery = new FlickrGallery();
   $id = $_REQUEST['id'];
   if (!empty($id))
   {
     $info = $gallery->getPhotoInfo($id);
     $title = $info['title'];
     $img = 'http://static.flickr.com/' . $info['server'] . '/' . $info['id']
       . '_' . $info['secret'] . '.jpg';
     $photoPage = 'http://www.flickr.com/photos/' . $info['owner']['nsid'] . '/'
       . $id . '/';
   }
?>

   <div class="photo-display">
     <p class="photo-title"><?php echo $title ?></p>
     <p class="photo-image"><a href="<?php echo $photoPage ?>"><img src="<?php echo
$img ?>" alt="<?php echo $title ?>" title="<?php echo $title ?>" /></a></p>
     <div id="photo-info-<?php echo $id ?>" class="photo-more"><a href="#"
onclick="displayInfo(<?php echo $id ?>); return false;">More info...</a></div>
   </div>
</body>
</html>
```

5. Finally, some CSS styles to add to `gallery.css`:

```css
.photo-info {
  width: 530px;
  text-align: left;
  margin-top: 1em;
}
.photo-info .photo-description {
  width: 530px;
  margin: 0;
}
ul.photo-tags {
  margin: 2em 0 0 0;
  background-color: #EEEEEE;
}
ul.photo-tags li {
  display: inline;
  margin: .5em 1em 0 0;
}
```

6. Now look at the gallery in your browser and navigate to a photo page. You will see a More info link under the photo, which, when you click in it, will show you something like Figure 6-5.

Figure 6-5

How It Works

In `info.php`, notice that the photo description may contain HTML, but the description as returned by phpFlickr has the characters `<`, `>`, `&` and `"` represented as the entities `&lt;`, `&gt;`, `&amp;`, and `&quot;` respectively. These are converted back to the appropriate characters before the description is displayed.

The JavaScript function `gallery.js` is called when the user clicks the More info link on the photo page. It creates an instance of the `Ajax.Request` object from the Prototype library. The `Ajax.Request` object acts as a wrapper around the variety of browser-specific ways to send an asynchronous HTTP request.

The `Ajax.Request` constructor is very straightforward. The first parameter is the page to which the request is being sent, the second is an object defining the details of the request. Here, it contains the parameters being sent and the method type to be used (usually `POST` or `GET`). Two event handlers are defined, to be called either on successful completion or on failure.

The onSuccess handler function uses another method defined in the Prototype library — $(). This is used to find an element with the document, given its ID. It is essentially shorthand for document .getElementById(). The handler function looks for a node in the original document with the id photo-info-ID, where ID is the photo ID, and replaces the contents of that node with the block of HTML received from the call to info.php.

The More info link on the photo.php page is contained within a <div> with an ID of the form photo-info-ID, where ID is the ID of the photo in question, and so is the element within which gallery.js will place the new HTML.

Enhancing the Gallery

The gallery is now beginning to take shape, but there are still a few improvements to make. To begin with, it would be nice to add some common elements to each page, such as a header and navigation. Because they are the same on every page, you don't normally want to have to edit each page every time you modify the header or the navigation — especially if you expand your application to have a larger number of pages. A good way around this problem is to place the common elements in separate PHP files and use include statements to include the content in each page.

Try It Out   **Adding Headers and Navigation**

In this exercise you're going to create some separate files for the heading and navigation, and then include them in each page.

1. Create a file, header.php, in your gallery directory:

```
<div id="gallery-header">Flickr Gallery</div>
```

2. Create a file, navigation.php, also in the gallery directory:

```
<ul id="gallery-menu">
 <li><a href="../index.php">Mashups Home</a></li>
 <li><a href="index.php">Gallery</a></li>
</ul>
```

3. Modify the existing PHP pages to include these pages. In the gallery directory, modify index.php:

```
<?php include (dirname(__FILE__) . '/../lib/gallery.php') ?>
<!DOCTYPE html PUBLIC "-//W3C//DTD XHTML 1.0 Transitional//EN"
   "http://www.w3.org/TR/xhtml1/DTD/xhtml1-transitional.dtd">
<html xmlns="http://www.w3.org/1999/xhtml">
<head>
  <title>Flickr Gallery</title>
  <link href="../css/main.css" rel="stylesheet" type="text/css" />
  <link href="../css/gallery.css" rel="stylesheet" type="text/css" />
</head>
<body>
<?php
```

```php
  $gallery = new FlickrGallery();
?>
  <?php include ('header.php') ?>
  <?php include ('navigation.php') ?>
  <ul class="photo-set">
  <?php
    $recentPhotos = $gallery->findRecentPhotos();
    foreach ($recentPhotos as $photo)
    {
      $title = $photo['title'];
      $img = 'http://static.flickr.com/' . $photo['server'] . '/' . $photo['id']
        . '_' . $photo['secret'] . '_s.jpg'
?>
    <li><a href="photo.php?id=<?php echo $photo['id'] ?>"><img src="<?php echo $img
?>" alt="<?php echo $title ?>" title="<?php echo $title ?>" /></a></li><?php
    }
?>
  </ul>
</body>
</html>
```

4. Then modify `photo.php`:

```php
<?php include (dirname(__FILE__) . '/../lib/gallery.php') ?>
<!DOCTYPE html PUBLIC "-//W3C//DTD XHTML 1.0 Transitional//EN"
  "http://www.w3.org/TR/xhtml1/DTD/xhtml1-transitional.dtd">
<html xmlns="http://www.w3.org/1999/xhtml">
<head>
  <title>Flickr Gallery</title>
  <link href="../css/main.css" rel="stylesheet" type="text/css" />
  <link href="../css/gallery.css" rel="stylesheet" type="text/css" />
  <script type="text/javascript" src="prototype.js"></script>
  <script type="text/javascript" src="gallery.js"></script>
</head>
<body>
<?php
  $gallery = new FlickrGallery();
  $id = $_REQUEST['id'];
  if (!empty($id))
  {
    $info = $gallery->getPhotoInfo($id);
    $title = htmlentities($info['title']);
    $img = 'http://static.flickr.com/' . $info['server'] . '/' . $info['id'] . '_'
. $info['secret'] . '.jpg';
    $photoPage = 'http://www.flickr.com/photos/' . $info['owner']['nsid'] . '/' .
$id . '/';
  }
?>
  <?php include ('header.php') ?>
  <?php include ('navigation.php') ?>
  <div class="photo-display">
    <p class="photo-title"><?php echo $title ?></p>
    <p class="photo-image"><a href="<?php echo $photoPage ?>"><img src="<?php echo
$img ?>" alt="<?php echo $title ?>" title="<?php echo $title ?>" /></a></p>
```

```
        <div id="photo-info-<?php echo $id ?>" class="photo-more"><a href="#"
onclick="displayInfo(<?php echo $id ?>); return false;">More info...</a></div>
    </div>
    </body>
    </html>
```

5. Finally, some new styles to add to `gallery.css`:

```css
#gallery-header {
    padding: 0.5em 2em 0.5em 2em;
    margin: 0;
    font-size: large;
    font-weight: bold;
    color: #000000;
    background-color: #EEEEEE;
    text-align: right;
}
#gallery-menu {
    border-top: 1px solid #EEEEEE;
    border-bottom: 1px solid #EEEEEE;
    list-style-type: none;
    margin: 1em 0 0 0;
    padding: 0;
}
#gallery-menu li {
    display: inline;
    margin: .5em 2em .5em 2em;
}
#gallery-menu li a:hover {
    background-color: #EEEEEE;
    text-decoration: none;
}
```

6. Take a look at the gallery `index.php` page in your browser, and you will see it is starting to look much smarter — as shown in Figure 6-6.

How It Works

The two files, `header.php` and `navigation.php`, contain snippets of HTML that will appear on every page in the gallery. Each time a PHP `include` directive is encountered —

```php
<?php include ('header.php') ?>
```

— the contents of the specified file are read and inserted into the main file. If the included file contains PHP code, that code is also executed, just as if it had been in the main file.

Where you have common elements that appear multiple times within a web site, the use of `include` statements like this can make the management of your web site much simpler. You can make site-wide changes without having to edit each page individually — all you need to do is edit the included file. Storing reusable content in a single file also ensures that all pages are consistent — there's only ever the one file to keep up to date.

The new CSS styles arrange the individual menu items in a horizontal row and set up the font and borders. The a:hover style is set so that the background color of the menu links changes to gray as you hover over them.

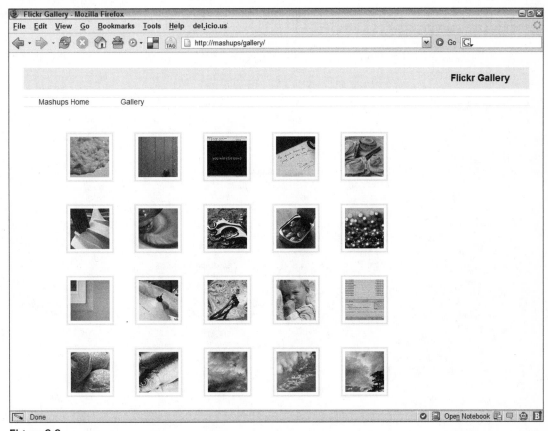

Figure 6-6

Smart Sets

The final enhancement to the gallery for this chapter is the addition of *Smart Sets*. Smart Sets are sets in which the content is not fixed, but is derived dynamically whenever the set is viewed. You'll be able to define how many photos should appear in each Smart Set, how the photos should be selected from your stream, and how they should be ordered.

Defining a Smart Set

In this exercise, you'll add Smart Sets to your existing gallery. You'll then be able to define as many sets as you want. Each dynamically generated Smart Set uses a number of parameters to determine which photos are included within it. They don't have predefined content—each one is built on demand as the page is viewed. This means that whenever you upload new photos to Flickr, they will automatically be incorporated into any relevant Smart Set.

1. Add a couple of methods to `FlickrGallery.php`:

```php
<?php

class FlickrGallery
{

    ...

    function showSmartSetThumbnail($linkPage, $title = "Set", $n = 20, $tags = "",
      $tagMode = "all", $sort = "date-posted-desc")
    {
      $s = "";
      $url = $linkPage . '?title=' . urlencode($title) . '&tags=' . urlencode($tags)
        . "&n=$n&tagMode=$tagMode&sort=$sort";
      // Get image to display
      $photos = $this->getSmartSet(1, $tags, $tagMode, $sort);

      if (is_array($photos) && count($photos) > 0)
      {
        $photo = $photos[0];
        $img = 'http://static.flickr.com/' . $photo['server'] . '/' . $photo['id']
          . '_' . $photo['secret'] . '_s.jpg';
        $s .= "<a href=\"$url\"><img src=\"$img\" /></a>";
        $s .= "<p class=\"smart-set-caption\">" . $title . "</p>";
      }
      return $s;
    }

    function getSmartSet($n = 20, $tags = "", $tagMode = "all",
      $sort = "date-posted-desc")
    {
      $ret = array();

      $args = array(
        'user_id' => $this->nsid,
        'sort' => $sort,
        'page' => 1,
        'per_page' => $n,
        'extras' => 'owner_name'
      );

      if (!empty($tags))
      {
```

```php
      $args['tags'] = $tags;
      $args['tag_mode'] = $tagMode;
    }

    $p = $this->flickr->photos_search($args);
    if ($this->flickr->getErrorCode())
    {
      echo ("Error fetching photos: " . $this->flickr->getErrorMsg());
    }

    if (is_array($p['photo']) && count($p['photo']) > 0)
    {
      $ret = $p['photo'];
    }

    return $ret;
  }

}

?>
```

2. Create a new file, smartsets.php, in your gallery directory.

```php
<?php include (dirname(__FILE__) . '/../lib/gallery.php') ?>
<!DOCTYPE html PUBLIC "-//W3C//DTD XHTML 1.0 Transitional//EN"
  "http://www.w3.org/TR/xhtml1/DTD/xhtml1-transitional.dtd">
<html xmlns="http://www.w3.org/1999/xhtml">
<head>
  <title>Flickr Gallery</title>
  <link href="../css/main.css" rel="stylesheet" type="text/css" />
  <link href="../css/gallery.css" rel="stylesheet" type="text/css" />
</head>
<body>
<?php
  $gallery = new FlickrGallery();
?>
<?php include ('header.php') ?>
<?php include ('navigation.php') ?>
<div class="smart-sets">
  <h1>Smart Sets</h1>
  <ul class="smart-sets-list">
   <li class="smart-set"><?php echo $gallery->showSmartSetThumbnail("smartset.php",
"Most Interesting", 20, "", "", "interestingness-desc") ?></li>
   <li class="smart-set"><?php echo $gallery->showSmartSetThumbnail("smartset.php",
"Cats", 20, "cat", "all", "interestingness-desc") ?></li>
   <li class="smart-set"><?php echo $gallery->showSmartSetThumbnail("smartset.php",
"Colorful", 20, "red,blue,green,orange,yellow", "any", "interestingness-desc")
?></li>
   <li class="smart-set"><?php echo $gallery->showSmartSetThumbnail("smartset.php",
"Red", 20, "red", "all", "date-taken-desc") ?></li>
   <li class="smart-set"><?php echo $gallery->showSmartSetThumbnail("smartset.php",
"Blue", 20, "blue", "all", "date-taken-desc") ?></li>
```

```
    <li class="smart-set"><?php echo $gallery->showSmartSetThumbnail("smartset.php",
"Green", 20, "green", "all", "date-taken-desc") ?></li>
    <li class="smart-set"><?php echo $gallery->showSmartSetThumbnail("smartset.php",
"Yellow", 20, "yellow", "all", "date-taken-desc") ?></li>
    <li class="smart-set"><?php echo $gallery->showSmartSetThumbnail("smartset.php",
"Orange", 20, "orange", "all", "date-taken-desc") ?></li>
    <li class="smart-set"><?php echo $gallery->showSmartSetThumbnail("smartset.php",
"Oldest", 20, "", "", "date-taken-asc") ?></li>
  </ul>
</div>
</body>
</html>
```

3. Now add some more styles to `gallery.css` to support this page:

```css
.smart-sets {
  width: 655px;
  text-align: center;
}
.smart-sets ul {
  list-style-type: none;
  width: 655px;
  margin: 2em 0 0 60px;
  padding: 0;
}
.smart-sets li {
  float: left;
  width: 131px;
  text-align: center;
  margin-bottom: 1em;
}
.smart-sets img {
  margin: 20px 20px 5px 20px;
  padding: 5px;
  border: 3px solid #EEEEEE;
}
```

4. Take a look at the `smartsets.php` page in your browser, and you'll see that it looks something like Figure 6-7.

How It Works

Two new methods are defined. The first, `showSmartSetThumbnail()`, is responsible for generating the square thumbnail for the set page. The second, `getSmartSet()`, is responsible for identifying the photos that belong in the set.

The `getSmartSet()` method takes a number of parameters that are passed straight into the phpFlickr `photos_search` method. Default values are set on all of the parameters in such a way that if the method is invoked with no parameters, it will simply return the 20 most recent photos.

The `showSmartSetThumbnail()` method calls `getSmartSet()` to identify the first photo in the set and then uses this image as the thumbnail to identify the set. It then generates HTML for the thumbnail that links to the page displaying the Smart Set, passing in all the parameters that define the Smart Set — this allows the use of a single parameterized page to display the set itself.

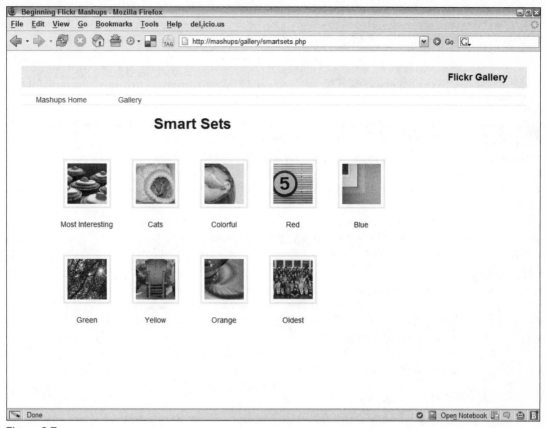

Figure 6-7

The `smartsets.php` page creates a list for which each list item represents a Smart Set—for each one, the `showSmartSetThumbnail()` method is invoked with a different set of parameters, each set defining a new Smart Set.

For example, the following item will display the thumbnail for a set entitled "Cats":

```
<li class="smart-set"><?php echo $gallery->showSmartSetThumbnail("smartset.php",
"Cats", 20, "cat", "all", "interestingness-desc") ?></li>
```

It will represent a set containing 20 photos, each tagged with *cat*, and they will be sorted in descending order of interestingness.

This item will display the thumbnail for a set entitled "Colorful":

```
<li class="smart-set"><?php echo $gallery->showSmartSetThumbnail("smartset.php",
"Colorful", 20, "red,blue,green,orange,yellow", "any", "interestingness-desc")
?></li>
```

This set will contain 20 photos, each tagged with one or more of the tags *red, blue, green, orange* and *yellow,* and they will again be sorted in descending order of interestingness. Each thumbnail links to a new page called `smartset.php`, which you will create next.

Now that you've created your Smart Set list, you need to write some code to display the individual sets themselves.

Try It Out   **Displaying the Smart Sets**

In this exercise, you'll add a PHP file to display the Smart Set.

1. For the Smart Set page itself, you need to create a new file, `smartset.php`, in your `gallery` directory:

```php
<?php include (dirname(__FILE__) . '/../lib/gallery.php') ?>
<!DOCTYPE html PUBLIC "-//W3C//DTD XHTML 1.0 Transitional//EN"
"http://www.w3.org/TR/xhtml1/DTD/xhtml1-transitional.dtd">
<html xmlns="http://www.w3.org/1999/xhtml">
<head>
  <title>Flickr Gallery</title>
  <link href="../css/main.css" rel="stylesheet" type="text/css" />
  <link href="../css/gallery.css" rel="stylesheet" type="text/css" />
</head>
<body>
<?php
  $gallery = new FlickrGallery();
?>
<?php include ('header.php') ?>
<?php include ('navigation.php') ?>
<ul class="photo-set">
  <?php
  $setTitle = $_REQUEST['title'];
  $n = $_REQUEST['n'];
  $tags = $_REQUEST['tags'];
  $tagMode = $_REQUEST['tagMode'];
  $sort = $_REQUEST['sort'];
  $smartSetPhotos = $gallery->getSmartSet($n, $tags, $tagMode, $sort);
?>
  <h1><?php echo $setTitle ?></h1>
<?php
  foreach ($smartSetPhotos as $photo)
  {
    $title = htmlentities($photo['title']);
    $img = 'http://static.flickr.com/' . $photo['server'] . '/' . $photo['id']
      . '_' . $photo['secret'] . '_s.jpg'
?>
    <li><a href="photo.php?id=<?php echo $photo['id'] ?>"><img src="<?php echo $img
?>" alt="<?php echo $title ?>" title="<?php echo $title ?>" /></a></li>
<?php
  }
?>
</ul>
</body>
</html>
```

2. The last thing left to do is to add the Smart Sets page to the main navigation. Update `naviga-tion.php` as shown:

```
<ul id="gallery-menu">
    <li><a href="../index.php">Mashups Home</a></li>
    <li><a href="index.php">Gallery</a></li>
    <li><a href="smartsets.php">Smart Sets</a></li>
</ul>
```

3. Navigate to one of the Smart Set pages in your browser, and you will see a finished page similar to that shown in Figure 6-8.

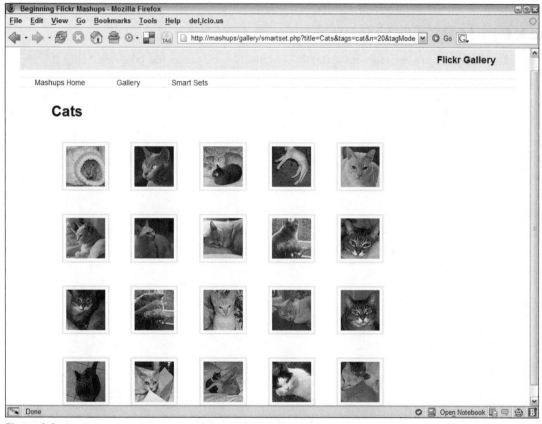

Figure 6-8

How It Works

The Smart Set page itself, `smartset.php`, is almost identical to the main `index.php` page—the only real difference is that it extracts the parameters needed for the call to `getSmartSet()` from the HTTP request. Where `index.php` uses the photos returned by `findRecentPhotos()`, this page uses the photos returned by `getSmartSet()`. The structure of the HTML generated is identical in both cases.

Summary

The Flickr API offers great potential for the development of mashups and remixes. Much of the functionality provided by the Flickr website is available to the API, enabling you to build complex applications quickly and easily. In this chapter, you have used the Flickr API to remix Flickr to produce a fully functioning photo gallery application. You have seen how to install and use the phpFlickr API kit, use AJAX to add content to a web page on demand, use `include` statements to separate out common content elements, and build dynamically generated sets of photos.

In Chapter 7 you will modify the gallery application further, but first, try the following exercises.

Exercises

1. Modify `info.php` to include details of both when the photo was taken and when it was posted to Flickr — be sure to format the dates into a sensible human-readable form.

2. On the photo page, you can click the More info link to reveal the extra details, but you can't close it again unless you reload the page. Add a Hide info link to return the page to its original state without having to reload the page.

Authenticating with Flickr

Viewing public photos on Flickr is one thing, but what happens if you want to view photos that are marked as private? Or perhaps you would like to update your photograph details on Flickr, changing the title or the description? The Flickr API enables you to do all of these things, but only after you authenticate yourself.

In this chapter you will see how the authentication process works, and then you'll update your photo gallery from Chapter 6 to allow you to update your photos' details on Flickr.

The Need for Secrecy

Before you can change any details on Flickr, or view photographs you have marked as private, it is only proper that Flickr take steps to ensure that you do actually have the right to do those things — by forcing you to log in. Anyone can view public photos on Flickr, but if you want to see photos marked as private, Flickr requires that you authenticate yourself. Once you are authenticated, Flickr can determine whether you have permission to see the photographs in question. To see this process in action, log out of Flickr and then enter the following URL in your browser.

```
http://www.flickr.com/photos/dopiaza/200228673/
```

There is a valid photo page at that URL, but the photo in question is marked as private. Because it is private, Flickr first needs to know who you are — so you are immediately directed to the login page. If you then log in, Flickr will then determine that you do not, in fact, have permission to view the photo and so present you with a "This page is private" message. (Just in case you're curious, you really shouldn't be too upset that you didn't get to see the picture in question — it's simply a plain white graphic with the word PRIVATE in the middle of it. You really didn't miss much.)

Systems to authenticate users can be built in various ways, but the ones you are most likely to encounter on the web involve having some unique identifier for every individual (typically an e-mail address or a user name) and a password. The identifier is potentially widely known and often public information. The password, however, is secret — it should only be known to the person concerned. So when you come to a web site such as Flickr that requires authentication, the process is usually straightforward — you enter your username and password, and the system checks those against its records. If the two match, you are allowed to proceed.

That's all very well, as you are interacting directly with Flickr, but what if you are using a third-party application? If you are using a third-party application and that application needs to make authenticated accesses to Flickr — perhaps so it can show you your private photos — how does it do that? The obvious answer would be for you to give the application your password, which it can then use to authenticate against Flickr and do whatever it needs to do, but there are problems with that approach. Your password is the key to your account. With it, you can do anything — delete photos, access billing information, even delete the account completely. Do you really trust the third party that much? Even if you do, are you absolutely sure that it takes proper care of your password — that it won't store it away somewhere that other, less scrupulous people could find it and take advantage of it?

Authenticating with Flickr

Flickr's authentication system overcomes some of these problems by ensuring that you never have to give any third-party application your password — you only ever give that to Flickr. Additionally, you can decide just what level of permissions you give to any third-party application — and then revoke those permissions later should you choose to do so.

Sound good? It is — it gives the end-user a great deal of control over how other applications can access their Flickr account. Nothing comes for free in this world, however, and there is a downside: you, as a third-party developer, have to do a little extra work in order to fit in with this scheme. Note that most API kits, including phpFlickr, will handle some of the details of authentication for you. In this chapter you'll be doing at least some of this yourself so that you can understand the process involved.

Configuring Your API Key

Before your application can take advantage of Flickr's authentication mechanism, you need to configure your API key — so, to kick off the process, go to Flickr's Your API Keys page at http://www.flickr.com/services/api/keys/.

Here you will see a list of all the API keys you have registered under your account, as shown in Figure 7-1.

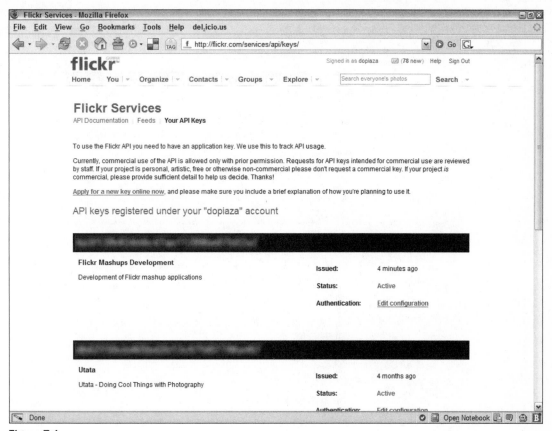

Figure 7-1

Click the Edit configuration link next to your API key and you will be taken to the API Key Authentication Setup page, as seen in Figure 7-2.

At the top of this page, underneath the API key, you will see a field entitled Shared Secret. The important word here is *secret* — you do not reveal the secret to anybody. The sharing is between you and Flickr — only you and Flickr know the secret, nobody else does. Take a note of your secret, and edit your apikey.php file to include it:

```php
<?php

$flickrApiKey = 'YOUR-API-KEY';
$flickrApiSecret = 'YOUR-API-SECRET';

?>
```

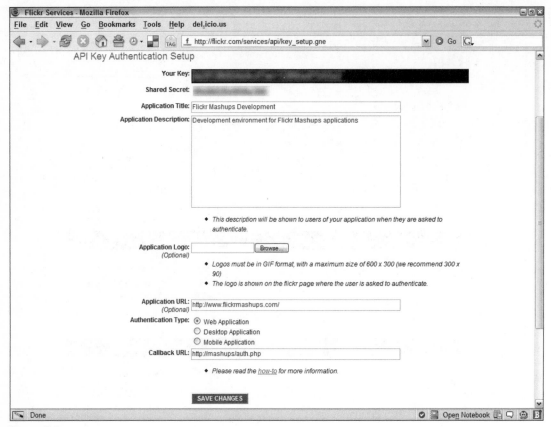

Figure 7-2

Below your shared secret is a form that enables you to configure your API key. The first few fields on this form let you enter a description of your application—enter some appropriate text in these. There is also space to specify a logo to be used. These details are all displayed to end users when they need to decide whether or not to grant access to your application, so be sure to enter something sensible here.

The next stage is to choose your *application type*. This chapter focuses on web applications, as they are the most common. The slightly different approaches used for desktop and mobile applications will be discussed later in this chapter. You should select Web Application at this point.

Finally, you need to set up a *callback URL*. This is a URL within your application that Flickr will call during the authentication process. For now, set it to a page that we will call `auth.php`, located in the top level of your mashups site. The value you enter here will depend on how you have set up your web server during development, but should look something like this:

```
http://localhost/auth.php
```

You'll be setting up the contents of the `auth.php` page shortly, but as far as configuring your key goes, you're all done.

> The URL you entered as the callback URL points to your development web server. If you are building an application to deploy elsewhere on the Internet, you may want to create two API keys with different callback URLs — one for development and one for live deployment.

A Typical Authentication Sequence

Now you've configured your key, let's take a look at what actually happens during the typical web-based authentication process. There are a lot of steps to go through here, and it all seems fairly complicated on first reading, but don't worry — it's nowhere near as difficult as it first sounds. You'll be building a custom library and using phpFlickr to handle a lot of the detail, so most of the time all of this will be hidden behind the scenes. For now, though, it's useful to walk through the sequence of events.

The very first thing that normally happens is that the user initiates a page request — maybe they just landed on your home page and you want to authenticate them immediately, or maybe they've just clicked a button called Show me my private photos. You now wish to authenticate them — find out who they are. To do this, you don't show them the page they have just asked for. Instead, you redirect them to a special authentication page on Flickr. The URL you send them to looks like this:

```
http://flickr.com/services/auth/
        ?api_key=YOUR-API-KEY&perms=PERMISSIONS&api_sig=API-SIGNATURE
```

Note that the URL is broken over two lines here for readability.

The address of the authentication page at Flickr is `http://flickr.com/services/auth/`. After that are three parameters. The first parameter, `api_key`, is your application's API key. The second, `perms`, is the permissions your application is requesting. Possible values for the `perms` parameter are:

❑ `read`: This is the permission to read private information such as details for photos marked as private.

❑ `write`: Permission to add, edit, and delete photo metadata (includes the `read` permission). This is the permission to modify attributes of photos, such as title and description, or notes. It also gives you permission to create, modify, and delete photo sets.

❑ `delete`: Permission to delete photos (includes the `write` and `read` permissions). This is the permission to permanently delete photos from Flickr.

The final parameter, `api_sig`, is the *signature* for the `method` call. This is the parameter that proves to Flickr that the request was indeed made by the application to which the API key being used was issued. How does it know that? The signature can only be generated if you know the one thing known to only you and Flickr — the shared secret. Here's how you calculate the signature:

You first alphabetically sort all the parameter names in the call you are making — in this case, `api_key` and `perms`. You then construct a string as follows:

1. First, you start with the shared secret.

2. Then, for each parameter in turn (alphabetically), you append first the parameter name and then the parameter value.

Finally, you take the MD5 hash of the resulting string.

So, suppose you have an API key of 1f2811827f3284b3aa12f7bbb7792b8d, and a shared secret of 4b3aa12f7bbb7792, and you require read permissions. You first create the string:

4b3aa12f7bbb7792api_key1f2811827f3284b3aa12f7bbb7792b8dpermsread

You then take the MD5 hash of that string — in PHP this is done with the md5 function. The MD5 hash is 2650f6827bc3ba51bd9a3873de57d23e, and is therefore the value of the api_sig parameter. So the URL used in this example is as follows:

```
http://flickr.com/services/auth/
      ?api_key=1f2811827f3284b3aa12f7bbb7792b8d
          &perms=read&api_sig=2650f6827bc3ba51bd9a3873de57d23e
```

Once again, this URL has been split over multiple lines for readability.

Having directed the user to the Flickr page, you have now handed responsibility for authenticating the user over to Flickr — Flickr will ask the user to log in if they are not already logged in, and if they have not already done so, they will then be asked to give your application the privileges it has asked for. They will see a screen something like that shown in Figure 7-3.

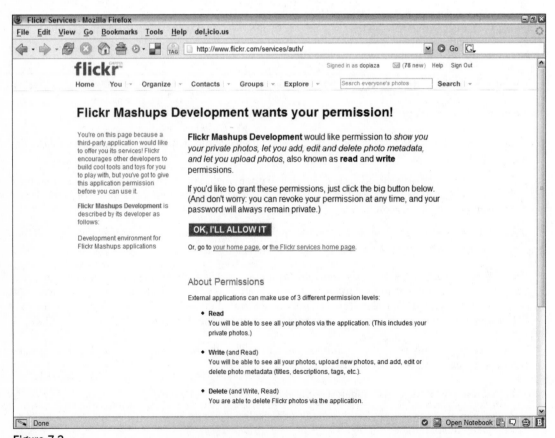

Figure 7-3

Once the user has been granted permission, Flickr needs to return control to your application. It does this by redirecting the user to the callback URL you specified when you configured your API key. A single parameter is passed back in the query string — the *frob*. The frob is a string and typically looks something like this:

```
2738983-e029b037199b03b03e89e
```

So, if your callback URL was `http://yourdomain.com/auth.php`, the user would be redirected to `http://yourdomain.com/auth.php?frob=2738983-e029b037199b03b03e89e`.

The frob is transient and is only valid for a maximum of 60 minutes. Upon receipt, your application should then call the `flickr.auth.getToken` method to exchange the frob for a token. This method must be signed in the same way the URL parameters were earlier.

The `flickr.auth.getToken` method takes the parameters `api_key`, `method`, and `frob`. Constructing a string out of the shared secret and the alphabetical list of parameters gives you this:

```
4b3aa12f7bbb7792api_key1f2811827f3284b3aa12f7bbb7792b8dfrob2738983-
e029b037199b03b03e89emethodflickr.auth.getToken
```

If you wish to use XML-RPC to talk to Flickr, there's something here that you need to make a special note of. You may remember from Chapter 4 that when you use XML-RPC the method parameter is sent separately in the message and not along with all the other parameters. For that reason, if you are using XML-RPC you must not include the method in the signature generation. For those of you using REST — which is what I am using in this book — the method parameter is included, as you can see in the example above.

The MD5 hash of our string of parameters is `bbef10bf2619921bb104190422a25fbe`, which you must then include as an extra parameter, `api_sig`, when you make the `flickr.auth.getToken` method call.

Once you have your token, you can use it to make authenticated calls. Each token is specific to a user and an application — once you have been issued a token, it can only be used in conjunction with your API key.

Now that you have your authentication token, you can make authenticated calls. Authenticated calls are the same as the non-authenticated calls that you have been using so far, but with two additional parameters: `auth_token` and `api_sig`. Each time you want to make an authenticated API method call, you need to pass in the authentication token you have received as an `auth_token` parameter and a signature, calculated as described above, as an `api_sig` parameter. This signing process ensures both that you are who you say you are (you need the shared secret to generate the signature) and that the user has given you the permission you need (the token embodies the level of permission granted to your API key by the user).

Authentication and API Kits

Most API kits worth their salt will handle a lot of the nitty-gritty details for you. PhpFlickr, for example, has methods and sample PHP files that will take care of getting the authentication token from Flickr, and then will automatically sign your method calls for you. At this point, you could simply start using the built-in methods within phpFlickr to perform authentication, but to fully understand the authentication process, it is worth building your own so you can see just how it works.

Building an Authenticator

In the previous sections, you saw how the authentication process worked. Now you'll see how to put together the actual code to make it happen.

Try It Out   Creating Your Own Authenticator

The first step in creating an authenticator is to create a `FlickrAuthenticator` class that will manage the whole authentication process. This class does two things:

❑   It determines whether the current user is already authenticated with the necessary permissions, and if not it hands them over to Flickr.

❑   It takes care of converting a frob to a token and storing it away for later use.

1.   Create a new file called `FlickrAuthenticator.php` in the system `lib` directory, as follows:

```php
<?php

class FlickrAuthenticator
{
  var $flickr;
  var $apikey;
  var $secret;
  var $auth;

  var $errorPage;

  function FlickrAuthenticator($apikey, $secret)
  {
    $this->apikey = $apikey;
    $this->secret = $secret;
    $this->flickr = new phpFlickr($apikey, $secret, false);
    $this->errorPage = 'http://' . $_SERVER['HTTP_HOST'] . '/error.php';
  }

  function authenticate($requiredPerms)
  {
    $doAuth = true;
    $token = $_SESSION['FlickrAuthenticationToken'];
    $this->setToken($token);
    if (!empty($token))
    {
      $auth = $this->flickr->auth_checkToken();
      if ($this->flickr->getErrorCode())
      {
        $this->setToken(NULL);
      }
      else
      {
        // We have a good token
        // Check we have the required privileges
        $perms = $auth['perms'];
```

```
      switch ($perms)
      {
        case "read":
          if ($requiredPerms == "read")
          {
            $doAuth = false;
          }
          break;

        case "write":
          if ($requiredPerms == "read" || $requiredPerms == "write")
          {
            $doAuth = false;
          }
          break;

        case "delete":
          if ($requiredPerms == "read" || $requiredPerms == "write"
            || $requiredPerms == "delete")
          {
            $doAuth = false;
          }
          break;
      }

      if (!$doAuth)
      {
        // No further authentication necessary, so store away
        // the results from checkToken
        $this->auth = $auth;
      }
    }
  }

  if ($doAuth)
  {
    // Need to authenticate - redirect to flickr
    $extra = $_SERVER['REQUEST_URI'];
    $apisig = md5($this->secret . "api_key" . $this->apikey . "extra" . $extra
      . "perms" . $requiredPerms);
    $url = 'http://www.flickr.com/services/auth/?api_key=' . $this->apikey
      . '&extra=' . $extra . '&perms=' . $requiredPerms . '&api_sig='. $apisig;
    header("Location: " . $url);
    exit(0);
  }
}

function updateCredentials($frob)
{
  $this->setToken(NULL);
  $token = $this->flickr->auth_getToken($frob);
  if (!$this->flickr->getErrorCode())
  {
    $this->setToken($token);
```

```
        $auth = $this->flickr->auth_checkToken();
        if ($this->flickr->getErrorCode())
        {
          $this->setToken(NULL);
          $this->error("There was a problem checking the authentication token: "
            . $this->flickr->getErrorCode() . " " . $this->flickr->getErrorMsg());
        }
      }
      else
      {
        $this->setToken(NULL);
        $this->error("There was a problem getting the authentication token: "
          . $this->flickr->getErrorCode() . " " . $this->flickr->getErrorMsg());
      }
    }

    function setToken($token)
    {
      $_SESSION['FlickrAuthenticationToken'] = $token;
      unset($_SESSION['phpFlickr_auth_token']);
      $this->flickr->setToken($token);
    }

    function error($message)
    {
      $_SESSION['error'] = $message;
      header('Location: ' . $this->errorPage);
      exit(0);
    }
  }
?>
```

2. Create a new file, error.php, in the top level of your mashups site.

```
<?php session_start(); ?>
<!DOCTYPE html PUBLIC "-//W3C//DTD XHTML 1.0 Transitional//EN"
  "http://www.w3.org/TR/xhtml1/DTD/xhtml1-transitional.dtd">
<html xmlns="http://www.w3.org/1999/xhtml">
<head>
  <link href="css/main.css" rel="stylesheet" type="text/css" />
  <title>Flickr Mashups</title>
</head>
<body>
  <h1>Error</h1>
  <p><?php echo $_SESSION['error'] ?></p>
</body>
</html>
```

3. Next you need to provide a page for Flickr to call via the callback URL. Create a file called auth.php at the top level of your mashups web site:

```php
<?php

include (dirname(__FILE__) . '/lib/apikey.php');
include (dirname(__FILE__) . '/lib/phpFlickr/phpFlickr.php');
include (dirname(__FILE__) . '/lib/FlickrAuthenticator.php');

$frob = $_REQUEST['frob'];
$extra = $_REQUEST['extra'];
$auth = new FlickrAuthenticator($flickrApiKey, $flickrApiSecret);
$redirect = '/';

if (!empty($frob))
{
  $auth->updateCredentials($frob);

  if (!empty($extra))
  {
    $redirect = $extra;
  }
}

header('Location: http://'.$_SERVER['HTTP_HOST'] .$redirect);

?>
```

How It Works

Let's now take a look at the individual bits of the `FlickrAuthenticator` class. The constructor is fairly straightforward — it takes in two arguments, the API key and shared secret, and uses those to construct an instance of phpFlickr. It also defines an error page:

```php
$this->errorPage = 'http://' . $_SERVER['HTTP_HOST'] '/error.php';
```

The purpose of the error page is to ensure there is some way to report back to the user errors found during the authentication process. The `$errorPage` variable is initialized to point to a file called `error.php` in the top-level directory of the web site — if your mashups are currently in a subdirectory, make sure you edit this statement to reflect the correct location of your error page.

The `authenticate` method should be called whenever your application wants to ensure that the current user is authenticated with a particular set of permissions. It takes one argument, which is a string containing the desired permissions — read, `write`, or `delete`.

The first thing the `authenticate` method does is see if the user is already authenticated — if they are, the class will already have a token for them. This token needs to be available across multiple HTTP requests, so the `FlickrAuthenticator` class stores the token in the user's session. `authenticate` checks the session to see if a token is present:

```php
$token = $_SESSION['FlickrAuthenticationToken'];
```

157

setToken is called for any token found, which ensures that phpFlickr will use that token to sign any method calls that are made:

```
function setToken($token)
{
    $_SESSION['FlickrAuthenticationToken'] = $token;
    unset($_SESSION['phpFlickr_auth_token']);
    $this->flickr->setToken($token);
}
```

The setToken method ensures that the correct token value is set in the session. It also invalidates the session variable phpFlickr_auth_token — this is where phpFlickr tries to keep track of tokens. Because you are overriding phpFlickr's own mechanism for obtaining tokens, you need to also clear this session variable — if you don't, phpFlickr will continue to try to use any existing token it has, possibly after the token has been revoked.

If a token is stored in the session, the flickr.auth.checkToken method is called to see if the token is still valid. If it is, the permissions granted to the token are compared against the permissions that were requested in the $requiredPerms argument — if the requested permissions are wider than those actually granted, then authentication will still need to take place so the user can be asked to grant the new permissions.

If the token is valid and has sufficient permissions, the $auth array returned in the call to flickr.auth .checkToken is stored so that it can be used later — the method response contains useful information such as the permissions granted to the token and the identity of the user to whom the token belongs:

```
<auth>
  <token>1698607-c0be5c01c44ea9ac</token>
  <perms>read</perms>
  <user nsid="50317659@N00" username="dopiaza" fullname="David Wilkinson"/>
</auth>
```

If no valid token with sufficient permissions is found, the user is redirected to Flickr's authentication pages:

```
$extra = $_SERVER['REQUEST_URI'];
$apisig = md5($this->secret . "api_key" . $this->apikey . "extra" . $extra .
"perms" . $requiredPerms);
$url = 'http://www.flickr.com/services/auth/?api_key=' . $this->apikey .
'&extra=' . $extra . '&perms=' . $requiredPerms . '&api_sig='. $apisig;
header("Location: " . $url);
exit(0);
```

Here, you can see the parameters for the redirection being built up and signed, exactly as described earlier — there is, however, one difference. The authentication URL allows for an extra options parameter, extra, to be passed. Flickr doesn't do anything directly with this parameter, but instead returns it to the application as a parameter when it redirects the user back to your application's callback URL.

Your application is free to use this extra parameter for any purpose you like. Here, it is used to identify the page the user was trying to access when authentication was requested — the value found in `$_SERVER['REQUEST_URI']`.

The `updateCredentials` method is invoked when a new frob has been received from Flickr, and is responsible for converting the frob to a token. When this method is invoked, any existing token is cleared out and the frob converted to a new token via the `flickr.auth.getToken` method. Finally, the validity of the token is confirmed with a call to `flickr.auth.checkToken`.

The `auth.php` file is very straightforward — it extracts the `frob` and `extra` parameters from the request and calls `updateCredentials` with `frob`, and then redirects the user to the path contained in the `extra` parameter. If no `extra` parameter was sent, the user is redirected to the root document in the current web site.

Now you have the authentication class and the callback URL all set up, try authenticating yourself.

Try It Out   **Authenticating Yourself**

In this exercise, you'll try authenticating yourself.

1.   Create a file called `7-1.php` in your gallery directory:

```php
<?php

include (dirname(__FILE__) . '/../lib/apikey.php');
include (dirname(__FILE__) . '/../lib/phpFlickr/phpFlickr.php');
include (dirname(__FILE__) . '/../lib/FlickrAuthenticator.php');

$auth = new FlickrAuthenticator($flickrApiKey, $flickrApiSecret);

$auth->authenticate("read");

?>
<h1>Authenticated</h1>
<p>You are logged in as
<strong><?php echo $auth->auth['user']['username'] ?></strong> with
<strong><?php echo $auth->auth['perms'] ?></strong> permissions.</p>
```

2.   Load the file into your browser and you should immediately be redirected to Flickr's authentication pages and asked to give your application `read` permission. After you've granted that permission, you should be redirected to the page you were originally trying to view, where you'll see something like that in Figure 7-4.

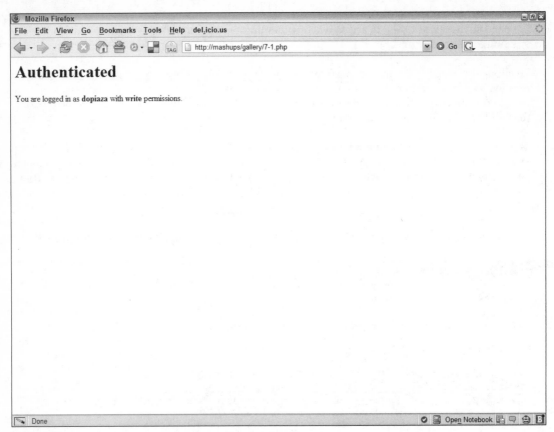

Figure 7-4

How It Works

When the page is loaded, the `FlickrAuthenticator` `authenticate` method is called. The first time you do this no token is set up, so the page redirects to Flickr. Once you have approved the application's access, Flickr returns you to the `auth.php` file specified in the callback URL, passing back a frob. This file calls the `FlickrAuthenticator` `updateCredentials` method to convert the frob into a token and then redirects you back to the test page above.

This time, when the page is loaded, the `authenticate` method finds a valid token stored in the session and so does not redirect you back to Flickr — instead, the rest of the script continues to execute. If you reload the page, you will see that it no longer redirects you to Flickr — the token in the session continues to be valid.

If you modify the page and change the requested permissions to `write`, like this:

```
$auth->authenticate("write");
```

you will find that on reloading the page, you are once again redirected to Flickr — this time to approve the new `write` permission.

Updating Your Photo's Details

Now that you have a working authentication system, you can update the gallery application created in the previous chapter to start using authentication. The Flickr API method `flickr.photos.setMeta` enables you to update the title and description of your photos, and it requires authentication with `write` permission.

Try It Out   Adding Authentication to the Gallery

The first thing to do is to integrate the `FlickrGallery` class with the `FlickrAuthenticator`. Both of these classes contain an instance of phpFlickr — but if you have multiple instances of phpFlickr, how can you ensure that when the instance belonging to the `FlickrAuthenticator` receives a valid token, the instance in the `FlickrGallery` will also be able to use that token? It would be possible to write some code passing the tokens around, but a more elegant and much simpler approach is to ensure that only one instance of phpFlickr is being used. You can modify the `FlickrGallery` class so that it doesn't instantiate its own copy of phpFlickr but instead makes use of inheritance to use the one inside `FlickrAuthenticator`. If you make the `FlickrGallery` class extend the `FlickrAuthenticator` class, all the authentication functionality will automatically be incorporated into `FlickrGallery`.

1.   Update `FlickrGallery.php` as follows:

```php
<?php

class FlickrGallery extends FlickrAuthenticator
{
  var $nsid = '50317659@N00';

  function FlickrGallery()
  {
    global $flickrApiKey;
    global $flickrApiSecret;

    $this->FlickrAuthenticator($flickrApiKey, $flickrApiSecret);
  }


...


  function setMeta($id, $title, $description)
  {
    $this->flickr->photos_setMeta($id, $title, $description);

    if ($this->flickr->getErrorCode())
    {
      echo ("Error setting metadata: " . $this->flickr->getErrorMsg());
    }
  }

  function checkAuthenticatedUser()
  {
    return ($this->nsid == $this->auth['user']['nsid']);
```

```
      }
}

?>
```

2. Update the `gallery.php` file to ensure that the `FlickrAuthenticator` class is included:

```php
<?php

require_once(dirname(__FILE__) . '/apikey.php');
require_once(dirname(__FILE__) . '/phpFlickr/phpFlickr.php');
require_once(dirname(__FILE__) . '/FlickrAuthenticator.php');
require_once(dirname(__FILE__) . '/FlickrGallery.php');

header("Content-Type: text/html; charset=utf-8");

?>
```

3. Now you need a page to allow the user to edit the title and the description, so create a new file called `edit.php` in your `gallery` directory:

```php
<?php
include (dirname(__FILE__) . '/../lib/gallery.php');
$gallery = new FlickrGallery();
$gallery->authenticate("write");
if (!$gallery->checkAuthenticatedUser())
{
  $gallery->error("You do not have permission to edit these details");
}
?>
<!DOCTYPE html PUBLIC "-//W3C//DTD XHTML 1.0 Transitional//EN"
  "http://www.w3.org/TR/xhtml1/DTD/xhtml1-transitional.dtd">
<html xmlns="http://www.w3.org/1999/xhtml">
<head>
  <link href="../css/main.css" rel="stylesheet" type="text/css" />
  <link href="../css/gallery.css" rel="stylesheet" type="text/css" />
  <title>Flickr Gallery</title>
</head>
<body>
<?php
  $id = $_REQUEST['id'];
  if (!empty($id))
  {
    $info = $gallery->getPhotoInfo($id);
    $title = $info['title'];
    $img = 'http://static.flickr.com/' . $info['server'] . '/' . $info['id']
      . '_' . $info['secret'] . '.jpg';
    $photoPage = 'http://www.flickr.com/photos/' . $info['owner']['nsid'] . '/'
      . $id . '/';
    $description = $info['description'];
  }
?>
<?php include ('header.php') ?>
```

```
<?php include ('navigation.php') ?>
  <div class="photo-edit">
    <form action="doEdit.php" method="post">
      <p class="photo-image"><a href="<?php echo $photoPage ?>"><img src="<?php
echo $img ?>" alt="<?php echo $title ?>" title="<?php echo $title ?>" /></a></p>
      <p class="photo-title-edit"><input name="title" type="text" id="title"
value="<?php echo $title ?>" size="50" />
      <p class="photo-description-edit">
        <textarea name="description" cols="50" rows="6" wrap="VIRTUAL"
id="description"><?php echo $description ?></textarea>
      </p>
      <p class="photo-description-edit">
        <input name="id" type="hidden" value="<?php echo $id ?>" />
        <input type="submit" name="Submit" value="Submit Changes" />
        <input type="reset" name="Reset" value="Reset" />
      </p>
    </form>
  </div>
</body>
</html>
```

4. The form action is set to be doEdit.php, which you now need to create in your gallery directory:

```php
<?php
include (dirname(__FILE__) . '/../lib/gallery.php');
$gallery = new FlickrGallery();
$gallery->authenticate("write");
if (!$gallery->checkAuthenticatedUser())
{
  $gallery->error("You do not have permission to edit these details");
}

$id = $_REQUEST['id'];
$title = $_REQUEST['title'];
$description = $_REQUEST['description'];

if (!empty($id))
{
  $gallery->setMeta($id, stripslashes($title), stripslashes($description));
}

header('Location: http://' . $_SERVER['HTTP_HOST'] . dirname($_SERVER['PHP_SELF'])
  . '/photo.php?id=' . $id);
?>
```

5. The last thing remaining is to place an Edit link somewhere so that you can actually get to your newly created edit page. The photo description is only displayed once the user has clicked the More info link — alongside these extra details would seem to be a good place to put the Edit link. Modify the info.php file:

```php
<?php

include (dirname(__FILE__) . '/../lib/gallery.php');
```

```
. . .

   <div class="photo-date-taken">Taken on: <?php echo
formatDateTaken($info['dates']['taken']) ?></div>
   <div class="photo-date-posted">Posted on: <?php echo
formatDatePosted($info['dates']['posted']) ?></div>
   <div class="photo-edit-link"><a href="edit.php?id=<?php echo $id
?>">Edit</a></div>
</div>
<?php
}
?>
```

6. Finally, to make it all look good, some additional CSS for the edit page should be added to the `gallery.css` file:

```css
.photo-edit {
   width: 530px;
   margin: 2em 0 0 60px;
   padding: 0;
   text-align: center;
}
.photo-edit .photo-image img {
   margin: 0;
   padding: 5px;
   border: 3px solid #EEEEEE;
}
.photo-edit-link {
   text-align: right;
}
```

7. To try this out, go to your third-party applications list at Flickr (http://www.flickr.com/services/auth/list.gne) and revoke any permissions your application currently has.

8. Open up the gallery in your browser and navigate to a photo page. Click the More info link and you should see the photo's description appear, along with an Edit link at the bottom of the page, as shown in Figure 7-5.

9. Click the Edit link and you will be redirected to Flickr to authorize your application. Once you have completed authorization, Flickr will return you to your application and you will be presented with the edit form, as in Figure 7-6.

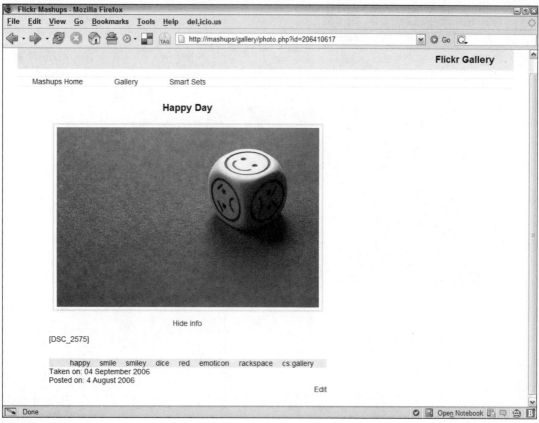

Figure 7-5

10. Edit the title and description in the form and submit your changes. You will be sent back to the photo page, where you should see your new title and description.

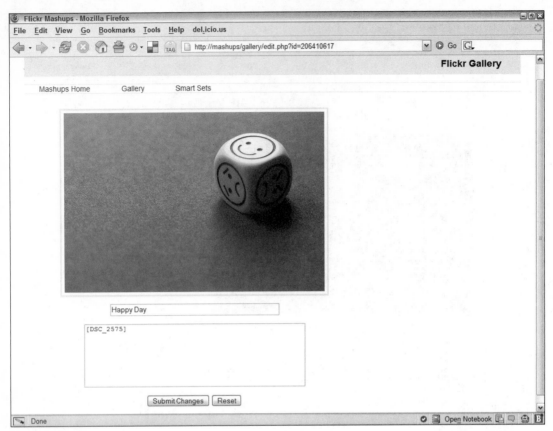

Figure 7-6

How It Works

The changes you made to `FlickrGallery.php` modify the class declaration so that `FlickrGallery` extends the base class `FlickrAuthenticator` and updates the `FlickrGallery` constructor to ensure that the base class constructor also gets called.

Two new methods are created. The first, `setMeta`, invokes the corresponding phpFlickr method and allows the title and description of a photo to be set. The second method, `checkAuthenticatedUser`, compares the NSID of the currently authenticated user with that of the user for whom the gallery is displaying photos.

> *Don't forget to change the NSID used by the `FlickrGallery` class to be your NSID; otherwise, you will not have permission to modify the photo's metadata.*

The new `edit.php` page creates a `FlickrGallery` instance and calls `authenticate`, asking for `write` permissions:

```
$gallery = new FlickrGallery();
$gallery->authenticate("write");
```

```
if (!$gallery->checkAuthenticatedUser())
{
  $gallery->error("You do not have permission to edit these details");
}
```

These checks *must* be done at the start of the document, before any output is sent — they will likely cause a redirect to take place, which is done by generating a `Location:` header. All headers must be sent before any other output takes place.

The rest of the page follows almost the same layout as the standard photo display page, except that the title and description are now editable form elements — note that the photo ID is also present in the form as a hidden field.

The `doEdit.php` script once again checks that the requesting user is currently authenticated with the appropriate permissions and then extracts the photo, title, and description from the request. It calls the `setMeta` method and redirects the user back to the photo page for this image, so that they can view the newly set title and description.

Other Authentication Mechanisms

The process described so far in this chapter is that used for web-based applications, and is the only one described in detail in this book. For non-web applications, the process is slightly different. The different approaches are summarized in this section, but if you want to use these, you should check the full details at Flickr's authentication pages at `http://www.flickr.com/services/api/misc.userauth.html`.

Desktop Application Authentication

The process for authenticating a desktop application is very similar to the one for authenticating a web-based application, but there is no callback URL to be specified — instead you use the `flickr.auth.getFrob` method to first get a frob. You then need to construct a URL for the user to go to in order to authenticate — this is done in exactly the same way as in the web-based application, but the URL here also includes the frob.

Once you have a URL, you need to direct the user to that web page — you can do this either by automatically opening the user's browser or by providing them with the URL to cut and paste into the browser's address bar. Once the user has completed authentication at the Flickr web site, they must return to your application and tell it that they have done so. Your desktop application can then proceed exactly as in the web-based application process by calling `flickr.auth.getToken`.

Mobile Application Authentication

The process for authenticating a mobile application is a little different, mainly to accommodate the limited user interfaces available to these applications, which often run on mobile phones with only a numeric keypad for data entry.

When you configure your API key for your mobile application, you first choose which set of permissions you need — read, write, or delete — and you are presented with an authentication URL of the form http://www.flickr.com/auth-12345.

You then need to send the user to the page at the authentication URL — perhaps by linking to there from your application's download page, or by asking them to visit it. Once they have authenticated and authorized your application, they are presented with a *mini-token,* which is a nine-digit number of the form 123-456-789. They must then enter this number into your application. Once the user has done this, your application can make a signed call to flickr.auth.getFullToken to exchange the mini-token for a normal token.

Summary

The Flickr authentication API offers a secure way to enable users to authorize third-party applications with various degrees of access to their Flickr photos. In this chapter you saw both how the authentication process works and how to implement an authenticated web-based application.

You learned how to configure your API key to enable authentication, built a PHP authentication class, saw how to sign authenticated API calls, and modified the gallery application to allow it to update photo metadata on Flickr

In the next chapter you will see how to use the Flickr API to upload photos to Flickr, but first, take a look at the exercises below to make some further modifications to the gallery application.

Exercises

1. On the edit.php page, allow the user to modify the tags used by the photo, as well as the title and description.

2. Currently the Edit link is shown to all viewers. Add a login link to the top of the page, and display the Edit link only if the current user both is logged in and is the user whose photos are being displayed.

Uploading Photos

In the previous few chapters you have seen how to view your photos on Flickr, and how to modify their metadata, but there is still one important piece missing. How do you get your photos there in the first place? Of course, you can always do this via Flickr's upload page, or with the Flickr Uploadr application, but in this chapter you will see how the uploading mechanism works and how to use it in your own applications — including the gallery application build in earlier chapters.

How Does Uploading Work?

The Upload API is regarded by Flickr as being separate from the main Flickr API, because it involves the transfer of binary data rather simple XML messaging. The Upload API has its own endpoint at `http://api.flickr.com/services/upload/`.

To upload a photo, you need to send four pieces of data to the Upload API endpoint:

- ❑ `api_key`: Your API key.

- ❑ `auth_token`: The authentication token for the user uploading photos — upload requires `write` access to be granted.

- ❑ `api_sig`: The signature for the API call — this value is calculated exactly as was described in Chapter 7.

- ❑ `photo`: The binary image data.

You can also use a number of optional parameters to set the photo's metadata:

- ❑ `title`: The title to be given to the photo.

- ❑ `description`: The description to be given to the photo.

- ❑ `tags`: A space-separated list of tags to be given to the photo.

- ❑ `is_public, is_friend, is_family`: The privacy level for the photo — use 0 for no and 1 for yes.

When calculating the api_sig *value for an upload request, you must include all parameters except those for the image data itself.*

The format of the request is a standard HTTP multipart form POST request — this is the same format as is sent when your browser uses an HTML form to perform file uploads. If you want to understand the fine details of building a multipart request, a good starting point is the HTML 4 Specification (http://www.w3.org/TR/html4/interact/forms.html#h-17.13.4.2), but in practice it is unusual to need to code such a thing from scratch — many libraries will do this for you. In this chapter we'll be using phpFlickr to handle the formatting of the upload request, but first, take a look inside a typical request so that you can see what is happening.

A typical request would look something like this:

```
POST /services/upload/ HTTP/1.1
Content-Type: multipart/form-data; boundary=27f3284b3aa12f234def
Host: www.flickr.com
Content-Length: 18294

--27f3284b3aa12f234def
Content-Disposition: form-data; name="api_key"

1f2811827f3284b3aa12f7bbb7792b8d
--27f3284b3aa12f234def
Content-Disposition: form-data; name="title"

My Uploaded Photo
--27f3284b3aa12f234def
Content-Disposition: form-data; name="auth_token"

537482-d1cf156c23903fa0
--27f3284b3aa12f234def
Content-Disposition: form-data; name="api_sig"

2650f6827bc3ba51bd9a3873de57d23e
--27f3284b3aa12f234def
Content-Disposition: form-data; name="photo"; filename="C:\photos\image.jpg"
Content-Type: image/jpeg


...
The raw image data appears here
...

--27f3284b3aa12f234def--
```

The first few lines are the HTTP headers that are sent; the body of the message itself doesn't begin until after the blank line. You can see that the message body is broken into sections — each delimited by an *encapsulation boundary*. The encapsulation boundary is a string consisting of two hyphens followed by a *boundary marker*. This boundary marker is a sequence of characters that can be any alphanumeric string (a few other characters are also allowed), but it *must not* appear in the data itself. The boundary marker is usually randomly generated and is defined in the Content-Type header of the HTTP request. The very last encapsulation boundary has a closing marker of two hyphens to indicate that no more sections follow.

Each section has its own set of headers. Here, most sections have only one header — Content-Disposition. The Content-Disposition header identifies each section as containing form data, and more importantly, it identifies the name of the data item. After the headers, each section then contains a blank line followed by the data themselves. For the image data, those data are the raw byte stream representing the image.

Creating an Upload Page

If you want to add new photos to your gallery, you currently need to go to the Flickr site and do it from there, or use one of the stand-alone tools such as Uploadr. Now that you've added some simple maintenance functions to enable you to edit your photo titles and tags, it would be nice to expand the gallery functionality so that you can upload new photos too.

Try It Out   **Uploading Your Photos**

In this exercise, you'll see how to add a new page to your gallery application to upload new photos.

1. To start with, you need to add a new method to FlickrGallery.php:

```php
<?php

class FlickrGallery extends FlickrAuthenticator
{
  ...

    function uploadPhoto($file, $title = null, $description = null, $tags = null,
      $isPublic = null, $isFriend = null, $isFamily = null)
    {
      $id = $this->flickr->sync_upload($file, $title, $description, $tags, $isPublic,
        $isFriend, $isFamily);

      if ($this->flickr->getErrorCode())
      {
        echo ("Error uploading photo: " . $this->flickr->getErrorMsg());
      }

      return $id;
    }
  }
?>
```

2. Next, you need an upload page — create a new file, upload.php, in your gallery directory:

```php
<?php
include (dirname(__FILE__) . '/../lib/gallery.php');
$gallery = new FlickrGallery();
$gallery->authenticate("write");
if (!$gallery->checkAuthenticatedUser())
{
  $gallery->error("You do not have permission to upload photos");
```

```
}
?>
<!DOCTYPE html PUBLIC "-//W3C//DTD XHTML 1.0 Transitional//EN"
  "http://www.w3.org/TR/xhtml1/DTD/xhtml1-transitional.dtd">
<html xmlns="http://www.w3.org/1999/xhtml">
<head>
  <link href="../css/main.css" rel="stylesheet" type="text/css" />
  <link href="../css/gallery.css" rel="stylesheet" type="text/css" />
  <title>Upload Photo</title>
</head>
<body>
<?php include ('header.php') ?>
<?php include ('navigation.php') ?>
<div class="photo-upload">
  <h1>Upload a Photo</h1>
  <form action="doUpload.php" method="post" enctype="multipart/form-data">
    <input type="hidden" name="MAX_FILE_SIZE" value="10485760" />
    <p class="upload-field">
      <label>Photo</label>
      <input name="file" type="file" size="50" />
    </p>
    <p class="photo-title-upload">
      <label>Title</label>
      <input name="title" type="text" id="title" size="50" />
    <p class="photo-description-upload">
      <label>Description</label>
      <textarea name="description" cols="50" rows="6" wrap="VIRTUAL"
id="description"></textarea>
    </p>
    <p class="photo-privacy-upload">
      <label>Tags</label>
      <input name="tags" type="text" id="tags" size="50" />
    </p>
    <p class="photo-tags-upload">
      <label>Privacy</label>
      <input type="radio" name="privacy" value="public" checked="checked"/>
Public<br/>
      <input type="radio" name="privacy" value="private" />Private<br/>
      <input type="radio" name="privacy" value="friends" />Friends Only<br/>
      <input type="radio" name="privacy" value="family" />Family Only<br/>
      <input type="radio" name="privacy" value="friendsfamily" />Friends and
Family<br/>
    </p>
    <p>
      <input type="submit" name="Submit" value="Upload Photo" />
      <input type="reset" name="Reset" value="Reset" />
    </p>
  </form>
</div>
</body>
</html>
```

3. Next, you need to create a form handler page, so create a file called doUpload.php in your gallery directory:

```php
<?php
include (dirname(__FILE__) . '/../lib/gallery.php');
$gallery = new FlickrGallery();
$gallery->authenticate("write");
if (!$gallery->checkAuthenticatedUser())
{
  $gallery->error("You do not have permission to upload photos to this account");
}

$size = $_FILES['file']['size'];
$filename = $_FILES['file']['tmp_name'];

$title = stripslashes($_REQUEST['title']);
$description = stripslashes($_REQUEST['description']);
$tags = stripslashes($_REQUEST['tags']);
$privacy = $_REQUEST['privacy'];

if (!empty($filename) && is_uploaded_file($filename) && $size > 0)
{
  $isPublic = 0;
  $isFriend = 0;
  $isFamily = 0;

  switch ($privacy)
  {
    case "public":
      $isPublic = 1;
      break;

    case "friends":
      $isFriend = 1;
      break;

    case "family":
      $isFamily = 1;
      break;

    case "friendsfamily":
      $isFriend = 1;
      $isFamily = 1;
      break;

  }
  $id = $gallery->uploadPhoto($filename, $title, $description, $tags, $isPublic,
    $isFriend, $isFamily);
}

header('Location: http://' . $_SERVER['HTTP_HOST'] . dirname($_SERVER['PHP_SELF'])
  . '/index.php');
?>
```

173

4. Now, in order to get to the upload page, you need a link to it, so add it to the main menu bar. Edit navigation.php:

```php
<?php
$user = $_SESSION['FlickrAuthenticatedUser'];
?>
<ul id="gallery-menu">
   <li><a href="../index.php">Mashups Home</a></li>
   <li><a href="index.php">Gallery</a></li>
   <li><a href="smartsets.php">Smart Sets</a></li>
<?php
if (!empty($user))
{
?>
   <li><a href="upload.php">Upload</a></li>
<?php
}
?>

   <li>
<?php
if (empty($user))
{
?>
      <a href="login.php">Login</a>
<?php
}
else
{
?>
      Logged in as <?php echo $user ?>
<?php
}
?>
   </li>
</ul>
```

The Upload link is only displayed if the user is currently logged in.

5. Finally, add a new CSS rule to gallery.css to enable the upload form to display correctly:

```css
.photo-upload label {
   display: block;
   font-weight: 600;
   margin-top: 0.5em;
   margin-bottom: 0.5em;
}
```

6. All the changes are now in place. Open up the gallery in your browser. If you are not already logged in, click the Login link in the menu bar — you should now see the Upload link. Click it and you will be taken to your new upload page, as in Figure 8-1.

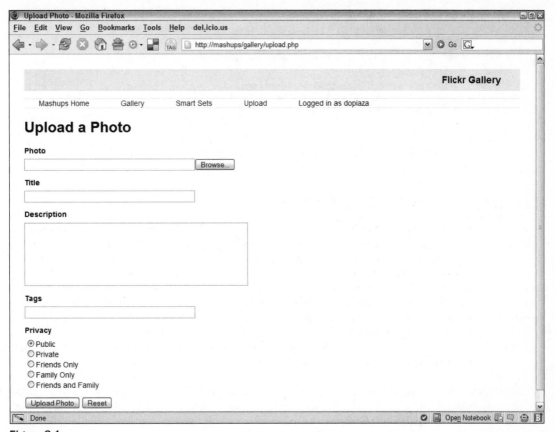

Figure 8-1

7. Browse your local disk until you find a photo to upload, add a little information in the title and description boxes and press the Upload Photo button. There will be a slight pause while your photo is uploaded, first to your web server, and then to Flickr. Once the process is complete, you will be redirected to the main gallery page where you should now see your photo.

How It Works

The `uploadPhoto()` method that you added to `FlickrGallery.php` takes a number of parameters. The first, `$file`, is the filename of the photo to upload — note that this code runs on the server, so this is the path to the file containing the photo *on the server*, not the client machine. The rest of the parameters are pretty much self-explanatory — they specify the title, description, tags, and privacy settings for the uploaded photo. `uploadPhoto()` doesn't do any processing of its arguments, it just passes them straight on to phpFlickr's `sync_upload` method to actually perform the upload.

`upload.php` is a fairly straightforward HTML form. It's worth noting that the form contains a file upload control:

```
<input name="file" type="file" size="50" />
```

Therefore, the form must specify an `enctype` attribute of `multipart/form-data`, like the following, rather than use the default value of `application/x-www-form-urlencoded`:

```
<form action="doUpload.php" method="post" enctype="multipart/form-data">
```

`doUpload.php` first of all checks that the user is authenticated with `write` permission, and then gets the size and location of the uploaded file. After checking the validity of the uploaded file, it extracts the metadata to be associated with the file from the request, and finally calls the `uploadPhoto()` method in `FlickrGallery` to upload the photo to Flickr.

Asynchronous Uploading

You might have noticed in the example in the previous section that the phpFlickr method you used was called `sync_upload`. PhpFlickr contains another method, called `async_upload`, that lets you perform an asynchronous upload. When you upload a photo using the synchronous method, the method does not return as soon as all the image data are sent to Flickr — Flickr has to perform a number of tasks first, including creating the set of different-sized images and storing it in the appropriate place on its servers. This process takes a little time and the Upload API does not return until it has finished. If you don't want your application to sit around waiting for Flickr to complete its processing, you can use the asynchronous version of the Upload API. With this, the API call returns as soon as all the data has been received at Flickr, leaving your application free to close the connection and continue doing other things while Flickr processes the uploaded photo in the background.

To specify that you want to use the asynchronous version of the API, you simply pass an extra argument, `async`, to Flickr in the body of your message — set the value to 1 for asynchronous uploading or 0 for synchronous. The phpFlickr method `async_upload` does this for you automatically.

If you upload photos asynchronously, you also need a way to find out when Flickr's processing is complete and the photos are available for viewing. The return value from the synchronous Upload API is the photo ID of the photo just uploaded, but when you use the asynchronous Upload API, you don't get a photo ID returned — instead you get a *ticket number*. This ticket number is a temporary identifier that lets you keep track of the progress of your uploaded photo — you can call the API method `flickr.photos .upload.checkTickets` to find out whether your upload is complete or not. The `checkTickets` method takes a list of ticket numbers and reports on the status of each one individually:

```
<rsp stat="ok">
  <uploader>
    <ticket id="324513135" invalid="1"/>
    <ticket id="324513136" complete="1" photoid="206410617" />
    <ticket id="324513137" complete="0" />
    <ticket id="324513138" complete="2"
  </uploader>
</rsp>
```

If a ticket was not found, the `invalid` attribute is set to 1; otherwise the `status` attribute indicates the progress of the upload. A `status` of 0 means that processing is not yet complete. A `status` of 1 indicates successful completion and the `photoid` attribute will be set to the photo ID for that photo. A `status` of 2 indicates that processing failed and the photo will not be available.

Replacing Photos

Alongside the Upload API, Flickr also provides a Replace API. This works in exactly the same way as the Upload API and has both synchronous and asynchronous versions. The Replace API endpoint is located at `http://api.flickr.com/services/replace/`, and the parameters for a `replace` call are as follows:

- ❑   `api_key`: Your API key.

- ❑   `photo_id`: The ID of the photo to be replaced.

- ❑   `auth_token`: The authentication token for the user who is replacing photos — `replace` requires `write` access to be granted.

- ❑   `auth_sig`: The signature for the API call — this value is calculated exactly as was described in Chapter 7.

- ❑   `async` (optional): Set to `1` for asynchronous uploading or `0` for synchronous.

- ❑   `photo`: The binary image data.

Note that you cannot change the photo's metadata when performing a `replace`.

PhpFlickr provides a `replace` method to allow easy access to the Flickr Replace API.

Summary

Flickr provides APIs to enable you to upload new photos and replace existing ones. In this chapter you saw how these methods differ from normal API calls in that they send binary data as part of the message body, and you also saw how to upload photos in both synchronous and asynchronous modes.

Your gallery application is now starting to take shape as a fairly functional application. In the next chapter we'll turn our attention back to the Flickr web site and you'll see how you can customize your own browsing experience using Firefox and Greasemonkey, but first, here's an exercise for you to try out another bit of the Flickr API.

Exercise

In this chapter you added upload functionality to the gallery. For this exercise, add a new screen to the application to enable you to replace an existing photo using the Replace API.

Remixing Flickr Using Greasemonkey

If there's anything about the Flickr web site that you wish was done just a little bit differently, this chapter is definitely for you. In this chapter you will learn how a Firefox extension called Greasemonkey can be used to customize the display of Flickr's web pages. You will create a set of Greasemonkey scripts that add both extra information and new functionality to Flickr. To use Greasemonkey, you will need to use the Firefox web browser — it will unfortunately not work in other browsers, such as Internet Explorer.

What is Greasemonkey?

Greasemonkey is an extension for the Firefox web browser that enables you to write user scripts that modify the behavior of the web sites you visit. Greasemonkey scripts are written in JavaScript, and look much like any other piece of JavaScript you might run in your browser, and you can use it to do most of the same things that you would in any client-side JavaScript.

You can find the official Greasemonkey web pages at `http://greasemonkey.mozdev.org/`.

Installing Greasemonkey

Installing Greasemonkey is very straightforward. First of all, you must make sure you have the latest version of the Firefox web browser installed — you can get this from `http://www.mozilla.com/firefox/`.

To install the Greasemonkey extension, go to the Greasemonkey web site at `http://greasemonkey.mozdev.org/` and click the Install Greasemonkey link.

Depending on your settings, Firefox may prevent Greasemonkey from installing automatically — in this case a bar will appear across the top of your browser window informing you of this, together with a button marked Edit Options. If you click this button, you are presented with a dialog box that enables you to authorize the site to install extensions on your computer, shown in Figure 9-1.

Figure 9-1

Add `greasemonkey.mozdev.org` to the list of allowed sites and close the dialog box. Now click the Install Greasemonkey link once more. This time you will see a dialog box asking if you want to install the extension, shown in Figure 9-2.

Figure 9-2

Click Install Now to complete the installation. Once Greasemonkey is installed, you will need to restart Firefox before you can use it.

Creating Your First Script

Creating a Greasemonkey script is as easy as writing a piece of JavaScript, so dive right in by creating a simple script.

Try It Out   **A Simple Greasemonkey Script**

In this exercise you'll create a simple script that will demonstrate how a Greasemonkey script can be made to execute when you visit certain web pages.

1. Create a file called `myfirstscript.user.js` and enter the following content:

```
// ==UserScript==
// @name        My First Script
// @namespace   http://www.dopiaza.org/flickr/greasemonkey/
// @description A simple first script
// @include     http://www.flickr.com/
// @include     http://flickr.com/
// ==/UserScript==

alert ("Hello! Welcome to Flickr!");
```

The name of the file you create for your Greasemonkey script is important — all Greasemonkey scripts must end with `.user.js`

2. Now you need to install the script. Open it in Firefox — you can do this in a variety of ways:

❏ Drag the file into the Firefox window.

❏ Type the full path to the file into the Firefox location bar.

❏ Select File⇨Open from the Firefox menus and navigate to the script.

3. Once you have opened the script, Greasemonkey should notice the `.user.js` extension and kick into action — you will see a Greasemonkey bar across the top of the browser window identifying the file as a Greasemonkey user script and asking if you want to install it. Click the Install button — you should then see an alert box confirming the script was installed.

4. Now, go to the Flickr home page at `http://www.flickr.com/` and you should see a new alert box pop up saying "Hello! Welcome to Flickr!" as you can see in Figure 9-3. Take a look at a few other pages on the Flickr site, and then come back to the home page. Each time you return to the home page, the alert box pops up.

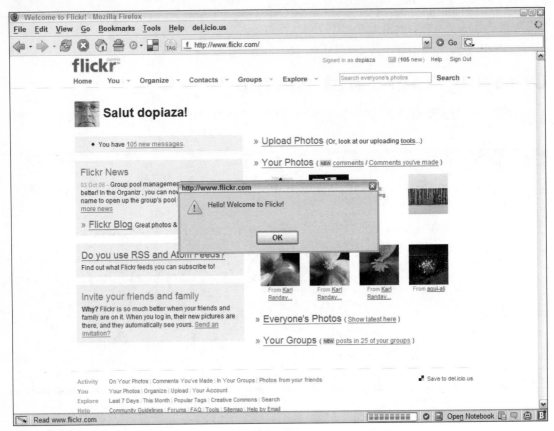

Figure 9-3

How It Works

The Greasemonkey script itself is very simple — it consists of a few comments, followed by a single line of Javascript:

```
alert ("Hello! Welcome to Flickr!");
```

This causes the alert box you saw to pop up. But why did it appear on the Flickr home page and no other? The answer lies in the comments at the start of the Greasemonkey user script.

```
// ==UserScript==
// @name        My First Script
// @namespace   http://www.dopiaza.org/flickr/greasemonkey/
// @description A simple first script
// @include     http://www.flickr.com/
// @include     http://flickr.com/
// ==/UserScript==
```

These comments are actually instructions to Greasemonkey describing how it should handle the script. All of these directives are optional, but most Greasemonkey scripts will include some, and often all of them.

❑ @name is the name of the script. This is what you see if you go to the Greasemonkey configuration screen — it's in the Firefox Tools menu under Manage User Scripts.

❑ @namespace is a URL used by Greasemonkey to distinguish between scripts that have the same name.

❑ @description is a human-readable description of the script shown when the script is selected in the Manage User Scripts dialog box.

❑ @include tells Greasemonkey on which pages the script should execute. The example here lists two pages http://www.flickr.com/ and http://flickr.com/ — it is necessary to list both variants of the URL because Greasemonkey treats them as separate pages. @include directives may include a wildcard in the form of an asterisk (*), so for example http://www.flickr.com/* would refer to all pages on the Flickr site.

❑ @exclude, not used in this example, specifies pages on which the script should not execute.

So, in this example, the script is run whenever the browser goes to either of the two pages listed in the @include directive: http://www.flickr.com/ and http://flickr.com.

You might want to uninstall this Greasemonkey script now — that alert box can start to get annoying after a while. If you open Tools ➪ Manage User Scripts, you can disable or completely uninstall any installed scripts.

Modifying Pages — A First Remix

Now you've seen how to create a very simple Greasemonkey script, it's time to move on to something more useful — your first Flickr remix using Greasemonkey. As you have seen in previous chapters, the key to accessing information on Flickr is the NSID. Every user and every group on Flickr has its own unique NSID, and this is the identifier you need when using most of the API methods. It is possible to find an NSID using the API, but it is often useful to be able to quickly find out the NSID of a user or group when you are testing, or just want to quickly try out a piece of code or an API method. In your first Flickr remix, you will create a Greasemonkey script that displays a user's NSID alongside their buddy icon.

Determining a User's NSID

In order to display a user's NSID, you first have to determine what it is. But how do you find out? A good place to start is on the user's main photostream page, where you can select View➪Page Source. Here you can see the HTML source for the page — there is a lot of HTML to look through, but the answer is buried away in here. If you look through this page carefully, you come to a piece of HTML that looks something like this:

```
<td class="Buddy">
    <img src="http://static.flickr.com/56/buddyicons/50317659@N00.jpg?1150665599"
alt="dopiaza's buddy icon" width="48" height="48" />
</td>
```

This is the HTML that displays the user's buddy icon at the top of the page. If you look at the URL for the buddy icon, you see that it also contains the NSID for the user. So once you have identified the buddy icon image, you can then determine the NSID.

What if the user hasn't set a buddy icon? In that case, they will still have the standard gray blockhead icon. You can still get the NSID from this, however: if you find a user who still has a gray blockhead icon set and look at the HTML for their photostream, you will find that their icon is displayed like this:

```
<td class="Buddy">
    <img src="http://www.flickr.com/images/buddyicon.jpg?50317659@N00"
alt="dopiaza's buddy icon" width="48" height="48" />
</td>
```

The user's NSID is still there, this time appended to the end of the usual blockhead buddy icon URL.

Try It Out   Finding the Images

Now that you can see how to get the NSID from the buddy icon, the question remains, how do you find the buddy icons themselves? To do that, you need to identify the different images in the page, which is what this exercise covers.

1. Create a new file called `findimages.user.js`, with the following content:

```
// ==UserScript==
// @name          Find Images
// @namespace     http://www.dopiaza.org/flickr/greasemonkey/
// @description   Find all images in a page
// @include       http://www.flickr.com/*
// @include       http://flickr.com/*
// ==/UserScript==

var imgElements = document.getElementsByTagName('img');

for (var i = 0; i < imgElements.length; i++)
{
    var img = imgElements[i];

    var src = img.getAttribute('src');

    GM_log("Found Image: " + src);
}
```

2. Open the file in Firefox and install the Greasemonkey script — either by clicking the Install button that appears or by selecting Tools⇨Install This User Script.

3. Open up the Javascript console by selecting Tools⇨Javascript Console, and clear any existing output by clicking the Clear button. Go to the Flickr home page (http://www.flickr.com/) in Firefox and observe the output to the Javascript console window — you should a long list of entries that look something like this:

```
http://www.dopiaza.org/flickr/greasemonkey/Find Images: Found Image:
http://www.flickr.com/images/spaceout.gif?0400849001151334252

http://www.dopiaza.org/flickr/greasemonkey/Find Images: Found Image:
/images/flickr_logo_gamma.gif.v1.2

http://www.dopiaza.org/flickr/greasemonkey/Find Images: Found Image:
```

```
/images/icon_unread.gif.v1.4

http://www.dopiaza.org/flickr/greasemonkey/Find Images: Found Image:
http://static.flickr.com/56/buddyicons/50317659@N00.jpg?1151240153
```

This is a list of all of the images in the page, including the buddy icon.

How It Works

This Greasemonkey script uses the same technique for finding elements in the web page that any other piece of client-side Javascript might use. It uses Firefox's standard Javascript implementation of the W3C DOM—the World Wide Web Consortium's Document Object Model Specification (`http://www.w3.org/DOM/`). A detailed description of how to use the DOM is beyond the scope of this book, but you can find many useful reference documents at the Mozilla Developer Center (`http://developer.mozilla.org/en/docs/DOM`).

The first thing the script does is get a list of all the image elements held within the current document—in other words, all instances of the `<img>` tag in the current web page:

```
var imgElements = document.getElementsByTagName('img');
```

The script then loops through each `img` element and extracts the value of the `src` attribute, which contains the path to the actual image being referenced:

```
var src = img.getAttribute('src');
```

Finally, the script calls a special Greasemonkey method, `GM_log`:

```
GM_log("Found Image: " + src);
```

`GM_log` is mainly used for debugging—it outputs a message to the Javascript console. Here it is used to demonstrate that all the images have successfully been identified.

Completing the Remix

Now you've seen some of the key elements of the script in action, it's time to put all the bits together and finish off your first Greasemonkey remix.

Try It Out   Displaying the NSID

In the final exercise in this section, you'll use everything you've learned to create a script that displays the user's NSID next to the buddy icon.

1. Create a new file called `showflickrnsid.user.js`, with the following content:

```
// ==UserScript==
// @name          Show Flickr NSID
// @namespace     http://www.dopiaza.org/flickr/greasemonkey/
// @description   Display user's NSID
```

```
// @include        http://www.flickr.com/*
// @include        http://flickr.com/*
// ==/UserScript==

var imgElements = document.getElementsByTagName('img');

var buddyIconPattern = /^http:\/\/static.flickr.com\/\d+\/buddyicons\/(.+).jpg/;
var blockheadPattern = /^http:\/\/www.flickr.com\/images\/buddyicon.jpg\?(.+)$/;

for (var i = 0; i < imgElements.length; i++)
{
  var img = imgElements[i];

  var imgClass = img.getAttribute('class');
  if (imgClass == 'person_hover_img')
  {
    // Just ignore this one - it's used when you hover over an user's icon
    continue;
  }

  // Check to see if this is a buddy icon image
  var src = img.getAttribute('src');
  var result = buddyIconPattern.exec(src);

  if (result == null)
  {
    // Try the second version, just in case they have no buddy icon set
    result = blockheadPattern.exec(src);
  }

  if (result != null)
  {
    var nsid = result[1];

    // We want the first containing tag that isn't an <a> tag
    var container = img.parentNode;
    while (container.nodeName != null && container.nodeName == 'A')
    {
      container = container.parentNode;
    }

    var node = document.createElement('span');
    node.appendChild(document.createTextNode(nsid));

    node.style.fontSize = 'xx-small';
    node.style.color = 'grey';

    container.appendChild(node);
  }
}
```

2. Install the script into Firefox as usual and take a look at some pages on Flickr — you will see that wherever you come across a buddy icon you will find the NSID for that user or group displayed alongside it, as you can see in Figure 9-4.

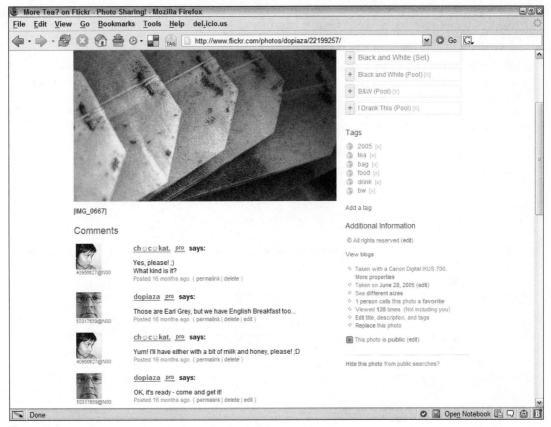

Figure 9-4

How It Works

This script largely follows the pattern of the previous one and starts by getting a list of all the `<img>` elements in the document.

It also defines two regular expression patterns:

```
var buddyIconPattern = /^http:\/\/static.flickr.com\/\d+\/buddyicons\/(.+).jpg/;
var blockheadPattern = /^http:\/\/www.flickr.com\/images\/buddyicon.jpg\?(.+)$/;
```

These regular expressions match the URLs used for buddy icons. In each pattern, the part in parentheses represents the NSID of the user.

For each image present in the page, the script needs to figure out if it is a buddy icon or not. The very first thing it determines is whether the `class` attribute of the `<img>` tag is set to `person_hover_img`. The reason for this isn't obvious until you see the effects. When you hover over a user's buddy icon, a popup menu appears, containing another copy of the buddy icon. That icon has a class of `person_hover_img`. You don't really want to display an NSID alongside this popup, so this check simply filters those out. If you're curious, try commenting out this check and observe the difference!

The next step is to execute the two regular expressions defined to see if either of them matches. If there is a match, it means that this image is indeed a buddy icon. If there is no match, the script moves on to the next image.

Now that you've found a buddy icon and extracted the NSID, the next step is to display the NSID. You can do this by creating a new HTML element (a `<span>` tag) that contains the NSID as a text element. The `span` element needs to be appended to the same container as the `<img>` element — this is usually a `<div>` or a `<td>` tag, depending on the particular page being viewed — so the parent node that contains the `<img>` tag needs to be identified.

```
// We want the first containing tag that isn't an <a> tag
var container = img.parentNode;
while (container.nodeName != null && container.nodeName == 'A')
{
  container = container.parentNode;
}
```

If the parent is an `<a>` tag, this is ignored and the next parent up the chain is used instead; otherwise the `<span>` would end up being part of the hyperlink too.

Finally, the new span element is created and inserted into the page.

```
var node = document.createElement('span');
node.appendChild(document.createTextNode(nsid));

node.style.fontSize = 'xx-small';
node.style.color = 'grey';

container.appendChild(node);
```

Using XPath

Another good way to find tags in a web page is by using Firefox's built-in XPath support. You can find information on using XPath within Firefox at the Mozilla Developer Center (`http://developer.mozilla.org/en/docs/XPath`).

Try It Out   **Using XPath to Find Tags**

In this exercise you'll create a script to locate all the images on the page, just as you did in the previous section, but you'll use XPath to do it.

1. Create a new file called `findimageswithxpath.user.js`, with the following content:

```
// ==UserScript==
// @name        Find Images with XPath
// @namespace   http://www.dopiaza.org/flickr/greasemonkey/
// @description Find all images in a page
// @include     http://www.flickr.com/*
// @include     http://flickr.com/*
```

```
// ==/UserScript==

var imgElements = document.evaluate(
  "//img[@width='75']",
  document,
  null,
  XPathResult.UNORDERED_NODE_SNAPSHOT_TYPE,
  null);

for (var i = 0; i < imgElements.snapshotLength; i++)
{
  var img = imgElements.snapshotItem(i);

  var src = img.getAttribute('src');

  GM_log("Found Image: " + src);
}
```

2. Install the script in Firefox and then open up the Flickr home page (http://www.flickr.com/) along with the JavaScript console. As before, the console will show a list of messages generated by the GM_log statement, each one identifying an image that was found in the document. This time, however, you will see that only the actual photographs displayed on the front page are shown in the console — the other graphics, such as the Flickr logo, aren't listed. That's because the XPath query explicitly asks for images that specify a width of 75.

How It Works

This example is identical to the previous "find images" example, except that it uses an XPath query instead of the getElementsByTagName method.

```
var imgElements = document.evaluate(
  "//img[@width='75']",
  document,
  null,
  XPathResult.UNORDERED_NODE_SNAPSHOT_TYPE,
  null);
```

The most common way to use XPath in Firefox is through the document.evaluate method. This method takes five parameters. The first is the XPath query itself. The query used here says "Search for all <img> elements that have the width attribute set to 75." It is possible to create a wide variety of queries using XPath, and the W3C documentation at http://www.w3.org/TR/xpath contains full details about the syntax.

The second parameter specifies the point from which the XPath query starts. Here the query covers the whole of the document, but if you want to search over just a subset, you can instead specify any element — perhaps one retrieved from a previous XPath search, or by a call to getElementsByTagName.

The third parameter is a reference to a namespace resolver function. Unless you have very specific needs, you probably won't ever need to use this. It is set to null here.

The fourth parameter indicates the type of result to be returned. In most cases, XPathResult.UNORDERED_NODE_SNAPSHOT_TYPE is the simplest means of accessing the search results. This does, however, return the matching nodes in what is essentially a random order. If the order in which you process the results is important, you may want to use `XPathResult.ORDERED_NODE_SNAPSHOT_TYPE` instead.

The final parameter enables you to specify an existing `XPathResult` object to use for the results. It is most common to specify `null` here, which causes a new object to be created.

The call to `document.evaluate` returns an instance of an `XPathResult` object, and the `snapshotItem()` method is used to access each individual node:

```
for (var i = 0; i < imgElements.snapshotLength; i++)
{
  var img = imgElements.snapshotItem(i);

  ...
}
```

Highlighting Comments: A Second Remix

Group discussions and comments on photos on Flickr are presented as a single long list and can get quite unwieldy as the list grows longer. Picking out the parts where you contributed can be difficult. Your next Flickr remix is going to subtly change the presentation of those pages to make it easy to find your own comments — you will create a Greasemonkey script to scan through all of the comments on a page and highlight any comments made by you by modifying the background color.

If you look at the source for any Flickr page that has comments, either a photo page or a group discussion page, you will see that all comments are held in a table and look something like this:

```
<tr valign="top">
  <td class="Who">
     <a href="/photos/dopiaza/" name="comment72157594178503351"><img
src="http://static.flickr.com/56/buddyicons/50317659@N00.jpg?1151240153"
alt="view profile" width="48" height="48" /></a>
  </td>

  <td class="Said">
    <h4><a href="/photos/dopiaza/">dopiaza</a>
    ...
  </td>
</tr>
```

Each comment has a table data cell with the class `Who`, which contains the buddy icon of the person making the comment. This means, as you saw earlier, that you can work out the NSID of each commenter. You just need to identify which of those comments were made by you — so somehow, the script needs to know what *your* NSID is. One way to let it know would be to hardwire your NSID into the script, but that's not a particularly portable solution — it would be much better if the script could determine the NSID of the currently logged-in user from the page content. If you look at the page source for any Flickr page, this turns out to be quite straightforward. At the top of each page is some Javascript that sets up a number of global variables. The part of most immediate interest is the line that sets the `global_nsid` variable — this is set to the NSID of the currently logged-in user.

```
global_nsid = '50317659@N00'
```

To access this JavaScript variable from a Greasemonkey script, you need to use the `unsafeWindow` variable. `unsafeWindow` is a direct reference to the `window` object in the web page. It is named as such to reinforce the fact that it is unsafe — it bypasses the usual mechanism that Greasemonkey employs to protect your script from attack from malicious web pages. It is, however, the only means of getting at the global variables defined in the web page, via something like this:

```
var myNsid = unsafeWindow.global_nsid;
```

In general, you should not use `unsafeWindow` if your script is likely to be executed in the context of on a page that you do not trust — its use opens up a number of potential backdoors through which your script can be misused. In this instance, there's probably little cause for concern. The Flickr staff aren't, on the whole, malicious in nature and using `unsafeWindow` here is probably OK.

You've now covered all the basic principles needed for this remix, so it's time to dive right in and look at the completed script.

Try It Out   **Highlighting Your Comments**

This exercise will create a script that will highlight your comments on a Flickr image.

1.   Create a file called `flickrcommenthighlighter.user.js`, with the following contents:

```
// ==UserScript==
// @name          Flickr Comment Highlighter
// @namespace     http://www.dopiaza.org/flickr/greasemonkey/
// @description   Highlight Flickr Comments
// @include       http://www.flickr.com/*
// @include       http://flickr.com/*
// ==/UserScript==


var buddyIconPattern = /^http:\/\/static.flickr.com\/\d+\/buddyicons\/(.+).jpg/;
var blockheadPattern = /^http:\/\/www.flickr.com\/images\/buddyicon.jpg\?(.+)$/;

var myNsid = unsafeWindow.global_nsid;

var commenters = document.evaluate(
  "//td[@class='Who']",
  document,
  null,
  XPathResult.UNORDERED_NODE_SNAPSHOT_TYPE,
  null);

for (var i = 0; i < commenters.snapshotLength; i++)
{
  var isMyComment = false;
```

```
      var tdCommenter = commenters.snapshotItem(i);

      // We are looking for the buddy icon contained within
      var images = tdCommenter.getElementsByTagName('IMG');

      for (var j = 0; j < images.length; j++)
      {
        var img = images[j];
        var src = img.getAttribute('src');
        var result = buddyIconPattern.exec(src);

        if (result == null)
        {
          // Try the second version, just in case you have no buddy icon set
          result = blockheadPattern.exec(src);
        }

        if (result != null)
        {
          // This is the buddy icon
          var nsid = result[1];
          if (nsid == myNsid)
          {
            isMyComment = true;
          }

          break;
        }
      }

      if (isMyComment)
      {
        // Need to restyle the comment to highlight it.
        // The parent container is the table row, and contains the commenter details
        // and the comment itself
        var container = tdCommenter.parentNode;
        container.style.backgroundColor = '#EEEEEE';
      }
    }
```

2. Install the script in your browser in the usual way, and browse through group discussions in which you have taken part, or photos that you have commented on. You will see your comments highlighted with a gray background, as opposed to the white background of other comments, as shown in Figure 9-5. I've chosen gray as it fits in well with the overall Flickr color scheme and doesn't look too out of place on the page. You are, of course, free to choose any color that suits you—just change the #EEEEEE in the script to the color of your choice.

Figure 9-5

How It Works

The script starts by finding all the table cells that are styled with the class Who — remember, these are the ones that contain buddy icons:

```
var commenters = document.evaluate(
  "//td[@class='Who']",
  document,
  null,
  XPathResult.UNORDERED_NODE_SNAPSHOT_TYPE,
  null);
```

The script then loops through each cell found, and for each one retrieves a list of images contained within:

```
var images = tdCommenter.getElementsByTagName('IMG');
```

193

Each image is then checked, just as before, to see if it is a buddy icon — if it is, the NSID is extracted and compared against that of the currently logged-in user. If they are the same, the isMyComment flag is set to true.

Finally, if isMyComment is set to true, the script locates the table row containing the comment and changes the background color to light gray.

Enhancing the Flickr Paginator

The final remix in this chapter looks at the Flickr Paginator — that's the list at the bottom of pages of links that let you jump to different page numbers, shown in Figure 9-6.

Figure 9-6

This remix enhances the Paginator by adding a text box that enables you to type in a page number and jump directly to that page.

If you go to a page on which the paginator appears (for example, your photostream) and view the source, the paginator looks something like this:

```
<div class="Pages">
  <div class="Paginator">
    <a href="/photos/dopiaza/page4/" class="Prev">&lt; Prev</a>
    <a href="/photos/dopiaza/">1</a>
    <a href="/photos/dopiaza/page2/">2</a>
    <a href="/photos/dopiaza/page3/">3</a>
    <a href="/photos/dopiaza/page4/">4</a>
    <span class="this-page">5</span>
    <a href="/photos/dopiaza/page6/">6</a>
    <a href="/photos/dopiaza/page7/">7</a>
    <a href="/photos/dopiaza/page8/">8</a>
    <span class="break">...</span>
    <a href="/photos/dopiaza/page145/">145</a>
    <a href="/photos/dopiaza/page146/">146</a>
    <a href="/photos/dopiaza/page6/" class="Next">Next &gt;</a>
  </div>
  <div class="Results">(2,628 photos)</div>
</div>
```

Each page number shown is a link (`<a>`), with the exception of the current page, which is a `<span>`. This remix will place an input text field immediately before the Next link.

Identifying the Paginator itself is straightforward; an XPath query of `//div[@class='Paginator']"` will do that. Finding the point at which the text box should be inserted is a little trickier. If you look at the paginator HTML above, you can see that the Next link is the very last tag in the paginator `div`. As far as Firefox is concerned, however, it isn't the last node inside that `div` — there is also a text node containing the carriage return and other whitespace. To cope with this, the script needs to identify the last *non-text* node present in the `div`. This is the Next link.

Try It Out   Enhancing the Paginator

This exercise will enhance the usefulness of the default Flickr paginator by adding a text box into which the user can enter a page number to jump to.

1. Create a file called `jumptoflickrpage.user.js`, with the following contents:

```
// ==UserScript==
// @name          Jump to Flickr Page
// @namespace     http://www.dopiaza.org/flickr/greasemonkey/
// @description   Jump to a specific Flickr page in a paginated set of pages.
// @include       http://www.flickr.com/*
// @include       http://flickr.com/*
// ==/UserScript==

var paginators = document.evaluate(
  "//div[@class='Paginator']",
  document,
  null,
  XPathResult.UNORDERED_NODE_SNAPSHOT_TYPE,
  null);
```

```
for (var i = 0; i < paginators.snapshotLength; i++)
{
  var paginator = paginators.snapshotItem(i);

  // Place the text box immediately before the "Next" item, which is the last
  // non-text element in the paginator (There is whitespace after it, which shows
  // up as a text node). It may be an anchor or a span, depending on whether we are
  // at the last page or not.
  var paginatorChildren = paginator.childNodes;

  var nextElement;
  for (var j = paginatorChildren.length - 1; j >= 0; j--)
  {
    if (paginatorChildren[j].nodeType == 1) // Element Node
    {
      nextElement = paginatorChildren[j];
      break;
    }
  }

  var inputBox = document.createElement('input');
  inputBox.setAttribute("type", "text");
  inputBox.setAttribute("size", "3");

  paginator.insertBefore(inputBox, nextElement);

  inputBox.addEventListener('keypress', function(evt)
  {
    var keyVal = evt.which;
    var key = String.fromCharCode(keyVal);

    if (key == '\r')
    {
      var pageNum = evt.target.value;

      // So, where are we now?
      var loc = window.location.href;
      // Remove any existing page number
      loc = loc.replace(/page\d+(\/)?$/, '');
      // Append the new page number
      loc += 'page' + pageNum + '/';
      // And go to the new page
      window.location.href = loc;
    }
    else
    {
      if (key != '\b' && isNaN(key))
      {
        evt.preventDefault();
      }
    }
  }, true);
}
```

2. Install the script into your browser and navigate to a Flickr page on which the paginator appears — a user's photostream page, for example. You should now see a text box included within the paginator. Type in a number and hit return, and you will be taken to the relevant page. You can see this in Figure 9-7.

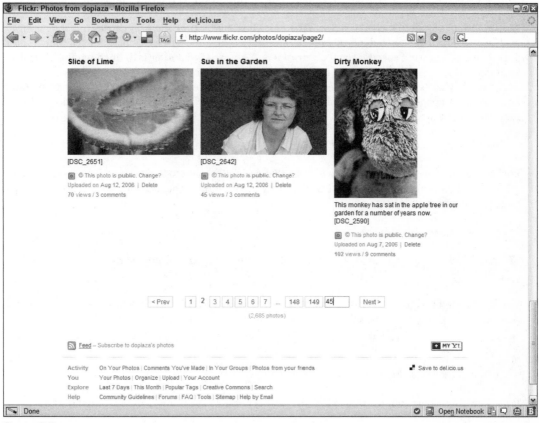

Figure 9-7

How It Works

The script uses XPath to identify any paginators in the page, and for each one modifies it by adding a text box.

The script identifies the location in which to insert the text box by working backward through the list of the paginator's child elements until it finds an element node. Element nodes have a node type of 1, as defined in the W3C DOM Specification.

```
for (var j = paginatorChildren.length - 1; j >= 0; j--)
{
    if (paginatorChildren[j].nodeType == 1) // Element Node
    {
```

```
        nextElement = paginatorChildren[j];
        break;
    }
}
```

Once the insertion point has been determined, a new input text box is created and added to the document.

The final step is to add an *event handler* to the input box. Every time the user carries out an action, such as pressing a key or clicking the mouse, an *event* is triggered. An event handler is a function that is executed whenever a specific event occurs. Here, a `keypress` handler is defined via the control's `addEventListener` method. This event handler will then be invoked every time the `keypress` event is triggered — whenever the user presses a key. It checks which key was pressed, and if it was the return key, the current page URL is modified to reflect the new target page. First of all, the location of the current page is obtained:

```
var loc = window.location.href;
```

Flickr pages that are paginated all have URLs that end with /pageXX/, where XX is the current page number. If the /pageXX/ part is missing, the first page is shown. The next step is to remove any existing page number from the URL:

```
loc = loc.replace(/page\d+(\/)?$/, '');
```

The regular expression /page\d+(\/)?$/ matches the string page followed by one or more digits and an optional trailing slash. If found, this string is removed from the URL.

Finally, the target page number is appended to the current URL and the web browser redirected to the new location:

```
loc += 'page' + pageNum + '/';

window.location.href = loc;
```

If the key pressed was not the return key, the script checks to see if it was either a digit or the backspace key:

```
if (key != '\b' && isNaN(key))
{
    evt.preventDefault();
}
```

If the key was not the backspace or a valid number, `evt.preventDefault()` is called. This prevents the default action for the event being taken — basically preventing the event from being passed any further along the chain of event handlers, so that the keypress is effectively discarded.

Learning More About Greasemonkey

This chapter has only scratched the surface of Greasemonkey. If you want to learn more about writing Greasemonkey scripts, Mark Pilgrim's excellent web site Dive Into Greasemonkey is by far the best place to start. You can find it at `http://diveintogreasemonkey.org/`.

Summary

In this chapter you saw how Greasemonkey can be used to modify Flickr's web pages. You have learned how to install Greasemonkey, create and install user scripts, locate elements in a web page using XPath, insert new HTML elements into the document, and create event handlers to introduce new behavior into the page.

In the next chapter, you'll look at a different way to use the images stored on Flickr. First, however, you might like to hone your Greasemonkey skills a little by trying the exercises below.

Exercises

1. The drop-down menus at the top of every Flickr page are a handy way to quickly navigate around the site. Write a Greasemonkey script that enables you to add some of your own custom locations to the drop-down menus. For example, add a link to the bottom of the Groups menu to take you to your favorite group. Add a link to the bottom of the Explore menu to take you to the API documentation page.

    Here are a few hints: if you look at the source for a Flickr page you will see a `<div>` with an ID of `candy_nav_button_bar`. This `<div>` contains all of those menus. Each drop-down menu has its own `<div>` — for example, the Explore menu is held in a `<div>` with an ID of `candy_nav_button_explore`. Within each menu `<div>` you will see the series of links that appear in the drop-down list — you simply need to append your links to these lists.

2. Greasemonkey's Jump to Page script works quite well, but gives strange results if you try to jump to a page that doesn't exist. For example, the paginator may only list 25 pages, but there's nothing to stop you trying to jump to page 26, or page 27, or page 2007. Modify the script so that you can jump only to a valid page.

Working with ImageMagick

In previous chapters you saw a variety of ways to present images sourced from Flickr in your web pages. So far we have focused on straightforward HTML-based presentations. In this chapter, you'll get to try something a little different — you'll see how to use the popular ImageMagick software to dynamically build your own graphics using images sourced from Flickr.

What Is ImageMagick?

ImageMagick is a suite of software that enables you to create and modify bitmapped images. Despite being specifically designed to work with images, ImageMagick doesn't have a graphical user interface in the way that applications such as Adobe Photoshop do; instead it is driven largely from the command line — or, more often, programmatically, via one of the many interfaces available. One of the most popular interfaces to ImageMagick is the PerlMagick library. PerlMagick provides a convenient object-oriented Perl interface to ImageMagick that we will be using in this chapter. Note that this chapter assumes that you have already set up Perl and the Perl Flickr API as described in Chapter 3.

ImageMagick is free software, and you can obtain both source and binary releases from the main ImageMagick web site at `http://www.imagemagick.org/`. Binary versions are available for a variety of platforms, including Microsoft Windows and many varieties of Unix, including Linux and Mac OS X.

Installation of ImageMagick and PerlMagick will vary depending on the platform you are running on, and you can find ImageMagick installation instructions at `http://www.imagemagick.org/script/binary-releases.php` and PerlMagick installation instructions at `http://www.imagemagick.org/script/perl-magick.php`. Pre-packed installation packages are available for a number of common platforms.

If you are using Microsoft Windows, you can download a Windows installer from the ImageMagick web site at `http://www.imagemagick.org/script/binary-releases.php`. There are different variants of the Windows installer — you can get versions to handle 8- or 16-bit images, and that are either statically or dynamically linked. Unless you are very sure you need something different, you should download the 16-bit dynamically linked version.

When installing under Microsoft Windows you will be asked at some point during the installation if you want to install the PerlMagick libraries — make sure you say yes to this.

If you are using Linux, most distributions will already include ImageMagick and PerlMagick — you should refer to your Linux distribution's installation instructions to see how to install these. If necessary, you can download an RPM file from the ImageMagick web site, together with installation instructions.

If you are using Mac OS X, you can find a packaged version of ImageMagick at http://www.entropy.ch/software/macosx/.

<table>
<tr><td>Try It Out</td><td>Mixing ImageMagick with Flickr</td></tr>
</table>

The easiest way to see how to use Perl to interface with both Flickr and ImageMagick is by example. Let's start by creating a quick Perl script that retrieves an image from Flickr and performs some basic processing using ImageMagick.

1. Create a file called 10-1.pl with the contents shown below. Note that this file is different from the PHP scripts you have been writing in that it is not executed by the web server. You run this from the command line, so it doesn't matter too much where you save it. Don't forget to enter your API Key, API secret, and NSID at the appropriate places.

```perl
#!/usr/bin/perl

use Image::Magick;
use Flickr::API;
use XML::Parser::Lite::Tree::XPath;

$apikey = 'YOUR-API-KEY';
$apisecret = 'YOUR-API-SECRET';

# Replace this with your NSID
$myNSID = '50317659@N00';

$flickr = new Flickr::API(
    {
        'key'    => $apikey,
        'secret' => $apisecret,
    });

$response = $flickr->execute_method('flickr.photos.search',
    {
        'user_id' => $myNSID,
        'per_page' => 1,
        'page' => 1,
    });

my $xpath = new XML::Parser::Lite::Tree::XPath($response->{'tree'});

@photos = $xpath->select_nodes('/photos/photo');

$image = Image::Magick->new;

if ($#photos >= 0)
{
```

```
    $photo = $photos[0];
    $url = 'http://static.flickr.com/' . $photo->{'attributes'}->{'server'} . '/'
        . $photo->{'attributes'}->{'id'} . '_' . $photo->{'attributes'}->{'secret'}
        . '_s.jpg';
    $image->Read($url);
}

$compositeImage = Image::Magick->new;
$compositeImage->Set(size=>'85x85');
$compositeImage->Read('xc:black');
$compositeImage->Composite(image => $image->[0], compose => 'Copy', x => 5, y =>5);

$compositeImage->Write(filename => 'image.jpg', quality => 85);
```

2. Run this script from the command line by typing the command `perl 10-1.pl`.

A new file should be created in the current directory. It will be the small square version of your most recent public photograph on Flickr, surrounded by a black border — something like that shown in Figure 10-1.

Figure 10-1

Remember that in Perl, the @ character is used to denote an array. Your NSID contains an @, so when you assign your NSID to the $myNSID variable, you must use single quotes around the string ('50317659@N00') to avoid variable expansion. If you use double quotes ("50317659@N00"), Perl will interpret that as an attempt to use the @N00 array.

How It Works

Let's take a look at that Perl script piece by piece to see what is happening here. The opening line

```
#!/usr/bin/perl
```

is only really of interest if you are running on a Unix system. It identifies the location of the Perl executable. It's good practice to put this in here, but for the purposes of this example, you can safely ignore it.

Next you have a list of the different Perl modules required by this script.

```
use Image::Magick;
use Flickr::API;
use XML::Parser::Lite::Tree::XPath;
```

The first two are reasonably obvious — they are the ImageMagick and Flickr API Perl libraries. The third is a little less obvious. The Perl Flickr API library returns an XML tree object, and one of the easiest ways to select the parts of the tree you are interested in is to use an XPath query. This third library provides the tools needed to do that.

Next, the script instantiates a `Flickr::API` object. The constructor for this takes a single parameter, which is a Perl *hash*, or associative array.

```
$flickr = new Flickr::API(
  {
    'key'    => $apikey,
    'secret' => $apisecret,
  });
```

The hash contains just two values — the Flickr API key and secret to be used. Once you have an instance of the `Flickr::API` object, you can invoke an API method:

```
$response = $flickr->execute_method('flickr.photos.search',
  {
    'user_id' => $myNSID,
    'per_page' => 1,
    'page' => 1,
  });
```

`Flickr::API` provides a method, `execute_method`, that is used to invoke Flickr API methods. It takes two parameters, the Flickr method to invoke and a hash containing the arguments for that method. Here, you are invoking the `flickr.photos.search` method to find the most recently uploaded public photo for the specified NSID.

The response returned by `execute_method` contains an instance of `XML::Parser::Lite::Tree`. This is a representation of the XML tree, similar to the one returned by phpFlickr. Rather than navigate this tree structure manually, you make use of the `XML::Parser::Lite::Tree::XPath` class to select the nodes you are interested in via an XPath query:

```
my $xpath = new XML::Parser::Lite::Tree::XPath($response->{'tree'});

@photos = $xpath->select_nodes('/photos/photo');
```

The XPath query used is `/photos/photo`, which will find all `<photo>` elements contained within the root `<photos>` element. Now, you only requested a single photo, so you would expect to find only one such node. You take the first (and only) element from the array and build the URL to the square photo stored on Flickr in the usual way:

```
$photo = $photos[0];
$url =  'http://static.flickr.com/' . $photo->{'attributes'}->{'server'} . '/'
  . $photo->{'attributes'}->{'id'} . '_' . $photo->{'attributes'}->{'secret'}
  . '_s.jpg';
```

Now for ImageMagick — first of all, an instance of an `Image::Magick` object is created:

```
$image = Image::Magick->new;
```

Then the image is read into the `Image::Magick` object from the constructed URL.

```
$image->Read($url);
```

This `$image` object is just a temporary place to store the image in a form you can use easily within ImageMagick. Next, you create a second `Image::Magick` instance that represents the final image:

```
$compositeImage = Image::Magick->new;
```

There are far too many methods available in the PerlMagick API to list here, but you can read about them in the online documentation. Here, you use a few of them to create a slightly modified version of our Flickr image. First, you set the size to 85 pixels square:

```
$compositeImage->Set(size=>'85x85');
```

Next, the new image is filled in with a solid color by reading in one of ImageMagick's internal *pseudo-image* formats, `xc:black`.

```
$compositeImage->Read('xc:black');
```

A pseudo-image is something that is treated by ImageMagick just like any other image, but is automatically generated. The XC pseudo-images are images consisting of a single solid color. You can see a full list of pseudo-image formats available on the ImageMagick web site at `http://www.imagemagick .org/script/formats.php`.

`$compositeImage` now contains a completely black 85 × 85 pixel image. The square image that was fetched from Flickr into the `$image` object is 75 × 75 pixels. If you copy that image onto the center of the black square, you should get a nice black frame around the edge of your photo. To do this you use the `Composite` method, which composites one image onto another. This method has many modes of operation — you just need a straightforward `Copy`. In order to get the black border around the photo, the image is positioned at coordinates (5, 5) — this should center the 75 × 75 pixel image within the 85 × 85 square.

```
$compositeImage->Composite(image => $image->[0], compose => 'Copy', x => 5, y =>5);
```

Note that the image copied is referred to as `$image->[0]`. An `Image::Magick` object can contain a number of different images, as you will see later in this chapter. This notation provides a convenient means of accessing those images.

Finally, you write the image out as a JPEG, using a quality of `85`.

```
$compositeImage->Write(filename => 'image.jpg', quality => 85);
```

Building a Group Badge

Now that you've seen an example of mixing together images from Flickr and ImageMagick, let's look at a more complex one. For the next project you will create another badge, this time to highlight a Flickr group pool. Each group on Flickr has a pool of photos contributed by the members — what better way to promote the group than to generate a badge showing recent submissions to the group pool? Such a badge would be perfect for inclusion on the group's main page on Flickr, in your Flickr profile, or perhaps if the group has a separate web site used to promote the group, then a badge would sit nicely there too. This badge will be different from those generated in Chapter 5, as it will consist of a single JPEG created using ImageMagick. Finally, you'll also create an HTML client-side image map to enable hotspots on the image, allowing the photos to link back to Flickr.

The badge you will be generating will be a fairly simple one. It will take the eight photos most recently added to the specified group's pool and arrange them around the edge of a three-by-three grid, with the group icon at the centre of the badge. You can see an example badge in Figure 10-2.

Figure 10-2

This badge will work for any group on Flickr with at least eight photos in the pool, but in this example we will use the Utata group — http://www.flickr.com/groups/utata/. If you want to try this out with a different group, just substitute your chosen group's NSID for the one used here.

Try It Out   Creating a Badge with ImageMagick

The basic process this script goes through in order to build the badge is very similar to that shown in the example above, so once again, we'll first present the badge building script in its entirety and then walk through the main steps to see what is happening.

1. Create a file called badge, with the following contents:

```perl
#!/usr/bin/perl

use FileHandle;
use Image::Magick;
use Flickr::API;
use XML::Parser::Lite::Tree::XPath;
use Getopt::Std;

getopt('d');

$apikey = 'YOUR-API-KEY';
$apisecret = 'YOUR-API-SECRET';

$groupNSID = '81474450@N00';      # Utata group NSID
$filename = 'badge';              # The output file name
$mapname = 'badge-map';           # The name given to the image map

$dir = './';
$dir = $opt_d if (defined($opt_d));

if ($dir !~ /\/$/)
{
    $dir .= '/';
```

```perl
}

$flickr = new Flickr::API(
  {
    'key'    => $apikey,
    'secret' => $apisecret,
  });

$photosCount = 8;

@recentPoolPhotos = ();
$recentPoolPhotosImage = undef;

buildBadge();

# Subroutines start here
sub getRecentPoolPhotos
{
  if ($#recentPoolPhotos == -1)
  {
    my $response = $flickr->execute_method('flickr.groups.pools.getPhotos',
      {
        'group_id' => $groupNSID,
        'per_page' => $photosCount,
        'page' => 1,
      });

    my $xpath = new XML::Parser::Lite::Tree::XPath($response->{'tree'});

    @recentPoolPhotos = $xpath->select_nodes('/photos/photo');
  }

  @photos = ();
  for ($i = 0; $i < $photosCount; $i++)
  {
    my $p = $recentPoolPhotos[$i];
    push(@photos, $p);
  }

  return @photos;
}

sub getGroupURL
{
  my $response = $flickr->execute_method('flickr.urls.getGroup',
    {
      'group_id' => $groupNSID,
    });

  my $xpath = new XML::Parser::Lite::Tree::XPath($response->{'tree'});

  my @groups = $xpath->select_nodes('/group');

  return $groups[0]->{'attributes'}->{'url'};
```

```perl
}

sub getGroupIconURL
{
  my $url = "";

  my $response = $flickr->execute_method('flickr.groups.getInfo',
    {
      'group_id' => $groupNSID,
    });

  my $xpath = new XML::Parser::Lite::Tree::XPath($response->{'tree'});

  my @groups = $xpath->select_nodes('/group');

  if ($#groups >= 0)
  {
    my $iconServer = $groups[0]->{'attributes'}->{'iconserver'};
    $url = "http://static.flickr.com/$iconServer/buddyicons/$groupNSID.jpg";
  }
  return $url;
}

sub getPhotoPage
{
  my ($p) = @_;
  my $url = 'http://www.flickr.com/photos/' . $p->{'attributes'}->{'owner'} . '/'
    . $p->{'attributes'}->{'id'} . '/';
}

sub getRecentPoolPhotosAsImage
{
  if (!defined($recentPoolPhotosImage))
  {
    @photos = getRecentPoolPhotos($photosCount);
    $recentPoolPhotosImage = Image::Magick->new;

    for $p (@photos)
    {
      my $img = 'http://static.flickr.com/' . $p->{'attributes'}->{'server'} . '/'
        . $p->{'attributes'}->{'id'} . '_' . $p->{'attributes'}->{'secret'}
        . '_s.jpg';
      $recentPoolPhotosImage->Read($img);
    }
  }

  return $recentPoolPhotosImage;
}


sub generateHTML
{
  my ($mapRef) = @_;

  my $s = "<img src=\"$filename.jpg\" width=\"225\" height=\"225\"
```

```perl
usemap=\"#$mapname\" border=\"0\" />\n";

  $s .= "<map name=\"$mapname\">\n";
  for $item (@$mapRef)
  {
    my $topleftx = $$item[0];
    my $toplefty = $$item[1];
    my $bottomrightx = $topleftx + $$item[2];
    my $bottomrighty = $toplefty + $$item[3];
    my $url = $$item[4];

    $s .= "<area shape=\"rect\" coords=\"$topleftx,$toplefty
$bottomrightx,$bottomrighty\" href=\"$url\" />\n";
  }
  $s .= "</map>\n";

  my $fh = new FileHandle "> $filename.html";
  if (defined $fh)
  {
    print $fh $s;
    $fh->close;
  }
}

sub addImage
{
  my ($image, $photo, $x, $y, $width, $height, $mapRef, $url) = @_;

  $image->Composite(image => $photo, compose => 'Copy', x => $x, y => $y);
  addMap($mapRef, $x, $y, $width, $height, $url);
}

sub addMap
{
  my ($mapRef, $x, $y, $w, $h, $url) = @_;
  my @location = ($x, $y, $w, $h, $url);
  push (@$mapRef, \@location);
}

sub buildBadge
{
  my @photoDetails = getRecentPoolPhotos();
  my $photos = getRecentPoolPhotosAsImage();
  my @map = ();
  my $mapRef = \@map;

  my $groupIconImage = Image::Magick->new;
  $groupIconImage->Read(getGroupIconURL());

  $image = Image::Magick->new;
  $image->Set(size=>'225x225');
  $image->ReadImage('xc:white');

  addImage($image, $photos->[0], 0, 0, 75, 75, $mapRef,
      getPhotoPage($photoDetails[0]));
```

```
      addImage($image, $photos->[1], 75, 0, 75, 75, $mapRef,
         getPhotoPage($photoDetails[1]));
      addImage($image, $photos->[2], 150, 0, 75, 75, $mapRef,
         getPhotoPage($photoDetails[2]));
      addImage($image, $photos->[3], 0, 75, 75, 75, $mapRef,
         getPhotoPage($photoDetails[3]));
      addImage($image, $photos->[4], 150, 75, 75, 75, $mapRef,
         getPhotoPage($photoDetails[4]));
      addImage($image, $photos->[5], 0, 150, 75, 75, $mapRef,
         getPhotoPage($photoDetails[5]));
      addImage($image, $photos->[6], 75, 150, 75, 75, $mapRef,
         getPhotoPage($photoDetails[6]));
      addImage($image, $photos->[7], 150, 150, 75, 75, $mapRef,
         getPhotoPage($photoDetails[7]));
      addImage($image, $groupIconImage->[0], 88, 88, 48, 48, $mapRef, getGroupURL());


      $image->Write(filename => $dir . $filename . '.jpg', quality => 85);

      undef $image;

      generateHTML($mapRef);
}
```

2. Now you are ready to run the script. From the command line, type `perl badge.pl`.

3. After a moment, two files should be created in the current directory — `badge.html` and `badge.jpg`. You can view `badge.html` just by opening in your browser. To embed it into a web page, use a PHP `include`:

```
<?php
  include ('/path/to/file/badge.html');
?>
```

4. If you want the generated files to be written to a different directory, use the `-d` argument: `perl badge.pl -d /path/to/output/directory`.

How It Works

The script starts off in pretty much the same way as the original example, but includes an additional Perl module, `Getopt::Std`, at the start. This module provides a simple interface for reading arguments off the command line. Here, you use the `-d` argument to specify the directory to save the badge to:

```
use Getopt::Std;

getopt('d');

...

$dir = './';
$dir = $opt_d if (defined($opt_d));

if ($dir !~ /\/$/)
{
```

```
    $dir .= '/';
}
```

The call to getopt() is used to specify the list of expected arguments. The value of any arguments found is then stored in a global variable $opt_x, where x is the argument letter. Here, you set $dir to be the output directory — defaulting to the current directory if no directory is specified. For convenience later on, you also check to ensure that the $dir ends with a trailing slash — adding one if necessary.

The script then initializes a few variables: $photosCount is the number of photos to be retrieved from Flickr, @recentPoolPhotos is the array in which the Flickr results get stored, and $recentPool PhotosImage is the Image::Magick object that the photos will be read into for processing.

Finally, the script calls the buildBadge() subroutine — this is the main subroutine that coordinates all the badge-building.

So, let's look at each subroutine in turn. First of all, a number of subroutines invoke the various Flickr API methods used. These all work in exactly the same way as the call to flickr.photos.search used in the example at the start of this chapter: the Flickr::API object is used to invoke a Flickr API method, and then an XPath query is performed to extract the relevant part of the response.

getRecentPoolPhotos() uses the flickr.groups.pools.getPhotos method to get the most recent photos posted to the group pool. This subroutine is called twice within the script, so the first time it is called, the results are cached in the @recentPoolPhotos array. getRecentPoolPhotos() first checks this array and retrieves details from Flickr only if the array is empty ($#recentPoolPhotos == -1). Upon receiving the results from Flickr, the script copies the results into the @recentPoolPhotos array for future use.

getGroupURL() is used to get the URL for the group page. You need this when you build up the image map — you want the group icon to link back to the main group page. The URL retrieved is the friendly URL for the group — of the form http://www.flickr.com/groups/utata/.

If you wanted to save an API call, you could use the less friendly form of the group URL, which uses the NSID: http://www.flickr.com/groups/81474450@N00/.

Getting the group's icon, on the other hand, always requires an API call. To construct the path to the group's icon, you need the ID of the server on which the icon is stored. getGroupIconURL() makes a call to Flickr's flickr.groups.getInfo method and uses the returned iconserver attribute to construct the appropriate URL:

```
my $iconServer = $groups[0]->{'attributes'}->{'iconserver'};
$url = "http://static.flickr.com/$iconServer/buddyicons/$groupNSID.jpg";
```

getPhotoPage() takes in a single parameter, which is the photo object received from Flickr. It extracts the owner and ID attributes from this object to then build the URL to the photo page. Note that, as with the group URL, you could use flickr.urls.getUserPhotos to get the friendly version of the URL to the users' photos — in other words, use http://www.flickr.com/photos/dopiaza/ instead of http://www.flickr.com/photos/50317659@N00/.

The eight photos displayed in the badge, however, are more than likely going to be from eight different people — that would be one API call for each photo, just to get the best URL. That seems like overkill when you already have a perfectly functional URL, so for the photo you'll use the version with the NSID in. So `getPhotoPage()` constructs the photo URL from the attributes it already has available:

```
my $url = 'http://www.flickr.com/photos/' . $p->{'attributes'}->{'owner'} . '/'
    . $p->{'attributes'}->{'id'} . '/';
```

The `getRecentPoolPhotosAsImage()` subroutine takes the photo list returned from Flickr by the `getRecentPoolPhotos()` subroutine, and reads it into an `Image::Magick` object.

```
@photos = getRecentPoolPhotos($photosCount);
$recentPoolPhotosImage = Image::Magick->new;

for $p (@photos)
{
    my $img = 'http://static.flickr.com/' . $p->{'attributes'}->{'server'} . '/'
        . $p->{'attributes'}->{'id'} . '_' . $p->{'attributes'}->{'secret'}
        . '_s.jpg';
    $recentPoolPhotosImage->Read($img);
}
```

The URL constructed is for the square version of the image — you're using that one here mainly because it's easy to tile with squares.

Now take a look at the `buildBadge()` subroutine. This starts off by defining an array, and then a reference to that array, in which you can then store details of the photo coordinates so that the image map can be created later.

```
my @map = ();
my $mapRef = \@map;
```

The next step is to collect together all the `Image::Magick` objects that are going to be used:

```
my $photos = getRecentPoolPhotosAsImage();

my $groupIconImage = Image::Magick->new;
$groupIconImage->Read(getGroupIconURL());

$image = Image::Magick->new;
$image->Set(size=>'225x225');
$image->ReadImage('xc:white');
```

`$photos` holds the object containing the eight images fetched from Flickr, `$groupIconImage` contains the group icon, and `$image` is the image that is used to build up the badge. The size of the badge is set to 225 × 225 pixels (that's enough to hold a 3 × 3 grid of images 75 pixels square), and it is initialized with a white background.

Next, all of the photos in the `$photos` object are added, one by one. The `addImage` subroutine is called to do this. `addImage` calls the `Image::Magick` Composite method to position the photo at the correct coordinates on the badge. After the photos have each been positioned on the badge, the group icon is placed in the center square:

```
addImage($image, $groupIconImage->[0], 88, 88, 48, 48, $mapRef, getGroupURL());
```

The group icon is 48 × 48 pixels, and so needs to be placed at (88, 88) in order to appear in the center.

As each image is added, `addImage` also calls `addMap` to store away the coordinates and dimensions of the photo, together with the URL to which it should link. This information is used to build the image map later.

When all the images and the group icon have been added, the badge is written out as a JPEG file:

```
$image->Write(filename => $dir . $filename . '.jpg', quality => 85);
```

The `$image` object is then undefined to free up any resources it was using. This isn't strictly necessary here — it will happen automatically when the script terminates, but if you were creating a number of different badges, it's an efficient thing to do.

Finally, `generateHTML()` is called. This subroutine creates a file containing the HTML to display the badge together with a client-side image map. It looks something like the code below.

```
<img src="badge.jpg" width="225" height="225" usemap="#badge-map" border="0" />
<map name="badge-map">
<area shape="rect" coords="0,0 75,75"
  href="http://www.flickr.com/photos/50317659@N00/208184656/" />
<area shape="rect" coords="75,0 150,75"
  href="http://www.flickr.com/photos/50317659@N00/206410617/" />
<area shape="rect" coords="150,0 225,75"
  href="http://www.flickr.com/photos/50317659@N00/185608819/" />
<area shape="rect" coords="0,75 75,150"
  href="http://www.flickr.com/photos/50317659@N00/179944011/" />
<area shape="rect" coords="150,75 225,150"
  href="http://www.flickr.com/photos/50317659@N00/179701217/" />
<area shape="rect" coords="0,150 75,225"
  href="http://www.flickr.com/photos/50317659@N00/159419108/" />
<area shape="rect" coords="75,150 150,225"
  href="http://www.flickr.com/photos/50317659@N00/148878960/" />
<area shape="rect" coords="150,150 225,225"
  href="http://www.flickr.com/photos/50317659@N00/141890381/" />
<area shape="rect" coords="88,88 136,136"
  href="http://www.flickr.com/groups/utata/" />
</map>
```

Building Better Badges

The badge built in this chapter is intentionally a fairly simply one. ImageMagick is a very powerful and versatile piece of software — in this chapter, we have only just skimmed the surface of its capabilities. If you want to dig deeper into ImageMagick, the PerlMagick interface is an ideal way to try out the different features quickly and easily. There is a great deal of information available via the ImageMagick web site at `http://www.imagemagick.org/` — if you can't find what you are looking for immediately, try using the search function on the site, which will more often than not manage to point you in the right direction.

The things you can do with ImageMagick are really only limited by your imagination. For example, Figure 10-3 shows a couple of badges designed by Karl Randay to showcase recent additions to the Utata group pool. As you can see, the images are laid out in a slightly different fashion, meaning that the basic badge design can be easily changed to accommodate incorporation into different page layouts.

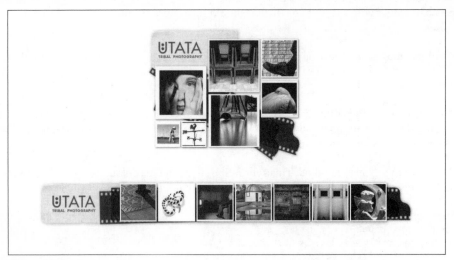

Figure 10-3

These badges were created by a script very similar to the one you saw in this chapter, but which first loads a background image into the `Image::Magick` object. The background images have placeholders to mark where the loaded images should go, as shown in Figure 10-4.

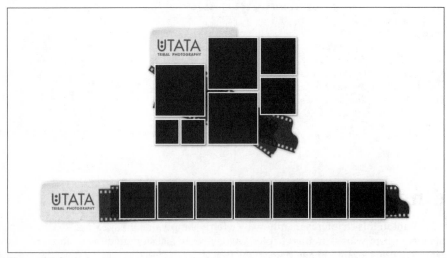

Figure 10-4

The script then resizes each image to the correct size and positions it over the placeholder square. Calculating the target coordinates for each of the images is somewhat tedious. Most image-editing packages make it easy by displaying the position of the cursor as you move it over the image.

More than Just Badges

Now you've played a little with ImageMagick, you don't have to constrain yourself to building badges — you can build any kind of image you like. Once you start playing around with manipulating the photos on Flickr, there's almost no end to the things you create — and of course, once you've created your new images you can also use the Upload API we looked at in Chapter 8 to automatically store your images in your Flickr account.

If you would like to see more examples of the kinds of images you can build, John Watson, in the guise of "fd's flickr toys," is one of the Flickr community's most prolific creator of Flickr mashups and remixes — you can see them in action at `http://bighugelabs.com/flickr/`. His web site enables you to convert photos into magazine covers, motivational posters, or even pieces of art with his "Hockneyizer," as you can see in Figure 10-5.

Figure 10-5

Summary

In this chapter you saw how the `Flickr::API` and `Image::Magick` Perl modules can be combined to create graphical elements made up of multiple images from Flickr. You learned how to invoke Flickr API methods using Perl, invoke ImageMagick functions using the PerlMagick interface, and build composite images using ImageMagick.

Before moving on to the next chapter, you should try making a badge of your own, so take a look at the following exercises.

Exercises

Half of the fun of applications such as ImageMagick is experimenting to see just what you can do with them. In this exercise, try designing and building your own badge — something you could incorporate into a website or your Flickr profile. Here are some suggestions:

❑ Produce a background graphic to set off your images (or persuade an artistically inclined friend to draw one for you), and build a badge that reads in the graphic and then superimposes images on it — just as you saw in the Utata badge examples above.

❑ Rather than build a group badge, create one using just your own photos. Try selecting what you think are your best photos for the badge.

❑ Try using a variety of sizes of images in your badge, rather than using just one size.

You may find the PerlMagick pages at `http://www.imagemagick.org/script/perl-magick.php` useful if you want to see the different methods available to you.

Part III
Mashing It Up

Visualizing the News

Flickr contains tens of millions of photographs taken by members all over the world, which must by now cover practically every subject imaginable. So — in theory at least — you ought to be able to find photos from Flickr that could be used to illustrate pretty much any subject you find discussed on the web. In this chapter you will build a mashup to try to do exactly that. In previous chapters you focused on retrieving data from Flickr; in this one you will gather data together from multiple sources. You will take news feeds from some of the major news sites, such as the BBC and CNN, and then automatically illustrate the news stories contained in those feeds with photos taken from Flickr.

The RSS Format

In Chapter 5 you saw how Flickr offers RSS as one of the formats used for its feeds, but there's much more to RSS than simply representing Flickr photostreams. RSS is an XML-based data feed format widely used for syndication of web sites. Originally devised by Netscape in 1999, RSS has a complex history and comes in many different versions. While each version has its own name, each one is confusingly abbreviated to RSS — you might hear RSS used to stand for *Really Simple Syndication*, *Rich Site Summary*, or *RDF Site Summary*, all depending on which version is being referred to.

Whichever version you use, RSS provides the same basic set of information — a feed consists of a channel and a series of items. The channel provides basic information about the feed, while each item is an individual piece of content.

In this chapter you'll build a mashup that takes feeds from a variety of news sites around the world. For the examples here you will use the feeds provided by BBC News. Remember, these news feeds provide up-to-the-minute information on current news stories, so the contents will change frequently — the structure, however, will remain the same. The main BBC News RSS feed is found at

```
http://newsrss.bbc.co.uk/rss/newsonline_world_edition/front_page/rss.xml
```

Let's take a look at how an organization such as the BBC uses RSS to represent news stories. Here's a typical extract from a news feed:

```
<rss version="2.0">
  <channel>
    <title>BBC News | News Front Page | World Edition</title>
    <link>http://news.bbc.co.uk/go/rss/-/2/hi/default.stm</link>
    <description>Visit BBC News for up-to-the-minute news, breaking news, video,
audio and feature stories. BBC News provides trusted World and UK news as well as
local and regional perspectives. Also entertainment, business, science, technology
and health news.</description>
    <language>en-gb</language>
    <lastBuildDate>Sat, 17 Jun 2006 14:24:42 GMT</lastBuildDate>
    <copyright>Copyright: (C) British Broadcasting Corporation, see
http://news.bbc.co.uk/2/hi/help/rss/4498287.stm for terms and conditions of
reuse</copyright>
    <docs>http://www.bbc.co.uk/syndication/</docs>
    <ttl>15</ttl>

    <image>
      <title>BBC News</title>
      <url>http://news.bbc.co.uk/nol/shared/img/bbc_news_120x60.gif</url>
      <link>http://news.bbc.co.uk/go/rss/-/2/hi/default.stm</link>
    </image>
    <item>
      <title>The Who recreate classic concert</title>
      <description>Rock band The Who recreate their legendary 1970 Live At Leeds
concert to launch their world tour.</description>
      <link>http://news.bbc.co.uk/go/rss/-/2/hi/entertainment/5086954.stm</link>
      <guid
isPermaLink="false">http://news.bbc.co.uk/2/hi/entertainment/5086954.stm</guid>
      <pubDate>Sat, 17 Jun 2006 00:19:14 GMT</pubDate>
      <category>Entertainment</category>
    </item>
    <item>
      <title>Gates to end daily Microsoft role</title>
      <description>Bill Gates says he will end his day-to-day role as head of
software giant Microsoft by 2008, to focus on his charity.</description>
      <link>http://news.bbc.co.uk/go/rss/-/2/hi/business/5085444.stm</link>
      <guid
isPermaLink="false">http://news.bbc.co.uk/2/hi/business/5085444.stm</guid>
      <pubDate>Fri, 16 Jun 2006 13:00:21 GMT</pubDate>
      <category>Business</category>
    </item>
  </channel>
</rss>
```

As you can see by the opening tag, this is RSS version 2.0. Other RSS versions have different formats, but you will still find the same key pieces of information within them. The <channel> tag contains elements that define the title of the feed, its description, and a URL to the feed's web site. The BBC offers a number of different feeds, such as world news, entertainment news, and technology news — each one of these feeds is essentially a different RSS channel. Within a channel are a number of items — each item has its own title, description, and link. In a feed such as this, each item is a news story, but the channel/item model also suits many other different kinds of data — from your grandmother's recipe collection to the change log from your source code control system. Pretty much any data source that can be broken down into a list is a potential candidate for RSS, and if you spend a little time browsing around the Internet, you will find no end of RSS feeds, with wildly varying subjects. They may all look a little different — RSS 0.91, 1.0, and 2.0 are all popularly used — but they are still RSS. There are other less common versions of RSS that you might still encounter — 0.90 and 0.93, for example.

So with all these slightly different formats around, surely writing a parser that can cope with all of them becomes more difficult? The answer is straightforward — let someone else do the hard work for you and use an existing RSS library to extract the data you need from the RSS feed.

Magpie

Magpie is an open-source project that greatly simplifies the process of extracting data from an RSS feed. It is very simple to use — all you have to do is pass it the URL of the feed and it will convert the feed data into a convenient PHP structure for you to use. It seamlessly handles all of the different versions of RSS for you, so you don't need to worry about the actual format of the feed itself. You can download Magpie from `http://magpierss.sourceforge.net/`.

Installing Magpie

Once you have downloaded it, installing Magpie is very straightforward. Create a new directory in the `lib` directory on your web server called `magpie`. Into this `lib/magpie` directory, copy all of the `.inc` files that were included in the Magpie distribution — `rss_cache.inc`, `rss_fetch.inc`, `rss_parse.inc`, and `rss_utils.inc`. There is also an `extlib` directory, which you should copy into the `lib/magpie` directory — this sub-directory contains just one file, `Snoopy.class.inc`.

Setting Up Magpie's Cache

Magpie has built-in caching of RSS feeds, meaning that it will fetch and parse RSS feeds only when there is new content, and avoids unnecessarily requesting content from the site supplying the RSS feed. This helps to improve the performance of your mashup, and the RSS providers will also look more kindly upon you for reducing the number of requests that you send.

Full instructions on setting up the cache are included in Magpie's installation instructions, which you can follow if you wish. For simplicity, though, you can just use your system's temporary directory to hold your cached files. This is typically `/tmp` on Unix-based systems and `c:\temp` on Microsoft Windows systems. You need to tell Magpie which directory to use for its cache, so you must add a statement to your Magpie scripts.

On Unix systems:

```
define('MAGPIE_CACHE_DIR', '/tmp/magpie_cache');
```

On Windows systems:

```
define('MAGPIE_CACHE_DIR', 'c:/temp/magpie_cache');
```

Try It Out   **Retrieving a Feed with Magpie**

In this exercise you will create a script to retrieve a feed from BBC News using Magpie.

1.   Create a new directory in the top level of your mashups site, called `visualizing-news`, for this chapter's files. In this directory, create a new PHP file called `11-1.php`, with the following content.

```php
<?php

require_once(dirname(__FILE__) . '/../lib/magpie/rss_fetch.inc');

header("Content-Type: text/plain");

$feed = 'http://newsrss.bbc.co.uk/rss/newsonline_world_edition/technology/rss.xml';

$rss = fetch_rss($feed);

print_r($rss);

?>
```

2.   If you then load the page into your web browser, you should see something like the following (although, hopefully, you will see more up-to-date news stories than these):

```
magpierss Object
(
    [parser] => Resource id #8
    [current_item] => Array
        (
        )

    [items] => Array
        (
            [0] => Array
                (
                    [title] => Safety fears as Shuttle date set
                    [description] => The US space shuttle Discovery will be
launched on 1 July, Nasa says, despite warnings it is not safe to fly.
                    [link] => http://news.bbc.co.uk/go/rss/-
/2/hi/americas/5091308.stm
                    [guid] => http://news.bbc.co.uk/1/hi/world/americas/5091308.stm
                    [pubdate] => Sat, 17 Jun 2006 21:32:45 GMT
                    [category] => Americas
                    [summary] => The US space shuttle Discovery will be launched on
1 July, Nasa says, despite warnings it is not safe to fly.
                    [date_timestamp] => 1150579965
                )

            [1] => Array
                (
                    [title] => Gates to end daily Microsoft role
                    [description] => Bill Gates says he will end his day-to-day
role as head of software giant Microsoft by 2008, to focus on his charity.
                    [link] => http://news.bbc.co.uk/go/rss/-
```

```
/2/hi/business/5085444.stm
                    [guid] => http://news.bbc.co.uk/1/hi/business/5085444.stm
                    [pubdate] => Fri, 16 Jun 2006 13:00:21 GMT
                    [category] => Business
                    [summary] => Bill Gates says he will end his day-to-day role as
head of software giant Microsoft by 2008, to focus on his charity.
                    [date_timestamp] => 1150462821
            )
    )


    [channel] => Array
        (
            [title] => BBC News | Technology | World Edition
            [link] => http://news.bbc.co.uk/go/rss/-/2/hi/technology/default.stm
            [description] => Visit BBC News for up-to-the-minute news, breaking
news, video, audio and feature stories. BBC News provides trusted World and UK news
as well as local and regional perspectives. Also entertainment, business, science,
technology and health news.
            [language] => en-gb
            [lastbuilddate] => Mon, 19 Jun 2006 10:19:55 GMT
            [copyright] => Copyright: (C) British Broadcasting Corporation, see
http://news.bbc.co.uk/2/hi/help/rss/4498287.stm for terms and conditions of reuse
            [docs] => http://www.bbc.co.uk/syndication/
            [ttl] => 15
            [tagline] => Visit BBC News for up-to-the-minute news, breaking news,
video, audio and feature stories. BBC News provides trusted World and UK news as
well as local and regional perspectives. Also entertainment, business, science,
technology and health news.
        )

    [textinput] => Array
        (
        )

    [image] => Array
        (
            [title] => BBC News
            [url] => http://news.bbc.co.uk/nol/shared/img/bbc_news_120x60.gif
            [link] => http://news.bbc.co.uk/go/rss/-/2/hi/technology/default.stm
        )

    [feed_type] => RSS
    [feed_version] => 2.0
    [encoding] => ISO-8859-1
    [_source_encoding] =>
    [ERROR] =>
    [WARNING] =>
    [_CONTENT_CONSTRUCTS] => Array
        (
            [0] => content
            [1] => summary
            [2] => info
            [3] => title
            [4] => tagline
            [5] => copyright
```

```
                )

        [_KNOWN_ENCODINGS] => Array
            (
                    [0] => UTF-8
                    [1] => US-ASCII
                    [2] => ISO-8859-1
            )

        [stack] => Array
            (
            )

        [inchannel] =>
        [initem] =>
        [incontent] =>
        [intextinput] =>
        [inimage] =>
        [current_namespace] =>
        [source_encoding] => ISO-8859-1
        [last_modified] => Mon, 19 Jun 2006 10:19:59 GMT

)
```

3. Now create a new PHP file in the `visualizing-news` directory, `11-2.php`, with the following content:

```php
<?php

require_once(dirname(__FILE__) . '/../lib/magpie/rss_fetch.inc');

$feed = 'http://newsrss.bbc.co.uk/rss/newsonline_world_edition/technology/rss.xml';

$rss = fetch_rss($feed);
$items = $rss->items;
?>

<h1><?php echo $rss->channel['title'] ?></h1>
<p><?php echo $rss->channel['description'] ?></p>
<ul>
<?php
foreach ($items as $item)
{
?>
  <li><strong><?php echo $item['title'] ?></strong><br/>
  <?php echo $item['description'] ?>
  </li>
<?php
}
?>

</ul>
```

4. Load this page into your browser. You will see the same feed as before, but this time formatted with the news items displayed as a simple list.

How It Works

The first few lines of the script simply read in the Magpie libraries and set the content-type for this web page to be plain text—that way the formatting from the `print_r` statement is preserved. The line that actually does all of the real work is this:

```
$rss = fetch_rss($feed);
```

This line calls the `fetch_rss` function in the Magpie library, passing in the URL of the RSS feed as a parameter. Magpie then returns a `magpierss` object, containing all the information from the feed. If you examine the output from the `print_r` statement, you can see the structure of the `magpierss` object. The two attributes of the most interest here are the `channel` and `items` arrays. `channel` is an associative array containing general information about the feed—title, description, and link. `items` is an array of the actual news items themselves, and as you can see, each item has its own title, description, link, and other metadata.

Now you've got hold of the feed, it's very simple to replace the `print_r` statement in the example above with some code to perform simple formatting, which is exactly what happens in the second script.

Finding Images on Flickr

Having now gotten your hands on the PHP structures containing the news items from the RSS feed, you can see that the title and description fields contain the text that describe the news story. If you choose some of the words found in those fields, you should be able to pass them on to Flickr and find any photos that use that set of words as tags. But which words should you use?

In the Microsoft news story, you can see the following text:

```
[title] => Gates to end daily Microsoft role
[description] => Bill Gates says he will end his day-to-day role as head of
software giant Microsoft by 2008, to focus on his charity.
```

A very simplistic approach to choosing keywords would be to try to pick out all the words that are names of people, places, or companies. To do that, just select all the proper nouns—in other words, anything that begins with a capital letter. If you do that, leaving the words in the order in which they appear, you have

```
Gates, Microsoft, Bill
```

A tag search on Flickr, looking for photos that have all those words as tags, should retrieve images that have a reasonable chance of actually being pictures of Bill Gates. Having only three keywords makes this a nice easy example, but what if the news story were instead about Wall Street's reaction to Bill Gates' announcement? By picking out capitalized words as keywords, you would then likely have a list of keywords that looked something like

```
Gates, Microsoft, Bill, Wall, Street, New, York, NASDAQ
```

The probability of there being a photo on Flickr that just happens to contain all those tags is relatively low. Clearly the search should look for photos that contain some, but not necessarily all, of those tags — in fact the more the better. You can do this by using the `flickr.photos.search` API method. If you set `tag_mode` to `any` and set `sort` to `relevance`, you end up with exactly what you want — the search will find photos that have one or more of the keywords as tags, but "sort by relevance" means that photos containing more of the tags will appear higher up the search results list.

Things still aren't perfect, though. Just having a high number of keyword matches doesn't guarantee you have the subject matter you are after — after all, that photograph of your Uncle Bill sitting on the wall after the street party in New York would likely score very highly too. Nevertheless, this approach is probably good enough to give some interesting results.

Try It Out   **Retrieving Relevant Images**

In this exercise you'll create a script to help you retrieve images from Flickr based on keywords, sorting them by relevance.

1. Create a new PHP file in the `visualizing-news` directory, `11-3.php`, with the following content:

```php
<?php

require_once(dirname(__FILE__) . '/../lib/phpFlickr/phpFlickr.php');
require_once(dirname(__FILE__) . '/../lib/apikey.php');

$flickr = new phpFlickr($flickrApiKey, $flickrSecret);

$keywords = array('bill', 'gates', 'microsoft');

$args = array(
  'tags' => join($keywords, ','),
  'tag_mode' => 'any',
  'sort' => 'relevance',
  'page' => 1,
  'per_page' => 6,
);

$photos = $flickr->photos_search($args);
$photoList = $photos['photo'];
?>

<ul>
<?php
foreach ($photoList as $photo)
{
  $squarePhoto = 'http://static.flickr.com/' . $photo['server']
    . '/' . $photo['id'] . '_' .$photo['secret'] . '_s.jpg';
?>
  <li><img src="<?php echo $squarePhoto ?>"></li>
<?php
}
?>

</ul>
```

2. If you look at that page in your browser, you should see a list of six images—hopefully, some of them will be of Bill Gates.

How It Works

This PHP script calls the `flickr.photos.search` method just as you saw before:

```
$args = array(
    'tags' => join($keywords, ','),
    'tag_mode' => 'any',
    'sort' => 'relevance',
    'page' => 1,
    'per_page' => 6,
);
```

The list of tags is built simply by converting the supplied list of keywords into a comma-separated string. `tag_mode` is set to `any` to ensure that any photos with one or more of the requested tags are returned. Finally, setting `sort` to `relevance` ensures that Flickr will sort the returned results with the best matches first.

For each photo, the URL for the small square (75 × 75 pixels) image is constructed, as described in Chapter 4.

```
$squarePhoto = 'http://static.flickr.com/' . $photo['server']
    . '/' . $photo['id'] . '_' .$photo['secret'] . '_s.jpg';
```

The results are then displayed as an HTML unordered list.

Putting Words and Images Together

Now that you've seen how to use Magpie to retrieve and parse an RSS feed, and then found relevant photos on Flickr, the time has come to put it all together into a completed mashup.

Try It Out   Creating the Mashup

In this exercise you will combine what you have learned in the two previous exercises to generate an illustrated news feed. You will use Magpie to retrieve a news feed and convert it into a PHP object. You will then look at the elements of that object and try to pick out some keywords that describe each news story. These words will form the basis of a Flickr search to retrieve photos that, with a little luck, will bear some relevance to the news story.

1. Create the `NewsItem.php` script in your site's `lib` directory. `NewsItem` is a PHP class that represents a single item in an RSS feed.

```
<?php

class NewsItem
{
  var $rssItem = null;
```

```
var $keywords = null;
var $photos = null;

// Flickr only allows 20 tags in a tag search
var $maxKeywords = 20;

// Some common words to ignore
var $commonWords = array(
  'a', 'an', 'the', 'it', 'is', 'for', 'to', 'he', 'she', 'in',
  'why', 'which', 'where', 'who', 'about', 'this', 'that', 'as',
  'his', 'her', 'as', 'i', 'me', 'my'
);

function NewsItem($rssItem)
{
  $this->rssItem = $rssItem;
  $this->photos = array();
}

function addPhoto($url, $link)
{
  array_push($this->photos, array('url' => $url, 'link' => $link));
}

function getPhotos()
{
  return $this->photos;
}

function getTitle()
{
  return $this->rssItem['title'];
}

function getDescription()
{
  return $this->rssItem['description'];
}

function getLink()
{
  return $this->rssItem['link'];
}

function getKeywords()
{
  if ($this->keywords == null)
  {
    $s = $this->getTitle() . " " . $this->getDescription();
    $words = $this->splitIntoWords($s);
    $this->keywords = $this->extractKeywords($words);
  }

  return $this->keywords;
```

```
}

function splitIntoWords($data)
{
  // Remove any possessive apostrophes
  $s = preg_replace('/\'s /', ' ', $data);
  // remove all except alphanumeric characters and spaces
  $s = preg_replace('/[^ \w]/', '', $s);

  return preg_split('/ +/', $s);
}


function extractKeywords($data)
{
  $words = array();

  foreach ($data as $word)
  {
    if (!in_array(strtolower($word), $words) && $this->isGoodKeyword($word))
    {
      array_push($words, strtolower($word));
    }

    if (count($words) >= $this->maxKeywords)
    {
      break;
    }
  }

  return $words;
}

function isGoodKeyword($word)
{
  // Discard immediately if it is a number
  if (preg_match('/^\d+$/', $word))
  {
    return false;
  }

  // Discard all common words
  if (in_array(strtolower($word), $this->commonWords))
  {
    return false;
  }

  // Does it contain any capital letters or numbers?
  if (preg_match('/[A-Z0-9]/', $word))
  {
    return true;
  }

  // If it is more than five characters, it must be a good word
```

```
      if (strlen($word) > 5)
      {
        return true;
      }

      return false;
    }
  }
?>
```

2. Create a file, NewsVisualizer.php, in the site lib directory. NewsVisualizer is the main PHP class for this mashup.

```php
<?php

class NewsVisualizer
{
  var $flickr;
  var $feedUrl;
  var $rss;
  var $maxPhotos = 6;
  var $maxStories = 5;

  // Constructor
  function NewsVisualizer($feedUrl)
  {
    global $flickrApiKey;
    global $flickrApiSecret;

    $this->flickr = new phpFlickr($flickrApiKey, $flickrApiSecret, false);
    $this->feedUrl = $feedUrl;
    $this->rss = fetch_rss($this->feedUrl);
  }

  function getTitle()
  {
    return $this->rss->channel['title'];
  }

  function getDescription()
  {
    return $this->rss->channel['description'];
  }

  function getLink()
  {
    return $this->rss->channel['link'];
  }

  function getItems()
  {
    $items = array();

    foreach ($this->rss->items as $item)
    {
```

```php
        $newsItem = new NewsItem($item);
        $photos = $this->findImages($newsItem->getKeywords());

        $photoCount = 0;
        foreach ($photos as $photo)
        {
          $squarePhoto = 'http://static.flickr.com/' . $photo['server']
            . '/' . $photo['id'] . '_' .$photo['secret'] . '_s.jpg';
          $photoPage = 'http://www.flickr.com/photos/' . $photo['owner']
            . '/' . $photo['id'] . '/';
          $newsItem->addPhoto($squarePhoto, $photoPage);
          if (++$photoCount >= $this->maxPhotos)
          {
            break;
          }
        }

        array_push($items, $newsItem);

        if (count($items) >= $this->maxStories)
        {
          break;
        }
      }
    return $items;
    }

    function findImages($keywords)
  {
    $args = array(
        'tags' => join($keywords, ','),
        'tag_mode' => 'any',
        'sort' => 'relevance',
        'page' => 1,
        'per_page' => $this->maxPhotos,
      );

    $photos = $this->flickr->photos_search($args);

    if ($this->flickr->getErrorCode())
    {
      // Display error message and return an empty set of photos
      echo $this->flickr->getErrorMsg() . " whilst searching for photos";
      return array();
    }

    return $photos['photo'];
  }
}
?>
```

3.   Create a file, `visualizing-news.php`, in the site `lib` directory. It simply ensures that the necessary libraries are included correctly and that the Magpie cache directory is correctly defined.

```php
<?php
require_once(dirname(__FILE__) . '/apikey.php');
require_once(dirname(__FILE__) . '/phpFlickr/phpFlickr.php');
require_once(dirname(__FILE__) . '/magpie/rss_fetch.inc');
require_once(dirname(__FILE__) . '/NewsItem.php');
require_once(dirname(__FILE__) . '/NewsVisualizer.php');

define('MAGPIE_CACHE_DIR', '/tmp/magpie_cache');
?>
```

Don't forget to change the location of the Magpie cache in this file to the correct location for your system.

4. Create `index.php` in the project's `visualizing-news` directory. This is the web page that displays the mashup.

```php
<?php
  // include any required files
  require_once(dirname(__FILE__) . '/../lib/visualizing-news.php');
?>
<!DOCTYPE html PUBLIC "-//W3C//DTD XHTML 1.0 Transitional//EN"
"http://www.w3.org/TR/xhtml1/DTD/xhtml1-transitional.dtd">
<html xmlns="http://www.w3.org/1999/xhtml">
<head>
  <title>Beginning Flickr Mashups: Visualizing the News</title>
  <link href="../css/main.css" rel="stylesheet" type="text/css" />
  <link href="../css/visualizing-news.css" rel="stylesheet" type="text/css" />
</head>
<body>
  <h1>Visualizing the News </h1>
  <?php
  // Initialise the feed URLs
  $feedList = array(
    'http://newsrss.bbc.co.uk/rss/newsonline_world_edition/front_page/rss.xml' =>
'BBC News',
    'http://newsrss.bbc.co.uk/rss/newsonline_world_edition/technology/rss.xml' =>
'BBC Technology News',
    'http://newsrss.bbc.co.uk/rss/newsonline_world_edition/entertainment/rss.xml'
=> 'BBC Entertainment News',
    'http://rss.cnn.com/rss/cnn_topstories.rss' => 'CNN News',
    'http://rss.imdb.com/news/' => 'Internet Movie Database News',
  );

  // See if a feed has been chosen
  $selectedFeed = $_REQUEST['feed'];
?>
  <form name="form" id="form" method="post" action="index.php">
    <select name="feed">
<?php
  $feedUrls = array_keys($feedList);
  foreach ($feedUrls as $feedUrl)
  {
?>
      <option value="<?php echo $feedUrl ?>" <?php echo ($feedUrl == $selectedFeed)
? 'selected="selected"' : '' ?>><?php echo $feedList[$feedUrl]?></option>
<?php
```

```
    }
?>
  </select>
  <input type="submit" name="Submit" value="Go" />
  </form>

<?php
  if (!empty($selectedFeed))
  {
    $visualizer = new NewsVisualizer($selectedFeed);
    $items = $visualizer->getItems();
?>
<div class="disclaimer">The images shown below were automatically chosen from
Flickr based on keywords found in the news feed. They do not bear any direct
relationship to the news feed or article and no such relationship should be assumed
or inferred.</div>
<div class="news-feed">
  <h2 class="news-feed-title"><?php echo $visualizer->getTitle() ?></h2>
  <p class="news-feed-description"><?php echo $visualizer->getDescription() ?></p>
  <ul class="news-items">
<?php
    foreach ($items as $item)
    {
?>
    <li class="news-item">
      <ul class="news-text">
        <li class="news-title"><a href="<?php echo $item->getLink() ?>"
target="_blank"><?php echo $item->getTitle() ?></a></li>
        <li class="news-description"><?php echo $item->getDescription() ?></li>
        <li class="news-keywords">Keywords: <?php echo join($item->getKeywords(),
", " ) ?></li>
      </ul>
      <ul class="news-images">
<?php
        $photos = $item->getPhotos();
        foreach ($photos as $photo)
        {
?>
        <li><a href="<?php echo $photo['link'] ?>" target="_blank"><img src="<?php
echo $photo['url'] ?>" /></a></li>
<?php
        }
?>
      </ul>
    </li>
<?php
    }
?>
  </ul>
</div>
<?php
  }
?>
</body>
</html>
```

5.   `visualizing-news.css` is the style sheet containing the style rules specific to this mashup. It should be created in the site's `css` directory.

```css
.disclaimer {
  font-size: small;
  margin-top: 1em;
  margin-bottom: 1em;
}

.news-feed {
  border: 1px solid #000066;
}

.news-feed h2 {
  padding: 0.5em 2em 0.5em 2em;
  margin: 0;
  font-size: large;
  font-weight: bold;
  color: #000000;
  background-color: #EEEEEE;
}

.news-feed-description {
  padding: 0 3em 0 3em;
}

.news-title {
  margin-bottom: 0.5em;
}

.news-description {
  margin-bottom: 0.5em;
}

.news-keywords {
  margin-bottom: 0.5em;
  font-size: x-small;
  color: #666666;
}

.news-item {
  list-style-type: none;
}

.news-text {
  list-style-type: none;
  margin: 0;
  padding: 0;
}

.news-images {
  margin: 0 0 1em 0;
  padding: 0;
```

```
  }

.news-images img {
  margin: 3px;
  padding: 3px;
  border: 2px solid #DDDDDD;
}

.news-images li {
  display: inline;
  list-style-type: none;
  margin: 5px;
  height: 91px;
  width: 91px;
}
```

6. To see the finished mashup in action, simply point your browser at the project's `visualizing-news/index.php` page and choose the RSS feed you want to view. You should then see something similar to Figure 11-1.

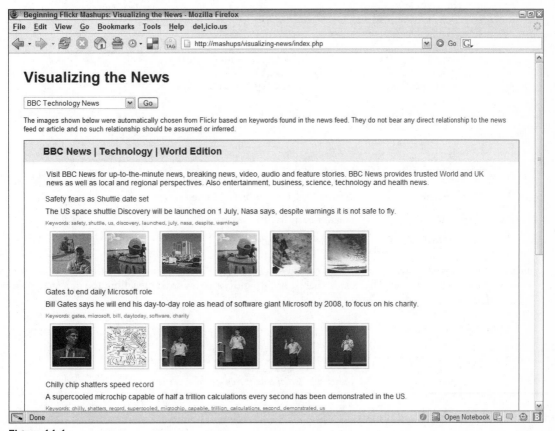

Figure 11-1

How It Works

The constructor for the NewsItem script takes a single argument—an element from the items array contained within a Magpie RSS object. For example:

```
// Use Magpie to fetch a feed

$rss = fetch_rss($url);

$items = $rss->items;

$firstItem = new NewsItem($items[0]);
```

Each NewsItem keeps track of the RSS item it represents and maintains an array of photos associated with the item. The NewsItem class also contains a number of helper methods to provide convenient access to the interesting parts of the RSS item, such as title and description.

The real work of the NewsItem class is initiated by the getKeywords method:

```
function getKeywords()
{
  if ($this->keywords == null)
  {
    $s = $this->getTitle() . " " . $this->getDescription();
    $words = $this->splitIntoWords($s);
    $this->keywords = $this->extractKeywords($words);
  }

  return $this->keywords;
}
```

Retrieving the keywords is a three-stage process:

1. Construct the string of text from which keywords will be chosen.
2. Split the text string into an array of individual words.
3. Extract an array of the keywords to be used.

The string of text from which keywords are chosen is simply a combination of the title and the description text from the RSS item. This text is then split into individual words, by calling the splitIntoWords method.

```
function splitIntoWords($data)
{
  // Remove any possessive apostrophes
  $s = preg_replace('/\'s /', ' ', $data);
  // remove all except alphanumeric characters and spaces
  $s = preg_replace('/[^ \w]/', '', $s);

  return preg_split('/ +/', $s);
}
```

This method makes two modifications to the string of text. First, it removes any possessive apostrophes in an attempt to improve the quality of the keywords used. (A search on the tag *Microsoft* will likely yield better results than a search on the tag *Microsoft's*.) To do this, it uses a regular expression to find the string 's followed by a space and then replaces all occurrences with a single space.

The second modification this method makes is to strip out any non-alphanumeric characters. It does this with another regular expression — /[^ \w]/. The special character \w matches any alphanumeric character, so [^ \w] will match any character other than a space or an alphanumeric character. Should any such character be found, it is replaced by an empty string.

Finally, the string is split into an array, with the regular expression / +/ — a sequence of one or more spaces — as the delimiter.

The extractKeywords method takes the array of words and picks out the ones to be used as keywords. It simply iterates through each item in the array, checks that the word hasn't already been picked as a keyword, and then calls the isGoodKeyword method to assess its suitability. When the maximum number of keywords is reached, or the supply of available words is exhausted, the function returns the list of keywords found.

The isGoodKeyword method conducts a series of simple tests to determine whether or not a given word should be used as a keyword or not. The tests are:

❑ Is the word a number? All words that consist entirely of digits are rejected.

❑ Is it in the list of well-known common words defined in the $commonWords array? All common words are rejected.

❑ Does the word contain any capital letters or numbers? Such words are deemed to be "interesting" and used as keywords.

❑ Is the word longer than five characters? Longer words probably make better keywords than short ones, so any words of six letters or more are accepted as keywords. This number is somewhat arbitrary — feel free to experiment with different values.

Any other words are automatically rejected.

The constructor for the NewsVisualizer class takes a single argument: the URL of the feed to process.

```
function NewsVisualizer($feedUrl)
{
  global $flickrApiKey;
  global $flickrApiSecret;

  $this->flickr = new phpFlickr($flickrApiKey, $flickrApiSecret, false);
  $this->feedUrl = $feedUrl;
  $this->rss = fetch_rss($this->feedUrl);
}
```

It kicks off by creating a new phpFlickr object, and then calls the Magpie fetch_rss method to create a new object containing the RSS feed.

The class then has some helper methods to easily access parts of the feed, such as the title and description.

The getItems method is used to get a list of NewsItem objects that represent the items in the RSS feed:

```
foreach ($this->rss->items as $item)
{
   $newsItem = new NewsItem($item);
   $photos = $this->findImages($newsItem->getKeywords());
```

The method iterates through the items array in the Magpie RSS object and creates a new NewsItem object for each one. The findImages method is then called, passing in the list of keywords from the NewsItem, to generate the list of photos that will be used. The square 75×75-pixel photo generated by Flickr is the one used in this mashup, so the URL to the square image is calculated with the information returned by the flickr.photos.search method, as is the URL to the user's photo page. Remember, the Flickr terms of service say you must link back to the photo page every time you display an image.

```
$squarePhoto = 'http://static.flickr.com/' . $photo['server']
   . '/' . $photo['id'] . '_' .$photo['secret'] . '_s.jpg';
$photoPage = 'http://www.flickr.com/photos/' . $photo['owner']
   . '/' . $photo['id'] . '/';
```

All photo URLs are registered with the NewsItem object, ready for display later.

In index.php, the names and URLs of the RSS feeds available for viewing are stored in an associative array called $feedList — the URL is the key, and the feed name is the value:

```
// Initialise the feed URLs
$feedList = array(
   'http://newsrss.bbc.co.uk/rss/newsonline_world_edition/front_page/rss.xml' =>
'BBC News',
   ...
);
```

The page then goes to display the form used to display the available feeds by iterating through this $feedList array. If a feed has been selected by submitting the form, the feed URL will be contained in $_REQUEST['feed']. As each <option> element in the feed selection form is generated, the URL for the feed is compared against the currently selected feed:

```
<option value="<?php echo $feedUrl ?>" <?php echo ($feedUrl == $selectedFeed)
? 'selected="selected"' : '' ?>><?php echo $feedList[$feedUrl]?></option>
```

If the two are the same, the selected attribute is set on the <option> element, thus ensuring that the drop-down list of feeds in the form shows the name of the feed currently being displayed.

If no feed has been selected yet, nothing more is displayed. If, however, a feed has been chosen — indicated by the $selectedFeed variable not being empty — the feed details are then retrieved by creating a NewsVisualizer object using the URL for the selected feed:

```
if (!empty($selectedFeed))
{
```

```
$visualizer = new NewsVisualizer($selectedFeed);
$items = $visualizer->getItems();
```

The rest of the page is devoted to formatting the feed contents, ready for styling by CSS. The feed itself is surrounded by a containing `<div>` with a class of `news-feed`. The feed items themselves are contained in an unordered list, and the photos used to illustrate the feed are contained in a nested unordered list within the feed item.

Summary

In this chapter you saw how to take data from a third-party source and use it to determine which photos to fetch from Flickr. You then took both the contents of the third-party data feed and the Flickr-hosted pictures and combined them to build your first true mashup — the mixing together of data from multiple sources.

In the next chapter you will see how third-party sourced data can be embedded directly into the Flickr page itself — but before you do that, you might like to try enhancing your current mashup even further by looking at the following exercise.

Exercise

When searching Flickr, the mashup currently only passes single-word tags into `flickr.photos` `.search`, so *Bill Gates* will appear as two separate keywords — *Bill* and *Gates*. This means that photos tagged with *Bill Gates* — two words combined as a single tag — will not be found by the search. Modify the mashup so that it can identify phrases such as *Bill Gates* and use them in the tag search as a single tag. Hint: a simple way to do this would be to cause the mashup to look for consecutive words that each begin with a capital letter.

Searching the Blogosphere

Much of Flickr's functionality is about supporting the social network that underpins it, a network that extends into the rest of the web as part of the blogosphere — the world of weblogs. Flickr actively encourages its use as a home for photos appearing on members' blogs — in fact, by default, all public photos uploaded to Flickr have a Blog This button so that any Flickr member can easily add photos from Flickr to their blog.

Although blogging a photo on Flickr is as straightforward as pressing a button, the problem of finding out where photos have been blogged is left to third-party web sites such as Technorati or Google. In this chapter you will see how to use Greasemonkey to query Technorati to find out just where photos have been blogged and embed the search results directly in photo pages.

What Is Technorati?

Technorati describes itself as "the authority on what's going on in the world of weblogs." It is a real-time search engine that tracks what is happening in the blogosphere. Most blogs are set up so that every time they are updated, they announce the change to the world by notifying various key servers. Technorati tracks these *pings*, as these notifications are known, and so can maintain a real-time index of the contents of the world's blogs.

If you go to the main Technorati web page at `http://www.technorati.com/`, you can not only see a rundown of what's going on in the blogosphere right now, but also search the blogosphere to find things of interest to you. The search function doesn't just enable you to enter keywords — you can also enter a URL to find any blogs that might contain a link to that URL. So, if you enter the URL to any Flickr photo page (`http://www.flickr.com/photos/dopiaza/29900246/`, for example), you will see a list of blogs that link to that photo. If you were to enter the URL of your photostream (`http://www.flickr.com/photos/dopiaza/`), you will see a list of all links to any of your photos.

Getting a Technorati API Key

Getting a Technorati API key is very straightforward — all you have to do is register on the main Technorati web site and then get your API key at `http://www.technorati.com/developersapikey .html`. Be sure to check through the terms and conditions of use for your key on the Technorati site.

Searching the Technorati Cosmos

Once you've got your Technorati API key, you're ready to try searching Technorati. A number of Technorati API queries are available, but the one that's needed here is the *cosmos* query. This query allows you to provide a base URL and returns all blogs linking to that URL.

Just like Flickr, Technorati provide a REST interface for its API, so trying out a query is as simple as entering a URL into your web browser. Try entering the following URL — substitute your Technorati API key for the text `YOUR-TECHNORATI-API-KEY`. Note that the URL is split over two lines here for readability — be sure to enter it as a single line in your browser:

```
http://api.technorati.com/cosmos?key=YOUR-TECHNORATI-API-KEY
    &url=http://www.flickr.com/photos/dopiaza/29900246/
```

You will see a response that looks something like this:

```
<?xml version="1.0" encoding="utf-8"?>
<!-- generator="Technorati API version 1.0 /cosmos" -->
<!DOCTYPE tapi PUBLIC "-//Technorati, Inc.//DTD TAPI 0.02//EN"
"http://api.technorati.com/dtd/tapi-002.xml">
<tapi version="1.0">
  <document>
    <result>
      <url>http://www.flickr.com/photos/dopiaza/29900246</url>
      <inboundblogs>2</inboundblogs>
      <inboundlinks>5</inboundlinks>
      <rankingstart>0</rankingstart>
    </result>

    <item>
      <weblog>
        <name>All Cupcakes, All The Time</name>
        <url>http://cupcakestakethecake.blogspot.com</url>
        <rssurl></rssurl>
        <atomurl>http://cupcakestakethecake.blogspot.com/atom.xml</atomurl>
        <inboundblogs>331</inboundblogs>

        <inboundlinks>456</inboundlinks>
        <rank></rank>
        <lastupdate>2006-06-30 13:38:35 GMT</lastupdate>
      </weblog>
      <nearestpermalink>http://cupcakestakethecake.blogspot.com/2005/08/cherries-
on-top.html</nearestpermalink>
        <excerpt> [IMG ]    Cupcakes    Originally uploaded by dopiaza.   Those are
```

```
cherries, right?</excerpt>
    <linkcreated>2005-08-03 16:06:57 GMT</linkcreated>
    <linkurl>http://www.flickr.com/photos/dopiaza/29900246/</linkurl>
  </item>

  ...

</document>
</tapi>
```

The XML document returned is a list of all the different blogs linking to the photo page that was specified in the url parameter sent in the request.

Talking to Technorati with Greasemonkey

You saw in Chapter 9 how to write some simple Greasemonkey scripts, but they concentrated on manipulating information already available on the Flickr page. For this mashup, you need to get your script to retrieve information from another site — Technorati. Fortunately, Greasemonkey makes this quite straightforward. You have already used part of the Greasemonkey API — the GM_log function to output messages to the JavaScript console. Now it's time to take a look at another Greasemonkey API function — GM_xmlhttpRequest. The GM_xmlhttpRequest function enables you to make arbitrary HTTP requests to any web site. The easiest way to understand it is to see it in action.

Try It Out   **GM_xmlhttpRequest**

In this exercise you'll use GM_xmlhttpRequest to perform a Technorati cosmos query when a Flickr photo page is loaded.

1.   Create a file, GM_xmlhttpRequestExample.user.js, with the following contents (remember to replace YOUR-TECHNORATI-API-KEY with your actual Technorati API key):

```
// ==UserScript==
// @name          GM_xmlhttpRequest Example
// @namespace     http://www.dopiaza.org/flickr/greasemonkey/
// @description   GM_xmlhttpRequest Example
// @include       http://www.flickr.com/photos/dopiaza/29900246/
// ==/UserScript==

var technoratiAPIKey = 'YOUR-TECHNORATI-API-KEY';

var url = 'http://api.technorati.com/cosmos';
var params = 'key=' + technoratiAPIKey + '&url=' + window.location.href +
'&limit=100';

GM_xmlhttpRequest(
  {
      method: "GET",
      url: url + "?" + params,
      headers:
      {
        "User-Agent": "Flickr-Technorati-Query"
```

```
        },
        onload: function(response)
        {
          GM_log ("Response:" + response.responseText);
        },
        onerror: function(response)
        {
          GM_log ("Error:" + response.status + " " + response.statusText);
          GM_log (response.responseText);
        }
  });
```

You'll notice that this script is set to execute only when one specific photo page is viewed. The only reason for this is to ensure that this test script doesn't flood Technorati with unnecessary traffic. If you want see the script work with a different photo page, just change the @include directive to reference your chosen page. Greasemonkey reads the @include directive only when the script is installed. If you edit the script after installation by clicking the Edit button in the Manage User Scripts dialog, you will also need to modify the Included Pages list in the Manage User Scripts dialog.

2. Install the script into Greasemonkey, and in Firefox, by going to the page `http://www .flickr.com/photos/dopiaza/29900246/` (or to your chosen photo page if you chose a different one).

3. Look at the JavaScript console (Tools⇨JavaScript Console) and you will see the response from Technorati displayed there.

How It Works

The first thing that the script does is set up the URL and parameters for the Technorati query. Three parameters are sent:

❑   `key`: Your API key.

❑   `url`: The URL of the page you want to search for — in this instance, it is the location of the currently viewed page.

❑   `limit`: The maximum number of results to return.

The `GM_xmlhttpRequest` function is then called. It takes a single parameter, which is an object with a number of fields defined:

❑   `method`: The HTTP method used. Usually, this will be either `GET` or `POST`.

❑   `url`: The URL to send the request to. Here, it is the Technorati REST endpoint for a cosmos search, with the parameters appended as the query string.

❑   `headers`: An associative array of HTTP header to send with the request.

❑   `onload`: A reference to a function to be called when the request has completed successfully.

❑   `onerror`: A reference to a function to be called when there is an error processing the request.

Once the Technorati request completes, the `onload` handler is called, which outputs the text of the response to the JavaScript console.

You can find a complete description of the GM_xmlhttpRequest function on the Dive into Greasemonkey site at http://diveintogreasemonkey.org/api/gm_xmlhttprequest.html.

Understanding the Response

When the GM_xmlhttpRequest call completes, it returns a response object, which is defined as having five fields:

❏   status: The HTTP status code of the response. A value of 200 means that the request completed normally.

❏   statusText: The HTTP status text of the response. This value is server-dependent.

❏   responseHeaders: A string containing the HTTP headers from the response.

❏   responseText: A string containing the body of the response.

❏   readyState: A field not currently in use.

The responseText field is where the information needed for this mashup is stored, but it is returned as a single string. The next step is to turn this string into a form it is easy to extract information from. As the response is an XML document, the obvious solution is to convert the string into a DOM that can then be used in the normal way.

Firefox comes with a built in DOMParser object (http://developer.mozilla.org/en/docs/DOMParser). This object has a number of methods, but by far the most useful here is parseFromString, which takes a string of XML and converts it to a DOM. Take a look at parseFromString in action.

Try It Out   Parsing the Response

In this exercise you'll create a JavaScript file to parse the XML you get back from GM_xmlhttpRequest.

1.   Create a file, DOMParserExample.user.js, with the following contents (remember to replace YOUR-TECHNORATI-API-KEY with your actual Technorati API key):

```
// ==UserScript==
// @name          DOMParser Example
// @namespace     http://www.dopiaza.org/flickr/greasemonkey/
// @description   DOMParser Example
// @include       http://www.flickr.com/photos/dopiaza/29900246/
// ==/UserScript==

var technoratiAPIKey = 'YOUR-TECHNORATI-API-KEY';

var url = 'http://api.technorati.com/cosmos';
var params = 'key=' + technoratiAPIKey + '&url=' + window.location.href +
'&limit=100';

GM_xmlhttpRequest(
  {
```

```
    method: "GET",
    url: url + "?" + params,
    headers:
    {
        "User-Agent": "Flickr-Technorati-Query"
    },
    onload: function(response)
    {
      var parser = new unsafeWindow.DOMParser();
      var dom = parser.parseFromString(response.responseText, "application/xml");

      var errors = dom.getElementsByTagName('error');
      if (errors.length > 0)
      {
        GM_log ("Technorati Error:" + errors[0].firstChild.nodeValue);
      }
      else
      {
        var items = dom.getElementsByTagName('item');
        if (items.length > 0)
        {
          for (var i = 0; i < items.length; i++)
          {
            var name = items[i].getElementsByTagName('name')[0];
            GM_log ("Found blog:" + name.firstChild.nodeValue);
          }
        }
        else
        {
          GM_log ('No blogs found');
        }
      }
    },
    onerror: function(response)
    {
      GM_log ("Error:" + response.status + " " + response.statusText);
      GM_log (response.responseText);
    }
  });
```

Once again, this script is set to execute only when one specific photo page is viewed. If you want to see the script work with a different photo page, just change the @include *directive to reference your chosen page.*

2. Install the script into Greasemonkey, and in Firefox go to the page http://www.flickr .com/photos/dopiaza/29900246/ (or to your chosen photo page if you chose a different one).

3. Look at the JavaScript console (Tools⇨JavaScript Console) and you will see a line saying Found blog for each blog that links to the photo page.

How It Works

This example is very much the same as the previous one — the only real difference is in the `onload` handler. The first step is to create a `DOMParser` object:

```
var parser = new unsafeWindow.DOMParser();
```

The `DOMParser` isn't directly available to Greasemonkey — it must be obtained from the application window via `unsafeWindow`. Once the script has created a new parser, the `parseFromString` method is used to convert the string into a DOM:

```
var dom = parser.parseFromString(response.responseText, "application/xml");
```

The second parameter to `parseFromString` is the content-type of the string being parsed — this is almost always `application/xml`.

Now you have a DOM object representing the response, you can access this object in exactly the same way that you access other DOM objects such as `document`. The first thing the script does is check to see if Technorati returned an error message:

```
var errors = dom.getElementsByTagName('error');
```

If no errors were returned, all `<item>` nodes are found. If you look at the format of the Technorati response, each item contains a name node — this contains the value you want to display:

```
<item>
  <weblog>
    <name>All Cupcakes, All The Time</name>
    ...
  </weblog>
</item>
```

For each item, the child `<name>` element is found:

```
var items = dom.getElementsByTagName('item');
if (items.length > 0)
{
  for (var i = 0; i < items.length; i++)
  {
    var name = items[i].getElementsByTagName('name')[0];
    GM_log ("Found blog:" + name.firstChild.nodeValue);
  }
}
```

The `<name>` element, in turn, has a single child element that is a text node containing the name of the blog. This value is printed out to the console.

Putting It All Together

Now that you've seen how to send a query to Technorati from within Greasemonkey, and how to extract fields from the result, you're almost set to build the mashup. One important thing remains — that's to decide where on the photo page you're going to put the blog information. It needs to be somewhere on the page that makes sense, and that is easy to locate within the Greasemonkey script. The Additional Information section in the right-hand column looks like a sensible place. If you look at the HTML for this column, you will see that it looks something like this:

```
<h4>Additional Information</h4>
  <p class="Privacy">
    <img src="/images/icon_public.gif" alt="This photo is public" width="15"
height="15" align="left" />
     <span style="font-size: 12px;">&#169;</span> All rights reserved
    (<a class="Plain"
href="/photo_settings.gne?id=29900246&photos_url=&context=set-72057594107731891"
title="Set privacy permissions for this photo">privacy</a>)
  </p>-

  <ul>
    <li class="Stats">Taken with a Nikon D100.<br /><a
href="/photo_exif.gne?id=29900246&context=set-72057594107731891" class="Plain">More
properties</a></li>

    ...

</ul>
```

Immediately below the privacy indicator looks like a good spot — the surrounding `<p class= "Privacy">` tag should be easy to find with an XPath query of `//*[@class='Privacy']`. The blog information can then be inserted after the close of the `<p>` tag, immediately before the start of the `<ul>`.

One final thing to consider before creating the mashup is just when the script should send its query to Technorati. It's probably not a good idea to send a request for each photo page that gets displayed. You're probably not interested in the blog information for every single photo you look at, and a query for each one could be considered excessive — especially if you're not always interested in the result. Remember, when accessing third parties, you should take care not to abuse the services they provide — send requests their way only when you actually need the information. A good compromise here is simply to add a link to each photo page saying "View blogs," and display the list of blogs only when the user clicks on the list.

Try It Out   Creating the Mashup

So, with all the key elements of the mashup covered, it's time to take a look at the completed Greasemonkey script.

1. Create a file, `QueryTechnorati.user.js`, with the following contents (remember to replace `YOUR-TECHNORATI-API-KEY` with your actual Technorati API key):

```
// ==UserScript==
// @name        Query Technorati
// @namespace   http://www.dopiaza.org/flickr/greasemonkey/
```

```
// @description    Query Technorati from Flickr photo pages
// @include        http://www.flickr.com/photos/*
// @include        http://flickr.com/photos/*
// ==/UserScript==

// *** Edit this ***
// You need to put your Technorati API key here
var technoratiAPIKey = 'YOUR-TECHNORATI-API-KEY';

var photoPagePattern = /^(.*\/photos\/[\w@-]+\/\d+\/)/;

// Check that we really are on a photo page
function checkPhotoPage()
{
  var isPhotoPage = false;

  if (photoPagePattern.exec(window.location.href))
  {
    isPhotoPage = true;
  }

  return isPhotoPage;
}

// Normalize the URL, removing any unneeded elements
function normalizeUrl()
{
  var url = window.location.href;
  var result = photoPagePattern.exec(url);
  if (result != null)
  {
    url = result[1];
  }

  return url;
}

// Add the "View blogs" link after the privacy element
function addLink(privacy)
{
  var parent = privacy.parentNode;
  var blogContainer = document.createElement('p');
  var blogLink = document.createElement('a');
  blogLink.setAttribute('href', '#');
  blogLink.setAttribute('class', 'Plain');
  var text = document.createTextNode('View blogs');
  blogLink.appendChild(text);
  styleElement(blogContainer);
  blogContainer.appendChild(blogLink);
  parent.insertBefore(blogContainer, privacy.nextSibling);

  blogLink.addEventListener("click", function(evt)
  {
    var waiting = document.createElement('span');
    waiting.appendChild(document.createTextNode('Waiting for Technorati...'));
```

```
      blogContainer.replaceChild(waiting, blogLink);
      showBlogs(blogContainer, waiting);
      evt.preventDefault();
  }, true);
}

// Retrieve the list of blogs and display them
function showBlogs(blogContainer, message)
{
  var url = 'http://api.technorati.com/cosmos';
  var params = 'key=' + technoratiAPIKey + '&url=' + normalizeUrl() + '&limit=100';

  GM_xmlhttpRequest(
  {
    method: "GET",
    url: url + "?" + params,
    headers:
    {
      "User-Agent": "Flickr-Technorati-Query"
    },
    onload: function(response)
    {
      blogContainer.removeChild(message);
      var parser = new unsafeWindow.DOMParser();
      var dom = parser.parseFromString(response.responseText, "application/xml");

      var errors = dom.getElementsByTagName('error');
      if (errors.length > 0)
      {
        var p = document.createElement('p');
        p.appendChild(document.createTextNode('Error: ' +
errors[0].firstChild.nodeValue));
        styleElement(p);
        blogContainer.appendChild(p);
      }
      else
      {
        var items = dom.getElementsByTagName('item');
        if (items.length > 0)
        {
          var list = document.createElement('ul');
          for (var i = 0; i < items.length; i++)
          {
            addBlog(list, items[i]);
          }
          blogContainer.appendChild(list);
        }
        else
        {
          var p = document.createElement('p');
          p.appendChild(document.createTextNode('No blogs found'));
          styleElement(p);
          blogContainer.appendChild(p);
        }
```

```
        }
        addTechnoratiCredit(blogContainer);
      },
      onerror: function(response)
      {
        var p = document.createElement('p');
        p.appendChild(document.createTextNode('There was an error retrieving blog
information'));
        styleElement(p);
        blogContainer.appendChild(p);
      }
    });
}

// Add this blog to the list
function addBlog(list, blog)
{
  var name = blog.getElementsByTagName('name')[0];
  var url = blog.getElementsByTagName('nearestpermalink')[0];
  var excerpt = blog.getElementsByTagName('excerpt')[0];

  var li = document.createElement('li');
  li.setAttribute('class', 'Stats');

  var a = document.createElement('a');
  a.setAttribute('href', url.firstChild.nodeValue);
  a.setAttribute('class', 'Plain');
  a.appendChild(document.createTextNode(name.firstChild.nodeValue));
  li.appendChild(a);
  li.appendChild(document.createElement('br'));
  li.appendChild(document.createTextNode(excerpt.firstChild.nodeValue));
  list.appendChild(li);
}

// Add a credit line, linking back to Technorati
function addTechnoratiCredit(blogContainer)
{
  var a = document.createElement('a');
  a.setAttribute('href', 'http://www.technorati.com/');
  a.setAttribute('class', 'Plain');
  a.appendChild(document.createTextNode('Technorati'));

  var p = document.createElement('p');
  p.appendChild(document.createTextNode('Search results by '));
  p.appendChild(a);
  styleElement(p);
  blogContainer.appendChild(p);
}

//Style a given node so that it matched the side bar
function styleElement(node)
{
  node.style.color = '#999999';
  node.style.fontSize = '11px';
```

```
    node.style.lineHeight = '15px';
}


// The script itself starts here
if (checkPhotoPage())
{
  var privacyElements = document.evaluate(
    "//*[@class='Privacy']",
    document,
    null,
    XPathResult.UNORDERED_NODE_SNAPSHOT_TYPE,
    null);

  if (privacyElements.snapshotLength > 0)
  {
    addLink(privacyElements.snapshotItem(0));
  }
}
```

2. After you've installed the script into Greasemonkey, you will see the View blogs link appear on each photo page. If you click the link, Technorati will be queried and you should see something like Figure 12-1.

Figure 12-1

How It Works

This is a much longer Greasemonkey script than the previous examples, so most of the code has been placed in functions for clarity. The main body of the script itself starts toward the end of the file and is just a few lines long. The very first thing the script does is to determine that it is on an actual photo page, rather than the photostream or some other page. It then performs an XPath query to look for the `<p class="Privacy">` tag described earlier. Once it has found this tag, it calls `addLink` to create the "View blogs" link.

The `addLink` function creates the HTML for the View blogs link and inserts it into the DOM — but that's not all. It also defines an event listener function that will be triggered whenever the user clicks on the link:

```
blogLink.addEventListener("click", function(evt)
    {
        var waiting = document.createElement('span');
        waiting.appendChild(document.createTextNode('Waiting for Technorati...'));
        blogContainer.replaceChild(waiting, blogLink);
        showBlogs(blogContainer, waiting);
        evt.preventDefault();
    }, true);
```

When triggered, this listener function replaces the View blogs link with a `<span>` element that says "Waiting for Technorati..." It then calls `showBlogs` to handle the retrieval and display of the blogs. Finally, `evt.preventDefault()` is called to prevent the click event from propagating any further. This stops the browser from trying to follow the link.

`showBlogs` is where the function starts to get interesting. It uses `GM_xmlhttpRequest` to send a Cosmos search request to Technorati — just as in the earlier examples. When a response is received, the "Waiting for Technorati..." message is removed, a DOMParser object is instantiated, and the `<item>` elements are extracted from the response. A new `<ul>` element is created and the details of each blog are added to it via the `addBlog` function. This, together with the `addTechnoratiCredit` function, simply creates new HTML elements containing the details to be displayed and inserts them into the DOM.

You may have noticed that CSS style information is added at a couple of points in the code. `<a>` tags are set to have a class of `Plain`, and the `<li>` elements have a class of `Stats`. These classes are just copied from the existing HTML to ensure that the newly inserted HTML doesn't look out of place. Some other elements are styled explicitly using the `styleElement` function:

```
function styleElement(node)
{
    node.style.color = '#999999';
    node.style.fontSize = '11px';
    node.style.lineHeight = '15px';
}
```

This function explicitly sets some of the styles to ensure that the elements match those already in the page. In case you are wondering, the numbers you see there are just copied out of the style sheets referenced by the photo page.

> The Greasemonkey script just created includes your Technorati API key. Be sure not to give your API key to anybody else — if you do, you will no longer be in control of how it is used and you could end up breaking Technorati's terms and conditions.
>
> If you want to distribute a script that needs an API key like this, you should always get the end user to sign up for their own key and use that in the script.

Summary

In this chapter you customized your view of Flickr by building a mashup that involves inserting information from a third-party site into a Flickr photo page. In doing so, you have learned how to use Technorati to find links to Flickr pages, use `GM_xmlhttpRequest` to send HTTP requests to other web sites from within Greasemonkey, and use the `DOMParser` to convert XML strings into a DOM.

In the next chapter you'll start to tackle a much more ambitious project, but before you embark on that you might like to try the exercise below to refine your Greasemonkey script even further.

Exercise

While running the Greasemonkey script built in this chapter, you may well have noticed that Technorati often returns multiple `<item>` elements for the same blog entry. Some of the `<item>` elements refer to the specific blog entry and others might just refer to the blog's home page. Modify the script so that it displays each blog only once, using the most specific link.

Displaying Your Photos with Google Maps

Throughout history, mankind has been fascinated by maps, trying to accurately portray, on a sheet of paper, a view of distant places — often places that the viewer of the map would never see. Today you can take photographs so that viewers will know how a location appears, but how can you describe to the viewer exactly where that location is? In this chapter you will see how to tag your photos with location information and then update the gallery application to display your Flickr photos on a map of the world so that people can see exactly where a given photo was taken.

What Is Geodata?

If you want your photos to appear on a map, one thing is clear — somehow you need to identify exactly where the photos were taken. On a graph, you use the x and y coordinates to pinpoint an exact location on the grid. On a map, you use latitude and longitude, both of which are measured in degrees. If you imagine a flat map of the world, it has the lines of latitude running horizontally, with 0° at the equator extending to 90° at the North Pole and –90° at the South Pole. The lines of longitude run perpendicular to the equator, with the 0° line passing through the English town of Greenwich. This line, known as the *Greenwich meridian,* or *prime meridian,* was officially designated the reference point for longitude measurements in 1884. Longitude measurements range from 0° at Greenwich through to +180° eastward and –180° westward. You can see how these lines of latitude and longitude are represented on a map of the world in Figure 13-1.

Every point on the globe can be uniquely identified by its latitude and longitude. The Statue of Liberty, for example, can be found at a latitude of 40.689156 degrees and a longitude of –74.044552 degrees. You might also sometimes see this written as +40° 41' 20.96", –74° 2' 40.39", where the fractional part of the degree is represented as minutes and seconds. Each degree is divided into sixty minutes (') and each minute is further divided into sixty seconds (").

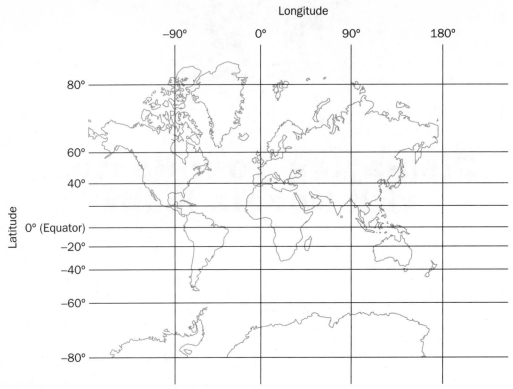

Figure 13-1

Using Google Maps

Google Maps enables you to view maps of pretty much anywhere in the world. You may already be familiar with the Google Maps web site, but let's take a quick look at the Google Maps interface. Open up your browser and go to `http://maps.google.com/`. You should see a screen that looks something like that shown in Figure 13-2. By default Google Maps opens up on a map of North America, but if you are accessing a localized version of Google Maps, `http://maps.google.co.uk/` for example, you may see a different map centered on your part of the world. If you do, don't worry—the only difference is the opening view; everything else still works in exactly the same way.

The first thing to try is moving the map about. Click anywhere on the map and drag the mouse—you should be able to move the map in any direction you choose. You can keep dragging to any part of the globe: keep on dragging in one direction, either to the left or right, and you will eventually circle the entire planet and end up back where you started from. Now drag the map until North America is shown again—just as in Figure 13-2.

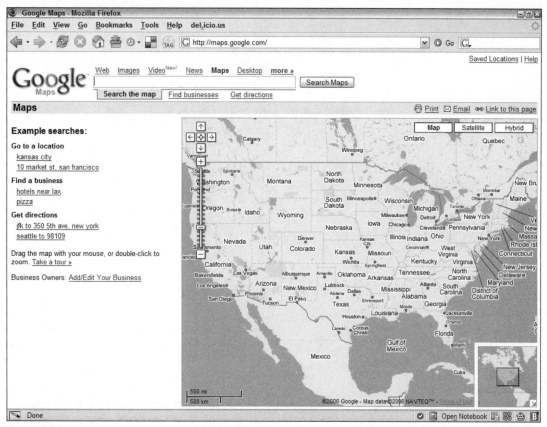

Figure 13-2

Another way to move in Google Maps is to double-click on the map somewhere. Try it now — pick a part of the map you want to take a closer look at and double-click. When you do this, you will notice two things. First, the map moves so that the point you clicked on is at the center of the screen. Second, the map zooms in slightly, giving you a closer view of the area. Pick a city shown on the map in front of you and double-click again on the city. Do this a few times: each time you double-click, the map recenters and zooms in a little closer, revealing more detail as it does so. The amount of detail available varies, depending on where in the world you are looking, but most North American cities will show detail all the way down to individual streets.

Now that you have zoomed in, how do you zoom out again? If you look to the top left of the map window, you will see a set of controls, shown in Figure 13-3.

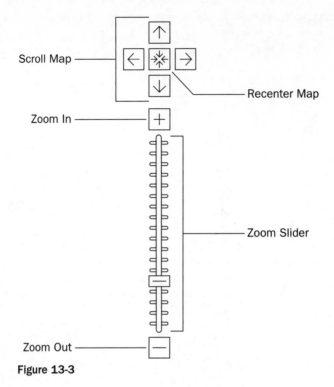

Figure 13-3

The slider control lets you adjust the level of zoom: drag it downwards to zoom back out. The four arrows at the top of the control panel each move the map a short distance in the corresponding direction. The center button inside the four arrow buttons returns you to your starting point — either the view that was shown when you first entered Google Maps, or the point you selected in a previous search.

Searching in Google Maps is very easy: simply type the name of the place you are looking for into the search box and the map will adjust to show you your target location. Try entering "Dallas, Texas" into the search box and pressing the search button — you should immediately see a street map of Dallas. You can search on other things than city and town names — try typing in "Golden Gate Bridge" or "Buckingham Palace" and you will be whisked away to those landmarks.

You can also jump to pages based on latitude and longitude. Remember the Statue of Liberty example from earlier? If you take the coordinates for that and type them into the search box:

```
40.689156, -74.044552
```

the map will recenter on to New York. Now drag the zoom slider all the way up to maximum detail, and you will see the Statue of Liberty at the very center of the map, as shown in Figure 13-4.

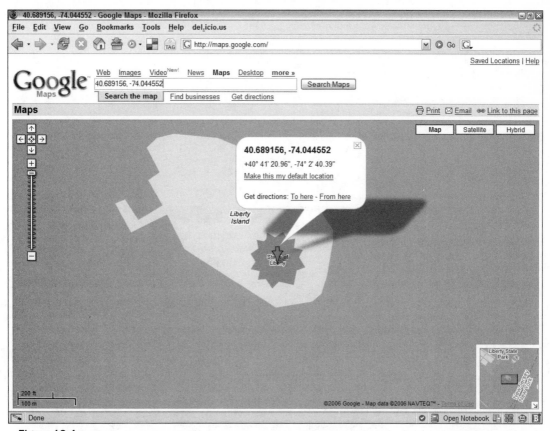

Figure 13-4

You can also use Google Maps to view satellite imagery of the area you are looking at. If you take your fully zoomed-in view of Liberty Island and click the Satellite button in the top right-hand corner of the map, the map switches to a satellite view of the island with the Statue of Liberty clearly visible. If you then click on the Hybrid button in the top right corner, you see the satellite view with an overlay shown — this overlay shows place names, together with street and road names. You can see this view in Figure 13-5.

If you want to find out the latitude and longitude of the point you are currently looking at in Google Maps, click Link to this page at the top of the map. The URL in the address bar will change to an address with a set of parameters that defines the current view — something like this:

```
http://maps.google.com/?om=1&z=9&ll=33.696923,-117.866821&spn=1.780039,2.320862
```

Within this parameter list, the `ll` parameter is the latitude and longitude of the center point of the map and the `z` parameter is the current zoom level.

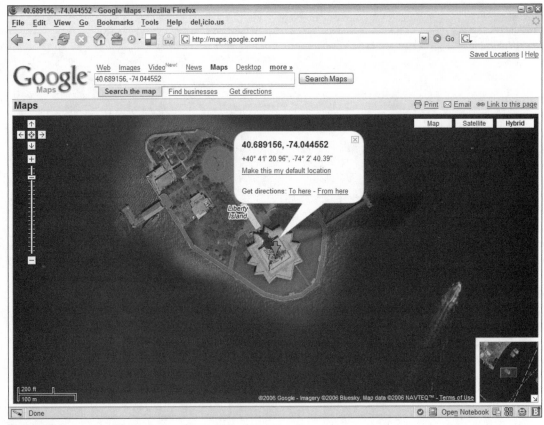

Figure 13-5

Getting a Google Maps API Key

Now that you've seen Google Maps in action, it's time to start using it in a mashup. Before you can do anything, however, you need a Google Maps API key. Getting a key is very simple — you just need to go to `http://www.google.com/apis/maps/`, where you can sign up for a key. In order to get a Google API key, you will need to create a Google account, if you don't already have one — you will be asked to either log in or sign up for an account when you apply for your API key.

You should note that a single Google API key is valid only for a certain URL prefix — you will be asked for this prefix when you sign up for your API key. This means that if you plan to develop your mashup locally and then deploy it on the Internet, you will need to sign up for two API keys — one with your local development URL and a second with the live URL you are using for your deployed application.

Once you've got a key, you'll find it looks something like this:

```
ABZIAAAAsb4CkrHTekHM7P4If9xZagjZgGqaUXO7s-DtJi6a9PbQNGFdG6ThAZDm0YW8Y9cDvCwlrBDNnUB
```

Now, put that key to use by building your first map.

Try It Out   Creating a Map

In this exercise, you'll start by creating the simplest map page that you can.

1. Create a new folder called maps in the top level of your web site, and create a new file called 13-1.html. Make sure you insert your Google Maps API key where it says YOUR-GOOGLE-MAPS-KEY.

```
<!DOCTYPE html PUBLIC "-//W3C//DTD XHTML 1.0 Strict//EN"
    "http://www.w3.org/TR/xhtml1/DTD/xhtml1-strict.dtd">
<html xmlns="http://www.w3.org/1999/xhtml">
  <head>
    <title>Flickr Mashups</title>
    <script src="http://maps.google.com/maps?file=api&v=2&key=YOUR-GOOGLE-MAPS-KEY"
      type="text/javascript"></script>
    <script type="text/javascript">

    /* <![CDATA[ */

    function doMap()
    {
        var map = new GMap2(document.getElementById("map"));
        var center = new GLatLng(0, 0);
        map.setCenter(center, 1);
    }

    /* ]]> */
    </script>
  </head>
  <body onload="doMap()" onunload="GUnload()">
    <div style="width: 512px; height: 400px;" id="map"></div>
  </body>
</html>
```

2. Load the page in your web browser, and you should see a map of the world, looking something like Figure 13-6.

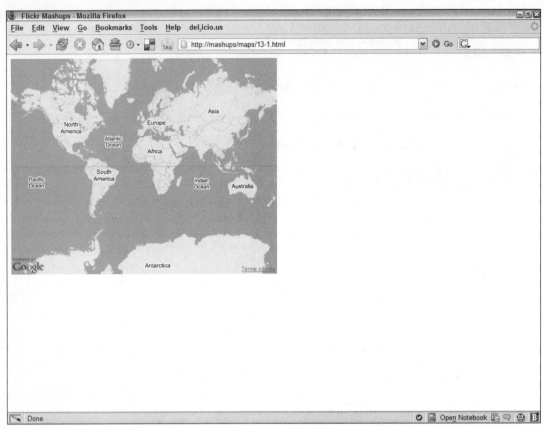

Figure 13-6

How It Works

Let's take a look a closer look at that HTML page. This time, we'll start at the bottom — if you look at the contents of the `<body>` tag, you'll see that there is almost nothing there, except for a `<div>` element:

```
<div style="width: 512px; height: 400px;" id="map"></div>
```

The `<div>` has no content, but it does have some attributes set. The `style` attribute sets the size of the `<div>` to be 512 × 400 pixels, and the `id` attribute defines the identifying name for the `<div>` — remember, every ID must be unique within the document. This `<div>` is where the map ultimately ends up. Let's now see how it actually gets there.

If you look in the `<head>` section of the document, you can see that a script is loaded from the Google Maps web site:

```
<script src="http://maps.google.com/maps?file=api&v=2&key=YOUR-GOOGLE-MAPS-KEY"
        type="text/javascript"></script>
```

This script is the Google Maps API library — every page you create that uses the Google Maps API must load this script. Your API key is included here as a parameter, and Google checks that the API key is valid for the site loading the script — if it isn't, an error message is displayed, and the script does not run.

Next is another JavaScript section that defines a new function called doMap(). The doMap() function instantiates a new GMap2 object:

```
var map = new GMap2(document.getElementById("map"));
```

The GMap2 class is the most important part of the Google Maps API — it represents an instance of a map on a page. Everything you do with Google Maps starts with an instance of GMap2. The constructor for GMap2 used here takes a single parameter — the element in which the map is to be placed. Here, you use document.getElementById() to locate the <div> with an id of map. This is the <div> defined in the body of your web page.

If you wish, you can put multiple maps on a page. Each map is then represented by an instance of the GMap2 object and each map must appear in its own element on the page — in other words, you should create separate <div> elements, each with its own unique id attribute, for each map on the page.

Once you've created a map instance, you need to tell the map what to display. Here, the script creates a new GLatLng object:

```
var center = new GLatLng(0, 0);
```

The GLatLng class represents a point on a map, consisting of a latitude and longitude. Note that, as is the convention on maps, the constructor for GLatLng takes the latitude as the first parameter and the longitude as the second. In this instance, however, the script just creates a point at 0° latitude, 0° longitude, which is a point on the equator, off the west coast of Africa. This is the point you want to center the map on, and to do so, you call setCenter:

```
map.setCenter(center, 1);
```

The first parameter to the setCenter method is the GLatLng object representing the center point of the map. The second parameter is the zoom level to use — 1 means that the map is zoomed out as far as possible.

Finally, the <body> tag itself defines two event handlers:

```
<body onload="doMap()" onunload="GUnload()">
```

The onload handler calls the doMap() function — in other words, once the page has finished loading, doMap() is invoked to create the GMap2 object, which is inserted into the <div> element. The onunload handler is invoked whenever the user navigates away from the page and calls the GUnload() function, which is part of the Google Maps API. GUnload() should always be called whenever a page incorporating Google Maps objects is unloaded — it tidies up a number of internal data structures used by the Google Maps API in an effort to work around a number of browser bugs that give rise to memory leaks.

You might have noticed that the JavaScript used here is encased in an XML CDATA section:

```
/* <![CDATA[ */

function doMap()
{
    var map = new GMap2(document.getElementById("map"));
    var center = new GLatLng(0, 0);
    map.setCenter(center, 1);
}

/* ]]> */
```

The CDATA start and end markers are both commented out (/* ... */) to avoid their interfering with the JavaScript itself, but why are they there? The reason is that the DOCTYPE for this document is XHTML, which is very strict about the format of the document. JavaScript code itself is not usually valid XHTML — it often contains unescaped entities such as angle brackets, both of which have special meaning in JavaScript ("less than" and "greater than," respectively). To ensure that you have a valid XHTML document, you should really enclose any inline JavaScript code such as these entities inside a CDATA section. If you don't do this, your page will probably continue to work, but it won't, strictly speaking, be valid XHTML — if you ever run your page against an XHMTL validator such as the one at http://validator.w3.org/, it will most likely fail validation without the CDATA tags.

Adding Controls to Your Map

You can drag the map you created in the previous example within the window to change its center point, but you may have noticed that you can't zoom in or out. To do this you need to add some more user interface elements, or *controls*, to the map.

Try It Out   **Adding Controls to the Map**

In this example you'll take your code and add a few controls to it.

1.   Create a new file called 13-2.html in your maps directory:

```
<!DOCTYPE html PUBLIC "-//W3C//DTD XHTML 1.0 Strict//EN"
    "http://www.w3.org/TR/xhtml1/DTD/xhtml1-strict.dtd">
<html xmlns="http://www.w3.org/1999/xhtml">
  <head>
    <title>Flickr Mashups</title>
    <script src="http://maps.google.com/maps?file=api&v=2&key=YOUR-GOOGLE-MAPS-KEY"
      type="text/javascript"></script>
    <script type="text/javascript">

    /* <![CDATA[ */

    function doMap()
    {
        var map = new GMap2(document.getElementById("map"));
```

```
        map.addControl(new GLargeMapControl());
        map.addControl(new GMapTypeControl());
        map.addControl(new GOverviewMapControl());
        var center = new GLatLng(48.858205, 2.294359);
        map.setCenter(center, 18, G_SATELLITE_MAP);
    }

    /* ]]> */
    </script>
</head>
<body onload="doMap()" onunload="GUnload()">
<div style="width: 512px; height: 400px;" id="map"></div>
</body>
</html>
```

Don't forget to substitute your Google Maps API key where specified.

2. Open up 13-2.html in your web browser, and you will see a close-up aerial view of the Eiffel Tower, just like that shown in Figure 13-7.

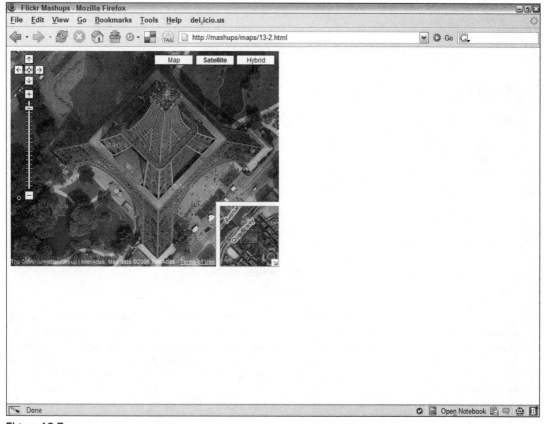

Figure 13-7

How It Works

This example is very similar to the earlier one — we've just added a few more details to the doMap() function. Three controls have been added to the map via the addControl method. The first, GLargeMapControl, is the pan-and-zoom control you saw earlier. (There's also a more compact version of this called GSmallMapControl, which is ideally suited for smaller maps.) The second control is a GMapTypeControl: these are the buttons that enable you to switch among Map, Satellite, and Hybrid views. The last control added is an instance of GOverviewMapControl. This control adds a small overview map in the bottom right-hand corner of the window that shows a thumbnail view of the area surrounding the region currently being viewed.

Finally, for this example, we've decided to opt for a slightly more interesting starting point — we are now centering the map on latitude 48.858205° and longitude 2.294359°. This is the location of the Eiffel Tower in Paris. The setCenter call used is slightly different this time:

```
map.setCenter(center, 18, G_SATELLITE_MAP);
```

To start with, we're zooming in quite close, at zoom level 18, in order to get a good view of the tower. We're also making use of the optional third parameter for setCenter, which enables us to choose the map type shown. G_SATELLITE_MAP is, of course, the satellite view. Other possible values that could be used here are G_NORMAL_MAP and G_HYBRID_MAP.

Building the Mashup

Now that you've seen how to embed a Google Map into a web page, you're a step closer to building your mashup. The next step is getting the geodata from Flickr — if you want to display a Flickr photograph on a map, you need to know the latitude and longitude for each photo to display.

Adding Geodata to Flickr Photos

Before you can retrieve location information from Flickr, you first need to be sure that you've actually added the necessary location details to your photos. The simplest way to do this is through Flickr's Organize feature. Log in to Flickr and click the Organize link in the main menu at the top of the screen. Once the organizer loads, click the Map tab at the top of the screen. The organizer then loads a map from Yahoo! Maps and displays it, along with a strip of your photos along the bottom of the window, as shown in Figure 13-8.

You can drag and zoom in and out of the map in much the same way as with Google Maps. To add location information to your photos, simply drag them from the strip at the bottom of the window onto the map at the appropriate location. When you add location data to your photos by dragging them onto the map, Flickr also records the *accuracy* with which the photo was placed. The closer you are zoomed in on the map when you place your photos, the more accurate the placement is deemed to be. With the map fully zoomed out to show the whole world, Flickr records an accuracy of 1. When the map is fully zoomed in, the accuracy is 16. You should always add location data at the maximum level of accuracy wherever possible.

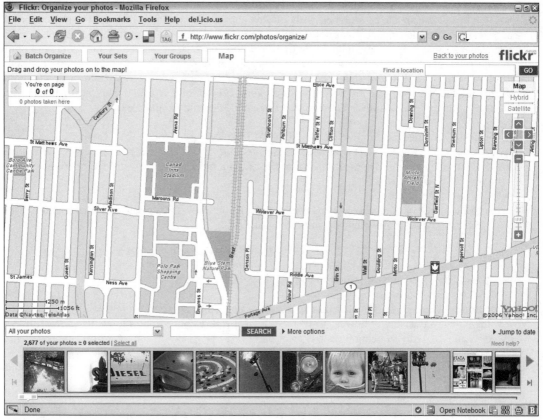

Figure 13-8

The level of detail available with the maps shown on Flickr varies depending on which part of the world you are looking at. Some people prefer to use third-party systems to add location data to their Flickr photos. A number of such systems exist: Yuan.CC Maps (`http://maps.yuan.cc/`) and loc.alize.us (`http://loc.alize.us/`) are two popular web sites often used for geotagging Flickr photos.

Retrieving Geodata from Flickr Photos

So once you've added your location data, just how you do retrieve it again via the API? The API method `flickr.photos.getWithGeoData` will return a list of the photos you have that have geodata associated with them. That sounds like just the ticket, until you realize that it requires authentication — meaning that it will work only for you, and then only if you authenticate first, which isn't really practical if you want to allow other people to view your location information. In fact, the easiest method is to use the `flickr .photos.search` method. If you pass in `geo` as the `extras` parameter to this method, the results will include location information where available — obviously no location information is returned for photos for which Flickr has no geodata stored. This approach seems promising, but on its own isn't really good enough. What you would actually like at this point is for the search method to return only photos that have geodata associated with them.

The `flickr.photos.search` method takes an optional parameter, bbox, which is the geographic bounding box of the area to be searched: only photos within this bounding box will be returned in of the search results. That also means that photos without geodata will not be returned when the bbox parameter is used, as Flickr has no way of knowing their location. Now, if you want all your geotagged photos to be returned regardless of where the location data are, you don't want to specify an overly restrictive bounding box. In fact, if you specify a bounding box large enough to cover the whole earth, you will find that the `flickr.photos.search` returns all geotagged photos within the bounding box (in other words, all of them) but excludes all photos that have no location data attached.

You can easily see this work in practice. Go to the API Explorer page for `flickr.photos.search` at `http://www.flickr.com/services/api/explore/?method=flickr.photos.search` and enter your NSID into the `user_id` field and `geo` into the `extras` field. Press the Call Method button and wait for the results to appear.

You should see a list of your photos appear in the results window. Each photo includes location information as attributes of the photo element, something like this:

```
<photo id="231699414" owner="50317659@N00" secret="f2ed044b79" server="92"
    title="Lollipops" ispublic="1" isfriend="0" isfamily="0" latitude="52.21284"
    longitude="-1.133437" accuracy="16"/>
```

The attributes `latitude` and `longitude` specify the geographic coordinates for the photo. The accuracy attribute is a measure of how accurate Google deems those coordinates to be. It can take any value between 1 and 16, with 16 being the most precise.

However, you didn't specify a bounding box value, so any photos that do not have location information still appear, but have each of their location fields set to 0:

```
<photo id="208184656" owner="50317659@N00" secret="3d4fb9c4b2" server="63"
    title="Float" ispublic="1" isfriend="0" isfamily="0" latitude="0" longitude="0"
    accuracy="0"/>
```

Now try again, but this time specifying a bounding box. The bounding box is a comma-separated list of four values specifying the geographic coordinates of the lower left-hand corner and the upper right-hand corner of the box — note that the order is bottom-left longitude, bottom-left latitude, top-right longitude, top-right latitude. A box that covers the whole globe would have a bottom-left coordinate of −180°, −90° and a top-right coordinate of 180°, 90°. So repeat the above call to `flickr.photos.search`, but this time also specifying -180, -90, 180, 90 as the bbox values. The default accuracy used when no value is specified is the maximum value of 16. If you have been using a lower level of accuracy when adding your photos, you might want to specify a lower value of accuracy as an additional parameter to the search.

When the results appear, you should see only photos that have location data.

Try It Out   Retrieving the Mapping Data

Now it's time to write some code. We slot the first piece of the puzzle into place by adding a new method to the `FlickrGallery` class to retrieve a list of geotagged photos:

1. Modify `FlickrGallery.php` to add the following method:

```php
<?php

class FlickrGallery extends FlickrAuthenticator
{
   ...

  function getWithGeoData()
  {
    $bbox = '-180, -90, 180, 90';

    $args = array(
      'user_id' => $this->nsid,
      'sort' => 'interestingness-desc',
      'bbox' => $bbox,
      'extras' => 'geo',
      'per_page' => 500,
      );

    $p = $this->flickr->photos_search($args);
    if ($this->flickr->getErrorCode())
    {
      echo ("Error fetching photos with GeoData: " . $this->flickr->getErrorMsg());
    }

    return $p['photo'];
  }
}
?>
```

Remember, if you are using a lower level of accuracy when you add geodata to your photos by not zooming in fully on the map, you may also want to add an `accuracy` parameter to the list of search parameters in the `flickr.photos.search` method call.

How It Works

The `getWithGeoData()` method works in pretty much the same way as all the other different `FlickrGallery` methods that search for photos. The only significant difference is the passing of the `bbox` parameter and the setting of `extras` to `geo`.

Processing the Geodata

Now you know how to actually retrieve the location information from Flickr, the next step is to somehow get those data into your map. Fortunately the Google Maps API provides some useful functions and classes, including an XML parser in the `GXml` class, to enable you to read in external data.

First you need to convert the photo data retrieved from Flickr into a form suitable for processing by your Google Maps application. Flickr itself uses XML in its responses to Flickr API methods, so you can just pass that XML straight back to Google Maps. There is a lot of information included in the response to `flickr.photos.search` that the map doesn't really need, however, so we will convert the Flickr results into a simpler XML structure.

Try It Out   **Adding the Data to the Map**

In this exercise you'll process the data that you've retrieved from the photos in your gallery, so you can add them to the map later on.

1.   Create a new file called `geo.php` in the gallery directory:

```php
<?php

include (dirname(__FILE__) . '/../lib/gallery.php');

$gallery = new FlickrGallery();

$photos = $gallery->getWithGeoData();

header ("Content-Type: text/xml");

echo "<?xml version=\"1.0\"?>\n";
echo "<photos>\n";

if (is_array($photos))
{
  foreach ($photos as $p)
  {
    echo "<photo " .
      "id=\"" . $p['id'] . "\" " .
      "latitude=\"" . $p['latitude'] . "\" " .
      "longitude=\"" . $p['longitude'] . "\" " .
      " />\n";
  }
}

echo "</photos>";

?>
```

2.   Enter the address of the `geo.php` page in your browser. You should see the generated XML structure, which looks something like this:

```xml
<?xml version="1.0"?>
<photos>
    <photo id="141890381" latitude="52.026482" longitude="-1.013328" />
    <photo id="231699414" latitude="52.21284" longitude="-1.133437" />
    <photo id="191649377" latitude="52.188187" longitude="-1.160227" />
    <photo id="226370215" latitude="52.958359" longitude="0.853414" />
    <photo id="132980705" latitude="52.189003" longitude="-1.161278" />
    <photo id="19551666" latitude="52.189003" longitude="-1.161278" />
    <photo id="148877823" latitude="52.972996" longitude="0.851462" />
    <photo id="237529084" latitude="52.225696" longitude="-1.178509" />
</photos>
```

How It Works

This PHP script calls the `FlickrGallery` method `getWithGeoData()` to retrieve a list of photos that include location data. It then sets the HTTP content-type header to be `text/xml`, to ensure that Google Maps interprets the data correctly as XML. Finally, the XML document is created.

The start of the document is the XML declaration:

```
<?xml version="1.0"?>
```

All valid XML documents should start with this line. Next, a `<photos>` element is output. Then, for each photo in the list retrieved from Flickr, a `<photo>` element is output, together with attributes containing the photo ID, the latitude, and the longitude. Finally, after each photo has been processed, the `<photos>` element is closed.

Laying the Groundwork

Before we continue, you'll use what you've learned so far to create a few files that will form the basis of the map page in the gallery.

Try It Out   Creating the Gallery Pages

In this exercise you'll create several files that will add a basic map to your gallery application.

1.   Create a file called `mapapi.php` in the `lib` directory:

```
<script src="http://maps.google.com/maps?file=api&v=2&key=YOUR-GOOGLE-MAPS-API-KEY"
    type="text/javascript"></script>
```

Make sure you put your Google Maps API key in here where indicated. The reason we've put this in as a separate file is to make it easy to change the API key for a different one—no matter how many pages you build with maps on them, the API key only appears in one place. Remember, the API key is different for each web site you run this file on—you will need different keys for your local development web server and your final deployment site.

2.   Now create a `map.php` file in the `gallery` directory:

```
<?php include (dirname(__FILE__) . '/../lib/gallery.php') ?>
<!DOCTYPE html PUBLIC "-//W3C//DTD XHTML 1.0 Transitional//EN"
  "http://www.w3.org/TR/xhtml1/DTD/xhtml1-transitional.dtd">
<html xmlns="http://www.w3.org/1999/xhtml">
<head>
  <title>Flickr Mashups</title>
  <?php include dirname(__FILE__) . '/../lib/mapapi.php' ?>
  <script src="../lib/js/map.js" type="text/javascript"></script>
  <link href="../css/main.css" rel="stylesheet" type="text/css" />
  <link href="../css/gallery.css" rel="stylesheet" type="text/css" />
</head>
<body onload="doMap()" onunload="GUnload()">
```

```php
    <?php include ('header.php') ?>
    <?php include ('navigation.php') ?>
    <div id="map"></div>
</body>
</html>
```

3. Now you need to do two more things before all the groundwork is in place. You need to update the style sheet, `gallery.css`, to add a new style ensuring that the map `<div>` is correctly sized:

```css
#map {
  width: 500px;
  height: 400px;
  margin: 1em;
}
```

4. Just for completeness, you should also update the `navigation.php` file to include a link to your newly created map page:

```php
<?php
$user = $_SESSION['FlickrAuthenticatedUser'];
?>
<ul id="gallery-menu">
  <li><a href="../index.php">Mashups Home</a></li>
  <li><a href="index.php">Gallery</a></li>
  <li><a href="smartsets.php">Smart Sets</a></li>
  <li><a href="map.php">Map</a></li>

    ...

</ul>
```

5. Now that all the bits are in place, it's time to get on to the real work. You now have to create the `doMap()` function that the `onload` handler will invoke. Start by creating a simple map, just as you saw in the earlier examples. Create the `map.js` file in the `lib/js` directory:

```javascript
function doMap()
{
    var map = new GMap2(document.getElementById("map"));
    map.addControl(new GLargeMapControl());
    map.addControl(new GMapTypeControl());
    map.setCenter(new GLatLng(0, 0), 1);
}
```

6. If you open your web browser, go to the gallery pages, and click the Map link in the main navigation, you should see a basic map page as shown in Figure 13-9.

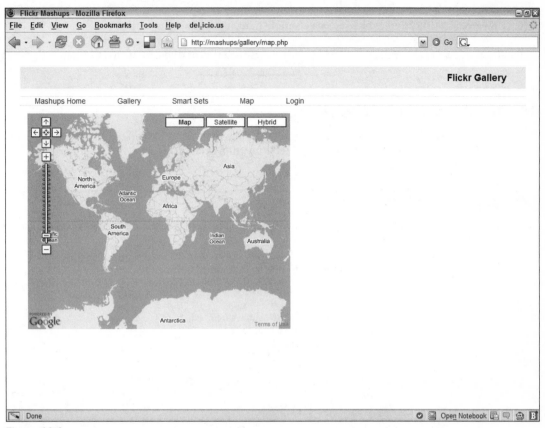

Figure 13-9

How It Works

The `map.php` file takes the same basic structure as the other pages in the gallery directory, but with some extra bits added to support the Google Maps mashup.

The main Google Maps JavaScript library is incorporated into the page via a PHP include:

```php
<?php include dirname(__FILE__) . '/../lib/mapapi.php' ?>
```

A second script is also included:

```html
<script src="../lib/js/map.js" type="text/javascript"></script>
```

The map.js file is where all the JavaScript for this mashup is kept—at the moment this file contains only the doMap() function, which creates a simple map, just as you saw earlier.

Finally, the onload and onunload event handlers are included and the <div> for the map is declared.

Adding Markers to the Map

Now you have an empty map, it's time to populate it. The first step is to read the XML data generated by your PHP script. The Google Maps API provides a function called GDownloadURL that retrieves the contents of a URL.

Try It Out   **Populating the Map**

In this exercise you'll use GDownloadURL to invoke your geo.php script and then use the GXml class to parse the XML data received into a DOM.

1.   Update map.js to add the following code to the doMap() function:

```
function doMap()
{
    var map = new GMap2(document.getElementById("map"));
    map.addControl(new GLargeMapControl());
    map.addControl(new GMapTypeControl());
    map.setCenter(new GLatLng(0, 0), 1);

    GDownloadUrl("geo.php", function(data, responseCode)
      {
        var xml = GXml.parse(data);
        var photos = xml.documentElement.getElementsByTagName("photo");

        var s = "";
        var n = Math.min(photos.length, 5);
        for (var i = 0; i < n; i++)
        {
            s += photos[i].getAttribute("id") + ", ";
        }

        alert("Ids received:\n\n" + s);
      });
}
```

2.   If you now look at the maps page in your browser, you should see the map load. Then there will be a slight pause as it calls the geo.php script, which in turn makes a call to Flickr to get the photo information. Finally, the alert should appear, showing you the photo IDs of the first five geotagged photos returned, as shown in Figure 13-10.

Now that you've established that the downloading and parsing of the XML file is working correctly, you can replace the handler function with code to do something useful with that data.

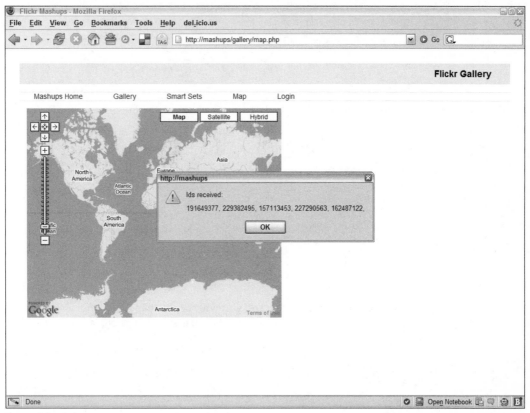

Figure 13-10

3. The Google Maps API provides a `GMarker` class that enables you to create and position markers easily on your map. You'll now see how to make use of this class to add markers at the location points for each of your geotagged photos. Update your `doMap()` function, replacing the test code you had earlier:

```
function doMap()
{
    var map = new GMap2(document.getElementById("map"));
    map.addControl(new GLargeMapControl());
    map.addControl(new GMapTypeControl());
    map.setCenter(new GLatLng(0, 0), 1);

    GDownloadUrl("geo.php", function(data, responseCode)
    {
        var xml = GXml.parse(data);
        var photos = xml.documentElement.getElementsByTagName("photo");

        for (var i = 0; i < photos.length; i++)
        {
            var id = photos[i].getAttribute("id");
            var latitude = parseFloat(photos[i].getAttribute("latitude"));
            var longitude = parseFloat(photos[i].getAttribute("longitude"));
            var point = new GLatLng(latitude, longitude);
```

```
        var marker = createMarker(point, id);

        map.addOverlay(marker);
    }
});
}
```

4. The next step is to write the `createMarker` function used in the previous example. Add this code to your `map.js` file:

```
function createMarker(point, id)
{
    var marker = new GMarker(point);

    GEvent.addListener(marker, "click", function()
    {
        marker.openInfoWindowHtml("<p>Photo Id: " + id + "</p>");
    });

    return marker;
}
```

5. Open up the map page in your browser, and you will see the map load. After a short pause, you should then see a set of markers appear — one for each geotagged photo, as in Figure 13-11.

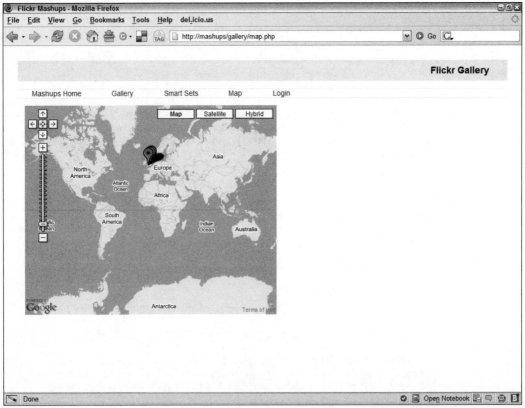

Figure 13-11

6. Center the map on one of the markers and zoom in closer to it, and then click on the marker. An Info Window should appear next to your marker, showing the ID of the photo at that location — something like that shown in Figure 13-12.

Try clicking on different markers — each time you click on one, the contents of the Info Window should change to show the correct photo ID.

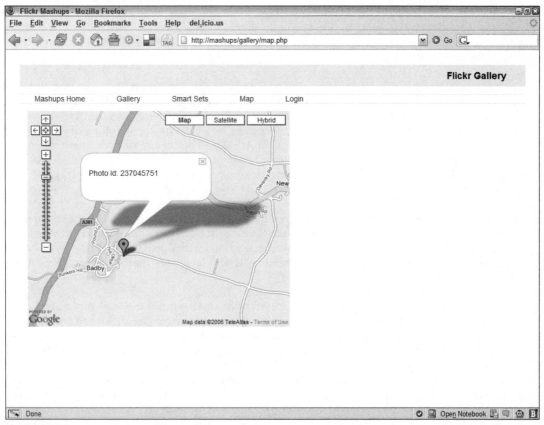

Figure 13-12

How It Works

When GDownloadUrl() is called, it takes two parameters. The first is the path to the page from which the XML data is fetched, and the second is a reference to a handler function that is called once the data is downloaded. As this is the only place the handler function is needed, it is declared inline.

The handler function starts by using the GXml class to parse the incoming data. This returns a DOM object representing the parsed XML document. The root element is accessed via the documentElement property, and so you can use this property to find all of the <photo> elements within the document.

```
var photos = xml.documentElement.getElementsByTagName("photo");
```

The next few lines in the function are temporary ones so you can check that the document is down-loaded and parsed correctly. They simply loop through the first five <photo> elements returned and col-lect the photo IDs into a single string, which is then displayed via a call to alert(). When developing mashups, it is often helpful to include a check like this from time to time, especially after a major step, just to ensure that things are working as you expect.

After you've replaced your temporary code, the updated download handler function now iterates through each photo returned, extracting the id, latitude, and longitude attributes. It then creates a new GLatLng object representing the location of the photo. A new function is then called, createMarker, which creates an instance of a GMarker object. Finally, this marker object is added to the map via the GMap2 addOverlay method.

The createMarker function takes two parameters: the GLatLng object representing the location of the photo and the Flickr photo ID. A new GMarker object is created at the photo location, and an event han-dler is defined for the marker. This event handler will be invoked whenever a click event occurs on the marker. Within the event handler, openInfoWindowHtml is called, passing in a string of HTML identify-ing the ID of the photo. The Info Window is a popup window that can appear over an instance of a GMap2 object. The GMarker object has a convenient helper function, openInfoWindowHtml, that opens the Info Window, positions it next to the marker on the map, and then adds the specified HTML to the Info Window.

You might notice something a little strange about the event handler you just defined. It uses the id parameter when displaying the HTML in the Info Window, but that id parameter is never stored any-where. The createMarker function will be called many times with different photo IDs, and when the event handler fires, some time later, createMarker will have long since finished executing. So how do you know you are using the correct value of id?

This construct, where the handler function is defined inside another function, is called a *JavaScript function closure*, and is the recommended means of handling tasks like this within Google Maps. Closures are a rel-atively complex topic and you can find a great deal of information about them on the web — just perform a Google search on "JavaScript Function Closure" to see a good selection of articles that talk about them in some depth. For now, the main thing to know is that the enclosed function continues to operate within the context of the outer function — all the variables defined within the outer function continue to be available to the inner function, even after the outer function has finished executing and has returned. The value that each of those variables is seen to have is the value it had when the outer function finished executing. This means that in this example, each instance of the click event handler will see that id has the value it had at the time that the createMarker function completed execution — in other words, the value of id within the event handler is whatever value was passed in for that iteration.

Some web browsers have problems with memory leaks when function closures are used, which is why it is important to call the GUnload function in the unload handler for your page — this ensures that the memory used within your Google Maps mashup is properly released.

Populating the Info Window

You now have an Info Window above each marker, but the contents of it aren't really very interesting. Let's now change the contents of the window to show something a little more useful — a thumbnail image of the photo, for example. All we need to do is generate the appropriate HTML.

Try It Out   **Displaying Information on the Map**

Rather than generate the HTML for the Info Window in the JavaScript code running in the browser, you'll use the same technique you used for retrieving the XML list of photos: you'll create a PHP file on the server to generate the appropriate data and then use GDownloadUrl to retrieve them for display.

1.   Create a file, geoview.php, in the gallery directory:

```php
<?php

include (dirname(__FILE__) . '/../lib/gallery.php');

$gallery = new FlickrGallery();

$id = $_REQUEST['id'];

header ("Content-Type: text/html");

if (!empty($id))
{
  $info = $gallery->getPhotoInfo($id);
  $title = $info['title'];
  $username = $info['owner']['username'];
  $realname = $info['owner']['realname'];
  $nameText = $username;
  if (!empty($realname))
  {
    $nameText = $realname . " (" . $username . ")";
  }
  $img = 'http://static.flickr.com/' . $info['server'] . '/' . $info['id'] . '_'
    . $info['secret'] . '_t.jpg';
  $photoPage = 'http://www.flickr.com/photos/' . $info['owner']['nsid'] . '/'
    . $id . '/';

?>
<div class="map-info">
  <p class="map-image"><a href="<?php echo $photoPage ?>"
    target="flickr-photo"><img src="<?php echo $img ?>" /></a></p>
  <p class="map-title"><?php echo $title ?></p>
  <p class="map-user"><?php echo $nameText ?></p>
  <p class="map-link"><a href="<?php echo $photoPage ?>"
    target="flickr-photo">View on Flickr</a></p>
</div>
<?php
}
?>
```

2.   Load the file into your web browser so that you can see the HTML it generates. You need to pass it the photo ID of the photo you are interested in, so choose one of your photos that will be appearing on the map. The URL you use to view this photo will depend on your local development environment, but should look something like this:

```
http://localhost/gallery/geoview.php?id=9563602
```

3. Once the page is loaded, look at the source for the page. You should see the generated HTML, which will look something like this:

```html
<div class="map-info">
  <p class="map-image">
    <a href="http://www.flickr.com/photos/50317659@N00/9563602/"
      target="flickr-photo">
      <img src="http://static.flickr.com/8/9563602_ef1017ae94_t.jpg" />
    </a>
  </p>
  <p class="map-title">Lynmouth Harbour</p>
  <p class="map-user">David Wilkinson (dopiaza)</p>
  <p class="map-link">
    <a href="http://www.flickr.com/photos/50317659@N00/9563602/"
      target="flickr-photo">View on Flickr</a>
  </p>
</div>
```

4. Each of the elements in the HTML has a `class` attribute specified to simplify styling using CSS. Modify `gallery.css` to add some new styles for the Info Window HTML:

```css
.map-info {
  width: 300px;
  height: 110px;
  font-size: 12px;
  color: #000000;
  background-color: #FFFFFF;
}

.map-image img {
  float: left;
  margin-right: 1em;
  margin-bottom: 1em;
  border: 1px solid #FFFFFF;
}

.map-title {
  font-size: 16px;
  font-weight: 800;
}
.map-link a {
  font-size: 10px;
}
```

5. Next, modify `map.js` to retrieve the generated HTML and display it in the Info Window — replace the existing `createMarker` function and add the new `displayMarkerInfo` function:

```javascript
function createMarker(point, id)
{
  var marker = new GMarker(point);

  GEvent.addListener(marker, "click", function()
  {
    displayMarkerInfo(marker, id);
  });

  return marker;
```

```
  }

function displayMarkerInfo(marker, id)
{
  GDownloadUrl("geoview.php?id=" + id, function(data, responseCode)
  {
    marker.openInfoWindowHtml(data);
  });
}
```

6. Reload the application in your browser and navigate to one of your markers. You will see that when you click on the marker, there is a slight pause while the HTML is retrieved before the Info Window opens up, as shown in Figure 13-13.

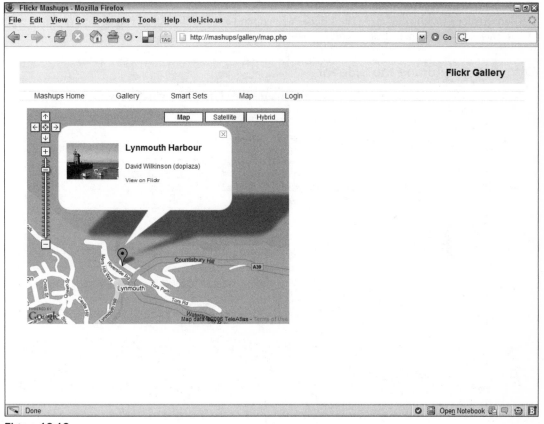

Figure 13-13

How It Works

The geoview.php script uses the FlickrGallery->getPhotoInfo method to retrieve the information for the photo and generates an HTML snippet ready for display in the Info Window. It generates the URL for the thumbnail version of the photo stored on Flickr — there isn't a great deal of space in the Info Window.

When you look at the HTML that `geoview.php` generates, you'll notice that the `<a>` tags open up the linked Flickr page in a new window. This is because the map state is lost if the user navigates away from the page containing the map. If the link opened in the same page, the user could click the Back button to return to the map, but at this point the map JavaScript would reinitialize and the user would no longer see the same view of the map as they did when they left it.

In `map.js`, the code to retrieve the HTML and display the Info Window has been moved into the new `displayMarkerInfo` function, which uses JavaScript function closures to access the correct marker once the HTML has downloaded.

Creating a Sidebar

For the next step in the mashup, you'll see how to create a sidebar containing HTML that can then be used to interact with your map. The sidebar will contain a list of the titles of all of your geotagged photos, each of which, when clicked, will appear in the map view.

Try It Out   Adding the Sidebar

In this exercise you'll create the sidebar that contains the HTML that will display clickable tags for each of your photos.

1. Modify `map.php` to include space for the sidebar:

```php
<?php include (dirname(__FILE__) . '/../lib/gallery.php') ?>
<!DOCTYPE html PUBLIC "-//W3C//DTD XHTML 1.0 Transitional//EN"
"http://www.w3.org/TR/xhtml1/DTD/xhtml1-transitional.dtd">
<html xmlns="http://www.w3.org/1999/xhtml">
<head>
<title>Flickr Mashups</title>
<?php include dirname(__FILE__) . '/../lib/mapapi.php' ?>
<script src="../lib/js/map.js" type="text/javascript"></script>
<link href="../css/main.css" rel="stylesheet" type="text/css" />
<link href="../css/gallery.css" rel="stylesheet" type="text/css" />
</head>
<body onload="doMap()" onunload="GUnload()">
<?php include ('header.php') ?>
<?php include ('navigation.php') ?>
    <div id="map-wrapper">
      <div id="map"></div>
      <ul id="marker-list"></ul>
    </div>
</body>
</html>
```

2. Replace the existing rules in `gallery.css` for `#map`:

```css
#map {
  width: 500px;
  height: 400px;
  margin: 1em;
}
```

with the following set:

```css
#map-wrapper {
    margin: 1em;
    width: 700px;
    height: 400px;
}

#map {
    float: left;
    width: 500px;
    height: 400px;
}

#marker-list {
    float: right;
    width: 197px;
    height: 398px;
    border: 1px solid #EEEEEE;
    list-style-type: none;
    margin: 0;
    padding: 0;
    overflow: scroll;
}
```

The map `<div>` and the `<ul>` marker list should now sit side by side within the containing `<div>` element.

3. In order to populate the list with the photo titles, you need to modify the format of the XML file that is generated so that it also contains the photo title as an attribute. Add an extra line to `geo.php`:

```php
<?php

include (dirname(__FILE__) . '/../lib/gallery.php');

$gallery = new FlickrGallery();

$photos = $gallery->getWithGeoData();

header ("Content-Type: text/xml");

echo "<?xml version=\"1.0\"?>\n";
echo "<photos>\n";
if (is_array($photos))
{
  foreach ($photos as $p)
  {
    echo "<photo " .
      "id=\"" . $p['id'] . "\" " .
      "latitude=\"" . $p['latitude'] . "\" " .
      "longitude=\"" . $p['longitude'] . "\" " .
      "title=\"" . htmlspecialchars($p['title']) . "\" " .
      " />\n";
  }
```

```
    }
    echo "</photos>";
    ?>
```

4. The next step is to build the list elements that sit within the `<ul>` element — each will be the title of a photo. Each title will also be contained within an `<a>` element so that when it is clicked, you will be able to call a JavaScript function to open the corresponding marker on the map. To do this, you will need to keep a track of which list items correspond to which photos.

   Edit `map.js` and add the following variable declarations at the top of the file:

```
var markers = new Array();
var photoIds = new Array();
```

   These two arrays will be used to keep track of which photo ID is represented by which marker.

5. Next, modify the `createMarker` function to store the relevant details in these two arrays:

```
function createMarker(point, id)
{
  var marker = new GMarker(point);
  markers.push(marker);
  photoIds.push(id);
  var index = markers.length - 1;

  GEvent.addListener(marker, "click", function()
  {
    displayMarkerInfo(index);
  });

  return marker;
}
```

6. Next, replace the existing `displayMarkerInfo` function with a new version that takes a single index parameter:

```
function displayMarkerInfo(index)
{
  var marker = markers[index];
  var id = photoIds[index];

  GDownloadUrl("geoview.php?id=" + id, function(data, responseCode)
  {
    marker.openInfoWindowHtml(data);
  });
}
```

7. Now to generate the list elements themselves — replace the `doMap()` function:

```
function doMap()
{
  var map = new GMap2(document.getElementById("map"));
  map.addControl(new GLargeMapControl());
  map.addControl(new GMapTypeControl());
  map.setCenter(new GLatLng(0, 0), 1);

  GDownloadUrl("geo.php", function(data, responseCode)
  {
```

```
      var xml = GXml.parse(data);
      var photos = xml.documentElement.getElementsByTagName("photo");

      var listHtml = "";

      for (var i = 0; i < photos.length; i++)
      {
        var id = photos[i].getAttribute("id");
        var title = photos[i].getAttribute("title");
        if (title == "")
        {
          title = "Untitled";
        }
        var latitude = parseFloat(photos[i].getAttribute("latitude"));
        var longitude = parseFloat(photos[i].getAttribute("longitude"));
        var point = new GLatLng(latitude, longitude);

        map.addOverlay(createMarker(point, id));

        listHtml += "<li><a href=\"#\" onclick=\"displayMarkerInfo(" + i
                  + "); return false;\">" + title + "</a></li>";
      }
      var markerList = document.getElementById('marker-list');
      markerList.innerHTML = listHtml;
    });
  }
```

8. After you've made these changes, reload the application in your browser. Once the markers appear, you should see the list of photo titles appear alongside the map. If you zoom in on the map and then click on one of the titles, the map will recenter so that the corresponding marker moves into view and the Info Window for that photo appears, as seen in Figure 13-14.

9. That's almost it for this particular mashup — but first there's scope for doing a last little bit of tidying up on your newly created list. All of those photo titles merge into one solid list, which can make it hard on the eyes to scan down the list looking for a particular photo. Simply adding a little spacing around each item can improve things enormously here, but another useful technique is to vary the background color of alternate rows in the list. The easiest way to do this is to add a CSS class to each list item as it is created. Modify the doMap() function as follows:

```
function doMap()
{
  ...

      map.addOverlay(createMarker(point, id));

      var className = (i%2 == 0) ? "even" : "odd";

      listHtml += "<li class=\"" + className + "\">"
        + "<a href=\"#\" onclick=\"displayMarkerInfo("
        + i + "); return false;\">"
        + title + "</a></li>";
    }
    var markerList = document.getElementById('marker-list');
    markerList.innerHTML = listHtml;
  });
}
```

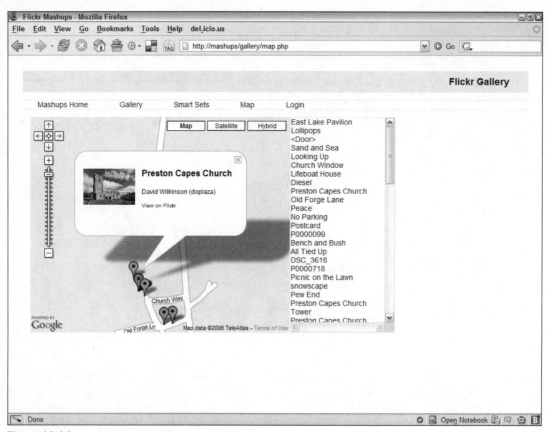

Figure 13-14

10. Modify `gallery.css` to add a couple of new style rules in order to provide a little spacing around the list elements and to change the background color of the even-numbered rows to be light gray.

```
#marker-list li {
  font-size: 12px;
  margin: 0;
  padding: 3px 5px 3px 5px;
}

#marker-list .even {
    background-color: #EEEEEE;
}
```

As you can see from Figure 13-15, these minor changes dramatically improve the appearance of the list.

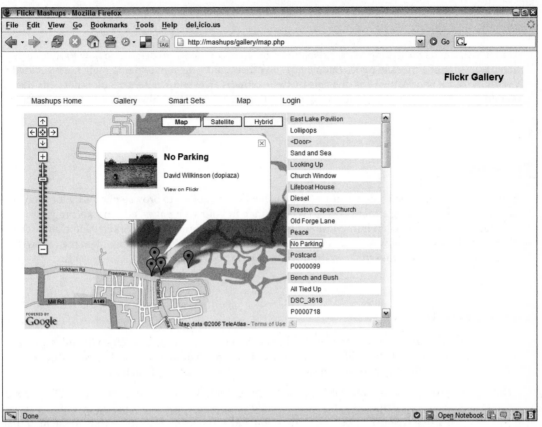

Figure 13-15

How It Works

In `map.php` you added a new `<ul>` element alongside the map, ready to store a list of all the markers placed. The whole map and list have also been wrapped inside a containing `<div>`. These elements are now sized and positioned using CSS.

In the modified `createMarker` function, each time a new marker is created, the marker object is pushed on to the end of the `markers` array and the corresponding photo ID is pushed on to the end of the `photoIds` array. The array index of the marker just added is calculated (it is the one currently at the end of the array) and this index is then passed as the parameter to `displayMarkerInfo` in the `click` event handler.

In the new version of `displayMarkerInfo`, both the photo ID and the marker to use are obtained by looking at the entry specified by the given index in each of the `markers` and `photoIds` arrays.

To create the list elements in the `doMap()` function, the list data is built up as a string of HTML in the `listHtml` variable. Each time a new item is added to the list, a new piece of HTML is appended to `listHtml`, of the following form:

```
<li><a href="#" onclick="displayMarkerInfo(n); return false;">Photo Title</a></li>
```

Here n is the index of the current list item. The onclick handler calls the displayMarkerInfo method with the appropriate index.

The code that adds formatting to the sidebar uses the loop counter, i, to determine how to style each list item. The value of i modulo two is calculated—in other words, the remainder left when i is divided by two. If the result is zero, then i is divisible by two, so this is an even row. If the result is not zero, then this is an odd row. A class attribute is added to each <li> element with the value even or odd accordingly.

Summary

In this chapter you added a new feature to the gallery—the ability to browse photos by location. You saw how to use the Google Maps API to embed a map in your web pages, add markers to your map at specific locations, display an Info Window showing details about specific markers, and change the view of the map by interacting with other HTML elements on the page. Now take a look at the following exercises to see some other ways you can improve your map.

Exercises

1. The list of photos retrieved from Flickr is sorted by interestingness. When the titles are displayed in the list alongside the map, it would be much more useful if they were displayed alphabetically. Change the code so that they are sorted into alphabetical order.

2. If you have a lot of geotagged photos, you might not want to try to show them all on a single map. You saw earlier on in this chapter how to display a map that opened up onto a particular region by selecting a particular center point and zoom level. Add some code to the map that retrieves only photos that are located within the area displayed in the map when it first opens, thus enabling you to show just a subset of your photos from a particular geographic area.

   You may need to refer to the Google API documentation at:

   http://www.google.com/apis/maps/documentation/

   in order to find the geographic coordinates of the area covered by the view on the screen.

Caching Your Data

So far, our focus has been on retrieving information from Flickr whenever it is needed. Sometimes, though, on-demand retrieval isn't necessarily the best way to get hold of the data you are after. Suppose for a moment that your mashup suddenly becomes extremely popular; perhaps it gets mentioned on a major web site such as Slashdot, Digg, or Boing Boing — mashups featured on sites like these can suddenly start to receive enormous amounts of traffic. How well will your mashup cope with the load? To a certain extent, this depends on where it is hosted, and the bandwidth and processing power available to it — but the way you write it can also make a huge difference to the way it performs under stress. In this chapter, I'll take a look at one of the most common, and often one of the most effective, ways of improving the performance of your mashup: caching data locally. I'll also provide a look at an example of a real-world Flickr mashup and examine the techniques used there to maintain site performance. Finally, you'll take some of the lessons learned and apply them to the Flickr gallery application you built in earlier chapters.

To Cache or Not to Cache

In the context of building Flickr mashups, *caching* simply means that when you retrieve a piece of information from Flickr, such as the results of a tag search or information about a photo, you do not discard that information when you are finished with it. Instead, you store the data away, and the next time your application needs to retrieve similar data — perform the tag search again, for example — it doesn't send a request to Flickr. Rather than repeat the request, it uses the local saved copy. In other words, the application remembers the answer from the previous search and assumes that the same result can be used again.

You should consider a number of factors before implementing data caching — after all, even the simplest of caching schemes will add extra complexity to your application. In the following sections I'll go over some of the questions you should be asking yourself.

Why Should You Cache?

Why bother caching data when you can just retrieve it from Flickr whenever you need it? It's certainly easier to build an application that just retrieves all the data it needs on demand, but that doesn't necessarily result in a well-designed application — if your mashup performs a search on Flickr every time somebody accesses a page, then an API call will be made to Flickr for every page load. Of course, it depends on the exact nature of your mashup, but in many cases the search performed and the results returned will be identical for each page loaded. If you take the front page of the gallery application built earlier in the book as an example, it's clear that the search results will change only when you upload new photos to Flickr. This might well be very infrequently, certainly when compared with the number of times the page is viewed. Remember that every API call to Flickr can add several seconds to the load time of your page. By retrieving the list of photos to display once, and then storing those results locally, you can improve the performance of your mashup quite dramatically.

Another thing to consider when using the API is the terms of use attached to your API key: Flickr states that your application shouldn't make an excessive number of calls — an average of one API call per second is generally considered to be an upper limit for what would be classed as acceptable. A popular application that requires several API calls to construct each page could easily find itself breaching that limit at peak times.

What Should You Cache?

Even if you decide that building a local cache is a good idea, there is still the question of just what data to cache. The first factor you have to consider is the lifetime of the data. Depending on how often you upload photos, the search results used by the gallery's front page might not change for days at a time, whereas a page showing the most recently uploaded photos to Flickr changes by the second. The next question you should consider is just how important it is that the data you use be absolutely up to date. In the gallery, is it really important that your latest photos show up instantly, or could they wait a couple of hours? If you are displaying the most recently uploaded photos, will showing those from a few minutes ago suffice? The actual answer will depend on your particular application, but in the vast majority of cases caching certain data items is both possible and desirable.

The decision to cache data is always a tradeoff — here, you are typically trading off the currency of the information against the time taken to get more up-to-date data. Take a look at a hypothetical example, that of a page that performs three separate tag searches to put together a series of photos and display the results back to the user. A brief experiment during the writing of this chapter showed that a simple tag search via the API for photos tagged *cat* took between two and three seconds to return a page of results. Performing three such searches would therefore be expected to take between six and nine seconds. Your application then has to parse the responses and process those data before the page can be generated. It is quite likely that this scenario would result in a page-generation time of a little under ten seconds *on the server* — this is before the page can even be returned to the user, whereupon it must be rendered in the user's browser and any images also downloaded and displayed. Those ten seconds in the world of Web 2.0 will seem like an eternity to a user sitting in front of a browser.

Now consider an alternative approach in which the results of the tag search are stored locally. The first time the page is viewed, Flickr must, of course, be consulted for the search results. These are then used to generate the requested page, but are also stored away locally. In terms of time taken, this page view is no different from the previous scenario. However, the next time the page is viewed, the locally stored copy of the search results is used — avoiding the multi-second wait for a response from Flickr. With a little care, it would be possible to generate such a page in a fraction of a second, resulting in a much better user experience than the long wait required in the uncached scenario.

Where Should You Cache?

Once you've made to decision to cache data, the final question is where to store it. For small quantities of data, you can always just write to disk and use the file system as a temporary storage area, but as the quantity and complexity of the data you are using rises, any file-based system becomes inefficient and difficult to use. For fast, efficient storage and retrieval of large quantities of data, a relational database is the only practical choice. Many database products are available, ranging in cost from free to many hundreds of thousands of dollars. In this chapter, we'll assume that you are developing on a budget and focus on database solutions at the free end of that range.

A Case Study

Before I move on, I'll provide a little context. I will take a brief look at a real-world example of a Flickr mashup — the Utata web site (`http://www.utata.org/`). Utata is a collective of photographers, writers, and like-minded people who share a compelling interest in the arts. The web site provides an environment in which the members' work can be displayed to an ever-growing audience. The site is intimately linked with Flickr — all photographs used on the site are stored on Flickr and the pages on the site are dynamically built with the Flickr API.

Like most real-world software projects, Utata wasn't a carefully planned development — it has changed and grown organically over time. The original requirements for the site were modest and easily supported. As time passed, new requirements continued to appear and the site, as well as the infrastructure behind it, has had to continually evolve to support the needs of its users.

Here I'll take a look at the background to Utata, how it has changed in the brief time since it was first created, and, most important, how its use of Flickr has had to change in order to accommodate those changes. In particular, you'll see how relying on the simple page-building techniques shown earlier in this book quickly became inefficient and more advanced use of data-caching was required to provide an acceptable level of performance.

The Origins of Utata

In the early part of 2005, writer and photographer Catherine Jamieson was growing tired of the hurly-burly of the other groups on Flickr. She wanted somewhere a little more relaxing to hang out and had failed to find anywhere suitable among the many thousands of groups already on Flickr — and so, like so many people before her, she started a group of her own. She invited some of her friends to join in and laid down a few house rules — the primary one of which was to be polite. When she was asked "Who should join?" she answered, "Whoever is polite and interested. *Notice polite is first.*" And so the group Utata was born, the doors flung open ready for people to join.

A diverse group of people steadily found their way into the group attracted in the main by the salon-style atmosphere of the group and the polite rule. With a shared interest in photography, it wasn't too long before the members were talking about working collaboratively and the idea of a group project was born. A theme was chosen: Trains — members were to submit photographs that fitted the theme. All the submitted pictures were held on Flickr and members posted them to a discussion thread in the Utata group. The quality of the photographs submitted was very high — it was clear that they needed to be displayed properly to the world outside of Utata, and so the Utata.org web site was born.

The Trains project was put together as a blog by means of the Moveable Type system published by Six Apart. The details for each photo in the project were entered by hand into Moveable Type and the result published as a series of web pages — one for each photo. The project itself was highly acclaimed and was featured on a number of web sites, including Yahoo! Picks. The actual construction of the project was, however, laborious. Utata members were keen to participate in more projects, but had to find a way to publish them that did not require quite so much manual data entry. The *tagging project* was born.

Tagging Projects

A tagging project is very simple in concept. A project theme is announced — Utata Silhouettes, for example — and people then take and upload photos corresponding to that theme. To identify that a given photo was part of the project, the owner adds a project-specific tag to the photo — utata_silhouettes in this example. Displaying a selection of photos on the Utata project page is then simply a matter of performing a tag search on the appropriate tag — just as you have seen in many of the projects featured in this book. From the returned list of tagged photos, a random selection displays on the project page.

This technique worked very well for a short while and tagging projects became a regular feature of Utata, usually being announced on a Friday so that members could spend their weekend taking photos. These regular weekend projects became so popular that by Monday, the tag being used would regularly feature in Flickr's Hot Tags list as one of those currently most popular. A great success — except that this very success was also to become the system's downfall.

Some people on Flickr are obsessed with getting as many views as possible on their pictures — they don't necessarily care where those views come from, or whether people actually like their photos, it's just the numbers that are important. One of the techniques employed by these people is to give their photos as many tags as possible, regardless of whether the tags are appropriate for the subject matter — the idea being to increase the probability that your photo will turn up in as many search results as possible and hence end up being viewed. Of course, the photo almost invariably bears no relation to the search terms, but increasing the view count is all that matters here. Many people find this behavior both bizarre and pointless, but nevertheless, it exists. A common source of suitable tags employed by these tag spammers is the list of currently popular tags on Flickr. And so, of course, the inevitable happened, and Utata project tags started to appear on photographs completely unrelated to the Utata projects. The projects weren't, on the whole, improved by having random phonecam snapshots of people dancing at nightclubs scattered throughout them. Clearly it was necessary to separate out the rogue photos.

Tracking Membership

The people misusing the project tags weren't members of Utata — they'd probably never even heard of Utata. They were simply copying tags off the Hot Tags page and adding them to their photos. One way to filter them out would be to cross-check the owners of the photos returned by the tag search against the membership of the Utata group — any photos owned by nonmembers would not be displayed.

This sounds good in theory, but is actually not that straightforward with the Flickr API. Currently, there is no way to get a list of members of a group. There has been talk on the Flickr API developer mailing list of Flickr providing such a method, but at the time of this writing, no such method is available. There is, however, a method gives you the list of public groups for a member — flickr.people.getPublicGroups. This method takes a member's NSID and returns a list of public groups of which they are currently members. Using this information, it is possible to write a method that identifies whether any given user is a member of Utata:

```
function isUtatan($person)
{
  global $utataNSID; // The NSID of the Utata group

  $ok = false;

  // Get public groups for this user
  $groups = $this->flickr->people_getPublicGroups($person);

  // And check all of their groups to see if they are in Utata
  if (is_array($groups['group']))
  {
    foreach ($groups['group'] as $group)
    {
      if ($group['nsid'] == $utataNSID)
      {
        $ok = true;
        break;
      }
    }
  }

  return $ok;
}
```

So, when Utata chose photos to display, it was simply a case of calling the isUtatan() method, passing in the NSID of the owner of the photo, and using only photos for which the method returns true. This proved very effective at filtering out the rogue photos — but was very slow. At that time, a typical project page laid the photos out in a grid with a larger central photo — as you can see in Figure 14-1.

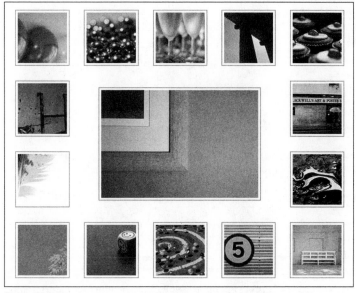

Figure 14-1

Building this page required something approximating the following sequence of actions:

1. Call `flickr.photos.search` using the project tag. If more than 500 photos match the search criteria, repeat for each page until the full list of photos is retrieved.

2. Choose a photo at random from the list. Call `isUtatan()` to check group membership for the photo's owner. If the check fails, choose a different photo and repeat.

3. Repeat Step 2 until 15 photos have been chosen.

4. Generate HTML to display photos.

A typical page built in this way would require around 16 API calls to build — often taking around thirty to forty seconds. This was clearly an unacceptable delay. It was time to start caching data.

The initial caching approach was very simple — the software would maintain a cache file consisting of a list of NSIDs for which it had previously checked group membership. Associated with each NSID would be a flag indicating whether the NSID was a member of Utata or not — something rather like this:

```
50317659@N00 y
43112796@N00 y
63233616@N00 n
10248938@N00 y
```

In the method `isUtatan()`, this cache file would first be checked to see if it contained the required information. If the NSID was not found in the cache, then the call to `flickr.people.getPublicGroups` was made as normal — but in this case, a new line containing the result for that member would be appended to the end of the cache file. This way, the Flickr API would need to be used only the first time a user was encountered. On subsequent occasions, the locally cached data would be used in preference. The new `isUtatan()` method looked something like this:

```
function isUtatan($person)
{
  global $utataNSID; // The NSID of the Utata group

  $ok = false;

  // Check cache first
  $isInCache = false;
  if (array_key_exists($person, $this->peopleCache))
  {
    $isInCache = true;
    if ($this->peopleCache[$person] == true)
    {
      $ok = true;
    }
  }

  if (!$isInCache)
  {
    // Get public groups
    $groups = $this->flickr->people_getPublicGroups($person);

    // And check all the groups to see if they are in Utata
```

```
      if (is_array($groups['group']))
      {
        foreach ($groups['group'] as $group)
        {
          if ($group['nsid'] == $utataNSID)
          {
            $ok = true;
            break;
          }
        }
      }
      $this->peopleCache[$person] = $ok;
      $this->savePersonToFile($person, $ok);
    }

    return $ok;
  }
```

The peopleCache member variable is an associative array of NSIDs and their membership status read in from the cache file at the start of the script. This method first checks to see if the requested member is present in the cache, and if so uses the cached value. If not, it retrieves the group list from Flickr, just as before. It then updates the in-memory copy of the cache, and also the file on disk with the new information.

With the new caching scheme in place, performance was dramatically improved. The first few accesses, while the cache was being built up, were still slow, but very quickly the cache grew to contain details of most of the regular contributors. Page generation was now down to a few seconds — most of which was the time taken to perform the tag search.

Introducing a Database

The disk cache file worked well, but Utata was just a few hundred members strong and membership was steadily growing. As the number of members increased, the disk cache would take longer to load. Also, page load times were also still longer than people would like — each project page required at least one call to flickr.photos.search, and sometimes more. If the list of photos used in a project could also be stored locally, that would eliminate the significant delay in building a page. The decision was made to switch over to a local database — all the locally held data would be stored there. It was easy to use, fast to access, and could store what was effectively an unlimited amount of data.

In addition to member information, information about project photos was stored in the database. A separate application was created to periodically perform tag searches for all the Utata projects and store the results in the database. A typical call to flickr.photos.search returned something like this:

```
<photo id="89833644" owner="50317659@N00" secret="1322015302" server="24"
title="Red Glass" ispublic="1" isfriend="0" isfamily="0" ownername="dopiaza"
latitude="0" longitude="0" accuracy="0" />
```

Each of those fields would be stored away in the database, ready for use later. Only photos belonging to registered Utata members would be stored in the database, thus avoiding the need to check ownership when the project pages were being viewed. With all of that information stored locally, it became possible to build a project page without accessing the Flickr API at all, and page creation times were now running at significantly under a second.

The application that performed the tag searches was scheduled to run periodically to ensure that the database was kept up to date, with each tag search taking place according to a defined schedule. Current projects would be refreshed every fifteen minutes; as they grew older, the refresh interval would change to once a day; and finally, as activity on the project tailed off, the project entries would be updated once every week. This approach kept API usage to a minimum while ensuring that the projects were always kept up to date within an acceptable period — data that were changing often were refreshed often, data that changed rarely were only refreshed weekly.

Utata Today

Utata has grown at an astounding rate. There are now over 6,000 members in the Flickr group, with new ones arriving every day. The Utata.org web site currently handles over 20,000 unique visitors every month, with a growth rate that shows no sign of slowing down. With practically every page on Utata.org being dynamically generated, it is clear that the original simplistic implementations would have long since failed to cope with the volumes of both data and traffic involved. The strategy of caching important data, however, has stood Utata in very good stead and should continue to support its growth for some time.

The basic infrastructure is still in place, keeping the Utata web site running. More and more functionality is added each month and today, the project pages are far more numerous and sophisticated than was ever envisaged during that very first Trains project.

Updating the Gallery

The Utata case study illustrates quite clearly how a project can very quickly go from humble beginnings to handling a significant volume of traffic. When you are building your mashups, it is useful to consider the ways in which they might end up being used. In this next section you'll take a look at some of the caching techniques that proved useful during the growth of Utata and see how they can be applied to the gallery application you built in earlier chapters.

The first step is to make sure that you have somewhere to store your data — it's time to install a database.

Installing MySQL

MySQL is a freely available database from the Swedish company MySQL AB. Over the past few years it has quickly become one of the most widely used databases on the Internet and it works quietly behind the scenes at many websites, including Flickr itself. You can download the latest version of MySQL from `http://www.mysql.com/`.

Microsoft Windows

Installation of MySQL under Microsoft Windows is very straightforward — simply download and run the installation package from the MySQL web site. Once the installer has installed the software, you will be asked if you want to configure your database server — you should say yes to this. The MySQL Server Instance Configuration Wizard then launches to help you set up your newly installed database. The first thing you are asked is whether you want to go through a detailed configuration or simply a standard configuration, as you can see in Figure 14-2.

For most people, the standard configuration will probably be perfectly satisfactory. If you decide to choose a detailed configuration, you will be asked a long series of questions. Unless you know what you are doing here, you should just choose the default on each screen. Whichever configuration path you choose, you will eventually get to a screen similar to that in Figure 14-3.

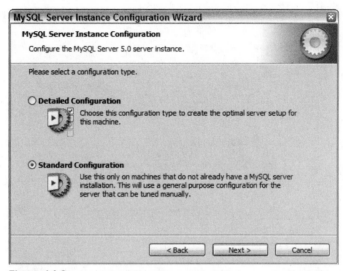

Figure 14-2

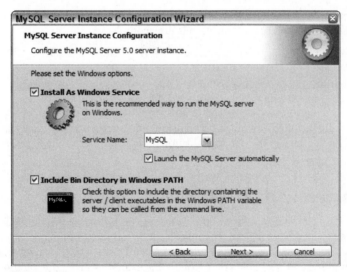

Figure 14-3

Be sure to check both the Install as Windows Service and Include Bin Directory in Windows PATH boxes.

Next you will be asked to set a root password, as shown in Figure 14-4.

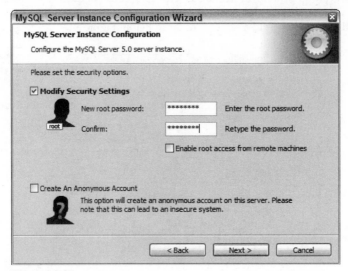

Figure 14-4

The root account is the one used to administer the database system. On a development machine, you could leave this as blank, but it is good practice to always set a root password, so you should do so here.

Once you have completed the wizard, you will be asked if you want to execute the configuration — go ahead and do this, your MySQL configuration is now complete.

Unix

All major distributions of Linux come with MySQL — you should check your documentation or your distribution's web site to see how to install the MySQL package.

The MySQL web site includes downloads and installation instructions for many other platforms, including Mac OS X. Consult the Downloads and Documentation sections of the MySQL web site for full details.

Getting Started with MySQL

Now you've got MySQL installed, I'll run through some of the basics of creating and using a simple database, including some basic SQL commands. Database administration and SQL is a large and complex topic and so we cannot hope to cover it in great detail here — I will, however, cover enough of the basics to get you going and to enable you to follow the examples given during the building of this mashup. When you're ready to learn more, many web sites and books are available to help you, and the MySQL web site itself is a good place to start. If you are already familiar with SQL, you should just take a few moments to familiarize yourself with the command-line utilities described here and then feel free to skip ahead a few pages and get started on the actual code.

Checking Your Installation

MySQL comes with a variety of command-line tools used to manage and interact with your databases. The first one I am going to look at is `mysqladmin`, a program used to perform a variety of administrative tasks on your database. Open up a command prompt and type the following command:

```
mysqladmin -u root -p version
```

This command causes `mysqladmin` to connect to the local database server. The `-u root` arguments tell it to connect to the database as the user `root`, while the `-p` argument tells it that a password is required. The final argument, `version`, tells `mysqladmin` to display the version and other status information about the database. When you execute the command, you will be prompted for a password. You should enter the root password that you set as part of the installation process. If you are running on a platform other than Windows and have installed MySQL via some other mechanism, it is likely that your default installation has no root password set — in which case, just press return when prompted for a password. You should see output that looks something like this:

```
C:\>mysqladmin -u root -p version
Enter password: *******
mysqladmin  Ver 8.41 Distrib 5.0.24a, for Win32 on ia32
Copyright (C) 2000 MySQL AB & MySQL Finland AB & TCX DataKonsult AB
This software comes with ABSOLUTELY NO WARRANTY. This is free software,
and you are welcome to modify and redistribute it under the GPL license

Server version          5.0.24a-community-nt
Protocol version        10
Connection              localhost via TCP/IP
TCP port                3306
Uptime:                 2 hours 6 min 42 sec

Threads: 1  Questions: 3  Slow queries: 0  Opens: 12  Flush tables: 1  Open tabl
es: 0  Queries per second avg: 0.000
```

If you see an error message that looks something like this, the server is not currently running:

```
C:\>mysqladmin -u root -p version
Enter password: *******
mysqladmin: connect to server at 'localhost' failed
error: 'Can't connect to MySQL server on 'localhost' (10061)'
Check that mysqld is running on localhost and that the port is 3306.
You can check this by doing 'telnet localhost 3306'
```

On Windows, you can start the server by typing the following command:

```
net start mysql
```

On other platforms, you should consult your local documentation to see how to start and stop the MySQL server.

Creating a Database

Now that you've verified that your MySQL server is up and running, it's time to create a database in which all your mashups data can be held. You do this with the `mysqladmin` command, as follows:

```
mysqladmin -u root -p create mashups
```

This time, instead of displaying version information, the command instructs the server to create a new database called `mashups`. Run this command to create the new database — you will be prompted for the root password. Once the command has completed, your new database will have been created.

Creating a Table

Now that you have a database, you need to be able to store and retrieve data into it. To do that, you need to run the `mysql` program — this is a command-line client application that enables you to manage your data using SQL. The syntax for the command to run the `mysql` application is very similar to that of `mysqladmin`. Type the following into your command prompt (once again, you will be prompted to enter your password):

```
mysql -u root -p mashups
```

The final argument here is the name of the database to connect to. When you run the command, you will be presented with a `mysql>` prompt, something like this:

```
C:\>mysql -u root -p mashups
Enter password: *******
Welcome to the MySQL monitor.  Commands end with ; or \g.
Your MySQL connection id is 8 to server version: 5.0.24a-community-nt

Type 'help;' or '\h' for help. Type '\c' to clear the buffer.

mysql>
```

The first thing you are going to do is create a *table* in your database. Tables are the structures in which your data are held. Each table is made up of a series of *columns*, with each column holding a single piece of data. For this example, imagine you are building a table that might be used by a grocery store to record items of fruit for sale. For each piece of fruit, you will need to hold three pieces of information:

❑ A stock code, which is an integer

❑ A description of the item, which is a string

❑ The price of the item, which is a floating-point number

So you need instruct MySQL to create a new table with three columns, one for each of those fields. To do this, you use the CREATE TABLE SQL command:

```
CREATE TABLE fruit
(
    stock_code INT,
    description VARCHAR(255),
    price DOUBLE
);
```

Here the SQL keywords are shown in uppercase so that they stand out — in practice, you can use either upper- or lower-case for them. Immediately following the command CREATE TABLE is the name of the table to create, fruit. There then follows a list of the columns to create, together with their data types. The three columns here correspond to the three data items required to be stored: stock_code is defined as type INT to hold the stock code of the item, description is defined as a VARCHAR(255) — a variable-length string of up to 255 characters — and price is defined as type DOUBLE. Many more data types exist than are used here — you can see details of them all in the MySQL documentation.

Enter the CREATE TABLE command at the mysql> prompt. Make sure you enter it exactly as shown. Each time you move onto a new line, you will see a -> continuation prompt. As soon as you enter the last line ending with the semicolon, the command will execute and you will see output like this:

```
mysql> CREATE TABLE fruit
    -> (
    ->      stock_code INT,
    ->      description VARCHAR(255),
    ->      price DOUBLE
    -> );
Query OK, 0 rows affected (0.09 sec)
```

If you make a mistake and need to run the command again, you may need to delete any existing table that was created. You can do this with the following command:

```
DROP TABLE fruit;
```

You should be very careful when you use the DROP TABLE command — your table will be immediately deleted, together with any data that were held in it.

Once you have created your table, you can confirm that it was created correctly by typing the following command at the mysql> prompt:

```
DESCRIBE fruit;
```

mysql will then display a description of your table, like this:

```
mysql> DESCRIBE fruit;
+-------------+--------------+------+-----+---------+-------+
| Field       | Type         | Null | Key | Default | Extra |
+-------------+--------------+------+-----+---------+-------+
| stock_code  | int(11)      | YES  |     | NULL    |       |
| description | varchar(255) | YES  |     | NULL    |       |
| price       | double       | YES  |     | NULL    |       |
+-------------+--------------+------+-----+---------+-------+
3 rows in set (0.00 sec)
```

Adding Data to Your Database

Now you have a table, you can write data into it using the INSERT command. Here's a typical INSERT statement to add information about a single item of fruit:

```
INSERT INTO fruit
  (stock_code, description, price)
  VALUES (1, 'Apple', 1.34);
```

As you can see, the INSERT statement contains a list of columns in the table, followed by a list of values to be placed in those columns — the order of the values specified in the parentheses corresponds to the order in which the columns are listed in the INSERT statement. If you enter this statement at the mysql> prompt, you will see this:

```
mysql> INSERT INTO fruit
    -> (stock_code, description, price)
    -> VALUES (1, 'Apple', 1.34);
Query OK, 1 row affected (0.11 sec)
```

You will notice that the response from the server says 1 row affected. The server is reporting the number of rows that were modified during the operation, and since you were inserting a single row, it reports that one row was affected by your statement.

In order to do anything useful with your database, you will need to store some more data in there. Add some more items to the table — here are some more INSERT statements. Enter each one of these in turn at the mysql> prompt:

```
INSERT INTO fruit (stock_code, description, price) values (2, 'Orange', 1.92);
INSERT INTO fruit (stock_code, description, price) values (3, 'Banana', 2.86);
INSERT INTO fruit (stock_code, description, price) values (4, 'Pear', 1.84);
INSERT INTO fruit (stock_code, description, price) values (5, 'Pineapple', 3.57);
INSERT INTO fruit (stock_code, description, price) values (6, 'Grapefruit', 1.19);
INSERT INTO fruit (stock_code, description, price) values (7, 'Lemon', 2.12);
INSERT INTO fruit (stock_code, description, price) values (8, 'Lime', 2.48);
```

Your table should now be populated with a wide variety of fruit items.

Viewing Your Data

Now that you have a number of different items of fruit in the database, you need to know how to view the data you have in there. For this, you use the SELECT statement. The simplest SELECT command you can perform is to retrieve all the data from a single table. To do this for the fruit table, type the following at the mysql> prompt:

```
SELECT * FROM fruit;
```

The asterisk here is a wildcard and means *all columns*. Here's what you should see on your screen:

```
mysql> SELECT * FROM fruit;
+------------+-------------+-------+
| stock_code | description | price |
+------------+-------------+-------+
|          1 | Apple       |  1.34 |
|          2 | Orange      |  1.92 |
|          3 | Banana      |  2.86 |
|          4 | Pear        |  1.84 |
|          5 | Pineapple   |  3.57 |
|          6 | Grapefruit  |  1.19 |
|          7 | Lemon       |  2.12 |
|          8 | Lime        |  2.48 |
+------------+-------------+-------+
8 rows in set (0.00 sec)
```

You can see that all the data entered via the `INSERT` statements were successfully recorded in the database. The `SELECT` statement returns a number of different *rows*, each of which corresponds to an item stored in the database table. Within each row is one column for every field stored against that item. The `mysql` program formats the results returned by the server into a table to make them easier to read.

If you are interested only in a single column, you can supply a column name:

```
mysql> SELECT description FROM fruit;
+-------------+
| description |
+-------------+
| Apple       |
| Orange      |
| Banana      |
| Pear        |
| Pineapple   |
| Grapefruit  |
| Lemon       |
| Lime        |
+-------------+
8 rows in set (0.00 sec)
```

You can also supply a comma-separated list:

```
mysql> SELECT description, price FROM fruit;
+-------------+-------+
| description | price |
+-------------+-------+
| Apple       |  1.34 |
| Orange      |  1.92 |
| Banana      |  2.86 |
| Pear        |  1.84 |
| Pineapple   |  3.57 |
| Grapefruit  |  1.19 |
| Lemon       |  2.12 |
| Lime        |  2.48 |
+-------------+-------+
8 rows in set (0.00 sec)
```

Searching Your Data

You can use `SELECT` to pick out specific items from the table using a `WHERE` clause. To find the description for the item with stock code 4, you would create a `SELECT` statement like this:

```
SELECT description FROM fruit WHERE stock_code = 4;
```

Note that equality is tested for by means of the equals sign, not two equals signs in a row as is common in many programming languages. If you try running that statement, you will see that only one row is returned from the database — the one that matched the specified condition of `stock_code` equal to 4:

```
mysql> SELECT description FROM fruit WHERE stock_code = 4;
+-------------+
| description |
+-------------+
| Pear        |
+-------------+
1 row in set (0.00 sec)
```

You can use all the usual comparison operators, such as <, <=, >, >= and !=. To find all items for which the price is greater than 2.0, do this:

```
mysql> SELECT * FROM fruit WHERE price > 2.0;
+------------+-------------+-------+
| stock_code | description | price |
+------------+-------------+-------+
|          3 | Banana      |  2.86 |
|          5 | Pineapple   |  3.57 |
|          7 | Lemon       |  2.12 |
|          8 | Lime        |  2.48 |
+------------+-------------+-------+
4 rows in set (0.00 sec)
```

To apply multiple conditions, you can use the Boolean operators AND, OR, and NOT in your queries:

```
mysql> SELECT * FROM fruit WHERE price > 1.0 AND price < 2.0;
+------------+-------------+-------+
| stock_code | description | price |
+------------+-------------+-------+
|          1 | Apple       |  1.34 |
|          2 | Orange      |  1.92 |
|          4 | Pear        |  1.84 |
|          6 | Grapefruit  |  1.19 |
+------------+-------------+-------+
4 rows in set (0.00 sec)
```

SQL offers a number of functions you can use inside your queries. For example, to find the most expensive item, you might use the MAX() function:

```
mysql> SELECT MAX(price) FROM fruit;
+------------+
| MAX(price) |
+------------+
|       3.57 |
+------------+
1 row in set (0.00 sec)
```

MySQL offers a great many functions, and full details on these and their usage can be found in the MySQL documentation.

Sorting Your Data

The SELECT statement also enables you to place an ORDER BY clause at the end, which will identify the columns used to determine the order in which the rows are returned. The order may be ascending (ASC) or descending (DESC). So to sort the items alphabetically, do the following:

```
mysql> SELECT * FROM fruit ORDER BY description ASC;
+------------+-------------+-------+
| stock_code | description | price |
+------------+-------------+-------+
|          1 | Apple       |  1.34 |
|          3 | Banana      |  2.86 |
|          6 | Grapefruit  |  1.19 |
|          7 | Lemon       |  2.12 |
|          8 | Lime        |  2.48 |
|          2 | Orange      |  1.92 |
|          4 | Pear        |  1.84 |
|          5 | Pineapple   |  3.57 |
+------------+-------------+-------+
8 rows in set (0.00 sec)
```

To sort by most expensive first:

```
mysql> SELECT * FROM fruit ORDER BY price DESC;
+------------+-------------+-------+
| stock_code | description | price |
+------------+-------------+-------+
|          5 | Pineapple   |  3.57 |
|          3 | Banana      |  2.86 |
|          8 | Lime        |  2.48 |
|          7 | Lemon       |  2.12 |
|          2 | Orange      |  1.92 |
|          4 | Pear        |  1.84 |
|          1 | Apple       |  1.34 |
|          6 | Grapefruit  |  1.19 |
+------------+-------------+-------+
8 rows in set (0.00 sec)
```

Modifying Your Data

To modify data in SQL, use the UPDATE command. You can use UPDATE without any conditions to make a global change to all rows in a table, but most often you will use it in conjunction with a WHERE clause to identify the specific items you want to modify. An UPDATE statement to set the price of bananas to 3.18 would look like this:

```
UPDATE fruit SET price = 3.18 WHERE stock_code = 3;
```

If you enter this command at the mysql> prompt, you will see the following:

```
mysql> UPDATE fruit SET price = 3.18 WHERE stock_code = 3;
Query OK, 1 row affected (0.03 sec)
Rows matched: 1  Changed: 1  Warnings: 0
```

No rows are returned by an UPDATE statement, but you can see how were affected. You should always be careful when running an update to ensure that your WHERE clause is correct—for example, if you had omitted the WHERE clause on the previous statement, you would have set the price of all items in the fruit table.

You can set multiple columns in a single query:

```
mysql> UPDATE fruit SET description = 'Seville Oranges', price = 2.94
    -> WHERE stock_code = 2;
Query OK, 1 row affected (0.05 sec)
Rows matched: 1  Changed: 1  Warnings: 0
```

Deleting Data

You can delete data with the SQL DELETE command. Like UPDATE, this command is most commonly used in conjunction with a WHERE clause. To delete the entry for pineapples, you would use the following statement:

```
DELETE FROM fruit WHERE stock_code = 5;
```

Once again, you should be very careful when using DELETE. If you omit the WHERE clause and accidentally enter the following code, you will delete all rows from the fruit table:

```
DELETE FROM fruit;
```

Talking to MySQL with PHP

You've now seen how to store and retrieve data from MySQL using the mysql program, but to use MySQL within your mashup you will need to be able to do all those things from within PHP. Fortunately, PHP comes with a MySQL extension, which provides a range of functions that provide you with full access to your databases. You should first make sure that the PHP extension is enabled in your installation of PHP by looking in your php.ini file. On Microsoft Windows systems, this will most likely be in either c:\php or c:\windows. On Unix-based systems, it is most commonly found in /etc.

On Windows, look for the following line:

```
extension=php_mysql.dll
```

On Unix, look for this one:

```
extension=mysql.so
```

You need to make sure this line is not commented out. If it is commented out, it will have a semicolon at the start of the line—delete this semicolon. If you modify the php.ini file, you will need to restart your web server for the changes to take effect.

You can verify that the MySQL extension is installed correctly by creating a PHP file with the following contents:

```php
<?php
phpinfo();
?>
```

Place this file in the document root for your web server and then open it in your web browser. Scroll through the document and, if the MySQL extension is enabled, you should see a section like that shown in Figure 14-5.

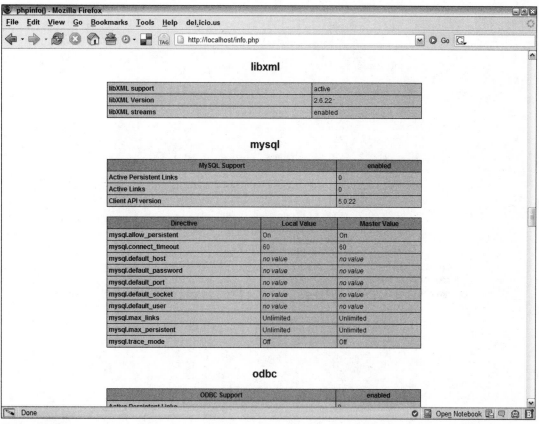

Figure 14-5

Once your MySQL extension is enabled, the easiest way to see how to use MySQL with PHP is with a brief example.

Try It Out   **PHP and MySQL**

In this example you'll create a brief script to see how you can make MySQL and PHP work together.

1.   Create a new file, `14-1.php`, in your `gallery` directory. Make sure you put your database password where it says `YOUR-PASSWORD-HERE`:

```php
<?php

$connection = mysql_connect('localhost', 'root', 'YOUR-PASSWORD-HERE');

if (!$connection)
{
  die ("Cannot connect to database server");
}

$ret = mysql_select_db("mashups", $connection);

if (!$ret)
{
  die ("Cannot access database");
}

$sql = "SELECT * FROM fruit ORDER BY description ASC";

$res = mysql_query($sql, $connection) or die("Invalid query: " . $sql);

?>

<table border="1">
  <tr>
    <th>Stock Code</th>
    <th>Description</th>
    <th>Price</th>
  </tr>

<?php

while($row = mysql_fetch_assoc($res))
{
  print "  <tr>\n";
  print "    <td>" . $row['stock_code'] . "</td>";
  print "    <td>" . $row['description'] . "</td>";
  print "    <td>" . $row['price'] . "</td>";
  print "  </tr>\n";
}
?>

</table>
```

2.   Load the page into your browser and you should see the contents of your `fruit` table, as shown in Figure 14-6.

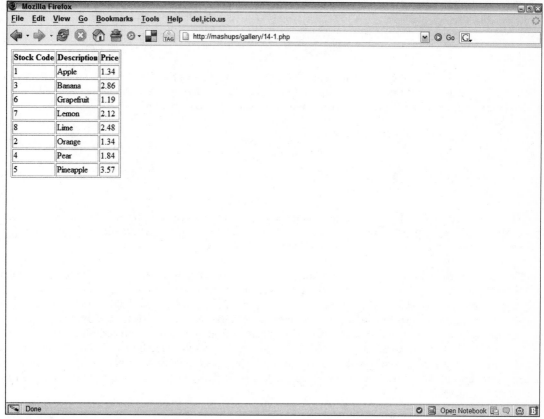

Figure 14-6

How It Works

The PHP script invokes a number of different MySQL functions. The first of these is `mysql_connect`, which is used to open a new connection to a database server:

```
$connection = mysql_connect('localhost', 'root', 'YOUR-PASSWORD-HERE');
```

The three parameters are the host name to connect to, the user to connect as, and the password for that user.

The next function used is `mysql_select_db`:

```
$ret = mysql_select_db("mashups", $connection);
```

This function selects the database to be used on this connection — in this case, your `mashups` database. A SQL string is then created to contain the query that will return all rows from the `fruit` table:

```
$sql = "SELECT * FROM fruit ORDER BY description ASC";
```

The rows will be sorted alphabetically by description. The query is then sent to the database server using the connection opened earlier:

```
$res = mysql_query($sql, $connection) or die("Invalid query: " . $sql);
```

You might notice the unusual syntax here. The or operator ensures that the second half of the statement is only evaluated if the first part returns false — so this is a convenient shorthand for generating an error message should the query fail. You could also write this statement more verbosely:

```
$res = mysql_query($sql, $connection)
if (!$res)
{
  die("Invalid query: " . $sql);
}
```

The two forms are functionally identical, and the choice of which version to use is largely one of style. In blocks of code in which you do not wish to distract the reader from the general flow of the code, the more concise version can often make the logic easier to follow.

The call to mysql_query does not immediately return all the data from the query — on a large database that might be many thousands of rows and far too much to handle in a single object. Instead, the returned value is a *result set*. A result set can be thought of as a pointer into the data in the database. At any given moment the result set points to a single row in the set of results returned by the query, and the contents of the currently pointed-at row can be retrieved from the database on demand — the data in each row aren't sent from the database until they are explicitly requested by the client. This means that the client application doesn't need to worry about having to store large amounts of data in memory at any one time; all that is handled by the database server. The client need only request the data as and when it needs them.

Finally, the script retrieves each row in turn, and formats it as a row in an HTML table:

```
while($row = mysql_fetch_assoc($res))
{
  print "  <tr>\n";
  print "    <td>" . $row['stock_code'] . "</td>\n";
  print "    <td>" . $row['description'] . "</td>\n";
  print "    <td>" . $row['price'] . "</td>\n";
  print "  </tr>\n";
}
```

The function mysql_fetch_assoc is used here, and takes a single parameter — the result set from the original query. This function retrieves the current row pointed at by the result set and stores the data values in an associative array. The key used for each value is the name of the column in the database and the value is the data value retrieved from the database. Once the row is retrieved from the database, the result set pointer is automatically moved on so that it points at the next row in the set of rows matched by the database query. Finally, when all matching rows have been retrieved and there are no more data to fetch, mysql_fetch_assoc returns false and the while loop terminates.

Caching Photos

In the gallery, the most common Flickr API method used is `flickr.photos.search`. For the first part of the gallery enhancements, you will eliminate many of the calls to `flickr.photos.search`, and instead rely on the use of a local database.

The Photo Table

You need a new table in your database to hold the photo information, so you must decide what information should be stored. If you take a look at a typical search response, it contains lines that look something like this:

```
<photo id="231699414" owner="50317659@N00" secret="f2ed044b79" server="92"
title="Lollipops" ispublic="1" isfriend="0" isfamily="0" latitude="52.21284"
longitude="-1.133437" accuracy="16" ownername="dopiaza" dateupload="1157196017"
datetaken="2006-08-28 14:23:43" datetakengranularity="0"/>
```

To get this result, the `extras` parameter in `flickr.photos.search` was set to `geo, owner_name, date_upload, date_taken`. The gallery application doesn't use all the fields that are returned, but as you have them available, you may as well store them all in the database.

Try It Out   **Creating the Photo Table**

In this exercise you'll create the table in your database to store information about your photos.

1.   Create a script called `create_photo.sql` to define a new table called `photo` in the database:

```sql
DROP TABLE IF EXISTS photo;

CREATE TABLE photo (
  photo_id VARCHAR(255) NOT NULL,
  photo_secret VARCHAR(255) NOT NULL,
  photo_server INT NOT NULL,
  photo_owner VARCHAR(255) NOT NULL,
  photo_owner_name VARCHAR(255) NOT NULL,
  photo_is_public TINYINT(1) NOT NULL,
  photo_is_friend TINYINT(1) NOT NULL,
  photo_is_family TINYINT(1) NOT NULL,
  photo_date_taken DATETIME NOT NULL,
  photo_date_taken_granularity INT NOT NULL,
  photo_date_upload INT NOT NULL,
  photo_title VARCHAR(255) NOT NULL,
  photo_latitude DOUBLE NOT NULL,
  photo_longitude DOUBLE NOT NULL,
  photo_accuracy INT NOT NULL,
  PRIMARY KEY  (photo_id)
);
```

Now execute the SQL command by opening up a command prompt, changing the directory to the location of your `create.sql` script, and running the following command:

```
mysql -u root -p mashups  < create_photo.sql
```

This command opens a connection to the database, reads in the contents of the SQL script, and executes it.

If you open up an interactive `mysql>` prompt by running the command

```
mysql -u root -p mashups
```

you can check the results of your create table statement by entering

```
DESCRIBE photo;
```

If all has gone well, you should see output that looks like this:

```
mysql> DESCRIBE photo;
+------------------------------+--------------+------+-----+---------+-------+
| Field                        | Type         | Null | Key | Default | Extra |
+------------------------------+--------------+------+-----+---------+-------+
| photo_id                     | varchar(255) | NO   | PRI |         |       |
| photo_secret                 | varchar(255) | NO   |     |         |       |
| photo_server                 | int(11)      | NO   |     |         |       |
| photo_owner                  | varchar(255) | NO   |     |         |       |
| photo_owner_name             | varchar(255) | NO   |     |         |       |
| photo_is_public              | tinyint(1)   | NO   |     |         |       |
| photo_is_friend              | tinyint(1)   | NO   |     |         |       |
| photo_is_family              | tinyint(1)   | NO   |     |         |       |
| photo_date_taken             | datetime     | NO   |     |         |       |
| photo_date_taken_granularity | int(11)      | NO   |     |         |       |
| photo_date_upload            | int(11)      | NO   |     |         |       |
| photo_title                  | varchar(255) | NO   |     |         |       |
| photo_latitude               | double       | NO   |     |         |       |
| photo_longitude              | double       | NO   |     |         |       |
| photo_accuracy               | int(11)      | NO   |     |         |       |
+------------------------------+--------------+------+-----+---------+-------+
15 rows in set (0.00 sec)
```

3. Now that you have your photo table defined, you need to populate it with photo information from Flickr. First of all, create a new file in your `lib` directory, `db.php`, containing all the database configuration details:

```php
<?php

$dbhost = "localhost";
$dbname = "mashups";
$dbuser = "root";
$dbpasswd = "YOUR-PASSWORD-HERE";

?>
```

This file contains the database host, database name, and user credentials needed to connect to the database. Don't forget to insert your database password where it says YOUR-PASSWORD-HERE.

4. Edit `gallery.php` in the `lib` directory to include the `db.php` file:

```php
<?php

require_once(dirname(__FILE__) . '/apikey.php');
require_once(dirname(__FILE__) . '/db.php');
require_once(dirname(__FILE__) . '/phpFlickr/phpFlickr.php');
require_once(dirname(__FILE__) . '/FlickrAuthenticator.php');
require_once(dirname(__FILE__) . '/FlickrGallery.php');

?>
```

5. Define a few variables in the `FlickrGallery` class. Edit `FlickrGallery.php` to add the following lines:

```php
<?php

class FlickrGallery extends FlickrAuthenticator
{
  var $nsid = '50317659@N00';
  var $connection = 0;

  var $useDB = 1;

  var $dbhost;
  var $dbname;
  var $dbuser;
  var $dbpasswd;

  function FlickrGallery()
  {
    global $flickrApiKey;
    global $flickrApiSecret;

    $this->FlickrAuthenticator($flickrApiKey, $flickrApiSecret);

    global $dbhost;
    global $dbname;
    global $dbuser;
    global $dbpasswd;

    $this->dbhost = $dbhost;
    $this->dbname = $dbname;
    $this->dbuser = $dbuser;
    $this->dbpasswd = $dbpasswd;
  }

  ...

}
?>
```

6. Now that you've declared the `$connection` member variable, you need a method to initialize it. Add the following method to the `FlickrGallery` class:

```
function getConnection()
{
  if (empty($this->connection))
  {
    $this->connection = mysql_connect($this->dbhost,
      $this->dbuser, $this->dbpasswd);

    if (!$this->connection)
    {
      die ("Cannot connect to database server: " . $this->dbhost);
    }

    $ret = mysql_select_db($this->dbname, $this->connection);

    if (!$ret)
    {
      die ("Cannot access database " . $this->dbname . " on " . $this->dbhostname);
    }
  }

  return $this->connection;
}
```

7. Now it's time for the important bit—the code to retrieve your photo details and store them in the database. Add the following two methods to your `FlickrGallery` class:

```
function flushDBPhotos()
{
  $sql = "DELETE FROM photo";
  mysql_query($sql, $this->getConnection()) or die("Invalid query: " . $sql);
}

function populateDBPhotos()
{
  $this->flushDBPhotos();
  set_time_limit(240);

  $q = "INSERT INTO photo"
    . " (photo_id, photo_secret, photo_server, photo_owner, photo_owner_name,"
    . " photo_is_public, photo_is_friend, photo_is_family,"
    . " photo_date_taken, photo_date_taken_granularity, photo_date_upload,"
    . " photo_title, photo_latitude, photo_longitude, photo_accuracy)"
    . " VALUES"
    . " ('%s', '%s', %d, '%s', '%s', %d, %d, %d, '%s', %d, %d, '%s',"
    . " %f, %f, %d)";

  $keepGoing = 1;
  $page = 1;
  while ($keepGoing)
  {
    $args = array(
      'user_id' => $this->nsid,
      'sort' => 'date-posted-desc',
```

```
        'page' => $page,
        'per_page' => 500,
        'extras' => 'date_upload, date_taken, owner_name, geo'
    );

    $p = $this->flickr->photos_search($args);
    if ($this->flickr->getErrorCode())
    {
        echo ("Error fetching photos: " . $this->flickr->getErrorMsg());
    }

    if (count($p['photo']) == 0)
    {
        // no more photos
        break;
    }

    foreach($p['photo'] as $photo)
    {
        $sql = sprintf($q, $photo['id'], $photo['secret'], $photo['server'],
            $photo['owner'], mysql_escape_string($photo['ownername']),
            $photo['ispublic'], $photo['isfriend'], $photo['isfamily'],
            $photo['datetaken'], $photo['datetakengranularity'],
            $photo['dateupload'],
            mysql_escape_string($photo['title']), $photo['latitude'],
            $photo['longitude'], $photo['accuracy']);

        mysql_query($sql, $this->getConnection())
            or die("Invalid query: " . $sql);
    }
    $page++;
    }
}
```

8. You need some means of invoking these new methods, so create an admin page for the gallery. Create a new directory called `admin` within the `gallery` directory. Within the `admin` directory, create a new file, `index.php`:

```
<?php include (dirname(__FILE__) . '/../../lib/gallery.php') ?>
<!DOCTYPE html PUBLIC "-//W3C//DTD XHTML 1.0 Transitional//EN"
"http://www.w3.org/TR/xhtml1/DTD/xhtml1-transitional.dtd">
<html xmlns="http://www.w3.org/1999/xhtml">
<head>
  <title>Flickr Mashups Gallery Admin</title>
  <link href="../../css/main.css" rel="stylesheet" type="text/css" />
  <link href="../../css/gallery.css" rel="stylesheet" type="text/css" />
</head>
<body>
 <h1>Gallery Administration
 </h1>
 <ul>
   <li><a href="refreshPhotoTable.php">Refresh Photo Table</a></li>
 </ul>
</body>
</html>
```

9. Then create another new file, refreshPhotoTable.php, also in the admin directory:

```php
<?php

include (dirname(__FILE__) . '/../../lib/gallery.php');

$gallery = new FlickrGallery();
$gallery->populateDBPhotos();

header ("Location: http://" . $_SERVER['HTTP_HOST'] . dirname($_SERVER['PHP_SELF'])
. "/index.php");

?>
```

10. It's finally time to try all this out. Open the admin index.php page in your browser, as shown in Figure 14-7.

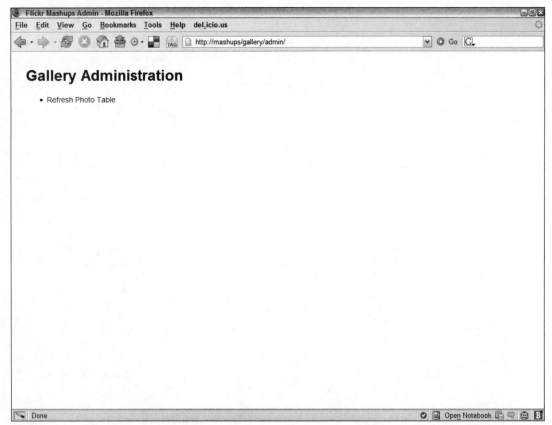

Figure 14-7

11. Click the Refresh Photo Table link. There should be a pause while the script runs and fetches all your photos; just how long it takes will depend on how many photos you have on Flickr. After a while, the screen will refresh as you are redirected back to the admin index page.

12. Quite a lot happened when you clicked on that link, but the effects aren't very visible. To reassure yourself that it all worked, go to a `mysql>` prompt and type the following:

```
SELECT COUNT(*) FROM photo;
```

13. The `COUNT()` function will tell you how many rows are in the table. You should find that there are now some data in your table — the exact number should be the same as the number of public photos you have in your photostream:

```
mysql> SELECT COUNT(*) FROM photo;
+----------+
| COUNT(*) |
+----------+
|     2419 |
+----------+
1 row in set (0.00 sec)
```

14. To see a little more detail, try this query:

```
SELECT photo_id, photo_title FROM photo ORDER BY photo_date_upload DESC LIMIT 10;
```

Clearly, in a case like this you don't really want to watch over two thousand rows of data scroll past, so the `LIMIT 10` modifier is added to the end of the query to limit the number of results returned to the first 10. You should see something like this:

```
mysql> SELECT photo_id, photo_title FROM photo
    -> ORDER BY photo_date_upload DESC LIMIT 10;
+-----------+--------------------------+
| photo_id  | photo_title              |
+-----------+--------------------------+
| 260568187 | Moo!                     |
| 251236008 | Web                      |
| 249695207 | Let There Be Light       |
| 243360958 | Braunston                |
| 243059430 | Pew End                  |
| 237529084 | Diesel                   |
| 237045751 | Red Seat                 |
| 231699414 | Lollipops                |
| 231694634 | Head in the Clouds       |
| 229382495 | 1934 Austin Ascot Saloon |
+-----------+--------------------------+
10 rows in set (0.01 sec)
```

How It Works

As you can see, there are a number of differences between the SQL in `create_photo.sql` and the `CREATE TABLE` statements you were using in the examples earlier. Take a look at those one by one.

The script starts with a line:

```
DROP TABLE IF EXISTS photo;
```

This command causes any existing table called `photo` to be deleted — but only if it already exists. This means that the script can be run repeatedly without generating an error — if the `CREATE TABLE` statement were to take place without removing an existing table of the same name, it would generate an error. Of course, any data held in the table will be lost, so you should exercise care when running scripts such as this.

317

Within the CREATE TABLE statement, a column is created for every field returned by the flickr .photos.search method. Here you can see that some new data types are being used. TINYINT(1) is a one-bit-long integer and is used for the Boolean fields. DATETIME is used to represent a date and time combination. Each field is also declared as NOT NULL, meaning that the field is never allowed to be empty (NULL); it must always contain a value.

Finally, the last line of the CREATE TABLE statement declares that the photo_id is the primary key for this table:

```
PRIMARY KEY (photo_id)
```

The primary key is the value that uniquely identifies the item represented in the row in the table. In the photo table, there is one row for every photo you have stored, so the photo ID will uniquely identify any given photo. You don't have to define a primary key for a table, but doing so will allow the database server to search your table more efficiently.

You will also see that we have adopted a naming convention here — each column in the table starts with a short prefix, photo_. This is really a matter of personal preference, but you may find that it is worth getting into the habit of naming your columns so that they always include a prefix specific to the table that contains them. By doing so, you will find that when you are dealing with a database containing many tables, complex queries become very much simpler to both write and understand.

The FlickrGallery class reads in a few database-configuration variables from the global values defined in db.php and stored as local member variables. Two other member variables are declared in FlickrGallery — $connection is where you'll store the database connection object, and $useDB is a Boolean flag that you will use to determine whether the data should be retrieved directly from Flickr, as they are currently, or from the database cache you are about to create.

The getConnection() code you added to FlickrGallery to initialize the database connection is identical to the code you used in the example earlier. The method first checks to see if the connection has already been initialized — if it hasn't, it goes ahead and connects to the database, storing the connection object in the local $connection member variable. This method can now be safely called multiple times in your PHP script and will open only one connection to the database.

The next two methods you added to FlickrGallery deserve to be discussed in a little more detail. The first method, flushDBPhotos(), clears out any existing photos from the photo table. The second method, populateDBPhotos(), is responsible for retrieving the list of photos from Flickr and storing them in the database.

I'll start with flushDBPhotos() as it is fairly simple — only two lines long. The first line defines the SQL to be executed:

```
$sql = "DELETE FROM photo";
```

This SQL statement has no WHERE clause, and so will cause all rows in the photo table to be deleted.

The second line of the method uses mysql_query to execute the SQL query:

```
mysql_query($sql, $this->getConnection()) or die("Invalid query: " . $sql);
```

The code here doesn't need to explicitly connect to the database—remember, the call to $this ->getConnection() will automatically initialize the connection if that hasn't been done already.

The populateDBPhotos() method is a little more complicated. The first step here is to call flushDBPhotos() to clear out any existing contents of the table. Once the table is empty, you can move on to retrieving the latest photo list from Flickr.

The PHP function set_time_limit() is then called to increase the maximum allowed execution time for this script. The value set is specified in seconds—you might need to adjust the value used here depending on the number of photos you have in your photostream and the speed of your local computer and network connection.

The main body of populateDBPhotos() is contained within a while loop. This loop continues to execute, once for each page of photos returned by flickr.photos.search. Once each page is processed, the page number, held in $page, is incremented and the next page of photos is fetched. The Flickr API allows up to 500 photos to be retrieved at a time, so even a large photostream with ten thousand photos in it can be read with only 20 calls to the API. Once the call to flickr.photos.search returns no more photos, the loop is terminated by means of a break statement.

The method will need to build up a large number of INSERT statements—one for each photo to be added to the database. To do this, you use PHP's sprintf() function to format the SQL, so at the top of the method the format string for the query is defined in $q:

```
$q = "INSERT INTO photo"
   . " (photo_id, photo_secret, photo_server, photo_owner, photo_owner_name,"
   . " photo_is_public, photo_is_friend, photo_is_family,"
   . " photo_date_taken, photo_date_taken_granularity, photo_date_upload,"
   . " photo_title, photo_latitude, photo_longitude, photo_accuracy)"
   . " VALUES"
   . " ('%s', '%s', %d, '%s', '%s', %d, %d, %d, '%s', %d, %d, '%s',"
   . " %f, %f, %d)";
```

The INSERT statement itself is quite long, simply because there are 15 fields to insert into each row, but it is no more complex than the shorter examples you saw earlier. Here's an example of what the INSERT statement looks like when the field values are filled in:

```
INSERT INTO photo (photo_id, photo_secret, photo_server, photo_owner,
photo_owner_name, photo_is_public, photo_is_friend, photo_is_family,
photo_date_taken, photo_date_taken_granularity, photo_date_upload, photo_title,
photo_latitude, photo_longitude, photo_accuracy) VALUES ('260568187', '809a77e9ff',
99, '50317659@N00', 'dopiaza', 1, 0, 0, '2006-10-04 12:01:56', 0, 1159961395,
'Moo!', 0.000000, 0.000000, 0)
```

For each photo in the array returned from the search, a SQL statement is constructed:

```
$sql = sprintf($q, $photo['id'], $photo['secret'], $photo['server'],
   $photo['owner'], mysql_escape_string($photo['ownername']),
   $photo['ispublic'], $photo['isfriend'], $photo['isfamily'],
   $photo['datetaken'], $photo['datetakengranularity'],
   $photo['dateupload'],
   mysql_escape_string($photo['title']), $photo['latitude'],
   $photo['longitude'], $photo['accuracy']);
```

Each parameter to `sprintf()` corresponds to one of the fields that needs populating in the format string.

You will notice that a couple of the parameters are wrapped in a call to `mysql_escape_string()`. These parameters are all strings that may contain special characters that need escaping. The character most likely to require special treatment here is the single quote (`'`). SQL uses single quotes as the delimiter for strings, so to embed single quotes in a SQL string, you need to escape them with a backslash (`\`):

```
'This is how to embed \'single quotes\' in a SQL string'
```

`mysql_escape_string()` ensures that all special characters are correctly escaped.

As each SQL statement is constructed, it is executed using `mysql_query()`.

The `refreshPhotoTable.php` script simply causes the `FlickrGallery` method `populateDBPhotos()` to be called, after which the user is redirected to the admin `index.php` page.

Using the Cache

You now have your database cache populated with your photos and connected to your gallery application. The next thing to do is start using the cache.

Try It Out — Using the Cache with the Gallery

Now that you have data in your cache, you can modify the existing code in the `FlickrGallery` class to start using it. Ideally, you want this change to be completely transparent to any web pages using `FlickrGallery`, so you'll take any rows returned from the database and convert them into an object identical to the kind returned by phpFlickr.

1. The phpFlickr object returned is just an associative array, so create a new method in the `FlickrGallery` class to turn a database row into a suitably formatted array object:

```
function buildPhotoFromRow($row)
{
    $photo = array();

    $photo['id'] = $row['photo_id'];
    $photo['secret'] = $row['photo_secret'];
    $photo['server'] = $row['photo_server'];
    $photo['owner'] = $row['photo_owner'];
    $photo['ownername'] = $row['photo_owner_name'];
    $photo['title'] = $row['photo_title'];
    $photo['ispublic'] = $row['photo_is_public'];
    $photo['isfriend'] = $row['photo_is_friend'];
    $photo['isfamily'] = $row['photo_is_family'];
    $photo['dateupload'] = $row['photo_date_upload'];
    $photo['datetaken'] = $row['photo_date_taken'];
    $photo['datetakengranularity'] = $row['photo_date_taken_granularity'];
    $photo['latitude'] = $row['photo_latitude'];
    $photo['longitude'] = $row['photo_longitude'];
```

```
    $photo['accuracy'] = $row['photo_accuracy'];

    return $photo;
}
```

2. Now that's in place, start with the `FlickrGallery findRecentPhotos()` method. Change the existing method to the following:

```
function findRecentPhotos($n = 20)
{
    $recentPhotos = array();
    if ($this->useDB)
    {
      $sql = "SELECT * FROM photo ORDER BY photo_date_upload DESC LIMIT $n";
      $res = mysql_query($sql, $this->getConnection())
        or die("Invalid query: " . $sql);

      while($row = mysql_fetch_assoc($res))
      {
        $photo = $this->buildPhotoFromRow($row);
        array_push($recentPhotos, $photo);
      }
    }
    else
    {
      $args = array(
        'user_id' => $this->nsid,
        'sort' => 'date-posted-desc',
        'page' => 1,
        'per_page' => $n,
        'extras' => 'owner_name'
        );

      $p = $this->flickr->photos_search($args);
      if ($this->flickr->getErrorCode())
      {
        echo ("Error fetching photos: " . $this->flickr->getErrorMsg());
      }

      $recentPhotos = $p['photo'];
    }

    return $recentPhotos;
}
```

3. Now load the main gallery page, shown in Figure 14-8.

    As you will see, it looks no different from before — the only difference is behind the scenes. No API calls were made to Flickr during the construction of this page; all the information needed was already held in the local database.

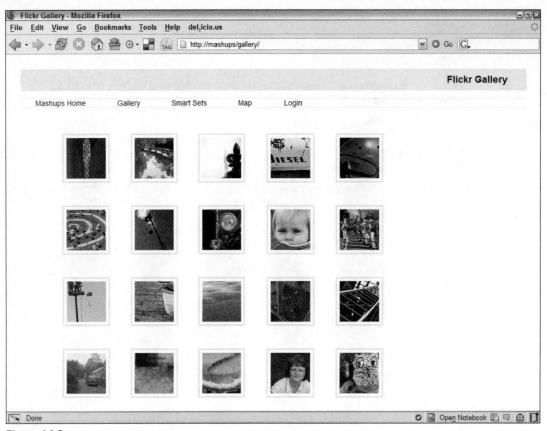

Figure 14-8

4. The other part of `FlickrGallery` you can now optimize to use your database cache is the `getWithGeoData()` method:

```php
function getWithGeoData($bbox = NULL)
{
  if ($bbox == NULL)
  {
    $bbox = '-180, -90, 180, 90';
  }

  $geoPhotos = array();
  if ($this->useDB)
  {
    $bounds = explode(",", $bbox);
    $sql = "SELECT * FROM photo WHERE photo_accuracy > 0"
      . " AND photo_latitude >= " . $bounds[1]
      . " AND photo_latitude <= " . $bounds[3]
      . " AND photo_longitude >= " . $bounds[0]
      . " AND photo_longitude <= " . $bounds[2];

    $res = mysql_query($sql, $this->getConnection())
```

```
              or die("Invalid query: " . $sql);

        while($row = mysql_fetch_assoc($res))
        {
          $photo = $this->buildPhotoFromRow($row);
          array_push($geoPhotos, $photo);
        }
      }
      else
      {
        $args = array(
          'user_id' => $this->nsid,
          'sort' => 'interestingness-desc',
          'bbox' => $bbox,
          'extras' => 'geo',
          'per_page' => 500,
          );

        $p = $this->flickr->photos_search($args);
        if ($this->flickr->getErrorCode())
        {
            echo ("Error fetching photos with GeoData: "
              . $this->flickr->getErrorMsg());
        }
        $geoPhotos = $p['photo'];
      }

      return $geoPhotos;
    }
```

5. If you open up the gallery map page in your browser, you should see no difference — except that the load time for the markers should be significantly less because the marker data are now being sourced locally, rather than retrieved from Flickr.

How It Works

The new code in `findRecentPhotos()` wraps an `if-then-else` block around the existing code that performs a Flickr search. If the `useDB` flag is set the database is used; otherwise Flickr is consulted as before. This means that you can switch your database cache on or off just by setting the `useDB` flag to 1 or 0 as appropriate.

The SQL query constructed here selects all the photos, sorted by upload date with the most recently uploaded first. It uses `LIMIT` to restrict the number of photos returned by the database to the number requested. It then iterates through the result set returned, calling `buildPhotoFromRow()` for each row, and stores the resulting photos in the `$recentPhotos` array, ready to return to the caller.

In the modified `getWithGeoData()` method, once again, the original code is wrapped in an `if-then-else` statement. If the database cache is to be used, the bounding box parameter, `$bbox`, is split into its component parts and a `SELECT` statement is constructed to find all photos that have geodata attached to them (`accuracy` has a non-zero value for photos with geodata) and whose latitude and longitude are within the bounding box coordinates. The matching rows are then fetched from the database and `buildPhotoFromRow()` called to convert the rows into photo objects.

Navigating Through Your Photos

You've made quite a lot of changes to the code now, but the application still looks exactly the same. The searching should be much faster now; the functionality of the application has not changed.

Try It Out   **Adding Navigation**

In this exercise you'll add a new feature that takes advantage of the data now being stored locally. On the `photo.php` page you will now add Next and Previous links that enable you to navigate through your photostream.

1.   You need to create three new methods in `FlickrGallery`. The first, `getPhoto()`, will retrieve a photo object for any photo with a given ID; the other two, `getNextPhoto()` and `getPreviousPhoto()`, will retrieve the next and previous photos in the sequence, respectively:

```php
function getPhoto($id)
{
  $photo = NULL;
  if ($this->useDB)
  {
    $sql = "SELECT * FROM photo WHERE photo_id = '"
      . mysql_escape_string($id) . "'";
    $res = mysql_query($sql, $this->getConnection())
      or die("Invalid query: " . $sql);
    if ($row = mysql_fetch_assoc($res))
    {
      $photo = $this->buildPhotoFromRow($row);
    }
  }

  return $photo;
}

function getNextPhoto($photo)
{
  $nextPhoto = NULL;
  $sql = "";

  if ($this->useDB)
  {
    // Get from recent photos
    $date = $photo['dateupload'];
    $sql = "SELECT * FROM photo"
      . " WHERE photo_date_upload > $date"
      . " ORDER BY photo_date_upload ASC LIMIT 1";

    $res = mysql_query($sql, $this->getConnection())
      or die("Invalid query: " . $sql);
    if ($row = mysql_fetch_assoc($res))
    {
      $nextPhoto = $this->buildPhotoFromRow($row);
    }
  }
  return $nextPhoto;
```

```
  }

  function getPreviousPhoto($photo)
  {
    $prevPhoto = NULL;
    $sql = "";

    if ($this->useDB)
    {
      // Get from recent photos
      $date = $photo['dateupload'];
      $sql = "SELECT * FROM photo"
        . " WHERE photo_date_upload < $date"
        . " ORDER BY photo_date_upload DESC LIMIT 1";

      $res = mysql_query($sql, $this->getConnection())
        or die("Invalid query: " . $sql);
      if ($row = mysql_fetch_assoc($res))
      {
        $prevPhoto = $this->buildPhotoFromRow($row);
      }
    }

    return $prevPhoto;
  }
```

2. Now add the Previous and Next links to the `photo.php` page. Edit `photo.php` in the `gallery` directory:

```php
<?php include (dirname(__FILE__) . '/../lib/gallery.php') ?>
<!DOCTYPE html PUBLIC "-//W3C//DTD XHTML 1.0 Transitional//EN"
"http://www.w3.org/TR/xhtml1/DTD/xhtml1-transitional.dtd">
<html xmlns="http://www.w3.org/1999/xhtml">
<head>
  <title>Flickr Mashups</title>
  <link href="../css/main.css" rel="stylesheet" type="text/css" />
  <link href="../css/gallery.css" rel="stylesheet" type="text/css" />
  <script type="text/javascript" src="../lib/js/prototype.js"></script>
  <script type="text/javascript" src="../lib/js/gallery.js"></script>
</head>
<body>
<?php
  $gallery = new FlickrGallery();
  $id = $_REQUEST['id'];
  if (!empty($id))
  {
    $info = $gallery->getPhotoInfo($id);
    $title = $info['title'];
    $img = 'http://static.flickr.com/' . $info['server'] . '/' . $info['id']
      . '_' . $info['secret'] . '.jpg';
    $photoPage = 'http://www.flickr.com/photos/' . $info['owner']['nsid']
      . '/' . $id . '/';

    $photo = $gallery->getPhoto($id);
    $prev = $gallery->getPreviousPhoto($photo);
```

```php
        $next = $gallery->getNextPhoto($photo);
    }
?>
<?php include ('header.php') ?>
<?php include ('navigation.php') ?>
<div class="photo-display">
  <p class="photo-title"><?php echo $title ?></p>
  <p class="photo-image"><a href="<?php echo $photoPage ?>">
    <img src="<?php echo $img ?>" alt="<?php echo $title ?>"
       title="<?php echo $title ?>" /></a>
  </p>
  <div class="photo-nav">
    <div class="photo-nav-prev">
    <?php
    if (empty($prev))
    {
    ?> <?php
    }
    else
    {
    ?><a href="photo.php?id=<?php echo $prev['id'] ?>">&lt; Previous</a><?php
    }
    ?>
    </div>
    <div class="photo-nav-next">
    <?php
    if (empty($next))
    {
    ?> <?php
    }
    else
    {
    ?><a href="photo.php?id=<?php echo $next['id'] ?>">Next &gt;</a><?php
    }
    ?>
    </div>
  </div>
  <div id="photo-info-<?php echo $id ?>" class="photo-more">
  <a href="#" onclick="displayInfo(<?php echo $id ?>); return false;">
    More info...</a>
  </div>
</div>
</body>
</html>
```

3. Finally, you just need a couple of extra styles in your `gallery.css` file:

```css
.photo-nav-prev {
  float: left;
  text-align: left;
}
.photo-nav-next {
  float: right;
  text-align: right;
}
```

4. Now load up the gallery page and view a photo. You should see Next and Previous links, as shown in Figure 14-9.

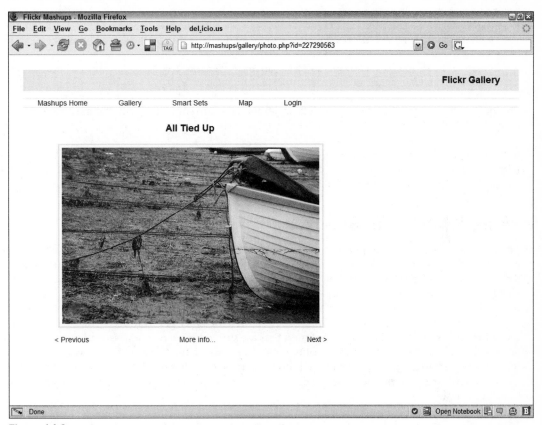

Figure 14-9

5. As you click on the two links, you can navigate up and down your photostream. Note that if you reach either end of the photostream and there is no next or previous photo to view, the corresponding link will not be shown.

How It Works

The `getPhoto()` method is pretty straightforward — it simply takes in a photo ID, looks up that photo in the database, and returns it as a photo object. In the SQL query, `mysql_escape_string()` is used to escape the `$id` variable — this is passed in as part of the URL as a parameter, and you should always escape data provided by a user to ensure that your SQL remains valid.

`getNextPhoto()` and `getPreviousPhoto()` are slightly more interesting. They both work in exactly the same way — the only different is in the SQL query they use to work out which photo to return. Both methods take in a photo object as a parameter and extract the upload date. To find the next photo in a sequence, a query like this is constructed:

```
SELECT * FROM photo WHERE photo_date_upload > $date
    ORDER BY photo_date_upload ASC LIMIT 1
```

This selects all rows in which the upload date is later than that for the current photo, and sorts those rows in order of increasing upload date. The first row that matches will be the next photo after the current one, by upload date. You are interested only in the next photo, so `LIMIT 1` ensures that only the first row is returned.

The previous photo is obtained in exactly the same way. The query used there is as follows:

```
SELECT * FROM photo WHERE photo_date_upload < $date
   ORDER BY photo_date_upload DESC LIMIT 1
```

This query will search for photos uploaded earlier than the current photo, with the most recently uploaded listed first.

In the new `photo.php`, the next and previous photos are retrieved and used to generate a new `<div>` with the class `photo-nav`. This `<div>` contains two other `<div>` elements containing the Previous and Next links, respectively. If either of the next or previous items is empty, then no link is generated.

Making Smart Sets Smarter

The final part of the gallery application to be improved is the Smart Sets. Currently, the main index page for the smart sets is the slowest page in the system to load, as it has to perform a Flickr search for each Smart Set defined. The problem is that you can't automatically generate these sets from the database using the information currently stored — you just don't have all the information required. Some of the Smart Sets are built around tags, but it's not practical to store tag information for each photo in your cache: you would have to call `flickr.photos.getInfo` for every photo stored, which could result in many thousands of API calls. And some Smart Sets are sorted by interestingness, and there is currently no way to establish a value for the interestingness of a photo via the Flickr API. So how can you improve the efficiency of Smart Sets? An obvious solution would be to gather the data in exactly the way they are gathered now — to perform the same `flickr.photos.search` method call as currently used and keep track of the results.

You already have details of all of the photos in your photostream recorded in the `photo` table — you clearly don't need to duplicate that information. In fact, the only thing needed to identify the contents of a Smart Set is a list of photo IDs.

Identifying Smart Sets

Whereas photos have a unique ID to identify them, Smart Sets don't. You need a way of uniquely identifying them so that they can be referred to in the database. One of the beauties of Smart Sets is the fact that you can create new ones on the fly just by adding a snippet of PHP to the Smart Sets page — whatever scheme you come up with must support this ability to create new Smart Sets at will.

The thing that uniquely identifies a Smart Set is the list of parameters used in the call to `flickr.photos.search` when creating it. If you could turn that list of parameters into a single easy-to-use value, that would make a suitable identifier.

The three things that go into the search query are the tags, the tag mode (`all` or `any`), and the sort order. You could create a string by joining these three things together like this:

```
$key = $tags . ":" . $tagmode . ":" . $sort;
```

This would result in a value for $key that would identify the correct Smart Set. This system could, however, result in some long and bizarre-looking keys. A slightly more elegant approach would be to take the MD5 hash of the string:

```
$key = md5($tags . ":" . $tagmode . ":" . $sort);
```

MD5 is a cryptographic hash function that returns a 128 bit value — usually represented as a string of 32 hexadecimal digits. A small change to the input string will cause a completely different MD5 hash to be generated. If you want to read a little more about the mathematics behind MD5, the Wikipedia article at http://en.wikipedia.org/wiki/Md5 is a good place to start. For your purposes here, however, all you need to know is that two different Smart Sets will give two different 32-byte hash values. The probability of two different Smart Sets resolving to the same MD5 hash value is so small that you can completely ignore it here.

Try It Out Storing Smart Sets

In this exercise, you'll use the techniques just discussed to create a new database to store your Smart Set contents for later use.

1. Create a new method in `FlickrGallery` to calculate a unique identifier for a Smart Set:

```
function getSmartSetKey($tags, $tagMode, $sort)
{
  $s = $tags . ":" . $tagmode . ":" . $sort;
  return md5($s);
}
```

2. Now create a new file called `create_smartset.sql`, in which you will put the SQL to create a new table in the database in which you can record your Smart Set contents:

```
DROP TABLE IF EXISTS smartset;

CREATE TABLE smartset (
  sset_key CHAR(32) NOT NULL,
  sset_photo_id VARCHAR(255) NOT NULL,
  sset_index INT NOT NULL
);
```

3. Create the table in your MySQL database by running the following command:

```
mysql -u root -p mashups < create_smartset.sql
```

You can then check that the table was created correctly using the `DESCRIBE` command:

```
mysql> DESCRIBE smartset;
+---------------+--------------+------+-----+---------+-------+
| Field         | Type         | Null | Key | Default | Extra |
+---------------+--------------+------+-----+---------+-------+
| sset_key      | char(32)     | NO   |     |         |       |
| sset_photo_id | varchar(255) | NO   |     |         |       |
| sset_index    | int(11)      | NO   |     |         |       |
+---------------+--------------+------+-----+---------+-------+
3 rows in set (0.01 sec)
```

You will notice that the sset_key column is defined as CHAR(32) instead of VARCHAR(32). You know that this field is of fixed length, so you can declare it as such. The sset_index column records the position of the photo within the set. You won't be using this field immediately, but it will come in useful later on, so include it here now.

4. Now you need a method to populate the smartset table. Add the following method to FlickrGallery:

```
function populateSmartSet($tags, $tagMode, $sort)
{
  set_time_limit(240);
  $key = $this->getSmartSetKey($tags, $tagMode, $sort);

  $keepGoing = 1;
  $page = 1;
  $n = 0;
  while ($keepGoing)
  {
    $args = array(
      'user_id' => $this->nsid,
      'sort' => $sort,
      'page' => $page,
      'tags' => $tags,
      'tag_mode' => $tagMode,
      'per_page' => 500,
      'extras' => 'date_upload, date_taken, owner_name, geo'
      );

    $p = $this->flickr->photos_search($args);
    if ($this->flickr->getErrorCode())
    {
      echo ("Error fetching photos: " . $this->flickr->getErrorMsg());
    }

    if (count($p['photo']) == 0)
    {
      // no more photos
      break;
    }

    $q = "INSERT INTO smartset"
      . " (sset_key, sset_photo_id, sset_index)"
      . " VALUES"
      . " ('%s', '%s', %d)";

    foreach($p['photo'] as $photo)
    {
      $sql = sprintf($q, $key, $photo['id'], $n);

      mysql_query($sql, $this->getConnection()) or die("Invalid query: " . $sql);
      $n++;
    }

    $page++;
  }
}
```

How It Works

If you look closely, you will see that this new method works in exactly the same way as the existing `populateDBPhotos()` method. The parameters required to generate the Smart Set are passed into the `flickr.photos.search` method call and the results inserted into the new `smartset` table. Once again, the maximum execution time for this script is increased by means of the PHP function `set_time_limit()`.

Given that you can create new Smart Sets at will just by adding the appropriate PHP to the Smart Sets page, it would be nice if you could populate the Smart Set cache automatically whenever a new Smart Set is encountered — so you won't actually populate our database with Smart Sets yet. Let's first take a look at how we view the Smart Set.

Viewing the Smart Set

The `smartset` table contains only photo IDs — you will need to get all the associated data for each photo from the photo table as well before you have all the photo details you need. To do this, you will use a feature of SQL called a *join*. A join literally joins together two different tables. The easiest way to understand this is to see it happen — let's create some test data to show a join in action.

Connect to the database as usual, using the following command:

```
mysql -u root -p mashups
```

You first need to create a dummy Smart Set entry, and for that you need to know the ID of one of your photos. Enter the following SQL command:

```
SELECT photo_id FROM photo LIMIT 1;
```

This will return the ID of one your photos, something like this:

```
mysql> SELECT photo_id FROM photo LIMIT 1;
+-----------+
| photo_id  |
+-----------+
| 260568187 |
+-----------+
1 row in set (0.00 sec)
```

Make a note of the photo ID you are shown by your query — it will be different from the one shown in the example here. Now make up a Smart Set entry:

```
mysql> INSERT INTO smartset (sset_key, sset_photo_id, sset_index)
    -> VALUES
    -> ('test', '260568187', 0);
Query OK, 1 row affected (0.03 sec)
```

Make sure you replace the photo id `260568187` with the photo ID returned by your SQL query.

You've now created data for a dummy Smart Set with a single entry. You can look at the data like this:

```
mysql> SELECT * FROM smartset;
+----------+---------------+------------+
| sset_key | sset_photo_id | sset_index |
+----------+---------------+------------+
| test     | 260568187     |          0 |
+----------+---------------+------------+
1 row in set (0.00 sec)
```

If you want to return information about the photo in the `smartset` table using a SQL join, you use a query like this:

```
SELECT sset_key, photo_id, photo_title FROM smartset, photo
  WHERE sset_photo_id = photo_id
```

In this query, you are looking at data across two different tables, `smartset` and `photo` — you can see them both listed in the FROM clause. You also need to tell the database how to relate the two tables together, and you do this by specifying a *join condition* in the WHERE clause. This join condition specifies the relationship that exists between the two tables — the condition that must be true for a row in one table to be referring to a row in the other. In this case, the common item is the photo ID — the `sset_photo_id` column in the `smartset` table represents the same identifier as the `photo_id` column in the `photo` table, so the join condition is `sset_photo_id = photo_id`.

If you run the query, you should see something similar to this:

```
mysql> SELECT sset_key, sset_photo_id, photo_title from smartset, photo
    -> WHERE sset_photo_id = photo_id;
+----------+---------------+-------------+
| sset_key | sset_photo_id | photo_title |
+----------+---------------+-------------+
| test     | 260568187     | Moo!        |
+----------+---------------+-------------+
1 row in set (0.02 sec)
```

As you can see, the SELECT has brought back columns from two different tables, but has correctly related the photo ID that was stored in the `smartset` table with the corresponding photo title from the `photo` table.

Try It Out   Viewing the Smart Set

Now you've seen how to use a SQL join to retrieve data from two different tables in your database, you can write the code to view a Smart Set.

1.   Change the existing `getSmartSet()` method in your `FlickrGallery` class as follows:

```
function getSmartSet($n = 20, $tags = "", $tagMode = "all",
  $sort = "date-posted-desc")
{
  $ret = array();

  if ($this->useDB)
  {
    $key = $this->getSmartSetKey($tags, $tagMode, $sort);
```

```php
    $sql = "SELECT COUNT(*) FROM smartset WHERE sset_key = '$key'";
    $res = mysql_query($sql, $this->getConnection())
      or die("Invalid query: " . $sql);

    if ($row = mysql_fetch_array($res))
    {
      $count = $row[0];
      if ($count == 0)
      {
        $this->populateSmartSet($tags, $tagMode, $sort);
      }
    }

    $sql = "SELECT * FROM smartset, photo"
      . " WHERE sset_photo_id = photo_id"
      . " AND sset_key = '$key' LIMIT $n";
    $res = mysql_query($sql, $this->getConnection())
      or die("Invalid query: " . $sql);

    while ($row = mysql_fetch_assoc($res))
    {
      $photo = $this->buildPhotoFromRow($row);
      array_push($ret, $photo);
    }
  }
  else
  {
    $args = array(
      'user_id' => $this->nsid,
      'sort' => $sort,
      'page' => 1,
      'per_page' => $n,
      'extras' => 'owner_name'
      );

    if (!empty($tags))
    {
      $args['tags'] = $tags;
      $args['tag_mode'] = $tagMode;
    }

    $p = $this->flickr->photos_search($args);
    if ($this->flickr->getErrorCode())
    {
      echo ("Error fetching photos: " . $this->flickr->getErrorMsg());
    }

    if (is_array($p['photo']) && count($p['photo']) > 0)
    {
      $ret = $p['photo'];
    }
  }

  return $ret;
}
```

2. Go to your web browser and open up the main Smart Sets page in the gallery. You will notice that it takes a little time to load — this is the first time the sets are being viewed and so the cache is being populated. Once the page has loaded, if you immediately reload it again, you should see that it loads almost instantly — all of the data are now stored locally and the page can be built without performing any searches via the Flickr API.

3. Go to your `mysql>` prompt, and you can now see the `smartset` data:

```
mysql> SELECT * FROM smartset LIMIT 10;
+----------------------------------+---------------+-------------+
| sset_key                         | sset_photo_id | sset_index  |
+----------------------------------+---------------+-------------+
| 9417f2554f324975fd99470e54b84411 | 29900246      |           0 |
| 9417f2554f324975fd99470e54b84411 | 12201606      |           1 |
| 9417f2554f324975fd99470e54b84411 | 44270733      |           2 |
| 9417f2554f324975fd99470e54b84411 | 92550411      |           3 |
| 9417f2554f324975fd99470e54b84411 | 24972438      |           4 |
| 9417f2554f324975fd99470e54b84411 | 104207697     |           5 |
| 9417f2554f324975fd99470e54b84411 | 30696249      |           6 |
| 9417f2554f324975fd99470e54b84411 | 17867492      |           7 |
| 9417f2554f324975fd99470e54b84411 | 12944696      |           8 |
| 9417f2554f324975fd99470e54b84411 | 72422441      |           9 |
+----------------------------------+---------------+-------------+
10 rows in set (0.00 sec)
```

4. Make a note of one of your Smart Set keys and try a different query using a join — make sure you replace the `sset_key` used here with one of your keys:

```
mysql> SELECT photo_id, photo_title FROM photo, smartset
    -> WHERE photo_id = sset_photo_id
    -> AND sset_key = '9417f2554f324975fd99470e54b84411'
    -> LIMIT 10;
+-----------+--------------------------------+
| photo_id  | photo_title                    |
+-----------+--------------------------------+
| 29900246  | Cupcakes                       |
| 12201606  | Burger                         |
| 44270733  | Celebration                    |
| 92550411  | Creme Egg                      |
| 24972438  | Double Chocolate Chunk Cookies |
| 104207697 | Straws                         |
| 30696249  | Banana Bread and Butter Pudding|
| 17867492  | New Boot                       |
| 12944696  | Ice Cream Cornet               |
| 72422441  | Cool as a Cucumber             |
+-----------+--------------------------------+
10 rows in set (0.00 sec)
```

How It Works

Once again, the existing code in `FlickrGallery` is enclosed in an `if-then-else` block. The code to retrieve the Smart Set contents from the database is then split into two parts. First of all, a query to count the number of photos in the set is created:

```
$sql = "SELECT COUNT(*) FROM smartset WHERE sset_key = '$key'";
```

The query is executed and the result returned via `mysql_fetch_array()`:

```
if ($row = mysql_fetch_array($res))
{
  ...
}
```

Note the use of `mysql_fetch_array()` rather than `mysql_fetch_assoc()` here. `mysql_fetch_array()` works in exactly the same way as `mysql_fetch_assoc()`, except that the results are returned as an indexed array rather than an associative array. Only one data item is returned as part of this query, so this will be found at `$row[0]`.

If the count returned is 0, you can assume that the database cache has not yet been set up for this Smart Set yet—this must be the first time that this set has been encountered. The set is then populated with a call to `populateSmartSet()`:

```
$this->populateSmartSet($tags, $tagMode, $sort);
```

Finally, a query is built to retrieve the required number of photos for this Smart Set from the database:

```
$sql = "SELECT * FROM smartset, photo"
     . " WHERE sset_photo_id = photo_id"
     . " AND sset_key = '$key' LIMIT $n";
```

The rows returned by this query will contain the whole set of columns from both the `smartset` and the `photo` tables. The results are converted into photo objects by calling `buildPhotoFromRow()`, and the resulting array of photo objects is returned.

Summary

You have now completed the modifications to your gallery application—very little may have changed in terms of what an end user sees, but behind the scenes, its capabilities have been greatly enhanced: all photos in your photostream are now stored in a local database to allow fast, efficient searching, and all Smart Sets are now stored locally, again, allowing them to be displayed to the user with very little delay.

You have learned a great many new things in this chapter:

- ❑ How to install the MySQL database server
- ❑ How to create SQL queries to create, read, modify, and delete data in database tables
- ❑ How to use the MySQL command-line tools to interrogate a database
- ❑ How to use PHP to interact with a MySQL database

This concludes the series of Flickr remixes and mashups explained in this book. You have seen and used a wide variety of methods, tools, and techniques for building software that interacts with Flickr in a wide variety of ways. Now it's time for you to move on and start putting the things you've learned here to good use—designing and building your own remixes and mashups. We have one final exercise left below, just so you can put your new-found database skills into practice, but after that it's over to you.

You may now want to take some of the ideas covered in this book and expand and improve on them, or perhaps you have ideas for new mashups of your own. Whatever you choose to do next, the possibilities are limited only by your own imagination. So what are you waiting for? Get mashing!

Exercise

The `photo.php` page shows Next and Previous links that enable you to navigate backward and forward in the photostream. When you view a Smart Set, it would be more appropriate if these links moved you through the set contents rather than the whole photostream. Change the way Next and Previous work so that the photo page behaves differently when you are viewing a Smart Set.

Here are a few hints (stop reading now if you prefer to solve this one on your own). You will need to identify within the photo page whether you arrived there while viewing a Smart Set or while viewing the photostream. You could do this by passing in an extra parameter identifying the set being viewed (if any). To find the next and previous items in the set, you will need to write some new SQL. You might find the `sset_index` column useful here.

Answers to Exercises

Chapter 2

Exercise 1

Once you've signed up to a new Flickr account and logged in, the Flickr home page at `http://www.flickr.com/` will look something like that shown in Figure A-1.

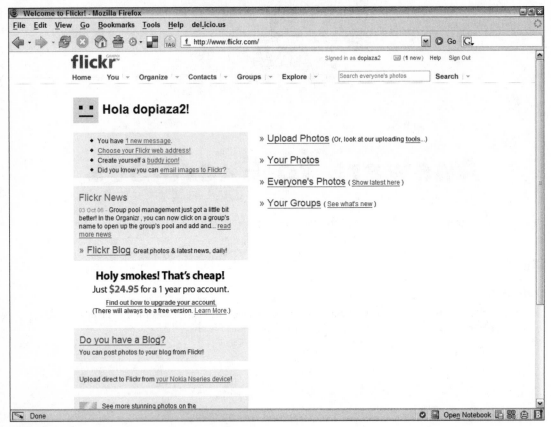

Figure A-1

If you click on the Upload Photos link, you will be taken to the Photo Upload page you saw in Figure 2-1. After you have uploaded one or more photos, go to your photostream page by clicking the You link in the menu at the top of the page — you should find it looks something like that shown in Figure A-2.

Figure A-2

Exercise 2

If you click on a photo on your photostream page, you will be taken to the photo page. You can add tags to the photo by entering them into the text box labeled Tags on the right-hand side of the page, as shown in Figure A-3.

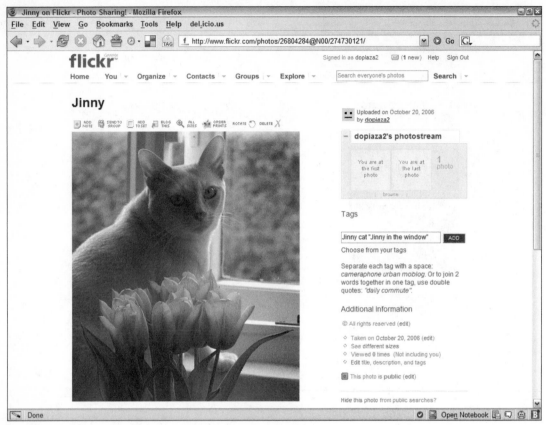

Figure A-3

Exercise 3

You can find a search box at the top of every page. Enter *cat* into it and click the arrow to the right of the word search. A drop-down list will appear showing the different areas you can search, as you can see in Figure A-4. Choose Everyone's Photos.

Figure A-4

You will see a search results page containing a list of photos about cats — you can see an example of such a page in Figure A-5.

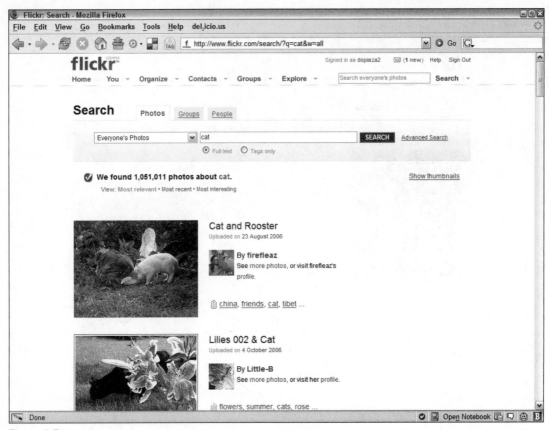

Figure A-5

If you change the search terms to *cat banana*, you will see a page of results featuring both those things —
as in Figure A-6.

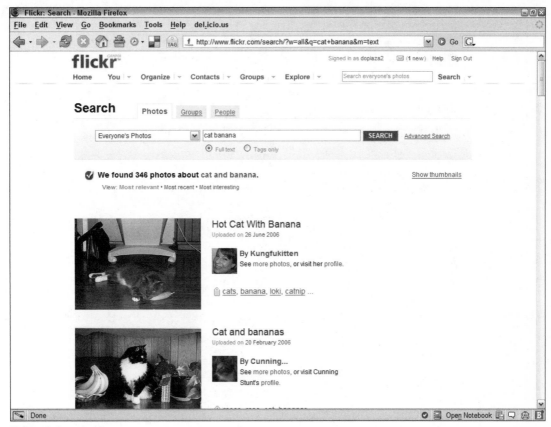

Figure A-6

It's actually quite difficult to find two common words that don't generate a match. I managed with *apricot* and *sardine*, as you can see in Figure A-7.

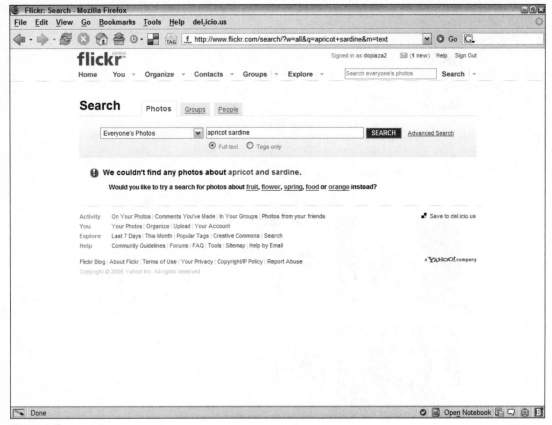

Figure A-7

Of course, with a million photos a day being uploaded to Flickr, there may well be a matching photo by the time you read this.

You can make this slightly easier by choosing to search on Tags only with the radio button under the search box — otherwise the search includes the photo titles and descriptions as well.

Exercise 4

From the search screen you saw in Exercise 3, click the People tab. Enter the name of the person you are looking for and press Search. A list of matches will appear, and from here you can jump to the person's Flickr page or profile. To add them as a contact, move your mouse over the user's buddy icon and click the arrow that appears, which will reveal a drop-down menu as shown in Figure A-8. Select the item that says "Add *user* as a contact."

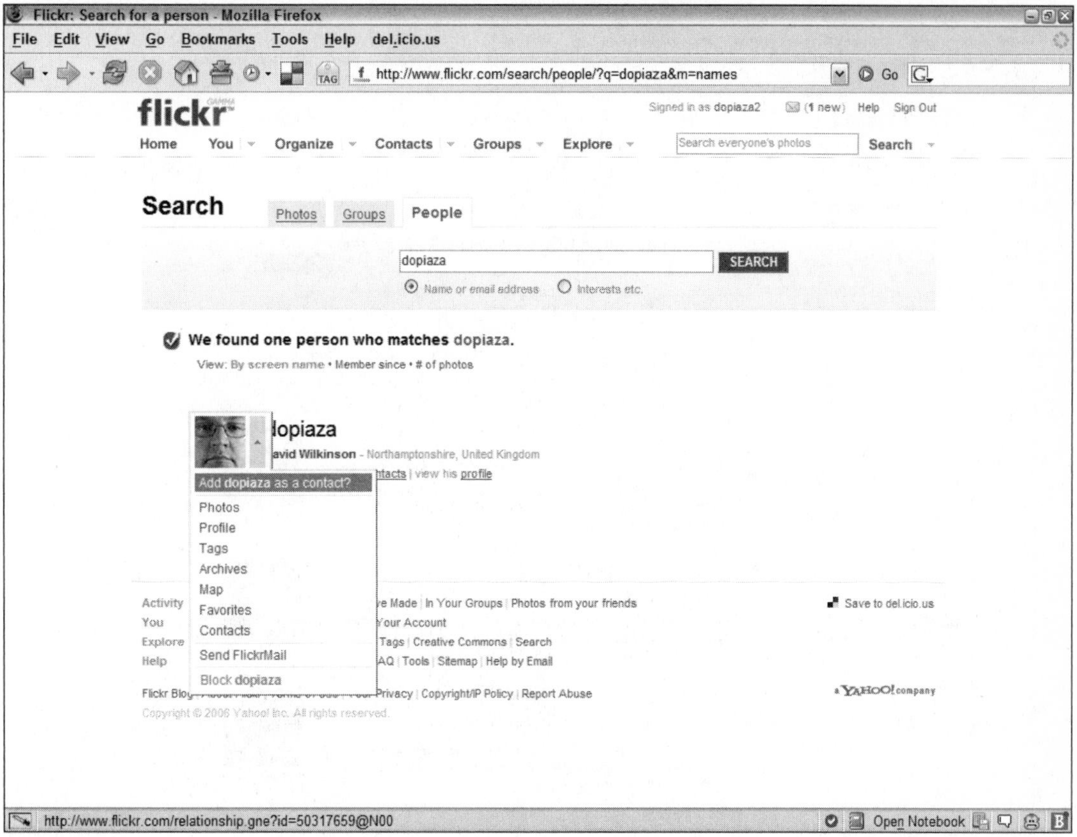

Figure A-8

Exercise 5

Again, from the search screen you saw earlier, click the Groups tab. Type **FlickrCentral** and click Search. You should see a screen something like that in Figure A-9 — with FlickrCentral somewhere in the search results.

Figure A-9

Click the group name for FlickrCentral and you will be taken to the main group page. Here you will see a large Join this group link. Click the link to join the group and you will then be able to participate in group discussions and add photos to the group pool.

Chapter 3

Exercise 1

Create a directory called `exercises` in the document root of your web site. Within this directory, create a file called `3-1.php` with the following contents:

```
<!DOCTYPE html PUBLIC "-//W3C//DTD XHTML 1.0 Transitional//EN"
  "http://www.w3.org/TR/xhtml1/DTD/xhtml1-transitional.dtd">
<html xmlns="http://www.w3.org/1999/xhtml">
<head>
  <link href="../css/main.css" rel="stylesheet" type="text/css" />
  <title>Flickr Mashups</title>
</head>
<body>
```

```
<h1>Exercise 3-1</h1>
<?php

// Create an array of 1000 numbers

$numbers = array();

for ($i = 0; $i < 1000; $i++)
{
  array_push($numbers, rand(1, 1000));
}

?>

<p>Array of <?php echo count($numbers) ?> numbers created.</p>

<?php

$total = 0;
foreach ($numbers as $n)
{
  $total += $n;
}

$average = $total / count($numbers);

?>
<p>The average is <?php echo $average ?></p>
</body>
</html>
```

View the file in your browser by entering the URL to the page. The actual URL will depend on how you configured your web server, but if you followed the instructions in Chapter 3, it will most likely be either `http://localhost/exercises/3-1.php` or `http://localhost:8080/exercises/3-1.php`.

The PHP script creates an array called `$numbers`. The `for` loop then iterates a thousand times, each time adding a random number between 1 and 1,000. A message is output verifying that the array was correctly created. A `foreach` loop then goes through the array, totals up all the numbers and then calculates and outputs the average.

Exercise 2

In your `exercises` directory, create a file called `3-2.php` with the following contents:

```
<!DOCTYPE html PUBLIC "-//W3C//DTD XHTML 1.0 Transitional//EN"
  "http://www.w3.org/TR/xhtml1/DTD/xhtml1-transitional.dtd">
<html xmlns="http://www.w3.org/1999/xhtml">
<head>
  <link href="../css/main.css" rel="stylesheet" type="text/css" />
  <title>Flickr Mashups</title>
</head>
<body>
  <h1>Exercise 3-2</h1>
  <p>Enter three numbers</p>
```

```
    <form method="post" action="3-2.php">
      <input type="text" name="num1" /><br/>
      <input type="text" name="num2" /><br/>
      <input type="text" name="num3" /><br/>
      <input type="submit" value="Submit" /><br/>
    </form>

    <?php
    $num1 = $_REQUEST["num1"];
    $num2 = $_REQUEST["num2"];
    $num3 = $_REQUEST["num3"];

    $total = $num1 + $num2 + $num3;
    ?>
    <p>The total is <?php echo $total ?></p>
  </body>
  </html>
```

View the file in your browser by entering the URL to the page. Once again, the actual URL will depend on how you configured your web server, but will most likely be either `http://localhost/exercises/3-2.php` or `http://localhost:8080/exercises/3-2.php`.

You should then see a page like that shown in Figure A-10.

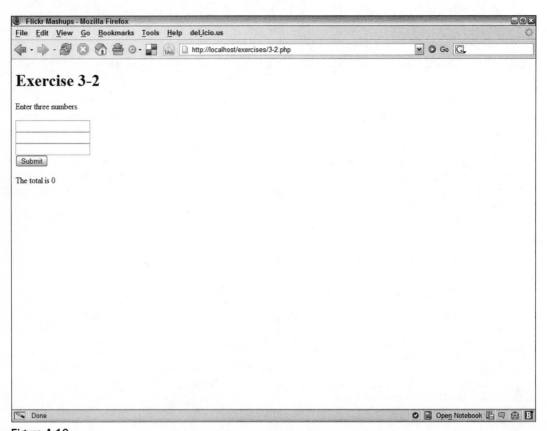

Figure A-10

Enter three numbers and press the Submit button—the total will then update. The PHP code in the file is very straightforward: each form field value is retrieved from the $_REQUEST object and the total calculated and then displayed.

Chapter 4

Exercise 1

```
http://api.flickr.com/services/rest/?method=flickr.photos.getRecent
    &api_key=YOUR-API-KEY&per_page=10
```

Exercise 2

Go to the API Explorer page for flickr.photos.search, which is at http://www.flickr.com/services/api/explore/?method=flickr.photos.search, and enter *cat* into the tags argument box and *interestingness-desc* into the sort argument box, and press the Call Method button.

This will find photos that are tagged *cat,* and sort them by interestingness, with the most interesting first.

Exercise 3

In the results returned in Exercise 2, look at the first photo tag returned and make a note of the id and secret attribute values.

Go to the API Explorer page for flickr.photos.getInfo, which is at http://www.flickr.com/services/api/explore/?method=flickr.photos.getInfo. Enter the ID and secret values you noted into the corresponding argument boxes and click the Call Method button.

Chapter 5

Exercise 1

Modify the badge.css file as shown below:

```
.badge {
  width: 250px;
}
.badge-title {
  font-size: 12px;
  font-weight: 600;
  text-align: center;
}
.badge p {
  margin: 0;
  padding: 0;
}
.badge-items {
  width: 250px;
  margin: 0;
  padding: 0;
}
.badge-item {
```

```
    display: inline;
    list-style-type: none;
}
.badge-item img{
  border: 1px solid #333333;
  width: 48px;
  height: 48px;
}
```

Exercise 2

Change the feed URL retrieved to `http://api.flickr.com/services/feeds/groups_pool` `.gne?id=81474450@N00&format=FORMAT`, where `FORMAT` is `php` or `json` as appropriate.

The modified `badge.php` is as follows:

```php
<?php

include("http://api.flickr.com/services/feeds/groups_pool.gne?id=81474450@N00&format=php");

$s = "";

$s .= '<div class="badge">';
$s .= '<p class="badge-title"><a href="' . $feed['url'] . '">' . $feed['title'] .
'</a></p>';
$s .= '<ul class="badge-items">';

$items = $feed['items'];

for ($i = 0; $i < count($items); $i++)
{
  if (preg_match('/(http:\/\/static.flickr.com\/\d+\/\d+_[0-9a-z]+)_m\.jpg/',
$items[$i]['description'], $result))
  {
    $image = $result[1] . '_s.jpg';
    $s .= '<li class="badge-item"><a href="' . $items[$i]['url'] . '"><img src="' .
$image . '" /></a></li>';
  }
}

$s .= '</ul></div>';

echo($s);

?>
```

The modified `javascript-badge.html` is as follows:

```
<!DOCTYPE html PUBLIC "-//W3C//DTD XHTML 1.0 Transitional//EN"
  "http://www.w3.org/TR/xhtml1/DTD/xhtml1-transitional.dtd">
<html xmlns="http://www.w3.org/1999/xhtml"><head>
  <title>Flickr Mashups: Javascript Badge</title>
```

```
    <link href="../css/main.css" rel="stylesheet" type="text/css" />
    <link href="../css/badge.css" rel="stylesheet" type="text/css" />
</head>
<body>

<script src="badge.js" type="text/javascript"></script>
<script src=
"http://api.flickr.com/services/feeds/groups_pool.gne?id=81474450@N00&format=json"
type="text/javascript"></script>

</body>
</html>
```

Chapter 6

Exercise 1

Modify `info.php` as follows:

```php
<?php

include (dirname(__FILE__) . '/../lib/gallery.php');

function decodeHTML($text)
{
  $s = str_replace("&lt;", "<", $text);
  $s = str_replace("&gt;", ">", $s);
  $s = str_replace("&quot;", "\"", $s);
  $s = str_replace("&amp;", "&", $s);

  return $s;
}

function formatDateTaken($d)
{
  // This is of the form YYYY-MM-DD HH:mm:SS

  $format = 'j F Y';
  $formattedDate = date($format, strtotime($d));
  return $formattedDate;
}

function formatDatePosted($d)
{
  // This is a unix timestamp

  $format = 'j F Y';
  $formattedDate = date($format, $d);
  return $formattedDate;
}

$gallery = new FlickrGallery();
$id = $_REQUEST['id'];
```

```
  if (!empty($id))
  {
    $info = $gallery->getPhotoInfo($id);
    $description = nl2br(decodeHTML($info['description']));
    $tags = $info['tags']['tag'];

?>
<div class="photo-info">
  <div class="photo-description"><?php echo $description ?></div>
  <ul class="photo-tags">
<?php
  if (!empty($tags))
  {
    foreach ($tags as $tag)
    {
?>
    <li><?php echo $tag['raw'] ?></li>
<?php
    }
  }
?>
  </ul>
  <div class="photo-date-taken">Taken on: <?php echo
formatDateTaken($info['dates']['taken']) ?></div>
  <div class="photo-date-posted">Posted on: <?php echo
formatDatePosted($info['dates']['posted']) ?></div>
</div>
<?php
}
?>
```

Add the following styles to `gallery.css`:

```
.photo-date-taken {
  margin-top: 1em;
  font-size: smaller;
  text-align: left;
}
.photo-date-posted {
  font-size: smaller;
  text-align: left;
}
```

Exercise 2

To do this, when inserting the new HTML fetched by the AJAX request, take a copy of the original content that is being replaced. When the Hide info link is clicked, remove the additional content and replace it with the original content.

Modify `gallery.js`:

```
var originalContent;

function displayInfo(id)
{
```

```
    var s = 'id=' + id;

    new Ajax.Request('info.php',
    {
      parameters: s,
      method: "post",
      onSuccess:function(response)
      {
        var node = $('photo-info-' + id);
        originalContent = node.innerHTML;
        node.innerHTML = response.responseText;
      },
      onFailure:function(response)
      {
        alert('Error: ' + response.status + ' ' + response.statusText);
      }
    });
  }
```

```
function hideInfo(id)
{
  // Restore original content
  var node = $('photo-info-' + id);
  // remove all children
  while (node.firstChild != null)
  {
    node.removeChild(node.firstChild);
  }
  node.innerHTML = originalContent;
}
```

Modify info.php to add the Hide info link:

```
<?php

include (dirname(__FILE__) . '/../lib/gallery.php');

...

if (!empty($id))
{
  $info = $gallery->getPhotoInfo($id);
  $description = nl2br(decodeHTML($info['description']));
  $tags = $info['tags']['tag'];
?>
<div class="photo-more"><a href="#" onclick="hideInfo(<?php echo $id ?>); return
false;">Hide info</a></div>
<div class="photo-info">
  <div class="photo-description"><?php echo $description ?></div>
  <ul class="photo-tags">
<?php
  if (!empty($tags))
  {
    foreach ($tags as $tag)
    {
```

```
?>
    <li><?php echo $tag['raw'] ?></li>
<?php
    }
  }
?>
  </ul>
  <div class="photo-date-taken">Taken on: <?php echo
formatDateTaken($info['dates']['taken']) ?></div>
  <div class="photo-date-posted">Posted on: <?php echo
formatDatePosted($info['dates']['posted']) ?></div>
</div>
<?php
}
?>
```

Chapter 7

Exercise 1

First, you need to add a new method to FlickrGallery.php to call the flickr.photos.setTags API method:

```php
<?php

class FlickrGallery extends FlickrAuthenticator
{

...

    function setTags($id, $tags)
    {
      $this->flickr->photos_setTags($id, $tags);

      if ($this->flickr->getErrorCode())
      {
        echo ("Error setting tags: " . $this->flickr->getErrorMsg());
      }
    }
}

?>
```

Modify edit.php to display the tags within the edit form:

```php
<?php
include (dirname(__FILE__) . '/../lib/gallery.php');
$gallery = new FlickrGallery();
$gallery->authenticate("write");
if (!$gallery->checkAuthenticatedUser())
{
  $gallery->error("You do not have permission to edit these details");
```

```
    }
?>
<!DOCTYPE html PUBLIC "-//W3C//DTD XHTML 1.0 Transitional//EN"
  "http://www.w3.org/TR/xhtml1/DTD/xhtml1-transitional.dtd">
<html xmlns="http://www.w3.org/1999/xhtml">
<head>
  <link href="../css/main.css" rel="stylesheet" type="text/css" />
  <link href="../css/gallery.css" rel="stylesheet" type="text/css" />
  <title>Flickr Gallery</title>
</head>
<body>
<?php
  $id = $_REQUEST['id'];
  if (!empty($id))
  {
    $info = $gallery->getPhotoInfo($id);
    $title = $info['title'];
    $img = 'http://static.flickr.com/' . $info['server'] . '/' . $info['id']
      . '_' . $info['secret'] . '.jpg';
    $photoPage = 'http://www.flickr.com/photos/' . $info['owner']['nsid'] . '/'
      . $id . '/';
    $description = $info['description'];

    $tags = "";
    if (!empty($info['tags']['tag']))
    {
      foreach ($info['tags']['tag'] as $tag)
      {
        $raw = $tag['raw'];
        // Note use of !== operator here
        if (strpos($raw, ' ') !== FALSE)
        {
          // Contains a space, so surround in quotes
          $raw = '&quot;' . $raw . '&quot;';
        }
        $tags .= $raw . " ";
      }
    }
  }
?>
<?php include ('header.php') ?>
<?php include ('navigation.php') ?>
<div class="photo-edit">
  <form action="doEdit.php" method="post">
    <p class="photo-image"><a href="<?php echo $photoPage ?>"><img src="<?php echo
$img ?>" alt="<?php echo $title ?>" title="<?php echo $title ?>" /></a></p>
    <p class="photo-title-edit"><input name="title" type="text" id="title"
value="<?php echo $title ?>" size="50" />
    <p class="photo-description-edit">
      <textarea name="description" cols="50" rows="6" wrap="VIRTUAL"
id="description"><?php echo $description ?></textarea>
    </p>
    <p class="photo-tags-edit"><input name="tags" type="text" id="tags"
value="<?php echo $tags ?>" size="50" />
    <p class="photo-description-edit">
```

```
        <input name="id" type="hidden" value="<?php echo $id ?>" />
        <input type="submit" name="Submit" value="Submit Changes" />
        <input type="reset" name="Reset" value="Reset" />
  </p>
    </form>
  </div>
  </body>
  </html>
```

Then modify doEdit.php to save the new tags:

```php
<?php
include (dirname(__FILE__) . '/../lib/gallery.php');
$gallery = new FlickrGallery();
$gallery->authenticate("write");
if (!$gallery->checkAuthenticatedUser())
{
  $gallery->error("You do not have permission to edit these details");
}

$id = $_REQUEST['id'];
$title = $_REQUEST['title'];
$description = $_REQUEST['description'];
$tags = $_REQUEST['tags'];

if (!empty($id))
{
  $gallery->setMeta($id, stripslashes($title), stripslashes($description));
  $gallery->setTags($id, stripslashes($tags));
}

header('Location: http://' . $_SERVER['HTTP_HOST'] . dirname($_SERVER['PHP_SELF'])
. '/photo.php?id=' . $id);
?>
```

Exercise 2

You can do this in a number of ways. The simplest way is to store the screen name of the currently logged-in user in the current session whenever they are successfully authenticated.

Modify the authenticate method in FlickrAuthenticator.php to do this:

```php
<?php

class FlickrAuthenticator
{

...

  function authenticate($requiredPerms)
  {
```

```
        ...

                if (!$doAuth)
                {
                  // No further authentication necessary, so store away
                  // the results from checkToken
                  $this->auth = $auth;
                  $_SESSION['FlickrAuthenticatedUser'] = $auth['user']['username'];
                }

        ...

          }

        ...

      }
      ?>
```

Then modify `navigation.php`:

```php
<?php
$user = $_SESSION['FlickrAuthenticatedUser'];
?>
<ul id="gallery-menu">
   <li><a href="../index.php">Mashups Home</a></li>
   <li><a href="index.php">Gallery</a></li>
   <li><a href="smartsets.php">Smart Sets</a></li>
   <li>
<?php
   if (empty($user))
   {
?>
   <a href="login.php">Login</a>
<?php
   }
   else
   {
?>
   Logged in as <?php echo $user ?>
<?php
   }
?>
   </li>
</ul>
```

Create a `login.php` page in the `gallery` directory to ensure that the user is authenticated and then redirect them to the gallery home page:

```php
<?php
include (dirname(__FILE__) . '/../lib/gallery.php');
$gallery = new FlickrGallery();
$gallery->authenticate("write");

header('Location: http://' . $_SERVER['HTTP_HOST'] . dirname($_SERVER['PHP_SELF'])
  . '/index.php');
?>
```

Finally, modify `info.php` to hide the Edit link if no one has logged in:

```php
<?php

include (dirname(__FILE__) . '/../lib/gallery.php');

...

$user = $_SESSION['FlickrAuthenticatedUser'];

$gallery = new FlickrGallery();

...

<?php
    if (!empty($user))
    {
?>
   <div class="photo-edit-link"><a href="edit.php?id=<?php echo $id
?>">Edit</a></div>
<?php
    }
?>
</div>
<?php
}
?>
```

Chapter 8

Exercise 1

The replace photo pages are very similar to the edit pages; the only practical difference is the need to keep track of the photo ID being replaced.

Add a new `replacePhoto` method to `FlickrGallery.php`:

```php
<?php

class FlickrGallery extends FlickrAuthenticator
{
    ...
```

```
    function replacePhoto($file, $photoId)
    {
      $id = $this->flickr->replace($file, $photoId);

      if ($this->flickr->getErrorCode())
      {
        echo ("Error replacing photo: " . $this->flickr->getErrorMsg());
      }

      return $id;
    }
}
?>
```

Create a new file, `replace.php`, in the `gallery` directory:

```
<?php
include (dirname(__FILE__) . '/../lib/gallery.php');
$gallery = new FlickrGallery();
$gallery->authenticate("write");
if (!$gallery->checkAuthenticatedUser())
{
  $gallery->error("You do not have permission to replace photos");
}
?>
<!DOCTYPE html PUBLIC "-//W3C//DTD XHTML 1.0 Transitional//EN"
  "http://www.w3.org/TR/xhtml1/DTD/xhtml1-transitional.dtd">
<html xmlns="http://www.w3.org/1999/xhtml">
<head>
  <link href="../css/main.css" rel="stylesheet" type="text/css" />
  <link href="../css/gallery.css" rel="stylesheet" type="text/css" />
  <title>Replace Photo</title>
</head>
<body>
<?php include ('header.php') ?>
<?php include ('navigation.php') ?>
<?php
$id = $_REQUEST['id'];
if (!empty($id))
{
?>
<div class="photo-replace">
  <h1>Replace Photo</h1>
  <form action="doReplace.php" method="post" enctype="multipart/form-data">
    <p class="upload-field">
      <label>Photo</label>
      <input name="file" type="file" size="50" />
    </p>
    <p>
      <input type="hidden" name="id" value="<?php echo $id ?>" />
```

```
            <input type="submit" name="Submit" value="Upload Photo" />
            <input type="reset" name="Reset" value="Reset" />
        </p>
    </form>
</div>
<?php
}
?>
</body>
</html>
```

Create a file to handle the form submission, doReplace.php, in the gallery directory:

```
<?php
include (dirname(__FILE__) . '/../lib/gallery.php');
$gallery = new FlickrGallery();
$gallery->authenticate("write");
if (!$gallery->checkAuthenticatedUser())
{
    $gallery->error("You do not have permission to replace photos for this account");
}

$id = $_REQUEST['id'];
if (!empty($id))
{
    $size = $_FILES['file']['size'];
    $filename = $_FILES['file']['tmp_name'];

    if (!empty($filename) && is_uploaded_file($filename) && $size > 0)
    {
        $id = $gallery->replacePhoto($filename, $id);
    }
}

header('Location: http://' . $_SERVER['HTTP_HOST'] . dirname($_SERVER['PHP_SELF'])
    . '/index.php');
?>
```

You need to modify info.php to provide a link to the replace.php page:

```
<?php

include (dirname(__FILE__) . '/../lib/gallery.php');


...
<?php
    if (!empty($user))
    {
?>
    <div class="photo-edit-link"><a href="edit.php?id=<?php echo $id
?>">Edit</a></div>
    <div class="photo-replace-link"><a href="replace.php?id=<?php echo $id
?>">Replace</a></div>
    <?php
```

```
    }
?>
</div>
<?php
}
?>
```

Finally, a couple of changes to the `gallery.css` file:

```
.photo-edit-link, .photo-replace-link {
  text-align: right;
}
.photo-upload label, .photo-replace label {
  display: block;
  font-weight: 600;
  margin-top: 0.5em;
  margin-bottom: 0.5em;
}
```

Chapter 9

Exercise 1

Create a script called `addcandymenus.user.js` and install it into Greasemonkey in the normal way:

```
// ==UserScript==
// @name          Add Candy Menus
// @namespace     http://www.dopiaza.org/flickr/greasemonkey/addcandy/
// @description   Add a variety of menus to Flickr's navigation
// @include       http://www.flickr.com/*
// @include       http://flickr.com/*
// ==/UserScript==

function addCandy(menuId, text, link)
{
  // Find the menu
  var menus = document.evaluate(
    "//div[@id='" + menuId + "']",
    document,
    null,
    XPathResult.UNORDERED_NODE_SNAPSHOT_TYPE,
    null);

  if (menus.snapshotLength > 0)
  {
    var menu = menus.snapshotItem(0);

    var a = document.createElement('a');
    a.setAttribute("href", link);
    a.setAttribute("title", text);
    a.appendChild(document.createTextNode(text));

    menu.appendChild(a);
```

```
    }
    }

    // The ids of the different menus are:
    //    candy_nav_button_you
    //    candy_nav_button_organize
    //    candy_nav_button_contacts
    //    candy_nav_button_groups
    //    candy_nav_button_explore

    addCandy("candy_nav_menu_groups", "Forums", "http://www.flickr.com/forums/");
    addCandy("candy_nav_menu_groups", "Utata", "http://www.flickr.com/groups/utata/");
    addCandy("candy_nav_menu_explore", "API Reference",
      "http://www.flickr.com/services/api/");
```

This script defines a function called addCandy() so that multiple links can easily be added. The addCandy() function uses XPath to find the menu with the specified ID and then appends a new link to the end of it.

You can see the script in operation in Figure A-11.

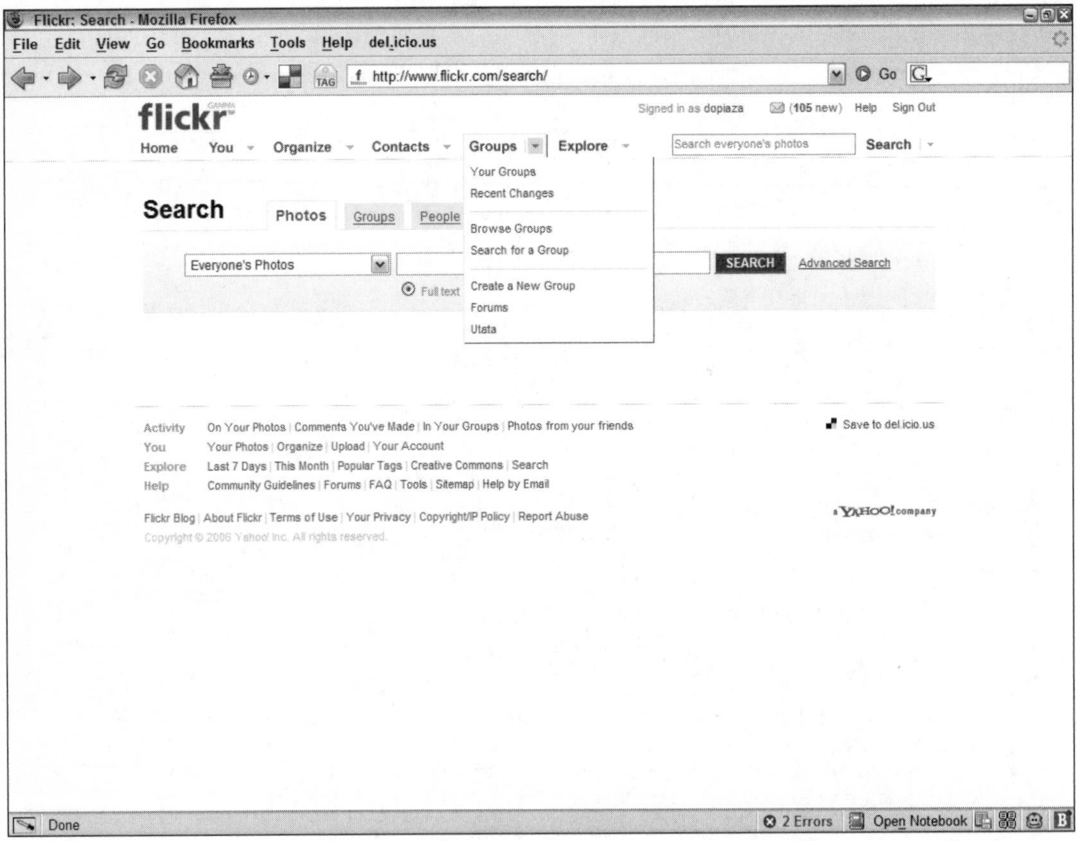

Figure A-11

Exercise 2

Here is the Jump to Page script with the modifications highlighted:

```
// ==UserScript==
// @name          Jump to Flickr Page Exercise
// @namespace     http://www.dopiaza.org/flickr/greasemonkey/
// @description   Jump to a specific Flickr page in a paginated set of pages.
// @include       http://www.flickr.com/*
// @include       http://flickr.com/*
// ==/UserScript==


var paginators = document.evaluate(
  "//div[@class='Paginator']",
  document,
  null,
  XPathResult.UNORDERED_NODE_SNAPSHOT_TYPE,
  null);

for (var i = 0; i < paginators.snapshotLength; i++)
{
  var paginator = paginators.snapshotItem(i);

  // Find the max page number
  var anchors = paginator.getElementsByTagName('A');

  // find the number of the last page linked
  var lastPageNum = 1;
  for (var j = 0; j < anchors.length; j++)
  {
    var children = anchors[j].childNodes;
    if (children.length > 0)
    {
      var child = children[0];
      if (child.nodeType == 3) // Text Node
      {
        var pageVal = child.nodeValue;
        if (!isNaN(pageVal))
        {
          lastPageNum = Math.max(lastPageNum, parseInt(pageVal));
        }
      }
    }
  }

  // Place the text box immediately before the "next" item, which is the last
  // non-text element in the paginator (There is whitespace after it, which shows
  // up as a text node. It may be an anchor or a span, depending on whether we are
  // at the last page or not.
  var paginatorChildren = paginator.childNodes;

  var nextElement;
  for (var j = paginatorChildren.length - 1; j >= 0; j--)
  {
```

```
      if (paginatorChildren[j].nodeType == 1) // Element Node
      {
        nextElement = paginatorChildren[j];
        break;
      }
   }

   var inputBox = document.createElement('input');
   inputBox.setAttribute("type", "text");
   inputBox.setAttribute("size", "3");

   paginator.insertBefore(inputBox, nextElement);

   inputBox.addEventListener('keypress', function(evt)
   {
     var keyVal = evt.which;
     var key = String.fromCharCode(keyVal);

     if (key == '\r')
     {
       var pageNum = evt.target.value;
       if (pageNum <= 0 || pageNum > lastPageNum)
       {
         evt.target.value = "";
         evt.preventDefault();
       }
       else
       {
         // So, where are we now?
         var loc = window.location.href;
         // Remove any existing page number
         loc = loc.replace(/page\d+(\/)?$/, '');
         // Append the new page number
         loc += 'page' + pageNum + '/';
         // And go to the new page
         window.location.href = loc;
       }
     }
     else
     {
       if (key != '\b' && isNaN(key))
       {
         evt.preventDefault();
       }
     }
   }, true);
}
```

The script calculates the last page number by getting a list of all the <a> tags within the paginator and identifying which of those contains a text node that is a valid number (a page number). The highest value found is then stored away for reference later.

When the return key is pressed, the entered page number is then checked to see whether it is within the valid range — if not, the event is discarded and the text box cleared.

Note that this approach introduces an interesting quirk if you are already on the last page of the set. The page you are currently viewing is not a hyperlink in the paginator; it's a <span> element. This means that the page number of the current page will not be returned in the list of <a> elements. This is usually of no consequence, unless you happen to be viewing the very last page in the set. In this case, the lastPageNum value calculated will actually be one less than the actual last page number. The effect of this is that when you are viewing the last page in a set, the largest number you can enter into the paginator is that of the penultimate page — but as you are already viewing the last page anyway, that doesn't seem to be such a great hardship.

Chapter 10

Exercise 1

The Perl mantra is "There's more than one way to do it," and that's certainly the case here. Here are a few suggestions, however, as to how you could achieve some of the things suggested in the exercise.

To use a background image, you need to produce a graphic in an appropriate form. ImageMagick can read many common formats, such as JPEG and PNG. Once you have your graphic, you need only read it into the ImageMagick object in which you are building the badge. In the example script in this chapter, the badge image was initialized to a plain white background:

```
$image = Image::Magick->new;
$image->Set(size=>'225x225');
$image->ReadImage('xc:white');
```

To use a background image, set the size to be that of the image and read in from the image filename:

```
$image = Image::Magick->new;
$image->Set(size=>'300x250');
$image->ReadImage('/path/to/your/image.jpg');
```

To use your own photos, simply replace the call to flickr.groups.pools.getPhotos:

```
my $response = $flickr->execute_method('flickr.groups.pools.getPhotos',
    {
      'group_id' => $groupNSID,
      'per_page' => $photosCount,
      'page' => 1,
    });
```

with a call to flickr.photos.search:

```
my $response = $flickr->execute_method('flickr.photos.search',
    {
      'user_id' => 'YOUR-NSID-ID',
      'per_page' => $photosCount,
      'page' => 1,
    });
```

If you want to choose what you regard as your best photos, you can either put these photos into a photo-set and retrieve that list with `flickr.photosets.getPhotos`, or you can simply tag each photo with a tag such as `badge_display` and add that tag to the call to `flickr.photos.search`:

```perl
my $response = $flickr->execute_method('flickr.photos.search',
  {
    'user_id' => 'YOUR-NSID-ID',
    'tags' => 'badge_display',
    'per_page' => $photosCount,
    'page' => 1,
  });
```

To resize your images, it is always better to start with a larger image and shrink it than to increase the size of a smaller image. The square image on Flickr is only 75 pixels to a side, so if you need a larger square image you should download one of the larger sizes and crop it to a square before reducing it to the correct size. The following Perl subroutine shows how to take a larger image and crop and resize it to a square. It takes two parameters — `$image` is the `Image::Magick` object containing the larger image (for example, the medium image from Flickr), and `$n` is the desired width.

```perl
sub cropToSquare
{
    my ($image, $n) = @_;
    ($origWidth, $origHeight) = $image->Get('width', 'height');

    $square = Image::Magick->new;
    $square->Set(size => $origWidth . 'x' . $origHeight);
    $square->ReadImage('xc:white');
    $square->Composite(image => $image, compose => 'Copy', x => 0, y => 0);

    $w = $n;
    $h = $n;
    $x = 0;
    $y = 0;
    if ($origWidth > $origHeight)
    {
        $w = floor($h * $origWidth/$origHeight);
        $x = floor(($w - $n)/2);
    }
    else
    {
        $h = floor($w * $origHeight/$origWidth);
        $y = floor(($h - $n)/2);
    }

    $square->Resize(geometry =>  $w . 'x' . $h . '!');
    $square->Crop(geometry =>  $n . 'x' . $n . "+$x+$y");

    return $square;
}
```

The subroutine copies the image into a new `Image::Magick` object and calculates how to resize the image so that the shortest side is the required crop size. It then crops in the longer dimension to produce a square image.

As the `cropToSquare` subroutine makes use of the `floor` function, you will also need to add a new package reference to the start of the file:

```
#!/usr/bin/perl
```

```
use POSIX;
use FileHandle;
use Image::Magick;
use Flickr::API;
use XML::Parser::Lite::Tree::XPath;
use Getopt::Std;


...
```

Chapter 11

Exercise 1

The solution presented here simply looks for consecutive words that each begin with a capital letter and then presents them as a single keyword. The individual words are also still added to the keywords list.

In `NewsItem.php`, modify the `extractKeywords` method to add the two new lines shown below:

```
function extractKeywords($data)
{
  $words = array();

  $names = $this->findFullNames($data);
  $words = array_merge($words, $names);

  foreach ($data as $word)
  {
    if (!in_array(strtolower($word), $words) && $this->isGoodKeyword($word))
    {
      array_push($words, strtolower($word));
    }

    if (count($words) >= $this->maxKeywords)
    {
      break;
    }
  }

  return $words;
}
```

Then create a new method called `findFullNames`:

```
function findFullNames($data)
{
  $names = array();
  $currentName = "";
```

```
    $count = 0;
    foreach ($data as $word)
    {
      $firstLetter = substr($word, 0, 1);
      if ($firstLetter == strtoupper ($firstLetter))
      {
        // This word begins with an upper case letter
        $currentName .= $word . " ";
        $count++;
      }
      else
      {
        // This word does not begin with an upper case letter
        if ($count > 1)
        {
          // But we have already found a run of two or more capitalized words
          array_push($names, trim($currentName));
        }

        $currentName = "";
        $count = 0;
      }
    }

    return $names;
}
```

This solution can spot names in many contexts, and produces better search results than the original code, but it is still fooled when it comes up against phrases such as "Microsoft's Bill Gates" — it treats this as "Microsoft Bill Gates." Experiment with different strategies for finding keywords and see which ones work best.

Chapter 12

Exercise 1

This solution assumes that the `<item>` entries with the longest `<nearestpermalink>` URLs will be the most specific links.

Modify the `showBlogs` function as shown below (the changed lines are highlighted):

```
// Retrieve the list of blogs and display them
function showBlogs(blogContainer, message)
{
  var url = 'http://api.technorati.com/cosmos';
  var params = 'key=' + technoratiAPIKey + '&url=' + normalizeUrl() + '&limit=100';

  GM_xmlhttpRequest(
  {
    method: "GET",
    url: url + "?" + params,
    headers:
    {
      "User-Agent": "Flickr-Technorati-Query"
```

```
    },
    onload: function(response)
    {
      blogContainer.removeChild(message);
      var parser = new unsafeWindow.DOMParser();
      var dom = parser.parseFromString(response.responseText, "application/xml");

      var errors = dom.getElementsByTagName('error');
      if (errors.length > 0)
      {
        var p = document.createElement('p');
        p.appendChild(document.createTextNode('Error: ' +
errors[0].firstChild.nodeValue));
        styleElement(p);
        blogContainer.appendChild(p);
      }
      else
      {
        var items = dom.getElementsByTagName('item');
        var filteredItems = filterItems(items);
        if (filteredItems.length > 0)
        {
          var list = document.createElement('ul');
          for (var i = 0; i < filteredItems.length; i++)
          {
            addBlog(list, filteredItems[i]);
          }
          blogContainer.appendChild(list);
        }
        else
        {
          var p = document.createElement('p');
          p.appendChild(document.createTextNode('No blogs found'));
          styleElement(p);
          blogContainer.appendChild(p);
        }
      }
      addTechnoratiCredit(blogContainer);
    },
    onerror: function(response)
    {
      var p = document.createElement('p');
      p.appendChild(document.createTextNode('There was an error retrieving blog
information'));
      styleElement(p);
      blogContainer.appendChild(p);
    }
  });
}
```

Create a new function, `filterItems`:

```
// Filter out the items we want to display
function filterItems(items)
{
```

```
      var filteredItems = new Array();

   for (var i = 0; i < items.length; i++)
   {
     var processed = false;
     var itemName = items[i].getElementsByTagName('name')[0].firstChild.nodeValue;

      // Do we have this blog name in the list yet?
      for (var j = 0; j < filteredItems.length; j++)
      {
        var filteredItemName =
filteredItems[j].getElementsByTagName('name')[0].firstChild.nodeValue;
        if (itemName == filteredItemName)
        {
          // We have a match. Let's compare the URLs
          var itemUrl =
items[i].getElementsByTagName('nearestpermalink')[0].firstChild.nodeValue;
          var filteredItemUrl =
filteredItems[j].getElementsByTagName('nearestpermalink')[0].firstChild.nodeValue;
          // We'll assume here that the longest URL is the most specific
          if (itemUrl.length > filteredItemUrl.length)
          {
            // The new item has a longer URL, so replace the old one.
            filteredItems[j] = items[i];
          }
          processed = true;
          break;
        }
      }

      if (!processed)
      {
        // We haven't encountered this one before, so append it to the list
        filteredItems.push(items[i]);
      }
   }
   return filteredItems;
}
```

Chapter 13

Exercise 1

When the list of photos is generated by the JavaScript on the client, it preserves the order of the photos from the XML, so you can simply sort the photos in `geo.php` before the XML is constructed:

```php
<?php

include (dirname(__FILE__) . '/../lib/gallery.php');

function sortPhotosByTitle($a, $b)
{
  return strcasecmp($a['title'], $b['title']);
```

```
    }

    $gallery = new FlickrGallery();

    $photos = $gallery->getWithGeoData();

    if (is_array($photos))
    {
      usort($photos, "sortPhotosByTitle");
    }

    header ("Content-Type: text/xml");

    echo "<?xml version=\"1.0\"?>\n";
    echo "<photos>\n";
    if (is_array($photos))
    {
      foreach ($photos as $p)
      {
        echo "<photo " .
          "id=\"" . $p['id'] . "\" " .
          "latitude=\"" . $p['latitude'] . "\" " .
          "longitude=\"" . $p['longitude'] . "\" " .
          "title=\"" . htmlspecialchars($p['title']) . "\" " .
          " />\n";
      }
    }
    echo "</photos>";
    ?>
```

Here you use PHP's `usort` function — this enables you to specify a custom function to compare two items in the array to be sorted. The `sortPhotosByTitle` function performs a case-insensitive compare on the `title` elements of the photo items.

Exercise 2

When the map is constructed, you can obtain the coordinates of the area covered by the map using the Google Maps API method `getBounds()`. The `doMap()` function in `map.js` is modified to use the result of calling `getBounds()` to calculate the coordinates for the bounding box:

```
function doMap()
{
  var map = new GMap2(document.getElementById("map"));
  map.addControl(new GLargeMapControl());
  map.addControl(new GMapTypeControl());

  // Add your new starting center point and zoom level here
  map.setCenter(new GLatLng(51.226238,-3.823586), 13);

  var bounds = map.getBounds();
  var southWest = bounds.getSouthWest();
  var northEast = bounds.getNorthEast();

  var s = "swlat=" + southWest.lat()
```

```
                 + "&swlng=" + southWest.lng()
                 + "&nelat="  + northEast.lat()
                 + "&nelng=" + northEast.lng();

      GDownloadUrl("geo.php?" + s, function(data, responseCode)
      {
        var xml = GXml.parse(data);
        var photos = xml.documentElement.getElementsByTagName("photo");

        ...

      });
    }
```

geo.php is modified to pass the bounding box coordinates into FlickrGallery:

```php
<?php

include (dirname(__FILE__) . '/../lib/gallery.php');

function sortPhotosByTitle($a, $b)
{
  return strcasecmp($a['title'], $b['title']);
}

$gallery = new FlickrGallery();

$swlat = $_REQUEST['swlat'];
$swlng = $_REQUEST['swlng'];
$nelat = $_REQUEST['nelat'];
$nelng = $_REQUEST['nelng'];

$bbox = NULL;

if (!empty($swlat) && !empty($swlng) && !empty($nelat) && !empty($nelng))
{
  $bbox = "$swlng, $swlat, $nelng, $nelat";
}

$photos = $gallery->getWithGeoData($bbox);
if (is_array($photos))
{
  usort($photos, "sortPhotosByTitle");
}

header ("Content-Type: text/xml");

echo "<?xml version=\"1.0\"?>\n";
echo "<photos>\n";
if (is_array($photos))
{
  foreach ($photos as $p)
  {
    echo "<photo " .
```

```
            "id=\"" . $p['id'] . "\" " .
            "latitude=\"" . $p['latitude'] . "\" " .
            "longitude=\"" . $p['longitude'] . "\" " .
            "title=\"" . htmlspecialchars($p['title']) . "\" " .
            " />\n";
    }
  }
  echo "</photos>";
  ?>
```

Finally, the `getWithGeoData()` method in `FlickrGallery.php` is modified to accept an optional bounding box parameter:

```php
<?php

class FlickrGallery extends FlickrAuthenticator
{
  ...

  function getWithGeoData($bbox = NULL)
  {
    if ($bbox == NULL)
    {
      $bbox = '-180, -90, 180, 90';
    }

    $args = array(
      'user_id' => $this->nsid,
      'sort' => 'interestingness-desc',
      'bbox' => $bbox,
      'extras' => 'geo',
      'per_page' => 500,
      );

    $p = $this->flickr->photos_search($args);
    if ($this->flickr->getErrorCode())
    {
      echo ("Error fetching photos with GeoData: "
        . $this->flickr->getErrorMsg());
    }

    return $p['photo'];
  }

}
?>
```

If you would like to experiment further with the Google Maps API, you could continue to improve this mashup in many ways. For example, the current solution will only load markers for photos within the original bounding box. When the user drags the map, photos outside the original area are not shown. The Google Maps API fires a `moveend` event when the map is dragged and a `zoomend` event when the zoom level has changed, so you can try adding event handlers for these events and then repeat the Flickr query to display a new set of markers for the area now covered by the repositioned map.

Chapter 14

Exercise 1

You need to change the code in the `FlickrGallery` class for `getNextPhoto()` and `getPreviousPhoto()`. Each of these should now take a new optional parameter, the Smart Set key:

```php
function getNextPhoto($photo, $key = NULL)
{
  $nextPhoto = NULL;
  $sql = "";

  if ($this->useDB)
  {
    if (empty($key))
    {
      // Get from recent photos
      $date = $photo['dateupload'];
      $sql = "select * from photo"
        . " where photo_date_upload > $date"
          . " order by photo_date_upload limit 1";
    }
    else
    {
      // Get from smart set
      // First find index for current photo
      $photoId = $photo['id'];
      $indexSql = "select sset_index from smartset "
        . " where sset_key = '" . mysql_escape_string($key) . "'"
        . " and sset_photo_id = '$photoId'";
      $res = mysql_query($indexSql, $this->getConnection())
        or die("Invalid query: " . $indexSql);

      if ($row = mysql_fetch_array($res))
      {
        $index = $row[0];

        $sql = "select * from smartset, photo"
          . " where sset_photo_id = photo_id"
          . " and sset_key = '" . mysql_escape_string($key) . "'"
          . " and sset_index > $index"
          . " order by sset_index limit 1";
      }
    }

    if (!empty($sql))
    {
      $res = mysql_query($sql, $this->getConnection())
        or die("Invalid query: " . $sql);
      if ($row = mysql_fetch_assoc($res))
      {
        $nextPhoto = $this->buildPhotoFromRow($row);
      }
```

```
      }
  }

  return $nextPhoto;
}

function getPreviousPhoto($photo, $key = NULL)
{
  $prevPhoto = NULL;
  $sql = "";

  if ($this->useDB)
  {
    if (empty($key))
    {
      // Get from recent photos
      $date = $photo['dateupload'];
      $sql = "select * from photo"
        . " where photo_date_upload < $date"
        . " order by photo_date_upload desc limit 1";
    }
    else
    {
      // Get from smart set
      // First find index for current photo
      $photoId = $photo['id'];
      $indexSql = "select sset_index from smartset "
        . " where sset_key = '" . mysql_escape_string($key) . "'"
        . " and sset_photo_id = '$photoId'";
      $res = mysql_query($indexSql, $this->getConnection())
        or die("Invalid query: " . $indexSql);
      if ($row = mysql_fetch_array($res))
      {
        $index = $row[0];

        $sql = "select * from smartset, photo"
          . " where sset_photo_id = photo_id"
          . " and sset_key = '" . mysql_escape_string($key) . "'"
          . " and sset_index < $index"
          . " order by sset_index desc limit 1";
      }
    }

    if (!empty($sql))
    {
      $res = mysql_query($sql, $this->getConnection())
        or die("Invalid query: " . $sql);
      if ($row = mysql_fetch_assoc($res))
      {
        $prevPhoto = $this->buildPhotoFromRow($row);
      }
    }
```

```php
    }

    return $prevPhoto;
}
```

In each case, if no Smart Set key is passed in, the function behaves exactly as before, retrieving the next or previous photo from the photostream, as appropriate. If a Smart Set key is passed in, a different piece of SQL is generated.

First of all, the sset_index for the current photo is obtained — this is the position in the Smart Set of the photo. Then this is used to generate a new query that will find the next highest or next lowest index as appropriate.

photo.php is modified to take an extra optional parameter, key, in the query string. This key is then passed into getPreviousPhoto() and getNextPhoto(). The Next and Previous links themselves are also modified to ensure that the key parameter is passed on as the user moves from photo to photo:

```php
<?php include (dirname(__FILE__) . '/../lib/gallery.php') ?>
<!DOCTYPE html PUBLIC "-//W3C//DTD XHTML 1.0 Transitional//EN"
   "http://www.w3.org/TR/xhtml1/DTD/xhtml1-transitional.dtd">
<html xmlns="http://www.w3.org/1999/xhtml">
<head>
   <title>Flickr Mashups</title>
   <link href="../css/main.css" rel="stylesheet" type="text/css" />
   <link href="../css/gallery.css" rel="stylesheet" type="text/css" />
   <script type="text/javascript" src="../lib/js/prototype.js"></script>
   <script type="text/javascript" src="../lib/js/gallery.js"></script>
</head>
<body>
<?php
   $gallery = new FlickrGallery();
   $id = $_REQUEST['id'];
   $key = $_REQUEST['key'];
   if (!empty($id))
   {
      $info = $gallery->getPhotoInfo($id);
      $title = $info['title'];
      $img = 'http://static.flickr.com/' . $info['server'] . '/' . $info['id']
         . '_' . $info['secret'] . '.jpg';
      $photoPage = 'http://www.flickr.com/photos/' . $info['owner']['nsid']
         . '/' . $id . '/';

      $photo = $gallery->getPhoto($id);
      $prev = $gallery->getPreviousPhoto($photo, $key);
      $next = $gallery->getNextPhoto($photo, $key);
   }
?>
<?php include ('header.php') ?>
<?php include ('navigation.php') ?>
<div class="photo-display">
   <p class="photo-title"><?php echo $title ?></p>
   <p class="photo-image"><a href="<?php echo $photoPage ?>">
      <img src="<?php echo $img ?>" alt="<?php echo $title ?>"
         title="<?php echo $title ?>" /></a>
   </p>
```

```
    <div class="photo-nav">
      <div class="photo-nav-prev">
      <?php
      if (empty($prev))
      {
      ?> <?php
      }
      else
      {
      ?><a href="photo.php?id=<?php echo $prev['id'] ?>&key=<?php echo $key ?>">&lt;
Previous</a><?php
      }
      ?>
      </div>
      <div class="photo-nav-next">
      <?php
      if (empty($next))
      {
      ?> <?php
      }
      else
      {
      ?><a href="photo.php?id=<?php echo $next['id'] ?>&key=<?php echo $key ?>">Next
&gt;</a><?php
      }
      ?>
      </div>
    </div>
    <div id="photo-info-<?php echo $id ?>" class="photo-more">
    <a href="#" onclick="displayInfo(<?php echo $id ?>); return false;">
      More info...</a>
    </div>
  </div>
  </body>
  </html>
```

Finally, `smartset.php` is modified to ensure that the key for the Smart Set is passed in as a parameter to the `photo.php` page:

```
<?php include (dirname(__FILE__) . '/../lib/gallery.php') ?>
<!DOCTYPE html PUBLIC "-//W3C//DTD XHTML 1.0 Transitional//EN"
  "http://www.w3.org/TR/xhtml1/DTD/xhtml1-transitional.dtd">
<html xmlns="http://www.w3.org/1999/xhtml">
<head>
  <title>Flickr Mashups</title>
  <link href="../css/main.css" rel="stylesheet" type="text/css" />
  <link href="../css/gallery.css" rel="stylesheet" type="text/css" />
</head>
<body>
<?php
  gallery = new FlickrGallery();
?>
<?php include ('header.php') ?>
<?php include ('navigation.php') ?>
<ul class="photo-set">
```

```php
<?php
  $setTitle = $_REQUEST['title'];
  $n = $_REQUEST['n'];
  $tags = $_REQUEST['tags'];
  $tagMode = $_REQUEST['tagMode'];
  $sort = $_REQUEST['sort'];
  $smartSetPhotos = $gallery->getSmartSet($n, $tags, $tagMode, $sort);
  $key = $gallery->getSmartSetKey($tags, $tagMode, $sort);
?>
<h1><?php echo $setTitle ?></h1>
<?php
  foreach ($smartSetPhotos as $photo)
  {
    $title = $photo['title'];
    $img = 'http://static.flickr.com/' . $photo['server'] . '/' . $photo['id'] .
'_' . $photo['secret'] . '_s.jpg'
?>
  <li><a href="photo.php?id=<?php echo $photo['id'] ?>&key=<?php echo $key ?>"><img
src="<?php echo $img ?>" alt="<?php echo $title ?>" title="<?php echo $title ?>"
/></a></li>
<?php
  }
?>
</ul>
</body>
</html>
```

Flickr API Methods

The following sections list the methods to be found in the different sections of the Flickr API, together with a brief description. New methods are regularly being added, so be sure to check `http://www.flickr.com/services/api/` for an up-to-date list.

Authentication

In order to perform certain API calls, Flickr needs to identify who you are in order to establish whether you have permission to perform the operation. These calls typically return private information or enable updates to be made to information stored on Flickr. Authentication is covered in detail in Chapter 7.

flickr.auth.checkToken	Get the credentials for an authentication token
flickr.auth.getFrob	Get a frob to use during authentication
flickr.auth.getFullToken	Get a full authentication token for a mini-token
flickr.auth.getToken	Get the authentication token for a frob

Blogs

You cannot set up a new blog via the API.

flickr.blogs.getList	Get the list of configured blogs for the calling user
flickr.blogs.postPhoto	Post a photo to the calling user's blog

Contacts

There is currently no way to add, remove, or modify contacts via the API.

flickr.contacts.getList	Get the full list of contacts for the calling user
flickr.contacts.getPublicList	Get the public list of contacts for a user

Favorites

flickr.favorites.add	Add a photo to the calling user's list of favorites
flickr.favorites.getList	Get a list of favorite photos for a user
flickr.favorites.getPublicList	Get the list of publicly visible photos for a user
flickr.favorites.remove	Remove a photo from the calling user's list of favorites

Groups

Although the API offers limited functionality for finding groups, it is not currently possible to browse or post to group discussions via the API.

flickr.groups.browse	Browse the group category tree
flickr.groups.getInfo	Get information about a group
flickr.groups.search	Search for groups

Group Pools

flickr.groups.pools.add	Add a photo to a group's pool
flickr.groups.pools.getContext	Get the next and previous photos in a group pool for a photo
flickr.groups.pools.getGroups	Get the list of groups to which the calling user can add photos
flickr.groups.pools.getPhotos	Get a list of photos found in a group pool
flickr.groups.pools.remove	Remove a photo from a group pool

Interestingness

flickr.interestingness.getList   Get the list of interesting photos for a given date

People

flickr.people.findByEmail	Get a user's NSID, given their e-mail address
flickr.people.findByUsername	Get a user's NSID, given their username
flickr.people.getInfo	Get information about a user
flickr.people.getPublicGroups	Return the list of public groups that a user is a member of
flickr.people.getPublicPhotos	Get the list of public photos for a user
flickr.people.getUploadStatus	Get remaining upload bandwidth and maximum file size for the calling user

Photos

flickr.photos.addTags	Add tags to a photo
flickr.photos.delete	Delete a photo from Flickr
flickr.photos.getAllContexts	Get a list of sets and group pools containing the photo
flickr.photos.getContactsPhotos	Get a list of recent photos from a contact
flickr.photos.getContactsPublicPhotos	Get a list of recent public photos from a contact
flickr.photos.getContext	Get the next and previous photos in the owner's photostream
flickr.photos.getCounts	Get a list of photo counts for specified upload date ranges
flickr.photos.getExif	Get a list of the EXIF tags stored within a photo
flickr.photos.getInfo	Get detailed information about a photo
flickr.photos.getNotInSet	Get a list of your photos that are not in any sets
flickr.photos.getPerms	Get the privacy and metadata permissions for a photo
flickr.photos.getRecent	Get a list of recently uploaded public photos
flickr.photos.getSizes	Get the available sizes for a photo

flickr.photos.getUntagged	Get a list of your photos that do not have any tags
flickr.photos.getWithGeoData	Get a list of your photos that have geodata attached
flickr.photos.getWithoutGeoData	Get a list of your photos that do not have geodata attached
flickr.photos.recentlyUpdated	Get a list of your photos that have been recently created or modified (includes being commented on)
flickr.photos.removeTag	Remove a tag from a photo
flickr.photos.search	Search for photos matching the specified criteria
flickr.photos.setDates	Set date information for a photo
flickr.photos.setMeta	Set the title and description for a photo
flickr.photos.setPerms	Set the privacy and metadata permissions for a photo
flickr.photos.setTags	Set the complete list of tags for a photo

Photo Comments

flickr.photos.comments.addComment	Add a comment to a photo
flickr.photos.comments.deleteComment	Delete a comment from a photo
flickr.photos.comments.editComment	Edit a comment on a photo
flickr.photos.comments.getList	Get the comments for a photo

Photo Licenses

flickr.photos.licenses.getInfo	Get the list of available photo licenses
flickr.photos.licenses.setLicense	Set the license for a photo

Photo Notes

To retrieve a list of notes for a photo, use the `flickr.photos.getInfo` *method.*

flickr.photos.notes.add	Add a note to a photo
flickr.photos.notes.delete	Delete a note from a photo
flickr.photos.notes.edit	Edit an existing note on a photo

Photo Transforms

flickr.photos.transform.rotate   Rotate a photo

Photo Upload

Photo uploads are covered in detail in Chapter 8.

flickr.photos.upload.checkTickets   Check the progress of photos being uploaded

Photosets

flickr.photosets.addPhoto   Add a photo to the end of an existing photoset

flickr.photosets.create   Create a new photoset for the calling user

flickr.photosets.delete   Delete a photoset

flickr.photosets.editMeta   Modify the title and description for a photoset

flickr.photosets.editPhotos   Set the complete list of photos and the primary photo in the photoset

flickr.photosets.getContext   Get the next and previous photos in a set for a photo

flickr.photosets.getInfo   Get information about a photoset

flickr.photosets.getList   Get the list of photosets for a user

flickr.photosets.getPhotos   Get the list of photos in a set

flickr.photosets.orderSets   Set the order of photosets for the calling user

flickr.photosets.removePhoto   Remove a photo from a photoset

Photoset Comments

flickr.photosets.comments.addComment   Add a comment to a photoset

flickr.photosets.comments.deleteComment   Delete a comment from a photoset

flickr.photosets.comments.editComment   Edit a comment on a photoset

flickr.photosets.comments.getList   Get the comments for a photoset

Reflection

flickr.reflection.getMethodInfo — Get information for a Flickr API method

flickr.reflection.getMethods — Get a list of available Flickr API methods

Tags

Methods to add and remove tags from photos are found in the Photos section.

flickr.tags.getHotList — Get a list of the hot tags for the current day or week

flickr.tags.getListPhoto — Get the tag list for a given photo

flickr.tags.getListUser — Get the tag list for a given user

flickr.tags.getListUserPopular — Get the popular tags for a given user

flickr.tags.getListUserRaw — Get the list of raw tags for the calling user

flickr.tags.getRelated — Get a list of related tags for a given tag

Test

flickr.test.echo — Echo all parameters back in the response

flickr.test.login — Check if the caller is logged in and return their username

flickr.test.null — Do nothing

URLs

flickr.urls.getGroup — Get the URL for a group's page

flickr.urls.getUserPhotos — Get the URL for a user's photostream

flickr.urls.getUserProfile — Get the URL for a user's profile

flickr.urls.lookupGroup — Get the NSID for a group, given its URL

flickr.urls.lookupUser — Get the NSID for a user, given their URL

Response Data Structures

This appendix describes some of the main data structures you will see returned from the various Flickr API methods. The Flickr API is regularly being updated, so be sure to check `http://www.flickr.com/services/api/` for the latest details.

Photos

The main kind of object that most people deal with on Flickr is, rather unsurprisingly, the photo. Each photo stored on Flickr has a number of key pieces of data associated with it. Note that not all API methods return all pieces of data. You should check the online API specification at `http://www.flickr.com/services/api/` to see what data are returned for each method call.

The photo can be returned in either summary or detailed format, depending on the API method used. Where the API returns a list of photos, each photo appears in summary form and usually takes the following format:

```
<photo id="160244291" owner="50317659@N00" secret="bd2ff55b61" server="70"
title="Wellington" ispublic="1" isfriend="0" isfamily="0"/>
```

The `flickr.photos.getInfo` method returns a more detailed view of the photo and looks something like this:

```
<photo id="160244291" secret="bd2ff55b61" server="70"
dateuploaded="1149452862"
isfavorite="0" license="2" rotation="0" originalformat="jpg">
    <owner nsid="50317659@N00" username="dopiaza" realname="David Wilkinson"
location="Northamptonshire, United Kingdom"/>
    <title>Wellington</title>
    <description>[DSC_1787]</description>
    <visibility ispublic="1" isfriend="0" isfamily="0"/>
    <dates posted="1149452862" taken="2006-06-04 14:07:19"
takengranularity="0"
lastupdate="1149942415"/>
    <editability cancomment="0" canaddmeta="0"/>
```

```
        <comments>3</comments>
        <notes>
            <note id="72157594161399287" author="50317659@N00" authorname="dopiaza"
x="313" y="144" w="50" h="50">Wellington had his eye on the camera...</note>
        </notes>
        <tags>
            <tag id="296457-160244291-16439" author="50317659@N00"
raw="wellington">wellington</tag>
            <tag id="296457-160244291-8427" author="50317659@N00"
raw="parrot">parrot</tag>
            <tag id="296457-160244291-594" author="50317659@N00" raw="bird">bird</tag>
            <tag id="296457-160244291-952" author="50317659@N00"
raw="animal">animal</tag>
            <tag id="296457-160244291-2476" author="50317659@N00" raw="big
bird">bigbird</tag>
        </tags>
        <urls>
            <url type="photopage">http://www.flickr.com/photos/dopiaza/160244291/</url>
        </urls>
</photo>
```

id

The id is returned as an attribute of the photo tag. It is the key piece of data that identifies each photo and each ID is unique across the whole of Flickr. Currently, IDs are allocated to photos sequentially upon upload, so you might think that you can identify when photos were uploaded relative to each other by comparing the photo IDs. You should not rely on this, though—Flickr staff have suggested that they may at some point start allocating photo ids nonsequentially.

Given that a photo ID uniquely identifies a single photo on Flickr, you would expect it to be simple to view any photo in your browser once you have the photo ID. Unfortunately, it's not quite that simple. The way Flickr photo page URLs are constructed means that you also need to know the owner of the photo. For example, the URL of the photo page for photo ID 160244291 is found here:

```
http://www.flickr.com/photos/dopiaza/160244291/
```

Without knowing that the owner of the photo is dopiaza, it is impossible to construct that URL. A quick and easy way to find the photo page is by going via the View All Sizes page. If you go to any of your photo pages on Flickr and click the All Sizes button above the photo, you get taken to a page that has a URL of the following form:

```
http://www.flickr.com/photo_zoom.gne?id=PHOTO-ID&size=1
```

Here, PHOTO-ID is the ID of the photo you are viewing. You can change this photo ID to that of any photo on Flickr, and so long as you have permission to view that photo, you will be shown it. So enter this URL using the ID of the photo you are interested in (you can ignore the size attribute):

```
http://www.flickr.com/photo_zoom.gne?id=160244291
```

You will be shown the photo's All Sizes page. This page has a handy "Back to the Flickr photo page" link to take you to the photo's main page. Note that this technique won't work if the photo is private, or if the owner of the photo has disabled downloads of their photos—it is, nevertheless, a useful trick to have up your sleeve.

owner

The owner is returned as an attribute of the photo tag when returned in summary format and contains the owner's Flickr NSID. This represents the account to which the photo was uploaded.

When the full photo details are retrieved, owner is a tag in its own right and has the following attributes:

nsid	The NSID of the owner
username	The screen name of the owner
realname	The real name of the owner, as set on the owner's profile
location	The location of the owner, as set on the owner's profile

secret

The photo secret is an attribute of the photo tag and is a hexadecimal number generated when a photo is uploaded to Flickr. This number is used to generate the URL that refers to the actual photo image itself. For more details of the photo URL, see the "Building URLs" section in Chapter 4.

server

The photo server is an attribute of the photo tag, and is a numeric value that identifies the server machine the image is stored on. This number is used to generate the URL that refers to the actual photo image itself. For more details of the photo URL, see the "Building URLs" section in Chapter 4.

title

When retrieved in summary format, title is an attribute of the photo tag. In the detailed format, title is a separate tag. In each case, it refers to the title of the photo as displayed on Flickr. On upload, the title is set based on the IPTC data embedded within the photo. If no IPTC title is set within the photo, the filename is used as the title.

description

The description tag is available only in the detailed photo format. It refers to the description of the photo as it is displayed on Flickr. On upload, the description is set based on the IPTC data embedded within the photo. If no IPTC description is set within the photo, the description field is left blank.

ispublic

In summary format ispublic is an attribute of the photo tag, but in detailed format it is an attribute of the visibility tag. It is set to 1 when the photo permissions are set to public; otherwise it is set to 0.

isfamily

In summary form, isfamily is an attribute of the photo tag, but in detailed form it is an attribute of the visibility tag. It is set to 1 when the photo permissions are set to private and visible to family; otherwise it is set to 0.

isfriend

In summary form isfriend is an attribute of the photo tag, but in detailed form it is an attribute of the visibility tag. It is set to 1 when the photo permissions are set to private and visible to friends; otherwise it is set to 0.

isfavorite

isfavorite is returned as an attribute of the photo tag and is relevant only when you are making an authenticated call. It is set to 1 if the authenticated user has marked this photo as a favorite; otherwise it is set to 0.

license

The license is returned as an attribute of the photo tag in detailed format and indicates which copyright license applies to the photo. It has a numeric value — you can get the list of available licenses and their associated values by using the flickr.photos.licenses.getInfo API method.

rotation

The rotation is returned as an attribute of the photo tag in detailed format and is set if the owner of the photo has used Flickr's rotate feature. It contains the number of degrees clockwise that the photo is rotated relative to the original.

originalformat

The originalformat is returned as an attribute of the photo tag in detailed format and indicates the format in which the original file was uploaded. Valid values are jpg, tif, and png.

dates

The dates tag is returned in detailed format and contains the following attributes, which define various dates:

posted	The date and time the photo was posted to Flickr
taken	The date and time the photo was taken
lastupdate	The date and time that the photo or any of its metadata, such as tags, comments, etc. were modified

Flickr passes dates around in two different formats, depending on the type of date being referred to. The *date posted* and *last update* dates are both represented as Unix timestamps. These are unsigned integers and represent the number of seconds since 00:00 on January first, 1970 GMT. Note that these timestamps are always held as GMT and it is your application's responsibility to format them and adjust for the user's time zone.

Date taken is passed around in MySQL `datetime` format. This is a string of the form:

```
YYYY-MM-DD HH:mm:ss
```

So, 7:02pm on the tenth of June, 2006 would appear as

```
2006-06-10 19:02:00
```

When passing one of these dates in as a parameter to a method call, you don't need to pass in a full date. The earliest matching date is assumed. So using the date

```
2006-06
```

is exactly the same as using the date

```
2006-06-01 00:00:00
```

The date taken is always in the time zone of the owner of the photo and should always be displayed as such.

A `takengranularity` attribute is also returned. Granularity is defined as the accuracy to which it is known that the date is true. In other words, it is possible to know that a photo was taken sometime in June 2004, but not know the actual day or time. Granularity is a numeric value and can take any value between 0 and 10. Only three values are currently used and supported by Flickr, but to ensure future compatibility, Flickr recommends that applications built to accept any value between 0 and 10.

The values currently in use are as follows:

Value	Meaning	Example
0	Fully specified date and time	2006-06-10 19:02:00
4	Year and month only	2004-06
6	Year only	1976

editability

The `editability` tag has two attributes that describe what attributes of the photo the currently authenticated user can edit.

cancomment	Can add comments to the photo
canaddmeta	Can add notes and tags to the photo

comments

The `comments` tag contains a count of the number of comments that have been added to the photo.

notes

The notes tag lists the notes that have been added to the photo. The value of each individual note tag is the text of the note itself, and the tag has the following attributes:

id	The unique ID of the note
author	The NSID of the author of the note
authorname	The screen name of the author of the note
x	The x coordinate of the top left corner of the note
y	The y coordinate of the top left corner of the note
w	The width of the note in pixels
h	The height of the note in pixels

All note coordinates have their origin at the top-left corner of the photo, and sizes are measured in pixels based on Flickr's medium image size, which is 500 pixels on its longest side.

tags

The tags tag contains a list of all the tags that have been added to the photo. Flickr tags are stored in two formats: the *raw* form, which is the tag exactly as entered by the user, and the *clean* form, which is the value used during a tag search or for constructing URLs — this version has any spaces and non-alphanumeric characters (such as the hyphen and the underscore) removed.

The value of each tag tag (that is, the XML tag that represents the Flickr tag) is the clean tag. tag has the following attributes:

id	The unique ID of the tag/photo combination
author	The NSID of the author of the tag
raw	The raw form of the tag

urls

The urls tag contains a list of relevant URLs, each URL having its own url tag and distinguished by the type attribute. Currently, there is only one URL present — that of type photopage. This is the URL of the main photo page for the photo in question.

extras

A number of the photo API calls that return a summary list have an optional extras parameter. This parameter is a comma-separated list of values, each of which represents an extra attribute to be retrieved. This allows more useful information to be returned in a single API call.

Currently supported fields are `license`, `date_upload`, `date_taken`, `owner_name`, `icon_server`, `original_format`, `last_update`, and `geo`. They return the following attributes:

Extras field	Attributes returned
license	license
date_upload	dateupload
date_taken	datetaken and datetakengranularity
owner_name	ownername
icon_server	iconserver
original_format	originalformat
last_update	lastupdate
geo	latitude, longitude and accuracy

People

Three data structures are used to represent people in Flickr: `user`, `contact`, and `person`.

The first, `user`, is returned by `flickr.people.findByEmail` and `flickr.people.findByUsername`, and looks something like this:

```
<user id="50317659@N00" nsid="50317659@N00">
    <username>dopiaza</username>
</user>
```

People returned as contacts via methods such as `flickr.contacts.getPublicList` return a data structure like this:

```
<contact nsid="94272988@N00" username="MarkyBon" iconserver="1" ignored="0"
realname="Mark Menzies" friend="1" family="0"/>
```

The final data structure, `person`, is returned by the `flickr.people.getInfo` call and contains much more detail:

```
<person id="50317659@N00" nsid="50317659@N00" isadmin="0" ispro="1" iconserver="4"
gender="M" ignored="0" contact="0" friend="0" family="0" revcontact="0"
revfriend="0" revfamily="0">
    <username>dopiaza</username>
    <realname>David Wilkinson</realname>
    <mbox_sha1sum>bb000a20aca3da32bcacb609b7f7c23557f286cd</mbox_sha1sum>
    <location>Northamptonshire, United Kingdom</location>
    <photosurl>http://www.flickr.com/photos/dopiaza/</photosurl>
    <profileurl>http://www.flickr.com/people/dopiaza/</profileurl>
    <photos>
```

```
            <firstdatetaken>1976-01-01 00:00:00</firstdatetaken>
            <firstdate>1108051836</firstdate>
            <count>2362</count>
    </photos>
</person>
```

nsid

The nsid attribute can be found in all formats and contains the NSID of the requested user. You may notice that some tags also contain an id attribute, which also contains the NSID. So which one should you use? The online documentation at http://www.flickr.com/services/api/ lists only the nsid as being returned and makes no mention of the id attribute, so it would seem sensible to refer to the nsid attribute in your code.

isadmin

The isadmin attribute is undocumented, but is currently set to 1 if the requested user is a Flickr staff member. The use of this attribute may change over time, so you should not depend on its behavior until it is formally documented.

ispro

The ispro attribute is set to 1 if the requested user has a pro account and 0 if they have a free account.

iconserver

The iconserver attribute contains the ID of the server holding the user's buddy icon. See the "Building URLs" section in Chapter 4 for details on using this attribute.

gender

The gender attribute is returned only when you make an authenticated call for information about a user other than the authenticated user, and returns the gender of the requested user as specified in their profile. The possible values for this attribute are as follows:

M	Male
F	Female
O	Other
X	Rather not say

ignored

The ignored attribute is returned only when you make an authenticated call for information about a user other than the authenticated user, and is set to 1 if the requested user is on the authenticated user's list of blocked users. If the requested user is not blocked, the attribute is set to 0.

contact

The `contact` attribute is returned only when you make an authenticated call for information about a user other than the authenticated user, and is set to 1 if the authenticated user has marked the requested user as a contact; otherwise it is set to 0.

friend

The `friend` attribute is returned only when you make an authenticated call for information about a user other than the authenticated user, and is set to 1 if the authenticated user has marked the requested user as a friend; otherwise it is set to 0.

family

The `family` attribute is returned only when you make an authenticated call for information about a user other than the authenticated user, and is set to 1 if the authenticated user has marked the requested user as a family member; otherwise it is set to 0.

revcontact

The `revcontact` attribute is returned only when you make an authenticated call for information about a user other than the authenticated user, and is set to 1 if the requested user has marked the authenticated user as a contact; otherwise it is set to 0.

revfriend

The `revfriend` attribute is returned only when you make an authenticated call for information about a user other than the authenticated user, and is set to 1 if the requested user has marked the authenticated user as a friend; otherwise it is set to 0.

revfamily

The `revfamily` attribute is returned only when you make an authenticated call for information about a user other than the authenticated user, and is set to 1 if the requested user has marked the authenticated user as a family member; otherwise it is set to 0.

username

The `username` attribute or tag contains the requested user's screen name.

realname

The `realname` tag contains the requested user's real name, as set in their Flickr profile.

mbx_sha1sum

The `mbx_sha1sum` tag is an SHA1 hash of the requested user's e-mail address. This is used to create FOAF profiles — the purpose of the friend of a friend (FOAF) project is to create "a Web of machine-readable homepages describing people, the links between them and the things they create and do." You can find more about FOAF at `http://www.foaf-project.org/`.

location

The `location` tag contains the requested user's location, as set in their Flickr profile.

photosurl

The `photosurl` tag contains the URL to the requested user's photostream.

profileurl

The `profileurl` tag contains the URL to the requested user's Flickr profile.

photos

The `photos` tag contains some summary information about the requested user's photostream. It acts as a container for the following tags:

firstdatetaken	The date taken of the earliest-taken photo in the user's photostream, represented in MySQL datetime format
firstdate	The date posted of the first photo in the user's photostream
count	The number of photos in the user's photostream

Photosets

Photoset information is returned by the `flickr.photosets.getList` and `flickr.photosets.getInfo` methods.

```
<photoset id="1448860" primary="67119347" secret="db16e276e9" server="29"
photos="27">
    <title>BBC Good Food Show 2005</title>
    <description>
BBC Good Food Show
NEC
Birmingham
UK

24th November 2005
    </description>
</photoset>
```

id

The id attribute contains the unique ID of the photoset.

primary

The primary attribute contains the ID of the primary photo in the photoset — that is, the photo used to represent the set on the photoset page.

secret

The secret attribute contains the secret for the primary photo in the photoset — that is, the photo used to represent the set on the photoset page.

server

The server attribute contains the server for the primary photo in the photoset — that is, the photo used to represent the set on the photoset page.

photos

The photos attribute contains a count of the number of photos in the set.

title

The title tag contains the title of the set, as displayed on the photoset page.

description

The description tag contains the description of the set, as displayed on the photoset page.

Groups

Information about groups on Flickr can be returned in a variety of formats. The flickr.groups.search method returns this set of summary information:

```
<group nsid="81474450@N00" name="Utata" eighteenplus="0"/>
```

The flickr.groups.pools.getGroups method, however, returns this set of summary information:

```
<group nsid="81474450@N00" id="81474450@N00" name="Utata" admin="1" privacy="3"
    photos="44958" iconserver="6"/>
```

Finally, detailed group information is returned by the flickr.groups.getInfo method:

```
<group id="81474450@N00">
    <name>Utata</name>
```

```
    <description>
        <b>UTATA</b> is a salon in the traditional sense. A parlor. THIS is a place
to talk. Tell stories. Ask questions. Be silly. Be serious. Learn. Teach. Grow.
Relax. Wind up or down. We talk about photography a lot, naturally. We try to grow.
Some of us are pros, some want to go pro, others want artistic fulfillment, some
are trying to be better photographers and some just come for the pie and
conversation.
    </description>
    <members>3315</members>
    <privacy>3</privacy>
    <throttle count="50" mode="month" remaining="45"/>
</group>
```

nsid

The `nsid` attribute contains the NSID of the group. You may notice that some method calls also return an `id` attribute that contains an identical NSID. The `nsid` attribute is the only one that is officially included in the Flickr documentation and so is the one you should use.

name

In summary format, `name` is returned as an attribute; in detailed format it is returned as a tag. In each case it contains the name of the group.

eighteenplus

The `eighteenplus` attribute is returned by some method calls, and is set to 1 if the group has been flagged as being suitable only for people eighteen years of age and older. For other groups, the attribute is set to 0.

admin

Some method calls will return an `admin` attribute, which is set to 1 if the authenticated user is an administrator of the group. For ordinary group members, the attribute is set to 0.

privacy

The `privacy` attribute indicates the level of privacy of the group. It is set to 1 for private groups, 2 for invite-only public groups and 3 for open public groups.

photos

The `photos` attribute indicates the number of photos in the group pool.

iconserver

The `iconserver` attribute contains the ID of the server holding the group's icon. See the "Building URLs" section in Chapter 4 for details on how to use this attribute.

description

The description tag contains the description of the group, as seen on the group's main page.

members

The members tag contains the number of members in the group.

throttle

The throttle tag contains details of any restrictions the group has on the number of photos that can be posted to the group pool by any member in a given time. The count attribute specifies the number of photos allowed. The mode attribute may take the values none, day, week, month, and ever. The remaining attribute is returned if the call is authenticated and indicates the number of photos that the authenticated user can still add to the pool.

If the mode attribute is none, the count and remaining attributes are not returned.

Licenses

Flickr maintains a list of licenses that can be attached to photos, and that are represented by the license tag.

```
<license id="4" name="Attribution License"
url="http://creativecommons.org/licenses/by/2.0/" />
```

id

The id attribute contains the unique ID for the license.

name

The name attribute contains the name usually used to describe the license.

url

The url attribute contains the URL that contains more information about the license.

Comments

Comments on sets and photosets can be retrieved by the API and are contained within the comment tag:

```
<comment id="296457-160244291-72157594155518379" author="22457768@N00"
authorname="Elan Photography" datecreate="1149457486"
permalink="http://www.flickr.com/photos/dopiaza/160244291/#comment72157594155518379
">absolutely brilliant!!</comment>
```

The body of the comment tag contains the actual text of the comment.

id

The `id` attribute contains the unique ID for the comment.

author

The `author` attribute contains the screen name of the author of the comment.

authorname

The `authorname` attribute contains the real name of the author of the comment, as defined in their profile.

permalink

The `permalink` attribute contains a URL that represents a permanent link directly to the comment — in other words, this URL should never change.

Useful Resources

In this appendix, you'll find a number of links to Web pages and other resources that can provide additional information about the topics in this book.

Flickr API Kits

A large number of API kits are available for Flickr. These kits are all developed by third-party authors and are not maintained or supported by Flickr. For support for any of these kits, you should contact the author. I've listed here some of the main API kits that are available.

ActionScript

Flashr is a comprehensive ActionScript 2 wrapper for the Flash API written by Kelvin Luck, distributed under a Creative Commons Attribution-NonCommercial-ShareAlike 2.0 license.

```
http://kelvinluck.com/projects/flashr-a-flickr-api-wrapper-for-flash
```

ColdFusion

CFlickr is a ColdFusion API kit that should work with ColdFusion MX 6.1 and later. It is distributed under the GNU General Public License and is available here:

```
http://chris.m0nk3y.net/projects/CFlickr/
```

Common Lisp

For all the parentheses fans out there, there is Flickr API binding for Common Lisp available under the GNU General Public License, which you can read about here:

```
http://schani.wordpress.com/2006/07/20/lisping-flickr/
```

Curl

Not to be confused with the command-line tool of the same name used elsewhere in this book, Curl is a platform for developing Rich Internet Applications, available from Curl Inc. (http://www.curl.com/). An API kit is available here:

```
http://www.curlr.org/
```

Delphi

Dimitris Giannitsaros has produced an API kit for Delphi, available under an MIT license here:

```
http://www.daremon.gr/flickr/
```

Java

flickrj is available under a BSD license here:

```
http://sourceforge.net/projects/flickrj/
```

jickr is available under an Apache license here:

```
https://jickr.dev.java.net/
```

.NET

Sam Judson's Flickr.Net API Library is available under the GNU Lesser General Public License from:

```
http://www.codeplex.com/Wiki/View.aspx?ProjectName=FlickrNet
```

Perl

There are a couple of CPAN modules available.

Cal Henderson's `Flickr::API` module is available under the Perl Artistic License at:

```
http://search.cpan.org/~iamcal/Flickr-API/
```

Christophe Beauregard's `Flickr::Upload` is freely available at:

```
http://search.cpan.org/~cpb/Flickr-Upload/
```

PHP

Dan Coulter's phpFlickr, which you have seen used extensively in this book, is available under the GNU Lesser General Public License here:

```
http://www.phpflickr.com/
```

Cal Henderson has produced a PEAR (PHP Extension and Application Repository) library for the Flickr API, which you can find here:

```
http://code.iamcal.com/php/flickr/readme.htm
```

Phlickr, a PHP5 library, is available under the GNU Lesser General Public License here:

```
http://sourceforge.net/projects/phlickr/
```

Python

Beej's Python Flickr API, licensed under the Creative Commons Attribution License, is available here:

```
http://beej.us/flickr/flickrapi/
```

Ruby

Rflickr provides a Ruby implementation of the Flickr API and is available under the GNU General Public License here:

```
http://rubyforge.org/projects/rflickr/
```

Flickr Development

There are a few different resources scattered about that should be of general use to developers of Flickr mashups. Your first port of call should always be the main Flickr services web page, where you can find the official documentation for everything about Flickr development, including the API, API keys, feeds, and much more:

```
http://www.flickr.com/services/
```

There is a developer's mailing list on Yahoo! Groups:

```
http://groups.yahoo.com/group/yws-flickr/
```

There is also an unofficial Flickr group about the API here:

```
http://www.flickr.com/groups/api/
```

Both the Yahoo! Groups mailing list and the Flickr group are regularly frequented by both Flickr staff and many of the leading API kit authors.

The Flickr Hacks group

```
http://www.flickr.com/groups/flickrhacks/
```

also often includes useful tips and tricks.

Flickr Mashups

Many Flickr mashups are out there already — there are far too many to try to list here, but here are a few of my favorites.

First, of course, there's my web site:

    http://www.dopiaza.org/

It contains a variety of bits and pieces. You'll find some useful tips and tricks there that relate directly to the contents of this book.

John Watson is one of Flickr's best-known mashups developers. His web site is here:

    http://bighugelabs.com/flickr/

It contains a wide range of Flickr toys.

Jim Bumgardner's Colr Pickr is a fascinating application that enables you to find pictures in certain Flickr groups based on what color they are. You can find this and various other interesting toys here:

    http://krazydad.com/colrpickr/

Retrievr is an amazing piece of software that lets you sketch a small drawing and then finds Flickr photos that look like your sketch. You can see it here:

    http://labs.systemone.at/retrievr/

Firefox and Greasemonkey

The main Firefox web site is found here:

    http://www.mozilla.com/firefox/

The Greasemonkey site is here:

    http://greasemonkey.mozdev.org/

Mark Pilgrim has published an online book called *Dive into Greasemonkey*, which should be considered essential reading for anyone building scripts in Greasemonkey. You can find it here:

    http://diveintogreasemonkey.org/

You can find a very large selection of Greasemonkey scripts here:

    http://userscripts.org/

The Flickr Hacks group is also generally used as a place to announce new Flickr Greasemonkey scripts:

    http://www.flickr.com/groups/flickrhacks/

When you are writing your own scripts, the Mozilla Developer Center contains documentation for all the different Firefox APIs you will most likely want to make use of, including DOM, DOMParser, and XPath. You can find the Mozilla Developer Center here:

```
http://developer.mozilla.org/
```

PHP

The main PHP web site is found here:

```
http://www.php.net/
```

On it you will find extensive documentation on PHP, containing pretty much everything you're ever likely to need to know on the subject of PHP development.

If you're looking to add extra functionality to PHP, you might want to take a look at PEAR, the PHP Extension and Application Repository, which provides a framework and distribution system for reusable PHP components. You can find this here:

```
http://pear.php.net/
```

Perl

The main Perl web site is here:

```
http://www.perl.org/
```

ActiveState's Windows version of perl can be found here:

```
http://www.activestate.com/
```

CPAN, the Comprehensive Perl Archive Network, is home to over 10,000 Perl modules:

```
http://cpan.perl.org/
```

MySQL

You can find MySQL, together with full documentation, here:

```
http://www.mysql.com/
```

A number of tools are available to help make the management of your MySQL databases much simpler. In particular, you might want to take a look at phpMyAdmin, which provides an administrative interface to MySQL. All you need is a PHP-enabled web server. PhpMyAdmin is distributed under the GNU General Public License, and you can find it here:

```
http://www.phpmyadmin.net/
```

ImageMagick

You can find full documentation for ImageMagick at the main ImageMagick web site:

```
http://www.imagemagick.org/
```

Here, in addition to the main site, Anthony Thyssen has an extremely comprehensive set of examples of how to use ImageMagick. His examples focus on running ImageMagick from the command line, but it is straightforward to translate these examples for the various APIs, including PerlMagick. His example pages are well worth reading if you want to explore ImageMagick further:

```
http://www.cit.gu.edu.au/~anthony/graphics/imagick6/
```

World Wide Web Consortium

The World Wide Web Consortium is the official body responsible for many of the standards in use on the Internet today, including HTML, XHTML, XML, XPath, CSS, and DOM, together with many other technologies. You can find all of the standards documents on their web site:

```
http://www.w3.org/
```

The standards documents do sometimes make fairly heavy reading — they're certainly not tutorials, but they are definitive.

Index

P